New York Places & Pleasures

an uncommon guidebook

NEW YORK
PLACES & PLEASURES

KATE SIMON

drawings by Bob Gill

Meridian Books, Inc.
New York

KATE SIMON

*Like so many New Yorkers, Kate Simon was born
elsewhere—in Warsaw, Poland. She was moved to
Manhattan as a child, received her education in the city's
schools, and has lived in many parts of New York City.
She likes to paint and travel widely, but always, as she
says, she returns "to the pleasures of the drunken course
of Pearl Street, the tattered refinements of Chelsea,
the blanked silence of warehouse streets in midday and
the skyscrapers huddled like gray elephants against
a purple twilight sky." Kate Simon has worked in various
capacities for book publishers, written reviews for*
New Republic, The Nation, *and other periodicals, and
revised Frances Toor's* New Guide to Mexico.
New York Places & Pleasures *is her first published book.*

M

First published June 1959 by Meridian Books, Inc.
First printing April 1959
© Copyright 1959 by Meridian Books, Inc.

Library of Congress Catalog Card Number: 59-7186
Manufactured in the United States of America
Typography and design by Elaine Lustig

CONTENTS

INTRODUCTION

A big city encountered for the first time is terrifying in its initial assault. Its variety of riches creates a paralysis of choice, its many *musts* a frantic sense of haste and of responsibilities unfulfilled. To know, on a first visit to Rome, that the Forum is waiting, and so are St. Peter's *and* the Sistine Chapel *and* the Coliseum *and* the Trevi Fountain *and* the Spanish Steps *and* the Keats Memorial, is often to have defeat accompany the challenge. A dogged persistence replaces pleasure, the feet and eyes slowly die as the mind retreats into impenetrable indifference. Later it all melds into a surrealist painting: the figures in the Sistine Chapel ceilings soar over the Forum, which is dimmed by the splashing of the Trevi Fountain, while Trajan's Column neatly bisects the canvas. Finally, you discover that, apart from the fear of seeming too bare of culture, you really don't care for Roman ruins or sculpturesque paintings tearing through a papal ceiling. You would much rather have spent more time following the lovely baroque curves of the Piazza San Ignazio, or sitting in the cafe hidden in the hedges above the Spanish Stairs, drowsy and contented in the golden afternoon of Rome. But time had run out.

New York City, of course, has its well-advertised *musts*, most of them fully deserving the enthusiasm they arouse as well as the lavish hyperbole—"biggest, tallest, richest, incredible, fantastic"—and these have been filmed, televised, and described so abundantly that even a first visit is a confirmation of strongly stamped impressions—a return, in a sense. The great lures are, mainly, the fashionable shops on the great avenues of midtown Manhattan, the glamorous night clubs and restaurants, the Empire State Building and Rockefeller Plaza. These diminish New York to a small, expansive El Dorado, a compact rectangle running north from 34th Street to Central Park South and east from Broadway to Park Avenue. But there is much more to be known, some of it possibly more appealing to certain temperaments, more suitable to certain pockets; the view from the top of the Empire State Building is indeed unbelievable, yet you may like better a man's-eye view of Bleecker Street; the blatant riches and wild energy of midtown may suit a Renaissance personality, but the quieter modesty of Brooklyn Heights may seem easier for an admirer of Emily Dickinson; some of the Fifth Avenue shops are great queens of noble beauty and vast riches, but there are people who find bargain counters more rewarding. In recognition of such happy differences, and with affection for the places and people less brightly illuminated in the city's publicity, the usual emphases have been reversed in this book, the brilliance of the famous rectangle dimmed and the color of the surrounding areas brought up.

New York City is too big and no one book is big enough to give more than a few facets of the impossibly complex, fluid whole—characteristics which preclude both comprehensiveness and immutability. The hope is that the visitor (and the New Yorker) will discover some of the less overpowering delights of the capricious, restless metropolis, with its exhilarating air and its ill-kempt streets, its beautiful skies rarely seen, a city exhausting to visit and difficult to live in, crammed with annoying, enchanting, and carefully anonymous people.

Before plunging you into the rest of this book, it seems only fair to make some concrete statement about its scope and point of view. It is by no means "the complete guidebook" nor does it aim to be. The basis for selection (other than the obvious one of space limitations) has been shaped by the observations and tastes of one curious and enthusiastic New Yorker, admittedly subjective and with a leaning towards the more modest attractions of the city.

An imposing list of books about New York City ranges from histories of street names, through word-paintings and nostalgic reminiscences, to massive compendia of statistics, and they all have their virtues. However, the traveller with a nonspecialist's interest in the city might find the following few useful and entertaining: For an exhaustive array of facts, figures, and listings, there is the *New York City Guide and Almanac,* published by the *Daily News*; for history and descriptive matter, browse in the *New York City Guide,* originally compiled by the W.P.A.; for the charm of historical oddities—early traffic

regulations, mainly in restraint of livestock, for instance
—try to find issues of the *Almanac for New Yorkers,*
published yearly in the late thirties, also compiled by the
W.P.A. and possibly collectors' items by this time. Lloyd
Morris' *Incredible New York* is a lively chronicle of the
last one hundred years in New York City, replete with
juicy details of social life; and *McSorley's Wonderful
Saloon* by Joseph Mitchell will introduce you to a gallery
of rare, indigenous individuals brilliantly and movingly
painted; and for the sheer pleasure of it read E. B.
White's masterful little book, *Here Is New York.*

*I am indebted to an endless list of people who gave time,
effort and information with great grace; unfortunately,
many of them are anonymous—a clerk in a store, a corner
policeman, a truck driver, a messenger boy on a bicycle.
It is pleasant to be able to thank again, in type, Mrs.
Waddell of the West Indian Day Association, Mr. Jesse
Walker of the* AMSTERDAM NEWS, *Mr. Friis of the Amer-
ican-Scandinavian Foundation, Mr. Borzecki of* NOWY
SWIAT, *Mr. Revelis of the* GREEK DAILY HERALD, *Mrs. Dorothy Homer and the rest of the staff of the Countee
Cullen Branch of the Public Library, Mr. Boni of "Trinacria" who gave me some of his luncheon wine and a bag
of sesame candies for strength against the cold wind,
the dry-goods merchant who offered me shelter among
the aprons against a storm on Orchard Street, the
many people whose uncles owned fascinating shops
which I* HAD *to see, the shopkeepers and headwaiters
who spilled colorful autobiographies in a kaleidescope of
accents, and all the other people who enthusiastically
led and misled me.*

KATE SIMON

Note: New York is an ever-changing city. Between the time
of investigation and the publication of this book, some shops and
restaurants may have undergone tranformation (new owners,
new hours, new policies) or even disappearance (a building
demolished, a change of fortune, a private disaster). This is one
of the hazards that beset all guidebooks, unfortunately, and that
must await corrected listings in later editions.

1

PAST INTO PRESENT

Major errors in timing and judgment made early New York City a Dutch town. Had not Francis I of France been frantically busy fighting Charles V of Spain in 1524, New York City might have been a French colony. In that year, Verrazano, the Florentine, sailed into New York Bay. Landing in a display of Renaissance grandeur, he took possession for his French employer of "this island, as also of the bay, river, and all countries, rivers, lakes and streams contiguous and adjacent thereunto, both those which have been discovered and those who may be discovered hereafter, in all their length and breadth." He declared all the land that he had seen, as well as that which he could imagine beyond it, subject to the laws and customs of His Majesty, immune from seizure and settlement by all other "potentates, princes, sovereigns, states and republics." Then he sailed away. It was one of the most splendid of futile gestures. It resulted in nothing, and it left the territory as wild and pristine as before.

Seventy-five years later, the States-General of the Dutch Republic offered a reward of twenty-five thousand guilders for the discovery of the Northeast Passage to China and Japan. The Dutch East India Company outfitted the *Half Moon*, appointed the Englishman Henry Hudson as her navigator, and shipped her off to the Arctic wastes beyond Norway. This was a fortuitous error: the frozen, desperate crew threatened mutiny, and Hudson turned westward, across the Atlantic to Maine and along the coast to Virginia. For a while, Delaware Bay seemed a likely opening to the "inland sea" he was seeking, but its barriers of current discouraged him and he sailed northward. He entered New York Bay in 1609 and followed the Hudson River in his expectation (an error which delights every schoolboy) of finding the Pacific Ocean or China or India. When his hopes failed to materialize, he went back down the river and home to Europe, leaving groups of Indians variously impressed with the power of European alcohol and firearms.

Within a few years, the enterprising Dutch had set up settlements along the river and at the southern tip of the island of the Mana-hatta Indians. Trade relations with

the Indians were established—trinkets and iron articles
for pelts and native food—and ships plied briskly between Amsterdam and New Netherland bringing baubles
and cooking cauldrons to the New World and carrying
back cargoes of fur and an occasional Indian as a souvenir of travel. The fur trade soon became too promising
to be left in the hands of a small company of merchants
and explorers at a time when the Dutch Republic needed
wealth to pursue its war with Spain. The obvious answer
was for the States-General to charter a West India Company to parallel the success of the older Dutch East India
Company in Asia. This was done in 1621, and rarely has
a commercial enterprise been granted so much power: it
could make war and effect treaties, establish colonies and
make alliances, raise an army and impose governmental
regulations. In other words, it was a surrogate of the
Dutch government, unless one chooses to think of the
government as a trading corporation and the West India
Company as one of its branches.

There was now land and trade, but where were the
people? The first group sent over were about thirty families of Walloons who had been religious refugees in
Leyden. They were shortly followed by about fifty people
who had been attracted by the company's advertised
inducements of free passage and employment. The next
step was to find a governor, and Peter Minuit, a former
employee of the East India Company, was appointed.
Although some of his enterprises as governor were sound
and far-seeing (he built a fort, distributed seeds and
tree grafts which were the beginnings of profitable farm-
ing, and established shipbuilding as a New World industry), Peter Minuit is remembered mainly as the man who
drove the shrewdest known bargain, twenty-four dollars
worth of beads, ribbons, and other shiny trinkets for the
island of Manhattan. He was a scrupulous gentleman, as
colonizers go, acknowledging the property rights of the
Indians; the history of exploration and colonization shows
few who stopped to bargain at all. Admirable and efficient as he was, Minuit could not populate the colonies
satisfactorily, so the Dutch West India Company reached
back into history and came up with a feudal plan, the

Patroon system: any person could take up a large area of navigable land and remain owner if, within four years, he could establish on it a settlement of over fifty people, these people to be his property for ten years of servitude. In the land-grabbing and power-grabbing and struggles to override the company's trading monopoly, Peter Minuit lost prestige and was recalled. He was replaced by young Wouter van Twiller, whose ambitions were more limited. Generous quantities of wine, food, and land were enough for him, so he was ultimately removed from office to enjoy himself with fewer official interruptions. Willem Kieft, the new broom, swept away the pleasures of the taprooms almost entirely; he swept away his Council and the influence of the church leaders, introducing arbitrary rule. His handling of relations with the Indians was tactless and even treacherous. Between Indian massacres and hasty removals to other colonies or back to Europe, the hard-won population of New Netherland was considerably reduced, and what was left was battered. Kieft was finally recalled.

The next minor conqueror was Peter Stuyvesant of the decorated peg leg, who stamped out popular amusements as well as political opposition and religious freedom. The immigrants who began to arrive in greater numbers between 1653 and 1664, members of various religious sects in difficulty, found a cold welcome. It was only by the intervention of the States-General (who had a practical eye to the financial potential of a larger settlement) that small groups of Jews and dissident Protestant sects were permitted to settle and worship.

In the meantime, the English colonies to the north and south of New Amsterdam were flourishing and the British kept a sharp eye on the Dutch settlement, making occasional abortive attempts to take it on an old claim —based on John Cabot's explorations—that it was British territory. Depleted by wars with the Indians and the bankruptcy of the West India Company, New Amsterdam was ripe for conquest. In 1664, the mother country's long commercial rivalry with England again reached the stage of open warfare (the Second Dutch War). An English fleet sailed into the harbor and New Amsterdam surrendered to the British. The name of the city was changed to New York, as the domain of the Duke of York, the brother of the then king, Charles II, and, of course, the Anglican Church was established. The city was reconquered by the Dutch in 1673, but the next year it was returned to the British, Holland giving up forever her claims to all of New Netherland.

As the city grew, under the rule of British governors of several degrees of competence and eccentricity, the problems multiplied, stemming from, and compounded by, violent changes in the British succession. Over the next century, however, despite governmental difficulties, plague, slave revolts, and panics, the city developed and settled into permanency. Churches and synagogues were established, a local city governing board was elected, a lighthouse and docks were built, ferries began to ply between New York and Brooklyn, New York and Staten Island, New York and New Jersey. There were street lights, a theater, a newspaper, and then an opposition newspaper; in 1757, out of its ripeness and self-importance, a history of New York was published. This growth came to a halt at the time of the American Revolution; New York lay sacked, lacerated, and gutted by fire through the British occupancy, which lasted until 1783. But her recovery was almost as rapid as her destruction. By 1790, New York City had become the capital of the state, the meeting place of the first Congress, and the seat of the Presidency itself. Its population was over 30,000.

During the following years, New York suffered periodic outbreaks of yellow fever and cholera, great fires and riots, and the ominous presence of a blockading British fleet during the War of 1812, and yet the city burgeoned breathlessly until the Civil War. The plagues drove some of the populace to outlying areas, expanding the limits of the city, pushing Potter's Field northward like a pawn on an ever-growing chess board. What had been King's College became Columbia College with a revived medical school and, later, a law faculty. Hospitals were built; a free school system was organized; more theaters, more newspapers, more ferries, charitable institutions, and banks were established to cope with the overwhelming size and complexity of the city. In 1803, New York was rich enough to afford a political scandal, the misappropriation of almost $44,000 in federal funds, from which it recovered to go on to greater and bolder theft. The demonstration of Robert Fulton's steamboat expanded ferry service and enlivened international trade, enabling the first department stores to offer a great variety of imports.

In 1825, the first ship to come from Buffalo through the Erie Canal and down the Hudson reached New York, giving the city a preferred position in western trade and control of the purse strings of the country. By the 1840's, New York was the new nation's leading port and shipbuilding center. There was enough "big" money to import grand opera and furnishings for great mansions, and to withstand a large-scale financial panic involving losses of about $60,000,000. In spite of this catastrophe, culture and finance thrived: the Philharmonic Society was founded, P. T. Barnum imported Jenny Lind to sing, the Crystal Palace was built to house a World's Fair, and the first baseball club was organized. The Board of Aldermen, known as "The Forty Thieves," inaugurated a high-riding period of government graft by accepting a bribe of $30,000 from persons very much interested in building the Third Avenue El (itself now as dead as the thieves). This was in 1854, and it must be some indication of the almost frightening prosperity of the city that fifteen years later, the Tweed Ring was able to take as much as $75,000,000 out of various municipal enterprises.

The Civil War threw New York City into a fervor of self-protection. She was rich and some of her wealth consisted of large debts owed by the South, debts which would be canceled by war. Several attempts to ward off the war were made by groups of merchants and the Chamber of Commerce, in proposed compromise and peace plans. It was also seriously suggested, and earnestly listened to, that New York City become a free state, mainly to cut taxes and remain uninvolved in the civil conflict. After Fort Sumter was fired on, there was a rash of patriotic demonstrations and, within the following month, 8,000 New Yorkers marched off to war, but as the war progressed, volunteers were lacking, and a draft call was issued in May of 1863, summoning 300,000 men. Registration was ordinary the first day, despite the wide resentment at the draft law's provision that enabled rich men to escape service through payment of $300. On the second day, a mob attacked the registration office; led by agitators, they went on to serious rioting, with Abolitionists and Negroes as their special victims. Negroes were beaten to death, a Negro orphanage was burned, and houses were looted. This went on for three days. When it was finally brought to a halt by the combined forces of police, militia, West Point cadets, and citizenry, $2,000,000 in property had been destroyed and a thousand people had perished.

The city recovered. After the Civil War, the exhibition of superlatives—fastest, biggest, richest—was reopened. It was possible for Jay Gould and Jim Fisk to make $11,000,000 profit by cornering the gold market and for American millionaires to ransack Europe for royal treasures gathered in omniverous loads and ultimately placed in marble *palazzi* of inhuman size. The Brooklyn Bridge was opened, a trolley line soon crossed it, and Brooklyn's identity as a separate city gradually diminished. In 1898 it was combined with the other boroughs—Manhattan, Queens, Richmond (Staten Island), and the Bronx—to form Greater New York. Tammany sank its fangs into the city government and bled it through graft and corruption for many years, giving way ultimately to depression and reform. Buildings grew taller, streets denser, and rapid-transit systems leaped over and across and under the city, stretching it in size as new settlements sprang up along their darting lines. These new neighborhoods consisted mainly of new ghettos to replace older ghettos of restriction or poverty.

In every known language, New York City has been called a "melting pot," a colorful phrase which by its vividness obscures the fact that, up to recent years, it wasn't quite true. By its very nature, historically and geographically, New York has been an immigrant's city, but it wasn't until the latter half of the last century and the beginning of this one that huge numbers of Europeans poured in great rivers to the Atlantic and across. Along with their bundles of household goods, they brought fear and optimism, despair and ambition, and a stubbornness which often had the face of courage. After walking, dragging, carrying, being folded into each other like old clothes in steerage holds, succumbing to typhus on the way, they arrived at Ellis Island to stand in awe of the Olympic immobility of immigration officials.

Having come to a new country, they returned to as much of the old as they could. They moved to neighborhoods where earlier immigrants from their old homelands had established strongholds; they formed benefit societies of their own people and established their own newspapers; they ate the familiar foods sold in shops undisturbed by the strangeness of American speech. The young ventured out because they were young, and embarrassed over their difference, but they were replaced over and over again by a new flood of *paisanos* and *landsleit*.

The foreign enclaves became small cities, self-sufficient and, by their foreignness, subtly impregnable. An Italian family left the village of Mulberry Street only to visit in the Italian town of Bleecker Street or the village of East 106th Street. Jews who had moved across the bridge to Brownsville returned for Passover dinner with the older settlers in Rivington Street or Suffolk Street on the lower East Side. Smaller groups, like the Chinese, lived all their lives within the squares of a few streets, pulled out only by the necessities of a job or rare commands from officialdom.

In a sense, the only melting pots were the elevated trains, the trolleys, and the larger factories—places of forced encounter arranged by the grotesque size of the city and the exigencies of breadwinning. Otherwise, there was little melting for many years. The elders of each colony formed a bastion; armed with old saws, warnings, threats, and sometimes the hysteria of xenophobia, they kept many of the young ringed in.

As the floods of immigration diminished, becoming an

inconsequential trickle by 1931, there were few rein-
forcements for these battalions. The newer generations,
awesomely superior in their American speech and styl-
ishness, won each successive battle for emancipation.
The whole city became theirs. It was then that the city
began in fact to become a melting pot; the walls of the
ghettos began to crumble, movement in and out of them
erased their rigid contours. The search for a new apartment was governed by economic considerations rather
than by Mama's fears, and the girls began to explore
the splendors of Klein's and Ohrbach's on Union Square,
even though Mama stayed faithful to the peddler who
collected enormous totals—at 50 cents or a dollar each
week—for his questionable wares. The sons reached out
of their neighborhoods to find fancier movie houses for
their dates. A neighborhood might still have (and still
often has) one predominant national color, but it is
streaked with others: a solid band of Italian shops is
interrupted by a Polish meat market; Irish saloons make
way for a Scandinavian delicatessen; a row of mailboxes
in an apartment house may show a dominance of Gins-
bergs, Kaplans, and Cohens, but scattered among them
will be a Jensen, a Citerella, a Sullivan.

By an engaging paradox, the blending of the old-
country populations into one another, destroying the
purity and self-containedness of the foreign areas, has
served to preserve their contributions. As the first and
second American generations spread and mixed with
each other, some common basic pleasures were shared.
Jewish women learned to cook good spaghetti because
their husbands insisted that it be *al dente,* a bit of gourmet sophistication they picked up from Italian co-
workers. The aromatic Jewish delicatessens all over the
city fill mouths which never formed a Yiddish word, and
New Yorkers whose fathers were Luigi, Ramon, Thad-
deus, now consider Chinese pork an American dish.

With the discovery of foreign cuisines, the sharing of
shopping information, the awareness of fiestas and celebrations, the New Yorker has learned to cherish the
founts of these goods, and enjoys eating and shopping

in Little Italy, in Chinatown, and on Orchard Street. These forays also afford him the expanded spirit of adventure inherent in foreign travel—at little expense and only the minor inconvenience of a subway ride. The middle-aged Chinese whose childhood playground was the dim, tight little halls of Chinatown might not deplore its replacement by a fresh, clean housing project, but many other New Yorkers might. Where would they take the kids for a walk and dinner on Sunday? Mulberry Street is dark and dormant, its restaurants are not superior to or cheaper than Italian restaurants in other parts of the city, but in an ambience of grocery stores hung with Italian salamis and cheeses, of sweet shops which smell of anise and serve *cassatta,* the restaurant food seems to have added flavors of authenticity and indigenousness; garlic is its own unconquerable self anywhere, on Mulberry Street it is charged with extra passion. Not the neighborhood Italians, but the Scotch-Irish couple from Brooklyn Heights, and the West Orange, New Jersey, family of Scandinavian descent, help to preserve what is left of Little Italy.

There are two groups in New York City who have not yet become parts of the free, restless flow, shift, and mixture. These are the Negro and Puerto Rican populations, largely still restrained in too-enclosed areas. Because it is economically difficult and socially almost impossible, a single Negro or Puerto Rican family can rarely move out of its ghetto into a new, good neighborhood; it is limited to settling with its group into an already depressed area, discarded by an earlier immigrant group. This does not necessarily mean an integration or blending but the superimposition of a new language and set of mores on an old slum. It is said commonly that the Puerto Rican newcomer will gradually follow the course of evolution which the Irish immigrant, then the Italian, and then the Jew followed: first feared, scorned, and victimized, then tolerated, then forgotten to the point where he himself becomes the one to fear, resent, and finally tolerate some still-newer group. This is inevitably true, with one important difference: the Puerto

Rican is also often a man of darker skin, and thus faces not only the classic struggle of the immigrant but carries the extra burden of the Negro; his progress from Puerto Rican to New Yorker will depend too on the speed and depth with which integration is accomplished in the rest of the United States.

2

NATIVES AND
OUTLANDERS

The Typical New Yorker?

The media of mass communications, with their lightning spread of information, as speedily spread misinformation. The New Yorker, as caricatured, fragmented, and distorted in fiction and the movies, is no more typical of New York than the apache is of Paris or the gigolo of Rome. For each success-bearing New Yorker, slickly dressed, shaved, and shined, his face carefully arranged in an expression of well-being, smooth and impenetrable as a marble egg, there is a man in the subway in a baggy coat, his collar frayed, his tie at a careless slant, and his face blue-stubbled and vulnerable with exhaustion. The tense, pill-gorged neurotic so frequently satirized is also the man who can stand patiently for a half hour or more in a rush-hour subway. He clutches, clings, and sways in a cauldron of steamy wet bodies on a summer day, his tired feet mashed by other feet, his ears bursting with noise, his eyes alert for the almost impossible seat. He will, nevertheless, when his station arrives, gently and patiently repeat "Getting out, excuse me" a dozen times as he slowly eases through the dense wall of bodies blocking the door. The woman who tears through a crowd at a sales counter with the heedlessness of a bulldozer, stands for hours in a movie line, gentling her restless children. The chic woman whose clothes look pasted on her in an approved New York design, her two strands of pearls placed precisely against her neck, her make-up as perfect as a fashionable portrait, is no more typical than the loosely made slattern who tucks her bathrobe up into its belt, throws a coat over it, and runs in her felt slippers to the grocer for a container of milk.

Stiff with controlled anger over the slow crawl of a bus, the New Yorker does not look out the window to amuse himself with the darts and flashes of life on the sidewalk; he concentrates on his fury. But some hours later, he can be found rooted before a new piece of construction, watching the monotonous grab, lift, and drop of a crane, the expression on his face that of a contented truant with eons of time to fritter away. The New Yorker hasn't much tolerance for slow service in

restaurants, but will put up almost uncomplainingly with
noise, crowds, heat, and cold.

Compared to most of the world's population, the New
Yorker is fanatically clean; it hurts him to appear in
public unshaven; he worries about body odor and considers it unspeakably barbaric not to bathe once a day;
he keeps his hair and teeth well brushed and his suit
pressed. But he lets his dog defecate on the sidewalk
and walks unseeing through wads of wind-blown rub-
bish. He will return to his old neighborhood and gaze
with nostalgia at the red brick box which was his boy-
hood school, but give no thought to the handsome (and,
occasionally, historic) buildings ruthlessly ripped out of
the city for taller buildings which have the luster of
expensiveness and newness.

Materialism, in its purest essence, is supposed to be
the hallmark of the New Yorker. He is pictured as
maimed in pursuit of the buck. But he is in reality a
romantic—it isn't the buck, which he could have earned
at home, in his safe small town, but the glitter of a
mound of gold, like Spanish treasure, which lures him.
To dream of being an actress is natural for any self-
respecting little girl; to want it with fanaticism, to leave
all safeties for it, is the drive of the romantic, as is a
conviction that drawing a little isn't enough—a painter
must live intensely with discomfort and disorder in
Greenwich Village in imitation of the Golden Age of
Montmartre. Thus, the little dreams stay at home and
the big ones come to New York.

The seasons, too, change the New Yorker's personality.
In the winter he creeps in on himself, his bones and
joints tighten, his eyes seem to turn inward as does his
flesh, to warm itself on itself. His personality curls inward like his body for protection from the cold; like
an animal, he crowds his being into a small, tight, private place, looking outward only to keep from being
battered by the traffic. In the summer he unfolds—he
becomes lazy and slow, loose and tropical. He is heat-
drunk and sloppily good-natured, moving among the
steaming buildings as if they were jungle trees and he
was ready to lie under one. Fall elicits the greatest vigor;

this is the time of the quest for a new and always improved life. Schools burst open and so do theaters and concert halls. Through this yearly renascence, following the torpor of summer, the New Yorker moves like a confident hunter—this will be the year of the business killing, of the block-long car (or, nowadays, the sportiest little foreign car), and the most fruity amour. His wife hunts with frenzied optimism for the furniture which will set her off as the elegant, cultivated lady she *truly* is, for the hat which will transfigure her, and the dress which will magically erase all inadequacies.

The fury of planning, searching, and nest-building mounts to the fireworks of Christmas and then, after New Year's, New York settles back, involuted and dormant, warmed by the glow of television in its cave, waiting for the indolences of Spring.

The Customer Is Always Wrong or Whatsamattawidyubud?

Along with its well-advertised distinctions, New York City scores rather high for a special variety of rudeness. It is a grating music sometimes given off by saleswomen, taxi drivers, bus drivers, and waiters—not by all of them, certainly, or even most, but enough to repel the uninitiated. The initiated New Yorker is indifferent to it, or amused, or snarls back, depending on how his life fits on his shoulders that particular day; he understands it as the disgruntlement of the debased aristocrat, the weariness of the elegant square peg in the coarse, round hole.

THE SALESWOMAN

The saleswoman is not rude because her feet hurt—everyone's feet hurt—nor from the usual wounds of love and money. Having dealt with women who have the leisure and façade she envies, she has come to imitate the most rarefied of them, borrows in reasonable facsimile their tricks of style, reads the same magazines, and assumes the aloof expression and languid response suitable to the fantasy. She earns an additional claim to the higher echelons of society through handling riches, an act which, by a 9:30-5:30 osmosis through class lines, transmutes her from a Fifth Avenue salesgirl to a Fifth Avenue heiress. When you ask this goddess to wait on you, you have smashed the glass slipper and thrown her into the cinders. Quite reasonably, Cinderella is angry with you.

THE WAITER

The New York waiter is also superior, but for different reasons. It is simply that he knows more than you do about everything. He disapproves of your taste in food and clothing, your gauche manners, your miserliness, and sometimes, it seems, of your very existence, which he tries to ignore. After you've been seated and the great presence has slowly approached and let its luster shine on you, you ask "How is the duck?" The presence turns its long lids on you, lets a pitying gleam emerge from under them, and intones, "Duck is an insi-i-i-pid animal," erasing at one stroke all ducks and your weakened ego. This waiter is often French or Italian and, though his native tastes may run to *pasta* and scratchy wine, he considers himself the sacred vessel of the secrets of Escoffier and Brillat-Savarin; his carefully maintained accent, he hopes, will join him to the great kitchens of Paris and Rome, though he may have come directly from a grim village in the Auvergne or in Sicily. The Jewish waiter is The Father—the father as doctor, the father as disciplinarian, the father as critic and, of course, protector; leaping from role to role, he makes an erratic and fascinating composite. When he is the protector, he will advise you to fold your coat neatly and put it on the nice chair there and he will guard it and watch "nobody should spill on it." As the disciplinarian, he will respond to "What kind of jam have you for the blintzes?" with "Jam is jam!" in the tone of outraged patience used to stop a nagging child. Should you order eggs fried rather than scrambled, as he approves of them, he will whip out his order book, keep his pencil ostentatiously poised, scrutinize you with the look of "you're going to be trouble but I'm ready for you," and mutter in a voice rich with sarcasm, "Ah, ha. Fancy customers!" The critic in him swings the lash wide: busboys are ignorant and lazy, bosses are oafs who rise to prosperity by trampling on waiters, customers are knaves or maniacs; in short, life would not be worth living except for the enchantments of complaining.

The doctor-father is his most engaging and annoying role. As if you were describing symptoms, he listens solemnly to your order, and then silently evaluates it. After a weighty pause, he offers you his learned advice: "If you're going to have the steak, you shouldn't eat soup with dumplings before, it'll lay heavy on your stomach. Have a little nice chicken liver first." "Maybe you shouldn't have fried chicken so late, boiled is better for you." "You want creamed spinach? Carrots is healthier." "No potatoes? Whatsamatter, you're not fat. It's not nice a woman should look like a stick." You will escape his solicitude only by succumbing to his superior knowledge of digestive matters, whether it pleases you or not.

THE TAXI DRIVER

While the saleswoman is a deposed duchess and the Jewish waiter an insatiable father and unappreciated savant, the New York City taxi driver carries a variety of personalities. As he triumphantly roars through a red light and purrs with satisfaction, "I coulda got a ticket," he sups of the glory of the bullfighter whose chest is stained but untorn by the close rush of the bull. "Don't worry," he assures you when you tell him you must make Grand Central in a few minutes: as a knight in checkered cap and old army jacket, he makes off on his crusade with jaw set and shoulders hunched, ready to do battle with time, distance, and other taxis. His progress, like Sir Galahad's, is full of adventuresome delays with almost supernatural overtones, and your anxiety gnaws at you as he seems to seek out all possible hazards—the broken traffic light, the street full of holes and excavation barriers, the routes of parades and demonstrations. But he usually gets you there on time, even if your request was unreasonable. However, to compensate for

your unreasonableness and his demanding adventure, he
expects an extra tip—no extra tip, no thanks. Nevertheless, it is impossible for a taxi driver to say nothing, so
he mutters, "Big sport. How could he afford a train ride?
Fancy luggage and no extra dime! Next time take a bus,
mister, it's cheaper."

Sometimes the cab driver is the Lord of New York,
viewing it with the pride and intimate knowledge of the
possessor of a suzerainty. He will talk about the "rackets"
in cryptic inside-dope terms, make veiled allusions—"If
people really knew what went on in this town's politics!"
—and speak longingly of the good old days of Jimmy
Walker as if personally bereaved. He will give the impression that all of New York is his and its best is a
little purse of secrets which he may or may not open
for you, depending on his royal whim. This is one of
the characters created by Broadway writers, based on
several florid personalities who served the theatrical
neighborhood, and now it is a legend in which many taxi
drivers are trapped. Because one or two taxi drivers have
had books published about their adventures during pro-
hibition, others are struggling similarly or at least talking like authors. Because one was quoted as a profound
primitive philosopher, many of them spout homely dull
bits of folk wisdom; the collective reputation for wit
impels lumpish attempts at humor.

Haggling over price either before or after a ride, as
in some foreign cities, is not part of the New York scene;
our taximeters can't be argued with as they grind out
their inexorable sums. The nearest equivalent is the
opening discussion of how to get where you're going.
You suggest going West on 49th Street to get to a theater.
Nope, impossible, 49th at this time of night is choked
with cars; the way to do it is go West on 47th, over to
Eighth, and cut back and around. It sounds a little irra-
tional, but you assume he is speaking from profound
technical knowledge and are reluctant to question a professional's judgment in his own métier. West 47th turns
out to be as clogged with cars as an old drain with rust,
nothing moves but the contained winds of your impatient temper, your dinner sours, and you rush to the

theater seat well immunized against the charms of the play and its actors. The taxi genie, however, drives away with the expression of one who has done his job well.

THE BUS DRIVER

The bus driver, on the other hand, balances the taxi man with his taciturnity. He seems to live in a perpetual state of controlled combustion. There is reason for it: he must drive a cumbersome vehicle through insane traffic as he collects fares, makes change, dispenses transfers, watches a front door and a side door, is asked incomprehensible questions in numerous uncertain accents, guards himself against the irate customer who missed his stop, and checks the bus passes of a loud crowd of schoolboys. There are few jobs which require one man to be responsible for so many nerve-wracking details, and the city bus driver must be forgiven his occasional irascibilities; it's easy when you've spent five minutes of any crowded bus ride watching him work.

Counterpoint: The Customer Could Be Right, Once!

The foregoing chamber of difficulties was described as preparation for people who are accustomed to friendly, less flamboyant types but the roll call is incomplete without mentioning the presence of pleasanter people.

At the *Hicks* soda fountain (16 E. 49th St., between Madison and Fifth; DC), there is a man behind the counter who wears a pink-striped shirt, a silly small bow tie, and rimless glasses. He dances a soda—the ice cream propelled into the glasses through a high arc, a graceful shift and step to the flavor dispensers, three rhythmic taps on the button, the glass thrust high with an arm twist and a swoop to the side for soda, an elegant turn of the nozzle and the body arcs in a prayerful waiting attitude. The soda is delivered with mock dedication and solemnity as nectar to the gods. While he moves through his choreography, he talks, and talks, often wittily, always engagingly.

Note For Diners' Club Members: After the address of Hicks (above), you will observe the initials "DC." This, of course, indicates that Diners' Club charge cards will be honored there. Throughout this book, especially in connection with the restaurants, the initials will be given for each establishment which has been identified to us as a Diners' Club member.

There is a bus dispatcher who has, for some time now, been stationed in front of Bloomingdale's at the 59th Street Lexington Avenue bus stop. He can lift a busload of tired disgruntled shoppers to a semblance of pleasantness by peering into the bus, catching sight of a girl in a green hat and admiring it loudly and extravagantly. He will change your dollar bill with, "And how are you today, beautiful?" There will be nothing flirtatious in his tone—he just wants you to feel good. "Have a good day, folks," will be his parting call as he pounds on the side of the bus to signal the driver to move off. He isn't witty, his phrases are pure cliché, his looks are rotund and ordinary, but he is the Light of Lexington Avenue.

The Outlander: How Not to Get Lost Too Hopelessly

The best way to get around in New York is to be both rich and patient, rich enough to take taxis (taxi fare is not as expensive as you might think, but the cost mounts as you traverse the city) and patient enough to endure their searching instinct for traffic snarls which become tight knots at noon, from 5 to 7 P.M., and just before theater-curtain time. If your purse isn't heavy, use buses or your feet for short distances, and ride the subways for longer ones. Riding the subways during rush hours (8 A.M. to 9:30 A.M. and 4:30 P.M. to 6:30 P.M.) requires heroism beyond the call of tourist duty. If you want to get some pallid idea of what it might be like, stand at the side of the change booth of a central station (42nd St. and Lexington Ave., for example) during the frantic hours and look around you, if you can stay on your feet long enough in the surging mob. That is as far as anyone not subway-conditioned should go during rush hours.

When you do use the subways, find out specifically

which branch of which line to use and also whether your destination is on a local or express stop. The IND line has four divisions: "A" (Eighth Ave.), "D" (Sixth Ave.), "E" and "F" (which go to Queens), plus various local branches; the IRT has two main divisions: Seventh Avenue and Lexington, with branches and local routes which end in widely separated areas, as do the various branches of the BMT. It is *very important* to find out specifically which branches of a line you will need to use. Have the line and the stop clearly marked for you on the subway map which you will have picked up, along with a sightseer's map and assorted leaflets, from the *Convention and Visitors Bureau* (90 E. 42nd St., just across from Grand Central Station—MU 7-1300). An "Official New York Subway Map and Guide" is available at the change booths of the subway system and "The Red Book" of the New York Telephone Company has an admirable map of the subway and elevated lines that cut across the city. Be wary of the buses, too; they make unexpected turns. A number of them thicken 42nd Street for a few minutes and then spread like frayed rope. Only the 42nd Street Crosstown bus (so marked) will take you across the length of it. The Fifth Avenue buses terminate their trips at various places, clearly indicated on the front. Avoid a Number 15 unless you actually want to go to Queens, and watch out for Number 5, which turns west on 57th Street and then makes its way up Riverside Drive. It's a lovely ride, but you'll never get to upper Fifth Avenue that way.

The Avenue That Isn't: On maps, and in a variety of official literature, you will encounter the name "Avenue of the Americas." This has been for many years the proper appellation for the avenue which runs north and south one block west of Fifth Avenue and one block east of Seventh Avenue.

In this book and elsewhere, and from the lips of virtually all New Yorkers, you will be meeting "Sixth Avenue." Officially, no such thoroughfare exists; it refers to the Avenue of the Americas. Regardless of official nomenclature, then, we will use here the old term which stubborn New Yorkers retain.

For finding the nearest cross streets on the avenues of the city we and "The Red Book" provide the following parlor game.

To find what street is nearest, take the house or building number, cancel last figure, divide by 2, add or subtract the key number found below. The result will be the nearest street (approximately, we might add).

Ave. A ....*Add* 3

Ave. B ....*Add* 3

Ave. C ....*Add* 3

Ave. D ....*Add* 3

1st Ave. .....*Add* 3

2nd Ave. .....*Add* 3

3rd Ave. .....*Add* 10

4th Ave. .....*Add* 8

5th Ave.

  Up to 200 ...*Add* 13

  Up to 400 ...*Add* 16

  Up to 600 ...*Add* 18

  Up to 775 ...*Add* 20

  From 775 to 1286...

    Cancel last figure

    and subt. 18

  Up to 1500 ..*Add* 45

Above 2000 ..*Add* 24

Ave. of the

  Americas ..*Subt.* 12

7th Ave. ....*Add* 12

  Above 110th

  St. ....*Add* 20

8th Ave. ....*Add* 10

9th Ave. ....*Add* 13

10th Ave. ....*Add* 14

Amsterdam

  Ave. ....*Add* 60

Audubon Ave. *Add* 165

B'way above

  23rd St. ...*Subt.* 30

Columbus

  Ave. ....*Add* 60

Convent Ave. .*Add* 127

Edgecombe

  Ave. ....*Add* 134

Central Park West ...*Divide house number by 10 and add 60*

Riverside Drive ......*Divide house number by 10 and add 72 up to 165th St.*

Ft. Washington

  Ave. ....*Add* 158

Lenox Ave. ..*Add* 110

Lexington

  Ave. ....*Add* 22

Madison Ave. .*Add* 26

Manhattan

  Ave. ....*Add* 100

Park Ave. ...*Add* 35

Pleasant Ave. .*Add* 101

St. Nicholas

  Ave. ....*Add* 110

Wadsworth

  Ave. ....*Add* 173

West End

  Ave. ....*Add* 60

Hard as it is to believe, the above system works. Don't strain it for perfection; but it will perform quite competently. As to the numbers on cross streets there is no set of mystic additions and subtractions. Cross streets run from a theoretical 1 east and west off Fifth Avenue in the center of the town up to the area of Central Park. If you reach beyond 500 you are either near or in one of the rivers.

To return to maps for a moment: those you get at the Bureau will be fine for general orientation, but you might need more detailed maps for walks. The *AAA* (Madison Ave. and 78th St., JU 6-2800; and branches at 109 E. 40th St., Statler Hotel, and Broadway and 62nd St.—all three JU 6-1166) has very good borough maps which they distribute to out-of-town visitors, whether members of AAA or not, and to New York City members; centrally-located bookshops and newsstands sell these same maps also. They may be more cumbersome than the schematic, smaller one, but essentially more useful and interesting.

Should you become helplessly enmeshed by the city's streets, buses, or subways, never ask a passer-by; he will never have heard of the place you want to reach or will have just arrived from Cincinnati himself. Look for a policeman or the man in the token booth of a subway station, or, if in extremis, call the Transit Authority (UL 2-5000).

A USEFUL NOTE: In addition to the information which this book affords you can supplement your advance knowledge of city events by checking the weekly column "Goings on About Town" in *The New Yorker;* the complete entertainment guide provided by *Cue Magazine;* "A Weekly Guide to Leisure Time in New York" provided in the Saturday edition of *The World-Telegram and Sun;* the surfeit of activity and entertainment advertising in the Saturday New York *Post;* and the concert, music, art, and general culture information abundantly described in the Sunday entertainment section of the New York *Times* and *Herald Tribune.*

TELEPHONE NOTE: The telephone numbers of the Transit Authority, the Convention and Visitors Bureau, and the AAA (listed in this chapter) are happily supplemented by other sources of information about the city's places and pleasures: The New York Public Library (Fifth Ave. at 42nd St. branch, OX 5-4200); The Brooklyn Public Library (Grand Army Plaza branch, ST 3-2300); the New York *Times* (LA 4-1000); New York *Herald Tribune* (PE 6-4000); the New York *News* Information and Travel Bureau (767 Second Ave., MU 2-1234). Also regardless of what kind of information you want about departments, agencies, or services you think should be available in New York City, if you call WH 3-3600 and ask for "Information Service" the chances are you will find out about them.

3
OASES

The visitor who spends only several days in New York is prepared, or should be, for a total expenditure of energy and money, and for utter collapse when he gets home. This excess makes for the bromidic: "It's all right for a visit but . . ." and the usual questions, "How can you live here? How can you keep up the pace?" New Yorkers rarely try to. We don't go to the theater every night, we don't shop every day, we go to night clubs rarely, and we experience visitors' depletion-fog only when we try to live as they do, accompanying them on incredibly greedy rounds. The New Yorker's constitution is no sturdier than any other's. In a short violent visit to Rome or Paris, he feels exactly as does the person from Oshkosh in New York. It is not only the frantic rushing to experience all one can, but also the assault of so many lives and events, unseen and unheard, pulsating around one, the exuberant varieties of people and enterprise, of millions of activities bubbling and throbbing in an immense caldron, unknown but felt—it is these that help cause the glutted exhaustion.

Parks

The visitor who stays longer will inevitably come to a time when he himself must run from, rather than welcome, the noise and crowd. The first obvious escape is his own hotel room. But that could give the feeling of being the only child not invited to the noisy party across the street. To elude the city and still be part of it is the trick. The parks, of course, answer the problem in good weather. Central Park in the center of the city, Prospect Park in Brooklyn, and Bronx Park to the north offer refuge, except on Sundays, when they are enchantingly peopled and too crowded to be restorative. If it must be a weekend day, find the obscurer corners, away from the baseball diamonds and the eating places and the zoos. Find the little gardens and small wooded paths, the areas which offer no enlightenment or entertainment, but which serve modestly as connective tissue for the livelier centers. The Bronx Zoo's multiplicity of sounds translates itself into an equally rich gathering of color in the Bronx Botanical Gardens, north of the Zoo, and the Brooklyn Museum on Eastern Parkway is flanked by lovely gardens threaded through with pleasant walks. In addition to the more easily accessible parks mentioned, there is Fort Tryon Park, above the Hudson in Washington Heights, Inwood Park, a bit north of that, Van Cortlandt Park at the northern end of the city, and wooded and almost rural areas in Queens and Staten Island.

A remarkable, almost wholly unknown and—considering the vaunted urbanity of New York—disingenuously rustic, phenomenon is the *Jamaica Bay Wildlife Refuge* (on Cross Bay Blvd., just south of North Channel Bridge, and easily accessible from borough parkways; open, as the Department of Parks describes it with unconventional imprecision, from "dawn until dusk"; visitor's permit obtainable from N.Y. State Conservation Dept., 270 Broadway—CO 7-2626). Situated on a reclaimed plot of 3200 acres containing islands and rivers, it houses numerous species of birds and offers ideal bird-watching for visiting Englishmen and New Yorkers taking up a country pastime.

Staten Island

Staten Island, to many New Yorkers, is a large sand bar holding only docks where the ferries pause before resuming the lovely round-trip ferry ride between South Ferry in Manhattan and St. George in Staten Island, each trip (they run frequently throughout the day) at the cost of an anachronistic nickel. Not so; within an undramatic compass, the Island contains a good variety of places and terrain, enough to fill several pleasant days of sight-seeing and wandering.

It is still surprisingly green and rural for a borough of New York and, although suburban developments are springing up quickly as transit communications with Manhattan improve, the large farms, the stretches of dour marsh, historic houses, and the little country stores will remain for some time, giving the cosmopolite a hardy taste of rural U.S.A. The best way to see the Island is, of course, by car. If you can't borrow or rent one, the local buses and an inconsequential amount of walking will get you to most of the places mentioned, but a car is infinitely better. Saturdays and Sundays are the best times to go, since some of the local monuments are open only on those days (lack of money and interest, as usual), even though the wait for the ferry may be longer and more harrowing than on weekdays.

An interesting trip through the Island may be made by following Richmond Road (leftward from the ferry stop), with a pause at the *Stillwell-Perine House* (built in 1679) and, in New Dorp, farther on, at the *Jacques Marchais Center of Tibetan Art*, whose temple and museum are open to the public rather rarely (3-5 Tuesdays and Thursdays, free; and the second and fourth Sundays of each month, 25¢). It's worth seeing if your hours coincide.

The road then takes a turn left, near which (at 63 Arthur Kill Rd.) sits the *Vorleezer House*, a dour, simple house once part of a busy primitive community whose ruins are still visible. Built prior to 1696, it was possibly the first elementary school in the United States. (Saturdays and Sundays, April-November, 2-5; and by appointment; adults 10¢, children free.)

Nearby, on Center Street in Richmond, stop for a long look at the *Staten Island Historical Society* (see page 128), and proceed southward to the Island's end (Tottenville) where, on a beautiful rise from the water's edge, fronting a view of New Jersey across the inlet, stands the *Billop Conference House*. The noblest mansion on Staten Island before the American Revolution, it later became famous as the scene of a meeting requested by Lord Howe to feel out the strength of American insistence on independence; Edward Rutledge, John Adams, and Benjamin Franklin met with him in September of 1776 and made, obviously, no concessions. Erected sometime before 1688, it was restored about twenty years ago and suitable period furniture was brought in. Except for an unrestored porch, the building looks as it did originally, at least on the outside: it isn't likely that the rich Billops,

in their fine house, had the kind of dull, mediocre furnishings now in it. But the house itself is good-looking
and the view imposing.

From the Conference House, pick up Arthur Kill Road
again and follow it as it wanders northward, through
rural communities of small houses and country stores,
with here and there a decayed aristocratic house, tur-
reted, convoluted, and maddened in the style of Hopper
and Charles Addams. Edging Rossville is a ships' bone-
yard, steel and wood rusting and bleaching, and right
near it, running along the road, a strip of old graveyard,
the stones at the same crazy angles as the worn masts,
as if to maintain a unity of funerary design.

One of the few places to eat on this end of Staten
Island is *Al Deppe's* "Clam Bar–Amusement Hall–Ice
Cream Stand" from which you can get onto Richmond
Avenue (watch the Richmonds; they are many and sometimes confusing) and ride into a completely different
terrain—marshlands with tall stands of sedge and then
orderly farms whose greenhouses and selling stands dot
the road. The horizontal quiet of the country doesn't
dampen the spirits of the lively *Farmers Market* on Saturday afternoon. What if the "fresh country" eggs come
from a warehouse in the city or the imported Sicilian
salami is marked "Armour," and the vegetable vender's
hands quicker than your eye? There *is* the rarity of a
used bookshop in its own separate shack, and everywhere the entertaining disorder of chocolate cookies
melting onto socks, artificial flowers bursting over salami,
sentimental chromos staring at work pants, and gaudy
streams of costume jewelry running everywhere.

Continuing on Richmond Avenue, you will find it soon
becomes Richmond Terrace as it curves east on the
northern end of the Island, hugging the waterfront, re-
vealing ships and shipyards, a spectacular view of Ba-
yonne Bridge, and farther on, the very famous view of
the New York skyline.

This is just an appetizer, a mere sampling of Staten
Island's charms. The well-arranged Zoo and the Staten
Island Institute of Arts and Sciences, the eminence of
Todt Hill, the Garibaldi Memorial, the resplendent Van-

derbilt Mausoleum in the Moravian Cemetery, the Sailors' Snug Harbor, are all still there and worth a return trip.

Sundry Other Shelters

Back in the city, there are more and other kinds of oases. The more popular and centrally located museums should be oases, but often are not, each crowded with its own caste of clientele. The *Museum of Natural History* and the *Hayden Planetarium* burst with little boys. The *Museum of Modern Art* accommodates hordes of young intellectuals, many of them more impassioned by the old movies than the new art. A more staid group (as befits the classics) fills the *Metropolitan Museum of Art,* particularly the rooms devoted to the great paintings and special exhibitions; here, too, the little boy and his friends play hide and seek among the Egyptian tombs and the knights in armor. There is, however, beautiful isolation and quiet in the rooms of Persian rugs and Oriental objects, among the ancient musical instruments, and the historic rooms of the American Wing. Another calming place in the Museum is the restaurant, situated on the main floor beyond the classical section. It surrounds a spacious pool in which young male muses of bronze ride on the backs of dolphin-fountains. The food, like most museum food, is ascetic, but the cool quiet affords compensation.

Those specialists' museums which are open to the general public, though inhabited mainly by small numbers of experts and devotees, offer the haven of silent long halls and the slightly triste charms of a diffident spinster, left too untouched. Try the *Hispanic Museum* or the *Museum of the American Indian* or the *Jewish Museum. The Cloisters* was altogether designed for escape: it sits on one of the crests of upper Manhattan, with walks and gardens fronting on a largesse of Hudson River views. Its medieval form and situation (like one of the castle-church-fortresses on the Garonne) and the medieval art it contains make the perfect remove from the present time and place. Its small well-ordered gardens, imitating those of the monasteries, the complete stillness of its ancient chapel, and the patiently-wrought felicity of its Unicorn tapestries temper haste and disquiet.

WHERE . . . WHEN . . . HOW: The vital statistics for each of the museums mentioned in this section (and for others, as well) are gathered together for convenience in the chapter especially devoted to museums, beginning on page 105. Note especially page 106, where data on locations, hours, fees, transportation routes, and the like are given for the major institutions.

Busy places in their off-time have their own particular enchantments as oases. There is Coney Island in the late fall and winter, the ferris wheels frozen in the sky, the carousel horses still and shrouded, the loops of roller coasters waiting in disuse, the smell of popcorn and frankfurters dispelled by winds, and the boardwalk a clear long stretch of shuttered stands and sea view. The Wall Street financial area on late Saturday afternoon or Sunday is a peaceful canyon; the elevators have stopped swallowing and disgorging thousands of people; the narrow crowded streets have lost their rivers of people and are now empty arroyos between the silent blind faces of tall buildings; the sky is small and elusive; and the only things of organic life are an occasional waterfront rat playing between the rivers, and the cat who awaits him. Nothing moves but the breeze which carries spice smells of Java and India, not quite trapped in the warehouses of Pearl Street.

The public libraries (N.Y. Public Library, branch and central library information, OX 5-4200) are good places for seclusion, except on Saturday afternoons, when the literate young traditionally take over.

The city's cafeterias (see page 133) are also good shelters. Unlike the libraries, they are not altogether free, nor are they peace-inducing during the popular mealtime hours. In the off-hours, however, you can sit and read a newspaper or just chew your cud for the price of a cup of coffee. It is best that you don't finish the coffee, so that the cup can stand before you as witness to your respectability. Should you make the mistake of finishing, the cup will be whisked away and you will be left without protection from a baleful eye or even an invitation to get going.

For sitting and staring without the need for the mask of a book or coffee, there are the bus and airline terminal waiting rooms, the benches in the Channel Gardens in Rockefeller Center, hotel lobbies, and the "Piazzale" Seagram on Park Avenue at 52nd Street. The Seagrams planned their new dark-gold (a Medici color) building to include the bravura Renaissance gesture of an expanse of plaza, fountains, a few trees, and a low marble-topped wall that makes good sitting. The waste of building space in this part of the city, where the value of land is that of diamonds elsewhere, is a startlingly magnificent piece of advertising, impressive to everyone and deeply valued by New Yorkers, especially by the couples decorously lunching out of paper bags on the broad comfortable wall.

The ease and pleasant torpor to be found in a hairdresser's chair or a barber shop are common knowledge and comfort, but lest you forget, this is a reminder; almost every city block has one or more of these temporary rest homes. And, following a more exact meaning of the word, there is the oasis of the saloon. Not the cocktail lounge or bar, roaring with excessive affability, jagged neon lights, and restless television images, but a saloon—taciturn, profoundly serious and exclusive, its welcome reserved for locals or the compatibles of one country or dialect. (You will not be unwelcome if you maintain a proper unobtrusiveness.) The most authentic and quiet of these are in old slum neighborhoods and are to be looked for if you wander in the rougher paths of the city. Not quite as basic, but reasonably like them are the Irish saloons on Third Avenue, between Sixtieth and Eightieth Streets. They are slowly diminishing in number, which doesn't diminish the greenness of the shamrocks on their signs, or the opacity of the green paint on their windows or the resounding purity of their names—Moriarty's, the Shannon Bar and Restaurant, Delaney's, Breffney's, O'Rourke's, Halloran's—or their thick, slowly gathered quiet, a quiet which no new place can have. There are others along Third Avenue, farther down, but some of the old saloons have been made self-conscious by an accretion of an enameled atmosphere, coy fittings of "Americana," and bar flies with extravagant vocabularies. Pass these by (after you've examined their exteriors which bear some handsome stained glass, cut glass, and pillars) and go north or east to Second Avenue, to the womb dimness of the *Old Landmark* at 1012 Second Ave., of *Cook's Bar and Grill* at 69th or *Ruderman's* at 70th. If you prefer the West Side, Eighth and Ninth Avenues abound in the Irish version of *gemutlichkeit* and so do Columbus and Amsterdam Avenues, farther north. The *Old Knick* at 91st (635 Columbus Ave.) has the proper tranquility, and so does the *Kelly Bros. Bar* at 83rd (481 Amsterdam); the latter has broken one rule by putting up a new sign recently, and another by being brightly lit, but it does sport some cut glass and a pleasant odor of age without being decrepit.

Should you be passing through town and need some nonalcoholic restoration, like getting cleaned up between trains, investigate the facilities of *Grand Central Station* or the *Port Authority Bus Terminal*, which are not nearly as all-encompassing as the Italian Albergo Diurnio, but have sections which serve similarly. At Grand Central, men can rent razors, shower, get hats cleaned, and suits pressed at the usual small sums just below the ramp leading down from Vanderbilt Avenue at 42nd Street. Women can't shower for some inexplicable reason, but there are dressing rooms in which to change and rooms equipped for baby-changing. (These latter, off the Women's Waiting Room, cost 25¢.) The *Port Authority Bus Terminal* (Eighth Ave., 40th-41st Sts.) doesn't discriminate: there are separate but equal showers for both men and women (50¢), off the rest rooms, and the use of soap and towels for a nickel. For more luxurious cleaning up and resting, a number of hotels offer day rates (from any time in the morning to 6:00 P.M.) at a cost that hovers around $5.00.

A not inappropriate end of a discussion of oases brings us to the simplest and most basic of all—the toilet and where to find it. In this respect, New York City lacks the civilized amenities of even small European towns: we have no comforting signs of "Señoras" and "Señores" guiding toward subterranean chambers in a main plaza. Except for a few little temples in WPA style, we have no little booths for men or dark medieval *cul de sacs* (except for the arches under the Brooklyn Bridge, which smell like the back streets of Dijon) nor the cafes which are large public houses and conveniently usable. It is an odd aspect of American Puritanism that the shops around Times Square can sell naked-lady playing cards, but no public toilet facilities are available for the people who buy them. Why we recognize sex but not elimination leads to some interesting conjecture, but not for a guidebook.

The city's central areas produce no special problems: hotels have rest rooms off their lobbies, *Horn and Hardart Automat* restaurants (38 at latest count; the phone books list addresses) can be used without cost, *Grand Central Station, Pennsylvania Station,* and the bus and airlines depots are well-equipped, though free booths become fewer with the years. The department stores are concerned mainly about women; they may have men's toilets, but those are well hidden, and men will find saloons more immediately hospitable. In sections away from the center of the city, it begins to cost: subway stations have toilets situated beyond the turnstiles so that relief must be paid for by a token (still 15¢ at press time) and possible supervision by a member of the Vice Squad; cafeterias require the price of a cup of coffee. Where there are no cafeterias and the subway stations are distant, and there are no department stores and few restaurants, as in Spanish Harlem and the lower East Side, the thing to do is look for a taxi and dash back to your hotel room, or stop people on the street, ascertain who is local, and beg to be invited to his home for a few minutes.

4

WALKS, AND A
RIDE OR TWO

The following section describes mainly walks, because in spite of civilization's advances, one's own feet are still the best conveyors for exploring. It is assumed that at some time during your stay, you will have covered some portions of Fifth Avenue, Madison Avenue, 34th Street, 42nd Street, 57th Street, and Broadway. If those, and the walks described, aren't enough, you might enjoy the elegant small houses in the East 60's and 70's off Fifth Avenue; the thoroughly Teutonic air of Yorkville (86th St. east of Lexington); the Hungarian and Czech neighborhoods below 79th Street on First and Second Avenues; the expensive, aristocratic boutiques of all kinds in the 50's between Sixth and Madison Avenues; the neglected charms of Chelsea, west of Eighth Avenue on 20th, 21st, and 22nd Streets; or the St. James quality of Gramercy Park and its surrounding streets, particularly 19th Street from Third Avenue westward, which was once (and could still be) called "The Block Beautiful." A really ambitious walker might tackle the bridges—the George Washington Bridge, over the Hudson at about 177th Street; the Brooklyn Bridge, which crosses the East River from just east of City Hall Park in Manhattan; the Williamsburg Bridge, which also crosses the East River, via Delancey Street in the lower East Side; these afford superb views and occasional gusts of clear, fresh air.

Any bus line in the city will take you through something of interest. If you have the time, go to the end of one line or other and back via a bus line on the next block (they run on almost every north-south avenue); the possibilities are endless for discovery and surprise.

Should you have a car at your disposal, drive the length of the city on both the East Side and West Side Drives, which skirt, respectively, the East River and the Hudson. The views of the edges of the city and the rivers are magnificent and worth the hire of a car, and a chauffeur, too. Be careful not to take any bridge or tunnel exits because you may be lost for weeks; consult the AAA or a garage attendant before you launch your car.

CAR-RENTAL NOTE: *Carey Cadillac Renting Co.* provides car and chauffeur for an afternoon, an evening, or a longer period (PL 5-6400; DC). Drive-yourself cars are available from many firms, including **Hertz** (MU 8-7744; DC) and *Avis* (TE 8-7518).

For a new slant on New York, try seeing Manhattan by air. Helicopter sightseeing trips leave the Heliport at West 30th Street and Twelfth Avenue (IL 8-7400) on Saturdays and Sundays. The glass-enclosed Bell 47J helicopter carries three people, plus the pilot, over a stretch of five to ten miles of Manhattan in six or seven minutes. You will be shown the Statue of Liberty, the financial district, the Empire State Building, the Chrysler Building, and the bridges and ships of the East River. $5 per person is the charge.

Around-the-Island Boat Trips

New York City is wonderfully lucky in its rivers. The Seine permits you the undersides of many small bridges and odd views—upward and distorted of Notre Dame and the Ile de la Cité—but it is mainly the river itself and its embankments that you view from the *bateaux mouches* of Paris; the excursion boats on the Thames are very pleasant, but it is a segmented London that you see; the Tiber is hardly navigable by anything but orange peel; and the Arno is, for most of the year, a moist laceration. The Hudson and East Rivers, though, girdle New York City with a band of water which afford two sets of spectacular and continuous views—from the city onto the rivers and from the rivers to the city. The best of the latter, unless you have access to a yacht, can be had from the little steamers that keep circling the island.

The boats present dramatically two concepts New Yorkers are likely to forget, trudging their ways through narrow terrestrial centers: New York is an immense port and a smallish island. From the rivers one can see the endless stretches of water leading into the Atlantic, the piers holding the great liners (like a gigantic stableful of huge, tired Percherons), the freighters heavy with bananas, waiting to be lightened, the tugs purposefully dragging barges of coal, like ants with large leaves. Then there is the city itself, or its many selves: the green embroidery of parks on its edges, the homogenized design of housing projects broken by the few remaining old houses and gardens off Sutton Place, the busy playgrounds and the rippled ribbons of cars on the encircling highways. Beyond them, like a volcanic upthrust, there are the peaks of skyscrapers backed by the solid cliffs of the Palisades and echoed horizontally by the bold, massive bridges.

This beautiful journey is an easy one to make: *Circle Line* boats (CI 6-3100) leave from Pier 83 at West 43rd Street and the Hudson River; *Day Line* boats (JU 6-5300) leave from Pier 81 at West 41st Street. Departures on both lines are from about 9:30 A.M. to 6:00 P.M. in the evening, leaving at intervals of an hour or less, during the summer months, and less frequently in the spring and fall (no winter sailings). Since the schedules of both lines differ a little, and they are so close to each other, getting on one line's boats or the other's should be easy at almost any time during the day. The 42nd Street crosstown bus (make sure it's that) will take you close to the piers. The charge is $2.50 for adults and $1.25 for children. A trip from Slip 2 at the Battery is considerably cheaper, but it means being more careful of your timing since the sailings are less frequent (at one and one-half hour intervals starting at 10:30 A.M.) and necessitates a subway ride, via the IRT, to South Ferry.

Take sunglasses, a sweater, and refreshments for your children; the trip takes about two and a half hours or a little more, and although refreshments and sandwiches are available, you won't want to take time for purchasing away from time for viewing. Take your deaf ear, too, in case the guide on your boat happens to be a personality kid (there are only a few of these, fortunately) who considers himself the most impressive experience of the trip.

Third Avenue International

The best fifteen-cent value in New York City (it will inevitably increase and still be a good value) is a ride on the Third Avenue bus from City Hall to 128th Street.

And should you get off to walk in any particular area
that attracts you and then get on again, the doubled or
tripled price is still a sightseeing bargain. Although the
removal of the Third Avenue El and its protective shadows have caused the secluded darkness of some sections
to put on more respectable, and duller, coats of paint,
it still remains a fascinating journey.

Fronting the terminal bus stop stands graceful City
Hall, serene, elegant, and startlingly antique among the
crags of gray skyscrapers, a lovely eccentric amidst the
sensible. The bus waddles northward, offering a quick
glimpse of the interlaced bands of Brooklyn Bridge, and
then wanders up Park Row, past shops of cheap musical
instruments, past pawnshops, and then past a corner of
Chinatown, which displays its Bowery side with two
movie theaters, two Chinese food markets, a sign on the
Bridge Clam House which advertises *scunghilli* and
spaghetti in Chinese as well as English, and a spacious,
antique barber shop which announces "Haircuts" in
Chinese, as well as—this time in Spanish—the fact that
it does tattooing. The color of the Bowery turns dimmer
then, in a strip of dingy saloons, flophouses, greasy luncheonettes, shops indifferently offering store fixtures and
cheap furniture, and employment agencies for the local
unemployables. To break the monotony comes the *Fat
Men's Shop* which is precisely as named ("Shirts to 22,
Sleeves to 38, Waists to 70"; 52 Third Ave.), and the wed-
ding-costume (hire or purchase) shops on Grand Street,
a dazzling row of billow, gaud, glitter, ebullience,
and intimate names—Marie, Marlene, Tessie—splashed
across the store fronts. Nearer 14th Street, pawnshops,
barber-supply houses, and cheap clothing shops take
dominance again, never obliterating, though, the ever-
present saloon. From 14th to 23rd, there is a gray stretch
of no particular character.

Things begin to happen again north of 23rd Street:
groceries which supply a local Middle-Eastern section
and its strip of restaurants (page 175) sport the names of
Turkish and Armenian proprietors (page 235); the International Gin-Seng Company indicates a small, tightly
packed group of Chinese who live on 28th Street be-

tween Third and Second Avenues only, and mostly on
the north side of the block at that; among the Easterners
and Middle-Easterners, Italian stores trumpet the availability of Hero sandwiches and Italian imports (page
233); here and there, heavy Hebrew letters indicate
kosher butcher shops; small Spanish signs and store-
iglesias (street-floor storefront evangelical churches) spot
the neighborhood. All together, they make an enchanting
mixture of colors, repeating one of the salient attractions
of the city.

The color turns to that of money near 42nd Street; the
antique shops come into view, first sporadically, and then
in a great, blinding burst of gilded chairs and mirrors,
crystal chandeliers, Capa da Monte fixtures, Chinese
vases, immense, gilded ships' figurehead women scream-
ing into a remembered wind, a huge red chair that might
have held a Teutonic chieftain as he drank his mead and
listened to a bard tell an ancient saga, rugs, Tarascan
figures (often fake) with sweet, foolish smiles on their
faces, and almost anything else old, odd, expensive, and
salable. Having been poor from the Bowery on, Third
Avenue now sings of luxury spending, its new tune
backed by the chorus of wealth emerging from the huge,
new office buildings filling the Grand Central Area.

After the profligate spree of 42nd to 62nd Streets,
among the antique stores and a few chic shops of very
high-style and choice "casual" clothing for high-style,
choice men, and with occasional down-to-earth dips to
Scandinavian groceries, seafood restaurants, and saloons,
Third Avenue settles into lower-middle-class decay: the
objets shops appear more raffish and hang in the limbo
between antique and junk, and the dusty, wistful charms
of thrift shops (page 219) come to the fore. And then
come the butcher shops. There are no known statistics
(except in meat-packing offices, possibly) of the number
of butcher shops or tons of meat consumed between 67th
and 90th Streets on the East Side, but the figures might
be startling. The inhabitants of the neighborhood cannot
be of one especially meat-addicted tribe, because any
newsstand in the area carries a startling diversity of
papers—the *Staatszeitung*, the *Irish Advocate*, the *Irish*

Echo, a Hungarian paper, *Novy Swiat,* the *Catholic News,*
and *La Prensa* among the more ordinary rest. It cannot
be a case of large spending, because, with the exception
of a growing number of buildings with luxury accommo-
dations, the area is preponderantly working class—the
Civil Service Leader (which informs about not-too-well
paid civil-service jobs) is more conspicuous than the
Wall Street Journal. Whatever the reason, there they are,
butcher shops decorated with Irish sausage, Hungarian
sausage, German wurst, kosher frankfurters, geese, ducks,
Polish ham, and glossy innards.

Having left the carnivorous Czechs, Hungarians, and
Germans who dominate 72nd to 88th Streets, the bus
enters a small but concentrated Irish area, considerably
reduced from an earlier size. There are close clusters of
saloons with shamrocks on the canopies, green paint on
the windows (the names on the lintels are Walsh,
O'Halloran, Pat McCann). The grocery stores have
names like "The Emerald Food Shop" and conspicuously
feature Irish stew, Irish bacon, Irish blood pudding, and
Irish fruit cake.

In the upper 90's, Third Avenue undergoes another
shift in mood, tone, and tongue: no more opulent butcher
shops featuring thirty-one varieties of sausage, no more
canisters of Irish tea, no more antique or even thrift
shops, just small, meagerly supplied groceries called
"Carmen," whose essential note is struck by a few plantains lying in the window. We have entered Spanish
Harlem, where "Call Me Sol" supplies children's and
women's clothing on long "lay-away" terms, and "El
Jardin del Arte" sells chromos and religious figurines and
repairs television and radio sets. Above 110th Street,
Third Avenue becomes the street of serious shopping
for *muebles, ropas,* and *televisiones,* while the smaller,
more interesting shops hide on the side streets (page
91).

The Manhattan portion of Third Avenue ends in the
stretch from 125th to 128th Streets, trailing off in tired
groceries, in a pawnshop or two, in hardware and tin-
ware and paint stores maintained for a meager living
and no show. Like the shops on the Bowery before they

were denuded of the El, they don't expect to be seen and don't give a damn what they look like; they are at the end of the line and stand listlessly beneath their slum houses waiting for almost anything to happen.

NOTE: Combinations with other trips can be many: Walks in Chinatown, Spanish and Italian Harlem, the Lower East Side, the very end of lower Manhattan, etc. (all described in this chapter).

Rims of Waters Walk

Having come (via IRT or BMT subways or Third Ave. or Broadway bus) to the southern end of Manhattan, and having explored the Stock Exchange, St. Paul's, Trinity Church, and City Hall on the excellent advice of the Visitors Bureau pamphlets (page 32), return to City Hall Park. Start southward on Broadway and into its adjoining ancient roadways which were gradually narrowed into threads by the increasing heights of their buildings—Liberty Street, Exchange Place, Pine Street— and look from east to west for slits of sky and river. As you continue south on Broadway, past the good men's furnishing shops, the elaborate stationery stores, the restaurants, the stool-and-counter coffee shops, you will notice that the banking houses give way to steamship lines and importing offices with name plaques that echo over great distances. At Bowling Green, there is a promise of openness shadowed by the bastion of the United States Customs House, and beyond that, suddenly, the openness of the sea.

Just north of Battery Park, toward the Hudson edge of the island, there is a ramp which stretches across a knotting of roadways, collecting and spreading the East and West Side Drives as they flow to and from Brooklyn. The imposing contrapuntal design of the roadways replaced, some years ago, the homelier charms of an Arab-tongued neighborhood and the lamented Washington Market. Not much is left of the former except a few signs and import offices and a stubborn shop, A. *Sahadi and Co.* (195 Washington St., which has the hookahs and pewter trays and honeyed nut cakes more commonly seen now in the East 20's and on Atlantic Avenue in Brooklyn. Of the Washington Market little is left but memories of elegant elderly gentlemen purchasing bear steaks and cuts of venison in season and inspecting the perfect fruits and exotic vegetables. At the corner of Washington and Vesey, an old grocer still maintains the color of the neighborhood as international food purveyor: he stocks canned tacos dinners, suet pudding, and spices and grains from all over the world, including a sack of Cassia Ficula whose sign recommends it as a laxative. And off Washington, at 235 Fulton Street, stands *Phil Alpert's* international cheese store and its neighbors, a few choice fruit and vegetable stores. The neighboring buildings, blind and silent during the day, burst into noisy energy after midnight when their stores of produce are released to run through the city (see pages 314-16).

Cut across eastward to Brooklyn Bridge, and stopping now and then to admire the changing views of the Bridge, follow its downtown side (Frankfort Street) toward the East River. This street and its small obscure offshoots, Gold Street, Jacob Street, Rose Street, have been the streets of the tanners and leather craftsmen from New York's very early days and it still is a leather center, smelling of hides and glue mixed with whiffs of herring from a nearby importer's. One of the smaller shops sells "Shoulders, Bellies, Splits, Strips, and Offal"; another specializes in colored pieces to sell by the pound to children's camps and handicrafters. Around the corner, on Williams Street, a firm confines its interests to kangaroo hides, while several others have followed the "do-it-yourself" drive by putting in tools and accessories for leathercrafting and other crafts.

As Williams meets Beekman, you will notice that the leather section has given way to paper and printing. Follow Beekman eastward to the river and you will find yourself just north of the *Fulton Fish Market*, which except for a few violent hours at dawn (see page 315) is shuttered and somnolent. It leaves its odor, though. As you stand in the square of Fulton Street, your head lightly enveloped in the smell of fish from the east, coffee from the west, and leather from the north, you might try to imagine the scene a century ago: the now-filled square then a slip crowded with every kind of vessel, carrying every kind of cargo from every known port, their officers in dignified city clothing mounting the stairs to dine at *Sweet's* (page 154) on the corner, others searching through the local chandlers' shops for rope and net replacements.

The flavor of foreign ports and strange tongues is not altogether gone by any means. It lingers in the small shops which carry freight hooks, seamen's oilskin suits, foghorns, and purposeful knives, and is harbored in an establishment (a vague word to cover a vague identity) called the *Eagle Bag and Burlap Co.* at 12 Fulton Street (page 239). Farther south on the river front and in some of the plazas built on the filled-in slips (John Street, Old Slip, Coenties Slip) are proud old houses with proud gold-on-black signs and old glass in many-paned windows. Their wares are still cordage, anchors, signal flags, marine letters, caulking materials, and marine hardware. Some are close-lipped, quiet places encased in old habits, some are slap-dash and lively, gay centenarians meeting modern times with water skis and yachting fancies. Look in at *B. Sack and Son* (54-55 South St.). They won't mind, unless you get tangled in the mounds of rope everywhere or permit yourself to be assaulted by one of the bundles of heavy supplies some giant keeps lowering from an overhead cache. Or go into *A. L. Don Co.* (37 South St.), and then look at the very old, solid sign of *De Grauw, Aymar and Co.* (34 South St.) and notice its high ledge, built to meet an ancient water line. Just above A. L. Don's, there is a seamen's supply shop, *Nifoussi Bros.* (39 South St.); it carries underwear, work clothes, boots, sea bags, and valises exactly like those found in the waterfront shops of Marseilles, of Naples, of Trinidad—and like those shops, is also run by multilingual Levantines and is as international as the sea itself.

A good place to finish this walk might be the *Seamen's Church Institute* at Coenties Slip (25 South St.). If you have the time, look through its *Marine Museum* (page 196) or, if you need a rest and a bite to eat, go down to

its cafeteria. Aside from a local file clerk or two escaping
for a coffee break, the clientele consists of groups of men
in fresh white shirts, few smoking and all talking quietly.
There is an almost disappointing lack of O'Neill torment
—no drunkenness, no knives, no roaring chanteys, no "ole
dabbil sea," just pleasant men between voyages, enjoying the Institute's hospitality and inexpensive food.

If you are not quite ready to return to your hotel, you
might walk into the streets west and north of Coenties
Slip, where you will find, among the giants, small houses
reminiscent of London courts and a few Greenwich Village streets. A few transplanted Villagers have actually
moved into them because the space is more generous,
the rents lower, and the nights and weekends quieter.
Stone Street or Beaver will lead you to the heavy solidity
of Hanover Square, on which imposing India House
stands as if planted there forever and, nearby, a building
whose ancient front still bears the carved letters, "Delmonico's," a name which at one time meant champagne,
pots of money, flavorsome food, and flavorsome scandal.
This combination of echoes of high life and confident respectability makes Hanover Square an eminent monument of American Victorianism.

LUNCH

Sloppy Louie's just south of Fulton (92 South St.); exceedingly fresh fish, some of which may be new to you, prepared in a variety of styles; inexpensive.

Seamen's Church Institute Cafeteria (25 South St.). Don't
be put off by the sign which limits it to the use of seamen
and their friends. Anyone who comes in is a friend.

For men only: *Volk's* (51 Cortland St., corner of Greenwich) and *McInnes* (67 Cortland); fine old saloon-type
restaurants which may admit women, but not comfortably.

*The Old Jewish East Side, Now Also Puerto Rican,
American Negro, Chinese, Filipino, Italian, and Gypsy*

Roughly, the section called the Jewish East Side (IND
"D" express train to Delancey St.) encompasses the area
bounded west to east by the Bowery and the East River

and north to south by Houston Street and the Brooklyn Bridge. This was the womb of the Jewish colonies which later spilled over into the Bronx and Brooklyn, urged by intense overcrowding and a proliferating mesh of transit facilities. Yet, for many years, no matter how many people it thrust across the bridges and along the elevated lines, the matrix kept gathering in new boarders among the *landsleit;* they made the little apartments more dense, they filled the little synagogues with the breast-beating clamor of Yom Kippur, they chatted with bewigged old ladies who took their Sabbath leisure on the stoops, and in the evenings they gathered in small local restaurants, spas of hot tea, where they discussed the future of the Jew and the working class (a common messianic fusion in those days). Ultimately, many of them left the sweat-shops which had supplied the only work they knew and became the smallest of business men, peddlers. From this status, the enterprising moved on to stores and push-carts in their new ghetto.

The stores remain, although most of the pushcarts are gone, and gone, too, are most of the little boys who played in the streets in skullcaps, and a good number of the kosher chicken stores where, on Thursday nights (for Friday morning preparation) large, lusty men with stained aprons would yell over the mounds of fresh-killed fowl to the approaching women: "Women! Women! I've got the hottest, fattest chickens! The Roth-schilds of chickens, beautiful as the daughters of Israel! Come and buy! Tear-r-r me apart in the r-r-rush, women!" In a corner of the store sat an old crone, her restless hands swiftly plucking feathers off the limp body in her lap. (The chickens were plucked *after* the purchase; no self-respecting Jewish housewife would buy a naked chicken and, as a matter of fact, one of the infallible tests of freshness involved blowing among the feathers after a set of preliminary pokes at the breast to ascertain the degree of plumpness.) Gone, too, are most of the little grocers who sold a half of a quarter of a pound of butter and one egg; their place has been taken by *bodegas* which sell *manteca* and *huevos*. The houses the old proprietors lived in are now used by Puerto Rican

and Negro families and by an increasing number of
Chinese families who cross the once impassable gap
between Mott and Forsyth Streets, via East Broadway.

The owners of the shops on Orchard Street, on Grand,
Allen, Delancey, and the smaller streets that run off them,
are Jewish still, although their domestic lives have followed the classic hegira: lower East Side to East Harlem, to the East Bronx, to the West Bronx, to upper Manhattan on the West Side (whence the next generation
moves to the suburbs). The clothing, yard goods, linen,
and shoe shops have changed in some respects to accommodate the new customers: bedspreads are apt to be
bolder in color and shinier, there are more extensive displays of bright toys and playful parlor ornaments of a
sort which the older Jews held in contempt as foolishness.
Yiddish is giving way to Spanish. The proprietors, like
their confreres in the Park Avenue market (page 92),
speak Spanish to the customers and Yiddish to each other,
and many signs which were bilingually English and Yiddish are now English-Spanish. The remaining Yiddish-
speaking customers are likely to be middle-aged Amer-
ican-born homing pigeons from upper Manhattan whose
Yiddish, never fluent, creaks and halts as they try to
recapture the memories of Poppa and Momma and cold
gefulte fish on Saturday afternoon (after the public
library and before the movies) in a railroad flat in the
East Bronx or Bensonhurst.

A good way to plunge into the heart of this multi-
tongued matter—not on Friday afternoon or Saturday,
Sundays are best—is to enter the *Essex Street Market* at
Delancey (right near the subway station). It is a nice,
big clean market and unremarkable except that it introduces the leitmotif of the present mixture—Puerto Rican
plantains, Chinese bean sprouts, kosher liver, and Italian
sausage. From the market, walk southward to Broome
Street and turn east. The very minor grocery of *Mr.
Hsiang Kee* (220 Broome), a charming man with few
teeth and little English who manages to communicate by
a steady shine of affability, is worth a visit. His stock is
small and completely unlike anything you're accustomed

to in a grocery; there are old eggs and older eggs, some in brine and some in shells blackened with age and decay. Among the jars of gingerroot and beancurd and cans of fish, are containers of roots and herbs which Mr. Hsiang tells you are to be cooked, preferably in the properly balanced combination of six, with meat and fish dishes, not so much for flavor as for their tonic effect. Medicines proper are packed in exquisite little boxes, not much bigger than dice and beautifully colored, worth buying as decorations or souvenirs.

Having exchanged smiles and bows with Mr. Hsiang, continue on Broome to Norfolk which, from Delancey south to East Broadway, is a piece of purity of the old era. In tight rows, as on medieval guild streets, stand the old shops which sell Hebrew religious articles and books. This is where the old men buy their new prayer shawls for the High Holy Days, where *yarmalkas* are purchased for Williamsburg youths (notice that some of them are back-belted in the style of the Ivy League cap) and where the devout buy Bar Mitzvah presents. Some of the proprietors are old men who speak little English and are rather worried about understanding it, others are youngish lightly-bearded scholars, whose gentle, cultivated English carries the mixed accent of many lands of temporary refuge rather than the lifts and stresses of Yiddish.

Turn back to Broome Street, still walking eastward toward Suffolk and Clinton. Here another guild cluster appears: in window after window, as close as possible to the glass in order to catch the full daylight, sit men and women bent in deep concentration over bits of darning, reweaving, and "stoteing" (an inexpensive substitute for weaving). In solitary silence, their heads down and their hand movements subtle, they sit almost motionless, like store-window mannequins who have toppled during the night. Turn south (to the right) on Clinton Street for a look at the sister of the sturdy bagel, the *Byalistoker pletzel*, fondly called "byalies" in the uptown luncheonettes. At 145 Clinton there is a bakery which sells them in their three or four shapes and sizes, hot and chewy, wholesale and retail. Across the street from the bakery is a noteworthy anomaly: a Jewish bar with a Jewish name, *Mendel's* (146 Clinton), curious because, traditionally, liquor played no part in Jewish life except for a glass of ceremonial wine, and older Jews had an abhorrence for more than the ritual cup because drunkenness was so often an important ingredient of Old World pogroms. Its habitués are the semiagnostics of the neighborhood, beardless, portly businessmen un-awed by the Yeshivah around the corner and American-ized into a well-developed taste for beer and saloon conversation. Back across at the corner, is the *G & M Kosher Caterers* (141 Clinton St.) which dispenses only kosher food and since the gamut of traditional dishes—*cholent, kreplach, kishka, kugel*—is somewhat meager for ranging New York tastes, the owners have added kosher meat balls and spaghetti as well as kosher chow mein, repeating the mixture of cuisine as it appears in cafe-terias and Italian *festas.* (Somewhere in this cheerful adoption of each other's food, the city's populace may be gestating an antisegregation moral.)

Continue a bit on Broome, past the *carnicerias* and kosher butcher, the storefronts of nonsectarian *iglesias,* the unused, long-dormant stores; on Attorney Street, just off Broome, you may come on a group of swarthy chil-dren with black curly hair and large eyes, soft, melting, yet wary; these will probably be the only children who will accost you with, "Gimme a nickel." They are obvi-ously not of the same stock as the Jewish children around, or the Puerto Rican or the Italian. They run in and out of stores which contain a few chairs, small tables, and low beds—furniture, walls, and all hung with brilliant strips of discordant cloth. They are gypsies, the progeny of the few remaining members of a once large if restless colony, now partially supplanted by a few Filipino fam-ilies who live above the stores.

Making small detours on the surrounding streets, wan-der back (westward) on Broome across Essex, following small enclaves of shops as they change in specializations from block to block—Essex to Orchard, elastics, boot-black supplies, zippers, buttons; Orchard to Allen, house dresses, aprons, nightgowns; Allen to Forsyth, up For-

syth, into Grand, and beyond to Delancey, interminable
lengths of yard goods. At this point it might be pleasant
to sit for a few minutes in the playground at Grand and
Forsyth. It has tree-shaded benches and, in the summertime, little arcs of water splash coolly into the children's
pool. If you're hungry, stop on Delancey Street, considered in its own sphere one of New York's important eating centers, like the East Fifties or Mott Street. Should
platters of Rumanian steaks or stuffed cabbage seem too
formidable, have a sandwich in one of the delicatessens
which thicken the ripe air of Delancey. Or, if you can,
wait a while until you reach the heights at *Katz's* on
Houston Street (see page 62).

Proceeding southward from Delancey, cutting a divert-
ing zigzag between Ludlow and Essex Streets, one en-
counters at 27½ Essex Street, around the corner from
Hester, a grocery of compelling orthodoxy—cheese, soup
mixes, and even the gelatin desserts are all kosher. One
of the last of a dwindling breed of shops lingers on at 41
Essex. Despite millions spent promoting ready-made cigarettes, there are still a number of urban die-hards who
roll their own, with or without the aid of little machines;
a number of them buy their materials in this old shop.
The front is adorned by two ancient bundles of tobacco
hung, seemingly forever, in its window and, for elegance,
ornate boxes of Russian cigarette papers which, the proprietor says, are quite usable, though of a pre-Stalin
vintage. A sort of red-cage arrangement inside the minute
store encloses the period cash register and jars of tobacco
used for blending individual mixes ("Not artificial sweetened, like uptown") for pipe smokers and the cigarette-
making customers. Much of the custom comes from Jewish patriarchs who formed their smoking habits in Czarist
Russia and cling to the Turkish tobaccos and Russian-
style paper tubes, and from dreamy Russian-Jewish intellectuals for whom the home-made, long-tubed Russian
cigarette, held between thumb and forefinger, makes a
mystic link between themselves and Pushkin. To round
out a meager stock, the owner has put in Italian matches
and novelty cigarette holders—a purchase of one of these
cheap objects or a box of the Turkish cigarettes made on

the premises could be your excuse for walking in, if you feel you need one.

Back on Ludlow Street, there is another sign of change: the dry cleaning shops which once had been exclusively Jewish, are now almost all Chinese. The social center of Ludlow near Canal approaching Chinatown, is the *Yuk One Coffee House* (17 Ludlow St.), a dim little shop whose sidewalk is fringed by a semicircle of old Chinese, sitting on boxes and kitchen chairs, their judicious conversations occasionally interrupted by an impulse to sing softly in unison.

One block east of Ludlow is the famous Orchard Street: at its south end (where you should be now) a dull, inert street, crowded with shops of sweaters, hose, inexpensive underwear and shirts, a good number of them wholesalers for dry-goods stores in other poor neighborhoods. This part of Orchard, up to Delancey, is the dusty stem of the luxuriant flower which burst forth a few blocks north, still splashing some of the color which enlivened so many pages written about immigrant Jews and New York. The pushcarts which used to block the gutters with total contempt for traffic are now sedate stalls attached to the shops, but offering the same enticing junk; an old shoe store where Talmudists once bought soft shoes with elastic sides is now the Casa Cubana Zapateria, which shows little snub-toed pumps with precarious heels and tinkling decorations; an eviscerated kid, its hooves conspicuously cloven, is no longer an unthinkable abomination here, and it hangs like an empty sack from a hook on Stanton Street, in front of a Puerto Rican butcher shop. The next block south, however, Rivington Street, is still the stronghold of kosher wine, the stores proudly advertising the surprising charms of "The Wine You Can Almost Cut with a Knife" and among the semi-solid wines are "appetizing stores," with vats of fat herrings and pink stretches of lox, the paté and caviar of many Jewish households. On Rivington, too (at 168, just off Orchard) is an ancient cubby which specializes in dried mushrooms, a reminder of the days when this ingredient went into almost every old-country soup pot.

Back on Orchard Street, the pants, shirts, house dresses,

and bedcovers tufted in peacock designs hang overhead like the banners of a great tourney. Under them there still ambles the winter's sweet-potato man (they're cheaper if you can make your purchase in Yiddish) and the summer's watermelon man, who may not, as in the old days, let you heft two or three slices to ascertain which is the best buy, but who will respect your right to deliberate and select "without the hands, please."

The north end of Orchard is marked by a broad shopping street known as "Houston" (Texas fashion) to outlanders, purists, and Anglo-Saxons; its friends and lovers call it "Howston" and the difference distinctly separates the "ins" from the "outs." Houston has a number of good food shops, but they are overtowered by three temples which, together, are a Mecca of the nostalgic.

Katz's Delicatessen (205 E. Houston St.) has been draping frankfurters in sauerkraut, loading steaming pastrami on rye, chopping mountains of potato salad, and cramming them into happy maws for over fifty years. Recently, it pushed through its bulging walls to become a huge L-shaped salon along whose inner side runs a set of counters heaped with anti-vitamin meats and an army-sized supply of sliced bread. The only way to see these counters is to stand behind the rows of backs waiting to be served and await your own turn to order a sandwich. (Don't try to edge your way in; this is a resolute crowd and not shy.) Then you take your sandwich to an empty seat at one of the long community tables. If you are chased from one of the tables by an elderly man in a whitish coat and a discouraged expression, don't be offended; he is a waiter and you've mistaken a service table for one of the free-for-alls meant for self-service customers. After engulfing a corned beef on club—several inches high and requiring a snake's hinged jaw—walk back to the take-out section. Its loaded counters, the large hanging scales, the many strings of salamis like a curtain of monster beads, the slices of meat for sampling flying across the counter, the eager noisy customers, the amiable countermen roaring bawdy gossip at each other as they weigh out bawdy-looking loops of "specials," the steamy, intimate air and speech—all fuse into a modern Breughel.

The Olympus of sturgeon and Nova Scotia salmon for many New Yorkers and for former New Yorkers who travel considerable distances to refresh themselves with the local nectar is found at *Russ and Daughters* (179 E. Houston St.). The elderly Mr. Russ, who still sits around the store (not because he must supervise the thoroughly efficient works but because he can't stay away), has several attractive, lively daughters who married several attractive, lively men. They work in the store at various times and together on busy Sundays, friendly, bright people whose voices bubble up a foam of warm greetings, paeans to sturgeon, sonnets to lox, and kind thanks. The friendliness and enthusiasm take some of the sting out of the prices, although their's are comparatively low in a generally fantastic scale, and as for quality—the experts grow soft-eyed and moist-mouthed when they describe the incomparable charms, first, of the Russ fish, and, then, of the Russ women.

A few doors west, *Ershowsky's Meat Market* (175 E. Houston St.) takes to itself the advantages of two worlds. It is open on Sundays in conformity with the Saturday closing traditional in this neighborhood and, in addition, has released itself from the trials of meticulous devotion to Jewish dietary laws. The front of the store is concerned mainly with coldcuts and frankfurters. The more serious purchases are made in the back room—actually a large meat locker and fairly cold—where there was (and there may still be) a man whose manner and matter of speech were a beguiling Semitic compound of rueful humor and gentle irony. He dressed in layers of heavy sweaters topped by a stained apron, and above his appealing moon face and innocent eyes he had stretched a woolen cap which ended in a meager little pompom. Saying "please" and "thank you" to him evoked: "Lady, do me a favor? Please don't say 'please' to me. I'll get used and I'll like it and soon I'll want everybody should say 'please' to me. And you know around here it's not a 'please' neighborhood, and I'll expect, I'll wait, and they wouldn't say it, and all the time I'll feel terrible. So better I shouldn't get used, so please don't spoil me, lady. Thank you anyhow."

Turning the corner, away from the rococo smells and tastes and personalities, go south on Allen Street to the disciplined, quiet geometry of ties horizontal and ties vertical, in shop after shop, many of them made by Middle Eastern Jews who live above the shops and meet in the little cafes on the street (page 313). Across the wide street are a few leftovers of what was once Copper Row, and above them windows bellied with pillows and comforters, made and remade by experts who learned their trade in the old country, stuffing the huge down puffs which were dragged through large sections of Europe into the steerage of many ships and past the eyes and hands of innumerable Ellis Island officials, to warm the alien winter. Back to Houston, now, where in small alleys protected from traffic, vigorous old Italians may be playing *boccie*, if the weather is good.

The proximity of the Houston Street Station (IND "D" train) would suggest that this is a reasonable place from which to leave the old Chinese singers, the gypsy children, the skullcapped booksellers, the goat-adorned butcher shop of the Dos Hermanos, Mr. Hsiang, the Russ ladies and their men, Ershowsky's man of the delicate sensibilities, and to return to the more homogenized world of central Manhattan.

Italian Markets and Slavic Streets

14th Street at First Avenue and south.
Via 14th Street bus, going east from any 14th Street station on any subway line or downtown bus.

If you can, start your First Avenue walk at Third Avenue and 14th Street simply to observe one of the many variants of New York City mixture as you walk east toward First Avenue: Jewish delicatessens, a Russian church, a Russian night club, an Italian pizza stall, an Italian restaurant, and Hungarian "home-cooking" establishments. As you turn southward on First Avenue, the ebullience of Italy takes over; the grocery windows are hung with heavy pennants of sausages and cheese, in front of the stores large sacks of beans, grain, and dried chestnuts slump among huge jars of cinnamon sticks, immense olives in wine, piñon nuts, and peppercorns. On the lids of the jars lie neat little bundles of dried oregano and rosemary and from among the sacks and jars and bundles sticks of dried bacalao rise like strange plants. The irresistible bakeries display little and big breads, brown and white ones, long and graceful breads, and stout, plain breads; some are crisscrossed in geometric patterns, some are coiled on themselves, some are crusty and rough, some are shiny and smooth. It is almost *de rigeur*, in this neighborhood, to buy a bread, stuff it with cheese or salami from the shop next door, and eat as you go.

Look in at the fish markets, at the mounds of minute snails, at the squid hanging from hooks like fatty gray rags, at the small fish lying in herringbone designs on their beds of ice. Further on, the cold white and grays of ice and fish give way to the loud orange, red, yellow, and green of vegetable and fruit stands, the spinach billowing from baskets onto pyramids of apples and oranges.

At 10th Street and First Avenue, there is a public market built as a WPA ingathering of the pushcarts which once clogged the streets but made them beautiful on cold nights, when the venders built fires in oil cans. Their faces and fruits were illuminated by the glow, and the row of fires and the dark beyond made the market street somehow a place of ritual. The inside market, though less magical now, is still worth seeing. In it stands an edifice built high of Italian cheese and salamis, a fortress of food topping a display of *prosciutto, mortadella,* and wrinkled sausages which look far less effectual than they taste.

Suddenly, at about 8th Street, there is a change of complexion: a large, orderly butcher shop offers Polish hams, raw bacon coated with paprika, and stuffed *kiszka* (which looks like, and is, large intestine); a Mr. Statiuk owns the shop. One of his compatriots must own the New Warsaw Bakery at the corner of 7th Street, another must have a half-interest in a saloon which calls itself "Your Place and My Place"—one of the names on the window is Polish and the other Italian, possibly a partnership that began in the local public school, disregarding the Italo-Polish border of East 8th Street.

A purity of physical type and old-country dress still persists in this area, particularly among the older people. The old Polish women, many of whom work as office-cleaners during the night, have wide pale faces, greenish eyes, and thin, light hair which they cover with wool kerchiefs of floral peasant designs. The old black-clad Italian women wear no hats or kerchief, except in church, proud of the thick, wavy hair which suits their significant faces.

This is a good place from which to plunge more deeply into the Slavic colony, mainly Polish and Ukrainian, sampling a few streets to get the quintessence of the whole, which extends from St. Mark's Place (the equivalent of 8th Street) to 4th Street, from Third Avenue eastward to Avenue B.

Each has two dominant social centers which can be divided roughly into body and soul: *The Polish National Home* (23 St. Mark's Pl.) coddles the flesh with games, dances, and a restaurant (see page 171) while *St. Stanislaus* (101 E. 7th St.), the oldest and largest Polish church in the city, runs a full-time parochial school, frequent lectures, and more decorous entertainments. For the Ukrainians, similar functions are maintained by the Ukrainian National Home at 140 Second Avenue and St. George's Ukrainian Catholic Church, a neo-classic structure at 22 East 7th Street, fronted by massive painted columns and topped by Byzantine onion bulbs.

Starting at 6th Street and First Avenue and walking westward toward Second Avenue, one notices the signs proclaiming various immigrant-aid groups, travel agencies, and lawyers with Slavic names. If you're there on a Saturday (the best day), look into the saloons. As in most bars with European patronage, they serve as club, political forum, information center, and sometimes, office, created for the leisured enjoyment of a few beers, man talk, and the absence of wives and children.

A few houses west of a minute shop which sells only incense for churches, there is an ordinary tenement whose only distinction is a fence which fronts an alley leading into an inner-court house. These were very common, and still exist, on the Lower East Side, where immigrants were once packed into the tightest possible areas. Out of a basement nearby leaps a sign: *Port d'Afrique* (310 E. 6th St.); near the window of this coffee shop and restaurant devoted to African cuisine and curries sits a handsome young Negro hand-lettering an announcement of an Afro-American cultural event. Across the street is the yellow-and-gilt storefront and Afro-Indian atmosphere of *Hassan's Coffee Shop*. These shops and the proprietors are part of the art and literary colony which tore away from Greenwich Village because rents were too high and apartments difficult to get, and moved eastward where there isn't much steam heat but plenty of companionable poverty and inexpensive gallery space.

Next door to Port d'Afrique is a theatrical costume shop whose displays are the ghost of gayer times, when Second Avenue was lined with crowded Yiddish theaters. Who uses the shop now is hard to say; possibly the St. Stanislaus group of Boy Scouts on 7th Street, when it puts on theatricals, possibly the local churches hire costumes for pageants, or maybe the proprietor is sleepily waiting for the return of the great Jacob Adler or the old Habimah Players. Should there be (and it isn't likely) a renaissance of the Yiddish theater, the players would have to find a new union building. The old one at 31 East 7th Street, with "Hebrew Actors Union" deeply carved into the façade, is now used by the Tall Folks Club, as calm a tenant as the old was volatile.

Having arrived via some digressions at Second Avenue and 6th Street, look north before you cross the avenue and scan the lovely cluster of mixture: between St. Mark's Place and 9th Street sits the *St. Mark's Cinema,* which sometimes shows Polish movies; one block below is a large new Chinese restaurant which serves Cantonese and Shanghai-style dishes, and below that stand the old temples of *blintzes* and *Byalistoker pletzels, Ratner's* (see page 164) and *Rapoports* (see page 164). Walk up Second Avenue to 7th Street and learn something of the Cyrillic alphabet by studying the drugstore sign: YKRAIHCbKA AПTEKA. When you've had enough, turn into 7th Street and walk east, back toward First Avenue. If a *Polish Medical Center and Dental Clinic* (maintained by the community) interests you, continue on to number 67; if it doesn't, then stop at 48 for a glance into the first of three interesting shops.

Arka's (48 E. 7th St.). The proprietor hasn't too much English (few of the shop people in this area do), but what he has is spoken in a gentle tone with slow patience. Like several other shops in the neighborhood, Arka's has Ukrainian books and records, machine-made pottery decorated in orange and brown cross-stitch designs, and the stitch-patterns, embroidery cloths, and silks which are in great demand locally. The older women in the area maintain a working interest in the traditional craft; on warm afternoons, groups of them sit on stools and boxes at the entrance to their houses, gossiping and embroidering, their headkerchiefs glowing in the late sun. It might be some of their handiwork which lies in the cases at Arka's—exquisitely fine stitching on pillow slips and handsome peasant blouses, some in the bright colors of rural crafts and a few in more sophisticated black and white, completely suitable (though unusual) to our mode of dress. Unusual, too, are the collection of Old World challis scarves in the traditional floral and Paisley designs (some of them large enough to use as shoulder shawls), and wool spreads and hangings in deep colors, patterned on old Ukrainian models, now woven in Switzerland. Notice also the inlaid and carved boxes whose minute, intricate decorations reach toward an Oriental mode, and some highly lacquered black candlesticks and vases, incised and painted in the styles of Ukrainian Easter eggs.

Howerla's Ukrainian Book Store (41 E. 7th St.) is crammed with old and new books—fiction, juveniles, how-to books, history—all in Ukrainian, sheet music and records, and also a collection of glossy, literal chromos of old patriots and heroes. The picture grows of Ukrainian people, not only self-confident and stubborn about the survival of their crafts, but bursting with words and opinions. Howerla's carries, in addition to Ukrainian periodicals published in New York, a surprisingly large set of weeklies from Scranton, Yonkers, and a few Canadian cities. Watch your step as you walk around the shop; it isn't very large, but the proprietor's son is small, agile, and a great lover of Ukrainian records; he may trip you on his scramble for the phonograph. Poppa often removes this hazard by perching the boy on his shoulders, going about his business somewhat in the manner of a parrot-mounting pirate.

Surma's Book and Record Shop (9 E. 7th St.) is bigger than the other similar shops on the street, with more orderly displays, and even some books in English on Ukrainian crafts and cooking. More stylishly "uptown" in general, but well supplied with embroidery patterns and silks, with Ukrainian Easter eggs and sunflower oil used by Slavs, with the cross-stitch pottery and the records and books in the local language. Here, again, the verbosity of Ukrainian opinion is astonishing, the periodicals ranging in origin from Toronto and Winnipeg to Buenos Aires, and reaching across from Paris.

The Slavic walk (with a little of every kind of people, as usual, making the picture less pure and more entertaining) leads ultimately to the improbable presence of New York City's oldest and most stubborn saloon, the famous *McSorley's Old Ale House* (15 E. 7th St.), whose dimness and dusty antiquity, pot-bellied stove and crooked pictures, rickety chairs, and silent, decrepit customers will stay frozen in time as Sloan painted it until they all fall gently together into a heap of dust. The insistence on staying unchanged is not at all out of deference to quaint, old "atmosphere"; the proprietors and clientele couldn't care less. It is the result of a line of strong-minded, irascible, conservative proprietors who liked things exactly as they had been for years and years. One terrible change has occurred, though: the name of a woman appears on the window as proprietor and, it is rumored, a woman who walks in now is not rushed out as in the old days. It is probable that she is frozen out instead, by inimical glances and frosty silence.

LUNCH:

Katz's, 205 East Houston Street (page 62)

Ratner's or *Rapoports,* 111 and 93 Second Avenue (page 164)

Sing Wu, 123 Second Avenue (page 154)

Greenwich Village

Fifth Avenue bus downtown to Washington Square; then walk south and/or west. (Also reached by subways and other bus routes—see page 326.)

Everything said of the Village is almost true. It isn't what it used to be, they say, but then it never altogether was; its fabled period as a womb of the arts refers to a time when the "artistic" Village was much smaller than commonly reported, when Carmine Street was the center of a French colony and Macdougal, Thompson, Bleecker, and Sullivan Streets were quite Italian, displaying on their Latin skins a few odd ornaments like the Provincetown Playhouse, Minetta Tavern, and a few saloons and their patrons. They say it is honky-tonk and exhibitionistic, which it is, but not in the reserved old streets like Bethune, near the Hudson, or Commerce or Morton or St. Luke's, which is a small section of Leroy. The Village is reputedly full of involved sex, public and private, but much of the appearance of decadence belongs to the boys and girls of stodgier neighborhoods who come here to try on the make-up, costumes, and manners of what they think is indigenous evil. They all seem to use an immutable costume—a compound of studied informality, rebellion, excessive shapeliness and shapelessness—which stays unchanged as each generation slips in and out of it. The Village shelters people looking for night clubs lit in dark poisonous colors and which serve meager drinks and the enticements of overripe girls in frayed G-strings or boys oddly dressed; it also contains an unusual number of good bookshops, vocal and impassioned PTA groups, and efficient young mothers who play chess in Washington Square, one hand stretching toward a pawn while the other rocks a baby carriage.

Like Chinatown and Rockefeller Plaza, Greenwich Village will probably appear as absolutely required on any New York City list and you may have a good idea of some of what you'll see—the miniscule Broadway that is 8th Street and the crafts and the jewelry shops on 4th Street. Don't neglect Macdougal Street, which is fast becoming the showiest street, with shops bearing the most outer-edge names—"Limbo," "The End," "Piñata

Party," "*Si Como No*" (page 241)—and displays that dwell heavily on discords in jewelry, somber things in leather (their craft conspicuously showing), folklore and folk arts, and unrestrained decor. Among them are honey-combs of coffee houses with Italian names, one of which serves borsch, pickled lox, and sour cream, while others offer for sale chess games with a master, at so much per game. Also, there is a guitar and lute maker and a few casual old Italian restaurants which appear to have come to Macdougal Street shortly after Columbus and intend to stay forever and unchanged.

For other stores of uninhibited styles inside and out, including one whose façade and adjoining sidewalk are painted in sections of shocking pink, shocking yellow, and shocking blue—like a Mexican basket made for the tourist trade—extend your walk back to 8th Street and across Seventh Avenue into Greenwich Avenue, with a short detour on Christopher which comes off Greenwich.

After a while, the Village may appear to you to be a huge, ill-planned store with paucity in some departments and excessive stock in others. That is the time to leave the self-conscious belt for a look at the old Jewish ceme-tary on 11th Street (between Fifth and Sixth Aves.), or a walk southward and westward to the old residential streets already mentioned and through Bleecker Street, between Sixth and Seventh Avenues. It is one of the few pushcart-market streets left in the city, although threat-ened with imminent improvement. The pushcarts trundle the same greens and the stores hang the same squid and salamis as other Italian markets do, but the others are rarely shopped by pairs of very clean boys wearing very tight pants and bulky, hand-knit sweaters, or women in thong sandals and earrings like black widow spiders.

LUNCH

Mother Hubbard on Sheridan Square (101 Seventh Ave. South) has very good hot apple pie. In an old, tableless clam bar on the west side of Macdougal between 3rd Street and Bleecker, one can enjoy clams on the half-shell, and nothing else. **The Bagel** (170 W. 4th St., west of Sixth Ave.) for inauthentic delicatessen. Some coffee houses on Macdougal serve lunch: try **Rienzi** (at 107) and **Lo Spuntino** (at 102).

ɴoᴛᴇ: Combine this walk, in season, with outdoor art show (page 324) or folk-singing (page 297). Remember that the Village will have nothing to do with Monday, so it sleeps it away and many shops stay closed. The days they are open are more likely to last from noon until 9:00 P.M. or 10:00 P.M. rather than the ordinary working hours (and some shops are open until midnight).

Ribbons, Cherries, and Fancies Walk
West 36th Street to 39th Street

Between Fifth and Sixth Avenues, on 36th to 39th Streets, lies the stuff that millinery dreams are made of, 38th Street constituting its retail core. Like the thrift shops, their windows have the Daliesque look of things separate and waiting to be related, of the unfinished sentence. There are canvas hat bodies, there are ribbons, there are wreaths of flowers, garlands of fruits, flames of feather, but rarely a hat. Although one or two shops in these tight-packed rows make hats to order, the emphasis is on the glitter which winds around them—ribbons, sequins, spangles, and lace filling windows with innocent glitter. Tangentially connected with these shops are logical offshoots—a shop limited to bridal accessories or theatrical materials or bags along with the ribbons. Around the corner, on Sixth Avenue, one finds the weightier matters of hatmaking: needles distorted for special handling, scissors oddly sized and shaped, grotesque irons for blocking and steaming, and all curiously fascinating, as if one were observing the development of a line of mutants.

Alternating with the strange tools and the gaud, on these streets you'll find some of the zestiest luncheonettes. A sandwich at one of them and a walk among the furbelows makes a pleasant break on the Macy's to Lord and Taylor shopping route.

The Village of Paddy's Market
West 40's and 50's on Ninth Avenue

Paddy's Market, on Ninth Avenue, from 36th Street to 44th Street, was a gypsy queen of markets when there was a Ninth Avenue El to take shoppers there easily, when solid households sent for their pheasants and especially blended coffees to the stores behind the pushcarts.

The Ninth Avenue El has succumbed to civic progress, the pushcarts to sanitation. They are gone. Instead, the efficient Port Authority Bus Terminal, in the center of the market, sheds a cool intelligent light which washes out some of the remaining color. Color still remains, though, in the stalls which extend from the shops (actually pushcarts which aren't pushed) and spill over with dandelion greens and feathery bulbs of finochio; in the cans of olives and capers and tomatoes lying in bright heaps on the sidewalks; in the shops themselves; in the proprietors and the customers.

This area is a good one for an international ear. You'll hear mainly Greek and Italian—the Italian that adds vowels, or swallows vowels, or maintains the pride of Siena. Now and then, you'll detect the rustling sibilants of Polish and varieties of mangled Spanish, the Castilian sententiously overdone and the Puerto Rican heedlessly underdone. At a vegetable stall, two partners argue in Yiddish. One has apparently overcharged a Puerto Rican woman for plantains and his partner protests; the seller says she doesn't know the difference; the partner with the conscience says slowly and weightily as he pulls in his pot belly and extends his five-foot-four height to the dignity of Jeremiah, "It doesn't matter. A person is a person," and he turns to the celery stalks which he begins to arrange in righteous rows.

Apart from the imported Near Eastern products (for which this section is one of the centers) and the superior meat in one old dignified butcher shop, the produce available in this area is rarely top grade and very often fairly near the bottom. This is the area where not-quite-

fresh bread and cooked foods are available at low prices
if one must buy them rather than the fresh breads con-
stantly turned out by the local Italian bakeries. Here,
too, are rows of butcher shops which specialize in so-
called "variety" meats: pigs' feet and testes, heads (at
10¢ a pound), necks, gizzards, and lungs. The raw hamburger is dotted with gristle and the bananas on the
stands tend to be speckled, but it is all edible and eaten
by a large number of people, not excluding young Village
couples who find even the Bleecker Street market a little
high for free-lance earnings.

Having nibbled at their edges, some of the stores are
now worth entering. Pick up some Greek pastry at the *Poseidon* (629 Ninth Ave.) or *Velissarion's* farther south
(at 532) or Italian *pasticiotti* at the *Domino Pastry Shop*
(near 38th St.) or pizza at *Romaniello's* (476 Ninth
Ave.). At the corner of 39th Street and Ninth Avenue
you'll have to hack your way through fruits and vegetables that rise like jungle fern to obscure the windows
of a store whose actual specialty is bread sticks—fat and
skinny, long and short, light and dark—in enough varieties for any *feinschmecker*. Sniff the fine ground Arabian coffee at the *Yemen Coffee House* (486 Ninth Ave.)
or, for expertise and reminiscences, turn west on 42nd
Street where (at 414) you'll find the *Dick Coffee Co.*
Mr. Dickholtz, its proprietor, started as a coffee-and-tea
salesman many years ago and is encyclopedic in the field.
If he isn't too occupied with roasting, grinding, and shipping, he'll be delighted to share his information about
teas, coffees, and the good old days of Paddy's Market,
or almost any subject except the two forbidden ones—
tea bags and instant coffee.

The Middle Eastern food stores which form, with the
Italian, the backbone of the market duplicate the community center spirit of the small-town stores in the old
country. Sometime during the noonday hours, lunch
already eaten, the Greek proprietors of local stores gather
in the *New International Importing Store* (517 Ninth
Avenue). They are seriously groomed merchants in dark
suits and high-collared shirts and, surrounded by Turkish

lakerda, Jugoslav carp, Greek wild onions and grape
leaves, and Cypriot honey, they sit in a circle around the
pot-bellied stove discussing with gravity the state of the
world and groceries. The same discussion may be going
on in Bulgarian at *Oriental Groceries,* almost next door,
or in Arabic at the *Yemen Coffee House.*

As in all markets, there is good eating of a simple kind
here. If the Greek or Italian pastries haven't sated you,
buy some Italian bread and salami or cheese, a pizza pie
or a hero sandwich (they grow in abundance here), or a
Homeric hero at *Manganaro's* (page 186), or a pastrami
sandwich at the ubiquitous Jewish delicatessen. If you'd
like a meal, the *Italian Kitchen* (472 Ninth Ave.) will
serve food as unassuming and robust as the local trades-
people who eat there.

Beyond Paddy's Market, Ninth Avenue fades into the
quiet anonymity of slum life in a period of reshaping.
The slums of Harlem and some areas in the East Side are
exuberantly sure of themselves: large groups of one-
language, one-face, one-memory make a solid root, and
the odd twigs that appear on its tree can be tolerated as
long as their number stays small and as long as the central culture keeps its bulwarks—the churches, the shops,
the restaurants—visibly near. The Ninth Avenue slums
have not such solid structure. They house small, disparate
groups, some the remains of an exodus, some just filter-
ing in, few solidly rooted. American Negroes live here,
Chinese, Puerto Ricans, Italians, Greeks, and the French
and Irish of older, larger groups; they circle each other
cautiously, subdued and watchful, like cats feeling each
other out.

This is not one of the most stimulating parts of the city,
but no place of people and houses can be dull, if you
have any interest to invest; give Ninth Avenue a few
more minutes. You might walk up the stairs to the *Seven
Arts Gallery Café* (596 Ninth Ave.), an exile from Macdougal Street, open from 2 P.M. to 2 A.M., if it is open at
all. At 670 there is a Spanish record and book store, its
stock including, as always in these stores, Spanish soaps,
perfumes, and postcards, treacly with sentiment. Out of

Spain and into poverty at 726, where there is a cobweb of a shop offering unclaimed laundry for sale, and selling it.

Eighth Avenue, moving eastward, is Broadway diminished, its skirt frayed and its tinsel battered. Broadway's explosions of light throw a dull glow on Eighth Avenue; the pizza palaces of Broadway are echoed by modest little slots on Eighth; the souvenir shops are naked, unsurrounded by Broadway's playlands; the jingle of Broadway money ends in the pawnshops on Eighth; the big sexy signs shrink to small bookshops featuring peculiar magazines and a pimpled clientele, all supervised by a proprietor who sits on a high seat, peering down disdainfully and distrustfully at his customers.

Another facet of sex appears in the *Tattoo Artist,* on the east side of Eighth, just north of 48th Street. The window and the interior are hung with framed tattoo designs—eagles, banners, mottoes, and hearts rigidly drawn and harshly colored. On a back wall hang two signs: "No hanging out" and "No tattooing if you are under 17." Apparently the desperate search for toughness of the uncertain young reaches into tattoo parlors also. As one watches (the operation is easily visible from the street), the act of tattooing and being tattooed does take on the somber, dedicated atmosphere of an ancient rite. The young priest is fair and tender-skinned; his blond, carefully coiffed and oiled head is bent over his needles in humble dedication, and his clear blue eyes are fixed and entranced. The postulant sits stiffly upright, his back a wall of strength, his teeth clenched and jaw jutting with the show and pride of masculinity, his eyes fixed, like the priest's, on the moving needles and the symbol emerging onto the flesh on his forearm. Both are wrapped in a deaf exclusion of the outer world, of anything but this solemn act of art, religion, and sex.

Eighth Avenue is also the workshop of Broadway. On the east side of the street, between 48th and 49th Streets, above the street level, is a row of shops which repair and sell all sorts of musical instruments. One shop (page 202) sells tricks and props to magicians, another rents out vaudeville costumes of the Weber and Fields vintage,

others are striving little halls which aspire to become
gorgeous dance studios from which a brilliant flood of
talent will glut Broadway. At the corner of 48th and
Eighth, take a good look at the old fire station whose
opposed red and green are muted by a thick leaven of
dust and age. Very near it, upstairs at 784, is another
antique, the *Nicosia Restaurant*, one of the Greek men's
clubs still left in this area. Just note it, don't go up. All
you'll probably find is a bare room housing a few old men
in black hats, tieless, silently playing cards in the time-
less solidity of Cézanne's cardplayers. A block or two up,
at 922, is a shop caught in limbo. Is it a music shop
descending in class or gazing hopefully upward? It is,
certainly, an olio of football cleats, fencing masks, drum-
sticks, small flags, guitars, and instrument cases. The
proprietor, bristling with anticipated insult, has pasted
up several signs which growl, "This is a first-class professional shop." It is hard to know exactly what that
means, except that he insists on a dignity he believes is
too rarely given him.

A beer in one of the plain-spoken saloons on Eighth
Avenue will punctuate your passage eastward toward
the splashy color of *Pizza Burger Pete* (2575 Broadway,
between 47th and 48th Streets), which has expanded its
repertoire of pizza and hamburgers to include such delicacies as Oriental spinach-and-cheese pies and Jewish
knishes. It is one of the favorite eating places of cowboys
during rodeo time; at off-hours they can be seen standing
quietly at the counters, steadily ruminating their way
through many squares of pizza. Stop, too, to examine
some of Broadway's underwear for women, especially
in the smaller shops. Like the last act of *Hamlet*, they
exaggerate and thus fall from their purpose; the eager arrangements of appliqués in odd places and the leering
mottoes, being too strained to titillate, only amuse.

47th Street will act as measure for most of the streets
that run between Sixth and Broadway in this neighborhood: on the corner there is a concentration of untiring
beauty culture—one establishment stays open until midnight, the other (muttering "Excelsior" now and then)
doesn't close at all. The rest of the street presents a fairly

typical mixture: one small Chinese restaurant, one of Naples, one Texo-Mexican chili house which places a penalty of 15¢ on any dish ordered without beans.

A quieter note is struck at 107 W. 47th Street where lives the *Connoisseur Tobacconist,* an old shop whose floor slopes down to meet dark faded cabinets dimly painted in peasant arabesques, and containing, among the tobacco jars, some fine old meerschaums and narghiles. At lunchtime the hospitable elderly proprietor gathers with a number of cronies over a can of salmon and a container of cottage cheese set on a small table. They mumble along in Yiddish in what should be a mellow scene—dark old room, gentle old men—but the atmosphere is cut through by a sudden outburst of clatter from the dim back; it appears that the back space is leased to a card-printing concern. Cutting across that noise shoots another, this time from the front of the store. A loud voice is roaring worries into an open public phone: "Where are those other three? I have only twenty-four and there's supposed to be twenty-seven. I'm ten minutes late awready, fa Chrissake!" Beyond the window stands a group of neatly dressed tourists, uncertain whether they may or may not enter the glass-domed bus before their shepherd does. Thus the tobacco-blending, card-printing shop has added to itself another dimension, a depot for sightseeing buses, imitating in a neighborhood most indigenously New York City, the multipurpose store of a very rural village.

The neighboring blocks, 48th and 49th, are large Neapolitan kitchens, divided into small restaurants which vary somewhat in price but not much in decor or menu. By the rule that where there are many Italian restaurants, there must be some Chinese, we also have those, and not much else except a few musical-instrument shops. At this point, it makes sense to cross Sixth on 47th and explore that block, east of Sixth Avenue. If it's time for a sandwich and the weather permits, go to the *Jeweler's Delicatessen* (51 W. 47th St.), whose narrow dimensions flower into a "garden." It has no grass and no flowers, but it does have a dense cluster of flowery umbrellas against white trelliswork, a bright red soft-drink con-

tainer, good rare views of the backs of buildings, and a
middle-aged, semiblonde waitress who says "Enjoy it,
dear" when she puts your sandwich before you. After
such pleasures and for contrast, you might stop in at the
Gotham Book Mart (page 275) or explore the *Jewelry
Mart.*

In recent years, the jewelry business has moved practically en masse to West 47th Street, leaving only a residue
of its activities in the old areas of Canal Street and
Maiden Lane. With the exception of a few coffee shops
and two honorable old inhabitants of the street—the *Del
Pezzo Restaurant* (page 143) and the *Gotham Book
Mart*, the whole of 47th Street between Fifth and Sixth
Avenues is a brilliant honeycomb of small stalls; some
specialize in pearls, some in gold and diamond combinations, some do engraving and resetting, while others
limit themselves to watch repairs. The strong light pour-
ing from the ceiling and meeting the glitter of the gold
and gems, the lively gestured conversations between
dealers, the enthusiastic bargaining and the incessant low
hum of whispered "deals" create the ebullience of Oriental sooks, an effect further colored by European and
Levantine accents.

Observe the repeated designs of two dark heads bent
solemnly over one diamond. Notice the young Hasidic
Jew in a crude shirt and without a tie, his pallor emphasized by his large black hat and his dark earlocks, timidly
following a confident full-bearded patriarch through the
aisles. He stands deferentially aside, to listen and learn
when the master, having found his customer, opens subtle
negotiations. Many of these earlocked and bearded
wanderers from Eastern Europe have, incidentally, no
set place of business: a little paperful of unset diamonds
is their stock, their vest pockets are their safes and stores,
and the only equipment they carry is a jeweler's eyepiece.
In good weather, they crowd the sidewalks outside the
exchanges, buying, selling, and arguing Talmudic inter-
pretation in a broad range of Yiddish dialects and idioms,
providing one of the last fertile research fields (since the
language is dying out) for a Jewish Henry Higgins.

The best places for an all-over interior view are the

balcony luncheonettes perched over the far ends of the exchanges at 2-8 West 47th or 36 West 47th. The best times to go are well before or after the lunchtime rush, when more ringside seats are available.

59th Street Walk

Sometime, while on a shopping trip to Bloomingdale's, or a walk through the near-Ming vases of Third Avenue or the gold-plastered alley of 57th Street, extend your walk through East 59th, starting from Third Avenue. For many years, the block between Second and Third was highly regarded by the *cognoscenti* for food shopping—not necessarily cheaper than elsewhere, but choice and varied. It still has that function in a diminished way: there is a long-established seafood shop; a fruit-and-vegetable stand of stable repute; *Lamanna's* (208 E. 59th St.), a long narrow store crammed with Italian imports; *Schweitzer's Coffee Co.* (204 E. 59th St.), which has been roasting and blending coffee for refined tastes over a long span of years; and a small grocery which contains a surprising number of connoisseur cheeses. This pattern of one-of-each-kind, making a small, fairly complete market, spreads into other enterprises and weaves a curious fabric; there is one Chinese restaurant, one Japanese novelties shop, a Calypso night club (or there *was* one), one modest gallery devoted to young painters, one good jewelry shop and, in one of the upstairs lofts, a collection of old clocks garnered and tenderly nursed by an expert who also teaches horology to a select few.

Beyond Second Avenue, a suggestion of homogeneity sets in with a row of small businesses involved in house-decorating, leaving a gap for the presence of an ultra-informal Italian restaurant ("for deliveries knock on glass with coin"), and all cosily nested against the roots of the Queensboro Bridge. And then 59th Street becomes something quite different, abandoned by time but not neglected. First appears the Mary Manning Walsh Home, old-fashioned low buildings in buff and terra cotta plaster work with meticulously placed and trimmed strips of hedge lining the sidewalk and boxes of pink geraniums in the windows. Below it sits a sedate row of small houses which continue around the corner to Sutton Place, chaste and elegant in dark gray with clear white trim, like a good tailored costume, making a contrast of frailty with a great round brick tower and the dark, labored lift of the bridge.

Three Harlems

Ask a middle-aged European intellectual (preferably French) to tell you what the word "Harlem" means and he'll give you a picture of a steaming pit a few blocks square, crowded with sinuous, shining black bodies twisted in the contortions of jazz and sex; exuberant and salacious, driven by the insistence of alcohol and saxophones; carefree, primitive, and low-down. It is a picture derived from the movies, books, and art, and bears a germ of verity, now anachronistic.

Twenty-five years ago and more, it was easy to find a party at almost any time, almost anywhere in the rectangle of 116th Street to 145th Street on and around Lenox and Seventh Avenues. The dollar you paid for unlimited drinks (small) made of incognito liquor masked by fruit juice paid your host's rent, and some of the rest of his keep if his parties were good. Sometimes they were simple and boisterously playful, sometimes dark and very quiet. There was one slight, neat man who lived in an apartment which consisted of one very large room and a smaller one, both dimly lit and furnished mainly with divans ranged along the walls. The decor consisted of a few beautiful boys of several shades of color, the most beautiful of them a tall, languid boy with a distant face, perfect and immobile. He wore a heavy seaman's sweater cut down across his shoulders and on his long, Nephertite neck a rope of large red beads; he was choice and selective and didn't disappear with a partner into the little room quite as frequently as the other boys.

It wasn't necessary to look for a rent party, however; every street had its speakeasy and some speaks had the relaxed clubbiness and almost naive good-fellowship that came with a steady intimate clientele. In time, one didn't go to drink primarily; one went to meet friends, to gossip and discuss love and politics against a background of now legendary piano-playing by Fats Waller or James P. Johnson. If one of the brotherhood succumbed to the oddities of the liquor, he was gently placed on a chair in some unused corner and gathered up by his cohorts when dawn slid across the East River. Except for the dramatic results of an occasional mistake in picking a girl or a business rival, nothing much untoward happened: the smaller speakeasies were restful and civilized, like the coffee houses of Dr. Johnson.

For a little more excitement, it was possible to go to any of a number of night clubs—big ones with ravishing chorus lines and entertainers of international reputations, or smaller clubs, unadvertised but by no means unknown. These latter had no fixed hours; they were considered open when two or more customers had gathered and closed when the last musician fell asleep in his chair. The liquor was best managed by the trick of swallowing without tasting and the cigarettes sold had an interesting flavor and tricky side effects. The music was blue and smoky and the entertainers were practitioners of rare talent: one stately creature with lovely legs and a deep bass voice specialized in collecting folded dollar bills off tables in a uniquely indirect manner and a surprising number of people spent valuable depression dollars to keep her (him?) in practice. If spectator sports turned pallid, there was always the Savoy Ballroom for Lindy-hopping whipped to frenzy by wild horns.

While the horns blew, though, other Harlems lived and worked, often in the unrelieved drabness of poverty. Beds were used in two and three shifts and "door-key kids" wandered the more companionable streets until their mothers came home from work, their houses again their own for a few hours. Non-Negro Harlems were busy with their polyglot lives, too. Just east of Eighth Avenue, around 125th Street, there was a Finnish colony which maintained a book-and-record shop, meeting halls, a restaurant, and a brisk program of folk dances and theatrical performances in Finnish. Not far away, there were German *Bierstube*, a Japanese restaurant or two, a couple of famous old English-style chop houses, Mexican chili joints, and streets of Italian and Jewish pushcart markets.

In spite of the mixture, however, there were three dominant Harlems: Italian, from 96th to 125th Streets, from Lexington Avenue to the East River; Puerto Rican, from 96th to 116th Streets, along Madison and Fifth Avenues, and westward; and Negro Harlem, filling the triangle made by St. Nicholas Terrace, 125th Street, and the Harlem River, the truncated apex formed by the short strip of 155th Street.

The years and economic and social development have made many changes. Italian Harlem has drastically shrunk; the Americanized young have left the neighborhood, and emigration has trickled down to a few old-country replenishments. A few regal old ladies in black still buy their dandelion greens and bundles of dried thyme from the Italian venders on Second Avenue; a few bakeries, now too large for their limited customers, still stuff Sicilian *canolli* and a few small restaurants still exude odors *a la Posilippo,* but the *funiculi-funicula* has gone out of the neighborhood, to return only for a few days in July during the fiesta of Our Lady of Mount Carmel (see page 328). Much of the neighborhood has been absorbed by enormous housing projects, with more to come, replacing the empty *latticini* and *salsiceria* shops and the rows of blank-eyed empty tenements awaiting the violence of demolition. Undoubtedly, the projects are worthy and even essential, but their infinite stretches of tall unadorned monoliths make dull viewing for a visitor unless he has a specialist's interest in them.

NEGRO HARLEM

Negro Harlem has lost its self-contained shape and also its hot glow, in part at least, for a wholesome reason: the slow, stubborn drive for desegregation in New York has hardly reached full fruition, but it has made it easier for Negroes to enjoy the pleasures of Broadway and the Village, to mingle with the crowds on Mott Street during the Chinese New Year's Festival, and to eat *calzone* and Italian ice on Mulberry Street in celebration of San Gennaro's miracle. It would have been more pleasurable, though, if these important advances could have arrived without sapping the noises and colors of Harlem; if *Smalls Paradise* (2294 Seventh Ave.), once crackling with bawd and vigor, were not reduced to being one of the many modest showcases of jazz groups; if Dickie Wells', which served up rare outrages all night had not been replaced by a *Wells* (2249 Seventh Ave.)—not even remotely related—which is also open all night and serves chicken and music, satisfactory but mundane. The sweet-potato men and the old fried-fish and sausage ladies, the venders of peanuts and barbecues—*Les Halles* of Harlem, restoring the wan body after a hard night—are gone and their function taken by listless little fish-and-chip joints. The greatest, most irreparable, blow to those of us who went there to learn jazz, drinking, and *Life*, is the loss of the Savoy Ballroom. When it was razed in 1958, Harlem became Rome without a Coliseum.

One of the few institutions left from the gaudy days is the *Apollo Theater* (253 West 125th Street, near Lenox Ave.). There is no other continuous vaudeville theater in New York City, nor any other with so enthusiastic an audience (except, of course, children's theaters). The program leans heavily on popular jazz styles, recently featuring "Rhythm and Blues," which is the old name for the obstinate beat in hymn-cum-hillbilly-cum-blues combination which seeped out of Harlem to become "Rock and Roll."

After a rotation of singers and dancers mainly differentiated from each other by the vocabulary of the master of ceremonies and their own particular oddities (a tap dancer introduced as "a very great genius" and billed as the "World's Most Consistent Dancer," dances indefatigably on, lightly stepping through a set of caricatures, neurotic twitches, and malformations in his struggle for uniqueness; a girl ushered in as "lovely and gorgeous" makes her distinction by obviously being a toothsome, dirty girl with a *perpetuum mobile* torso and a begging, breathless mouth), the lights go on and the audience scrounges back in its seats, ready. Another master of ceremonies comes out and sweetens the crowd with a few jokes about pawn tickets, toilets, beds, and Faubus, and soon launches the amateurs. They come hopefully from New Jersey, from the Bronx, from Louisiana, from Massachusetts, from Tennessee, and most of them assiduously imitate current popular styles of entertainment, so be prepared to see a lot of one kind of act. The fall of 1958, for instance, was the season of the male quartet, which zoomed and moaned behind one separate voice of treacle. Their clothing varied, of course, and some of them had more imaginatively lustrous hair styles than others; some wound up their songs in thin falsettos and others swooped to Russian basso range, but the set, stiff hand gestures, the lugubrious, rubbery melodies, and the hiccup break in the vowels were pretty much the same in each group.

Interspersed with the boy quintets were variations of an old sad theme—the entertainer who, in his mind, stands on a stage of gold and graciously acknowledges the plaudits of an immense crowd of rich, beautiful, sensitive, titled people; he performs exquisitely, each movement of perfect felicity, each sound true and moving; he and his audience are together in a state of grace; at the end of the act there is a deep silence of awe, then the millions rise, applaud and shout, and the women's faces shine with tears. But it doesn't happen that way. More usually the singer's voice dries into a fall of splinters and the dancer's fluid grace tightens into marionette angles; the trained dog refuses the hoop and its stout, blonde, pink-ribboned trainer desperately gropes back to an earlier self-portrait and floats à la Duncan across the stage, then sensing that as too pallid, twists her unwilling body into bumps and grinds. The audience, in the meantime, responds with impolite honesty, quite brutal: it jeers, whistles, laughs, and shouts the performers off. But it can be as joyously enthusiastic as it is derisive. One fat little girl drummer of about ten, a member of a mother-and-daughter jazz combination (good, too) carried the house off; it cheered and screamed and stamped its feet, insisting on an encore. So it goes on Wednesday nights in Harlem, hot crossfires of causes and effects, with not one cool breath of indifference. The last regular show goes on at about 9:30 P.M. and on Wednesday nights is followed, at 11:00 P.M., by the amateur show.

You could make an entertaining evening in Harlem by building around the last performance at the Apollo (preferably on amateur night). Dinner could be selected from:

The Shanghai Cafe (page 152) for northern Chinese food.

Bombay India Restaurant (465 W. 125th St., at Amsterdam) for curries and poories.

Place Pigalle (1965 Amsterdam Ave.) for good steaks and sea food.

Frank's Oyster and Chop House (313 W. 125th St.), an old and highly-respected Harlem institution with a consistently good kitchen and a more varied menu than its name implies.

New Flash Inn (154th St. and Seventh Ave.) for charcoal broiled meats, cooked on a sort of open hearth.

Ebony Lounge (1702 Amsterdam Ave., near 144th St.) for general American stand-bys.

El Mundial (222 W. 116th St.) is for *paella* and Spanish sausage.

Smalls Paradise (2294 Seventh Ave., at 135th St.) has already been mentioned as one of the fabled places of the Twenties and Thirties. Although much subdued, it is still a place of talented jazz, performed by changing small groups.

The Great Count Basie, too, maintains a jazz stronghold at 2245 Seventh Avenue (near 132nd St.), known with direct simplicity as *Count Basie's Bar;* once in a frequent while the regular group is joined by one of the old magic names of jazz, sitting in for the sheer joy of it.

The *Baby Grand Cafe* (319 W. 125th St.) functions more in the traditional night-club style with full shows always on tap and changing lists of performers and the frenetic air indigenous to night clubs. (Watch that cover charge!)

Somewhat in the night-club format is the *Palm Cafe* (209 W. 125th St.), from which Radio Station WOV broadcasts its late nightly programs of singers and jazz combinations. Even if you can't make broadcast time, stop in for a drink or a bite, if only to gape at the long bar bathed in sexy neon vapors of soft colors.

Try celebrity hunting at the **Red Rooster** (2354 Seventh Ave., at 138th St.) where Harlem's current great names meet for business, gossip, and display.

An attack of late hunger can be very satisfactorily allayed at the Palm Cafe and the Red Rooster. A very, very late one, verging into breakfast, can be handled at the aforementioned **Wells** (2249 Seventh Ave., next door to Count Basie's).

Despite shifts of population encouraged by the large number of housing projects still leaping up in Harlem, and by the slow but steady opening of other city areas to Negroes, two solid institutions have remained and functioned for many years as unifying cores of the community—the **Harlem Branch of the YMCA** (180 W. 135th St.) and the **Countee Cullen Branch of the Public Library** (104 W. 136th St.).

In addition to its broad athletic program, which runs the sports gamut from aquatics to wrestling (including judo and tumbling), the Y has extensive programs of arts and crafts, classes and clubs, amateur theatricals, and good professional concerts.

At a time, about thirty years ago, when the American Negro was discovering his many-limbed cultural roots, when he was writing poetry for and about his people, when the blues and spirituals were being re-examined by intellectuals—not as the moans of primitives, but as indigenous sources of American music, the Countee Cullen Branch of the Public Library was the agora of Harlem. It was here that much of the excitement of discovery and ensuing exchanges and discussions of the new ideas went on and still go on, now in a muted key.

This branch, named for the Negro poet, houses the Schomburg Collection of Negro Literature and History which is, as its name makes evident, devoted to printed matter (and more recently, recordings) by and about Negroes. Arthur A. Schomburg, a Negro dealer in rare books, gathered, over many years, much material on Negro matters and this became the core of The Negro Society for Historical Research, of which Schomburg was the librarian. In 1926, the collection was acquired by the Carnegie Foundation and deeded to the New York Public

Library; Schomburg stayed with his books, as curator, until his death in 1938.

Among the treasures of the collection is a volume of verse in Latin, written by a Negro and published in Granada in 1573; a history of ancient Spain and Africa, published in 1614; a remarkable picture file, and various African grammars. There are old programs and playbills, sheet music and records, pamphlets and broadsides, and an impressive file of American Negro newspapers dating from 1827. Current newspapers from all over the world are microfilmed when they are two years old and the Branch maintains a reading machine to facilitate their study. It hardly needs saying that this is an invaluable collection for the researcher, but it is also an awesome experience for the nonspecialist to browse through this monumental record of a people.

In recent years, the Countee Cullen Library divided into two separate but linked entities: the Schomburg Collection remained in the old building of Carnegie neo-classic library style, and the public library proper moved into a dignified modern adjoining building with a cool, well-lit and well-equipped reading room, an auditorium, and meeting rooms. On a balcony running across two sides of the tall room is an art gallery in which the work of Negro artists is shown and the public rooms are used for library-sponsored activities: drama groups, artists' and writers' workshops, children's story programs and concerts, as well as community activities such as meetings of local medical associations, discussions of the work of Negro architects, and, quite fittingly, Phi Beta Kappa scholarship examinations.

In spite of the many activities, the Countee Cullen Branch is not the ebullient place it once was; the shouting has died down, the ferment no longer boils, but it still maintains its neglected pride, like an abandoned bluestocking, waiting for the project people to settle down and produce another generation of exciting intellectuals as in the old days.

Scattered through the streets of Harlem, and at one time the subjects of envy and scorn among the native Negroes, are groups from the British and French West

Indies. Their pattern of living and settling was, however, a little different from that of early Jewish and Italian immigrants: it began the same way—they sent much of their earnings back to the islands for the support of their families—but differed in that many kept their children on the islands until they were quite grown, by which time the parents had established steady jobs or small businesses, like boarding houses or tailoring shops. They could then afford higher education for their children and, inevitably, a sizable professional group arose among them. The envy this stimulated, plus a xenophobic scorn of the British speech, the good West Indian manners and, especially, the thrift, caused epithets like "monkey" and "Jews of Harlem" to be applied to them by their American Negro neighbors. Among the West Indians themselves there was some discrimination: Trinidadians wouldn't join in civic enterprises with Barbadians, and vice versa, and so on through a chain of distorted links, with the French-speaking people most isolated of all, haughtily cloaked in the incomparable superiority of their "French culture." Although not altogether gone, much of the name-calling has stopped since hopes of desegregation have illuminated the smaller alleys of intergroup prejudice.

Unfortunately, there is little in Harlem of West Indian flavor for the visitor to enjoy; there are no restaurants where the savory West Indian cuisine can be tasted, no theater or club where the authentic dances of the Islands can be seen or the music heard regularly. The carnival spirit breaks through publicly, though, between January and March, when Calypso contests are held on week-end nights (most often, Saturdays) at any or all of the following places:

Park Palace (3 W. 110th St.—any Fifth Ave. bus except numbers 5 or 15, to 110th St.).

St. Nicholas Arena (66th St. between Broadway and Central Park West—Broadway bus to 66th St.).

Rockland Palace (155th St. at Eighth Ave.—Eighth Ave. IND local).

On Labor Day the annual West Indies Day Parade turns Harlem into Trinidad after Mrs. Jessie Waddell, its prime mover and founder, has cajoled, charmed, and monitored the participating groups into a cohesive whole (see page 331).

SPANISH HARLEM

The best time for a Spanish Harlem walk is a Saturday afternoon, not too late, in late spring or early summer, when life is lived almost entirely out of doors from early morning to late into the night. The market is at its most brilliant on Saturdays (and the pickpockets most adept and busy, so don't look expensive; carry only a necessary amount of money with you) and the stoops on the side streets crowded with young people free from work and school, forming impromptu ensembles of voices and guitars, singing softly of *"El Camino Verde";* the tune is plaintive and Mexican and the underlying rhythm Afro-Cuban. In the evening, if you're still around, go to 110th Street between Madison and Fifth where, on a fair evening, tables are brought out into the street for checker playing and eating, the street itself becoming the plaza left behind in Puerto Rico. Later, most of the people on the block, strumming guitars and softly pounding small drums, make their way to the Harlem Meer in Central Park and, from the rowboats on the Meer, send the music across the lake and back into the streets. When the park closes, the entourage returns and the party continues outside the houses. Incidentally, 111th Street is not welcome to this party; 110th Street, which considers itself a respectable old settlement, has fear and contempt for the disordered, restless village of the next block, accusing it of a magnificent list of vices; judging from the newspaper stories and other sources of local gossip, they might possibly be right.

Spanish Harlem begins to make its appearance as far south as 93rd Street on the East Side: the green-trimmed Emerald Food shops (vestiges of a thickly Irish settlement) give way to groceries named "Carmen," and "Comidas Criollas" crowd out hamburgers. Irish bacon and Irish blood pudding struggle back at 95th Street on Third Avenue but, at 96th, relinquish the field entirely to the *bodegas* and *carnicerias.*

The whole of Spanish Harlem has a homogeneity of
language and poverty: nondescript little bars and shops
with gorgeous names and dingy windows, tenements of
dusty gray or red brick overtowered by tall project blocks
and flanked by vast gaping holes waiting to be filled with
additional housing projects. But in the general drabness
there is much to see and experience. Take a Madison
Avenue bus up to 102nd Street, where the *Azteca* movie
house will, as likely as not, be showing a film featuring
Cantinflas. Walk up Madison and turn a bit west on 105th
Street, where you'll find one of the many storefront
churches which spring up and disappear with ephemeral
speed in Harlem. This one is the Bethania Christian
Church, which has affiliations, but others you will see,
with sonorous, improbable names uncertainly painted on
whitewashed tin walls or dim windows, are private enterprises run by itinerant preachers who stir up a small blaze
of faith and glory and, when the local enthusiasm and
the cash "take" diminish, disappear and try elsewhere.

Back on Madison Avenue and still going northward,
notice the luncheonettes steaming in the heavy oil used
for making *cuchifritos* and *mofongo* which, along with
various *pastelles*, are the hot dogs and hamburgers of this
area; *mofongo* is fried, mashed plantain, rolled into balls
and covered with a sauce; *cuchifritos* is a very poor man's
dish of fried bits of entrail, heart, ear, snout, etc. Pass
these delicacies by unless you have a steel-clad stomach
and are impervious to overripe cooking odors; feast instead on the lovely nostalgic names of the shops: a record
shop called *La Virgen del Carmen,* the *Vista Alegre* food
store and, as you turn eastward on 110th Street, *La Flor
de Mayo,* which is a small moving company with nothing
of the promise of spring or flowers about it; at the corner
of Park and 110th is *La Casa del Oro,* an oddly ambitious
sign to hang over a row of skimpy, cheap skirts, one
might think, but not for 110th Street. Before you come to
La Casa del Oro, however, you will have passed two
churches, *La Iglesia Hermosa* and a branch of the Pente-
costal Church, both of which have the same home-made,
improvised look of the dress of the local women—of poor
materials, poorly cut, but confidently overdecorated.

THE PARK AVENUE MARKET AND ITS ENVIRONS

Just before you reach the big market which runs under the Grand Central tracks as they lift from underground, on Park Avenue between 110th and 116th Streets, you will see a small shop called a *Botanica,* a name sometimes translated as "botanical garden," which it certainly isn't, or "religious store," which it just barely is. The windows tend to feature displays of religious figures in plaster painted in sentimental pale pinks and blues, or chromos a little more blatant in color. But since almost every other shop sells plaster saints—beauty parlors, general stores which live on the lay-away plan, radio repair shops, and photographers—the stock must be supplemented, and so you find books in some *botanicas,* roach and bedbug powder in others; some sell hair preparations and perfume, some have small stocks of all these articles, but they all sell dream books, herbs, incense, and the ingredients of magic potions. They are as unique and indigenous to Puerto Rican neighborhoods as *Wurstgeschaften* to Yorkville or bagel factories to the Jewish East Side, and more foreign in flavor than either. By all means snoop around in one for a few minutes.

The overflow from the indoor market spills over onto the west side of Park Avenue and east and west on 116th Street in an exuberant, disordered flood of wrinkled remnants, plantains, lotions, avocados, brushes, and cans of chiles. The food stands sizzle with American hot dogs, Neapolitan pizza, Latin-American *empanadas* and, occasionally, Mexican tamales; for drinks, there is the ever-present Coke, egg-cream (born on the lower East Side), or *tamarindo.* A large, life-like painting of a pig announces the presence of a roast-pork shop and if they have *chicheron* left, try some. It is cracklings, sold in sheets and very good for nibbling as you walk. Accompanied by the rhythm of Puerto Rican *decimos* emerging from an insistent radio, you gather up the color of green plantains, little yellow bananas, little red bananas, and almost black large ones, the glitter of oilcloth by the yard, the shine of pots and pans, the red of bottles of hot sauce in a row, the strong blues and yellows and

reds of toys. All the color seems to gather up and burst
in a frenzy at the *Radiante Bar* (at 116th St.), an uninhibited Latin fantasy of color, crenelations, latticework,
topped off by an immense crude medallion of male and
female heads, cosily nested in silhouette.

At this point it might be a good idea to go into the
market (avoiding the northernmost section which is devoted to meat and fish and smells it) to look at the food
eaten in this part of the city. Besides the familiar fruits
and vegetables on display, cheap and not choice, but thoroughly edible, there are bins on bins of plantains, cow-
peas, dasheen, cassava root, all sorts of peppers for chile,
and stalks of sugar cane for chewing on as candy; on other
stands are stacks of dried cod and strings of hot and
sweet Spanish sausage. The shopping stalls are separated
by little eating stands which serve *pescado en escabeche*
(often pronounced "saviche"), *pastelillos de papa o de
carne,* and the rest of the range of *comidas criollos.* The
radios roar mambos and merengues, the customers haggle
with vim and laughter, the venders shout their bargains,
the overwhelmed babies cry, and color sparks off the
fruit, off the pink rayon skirts of the women, and off the
explosive hues of their headkerchiefs.

The east aisles of the market constitute the clothing
departments: here you will find inexpensive work pants,
sweaters, corsets, children's clothing, yard goods, ornaments and, in the winter time, long woolen underwear.
The owners of these stalls (and those surrounding the
market) are mainly Jews who speak Spanish, Italian, and
English to their customers and Yiddish among themselves. One of the men who sells yard goods and sewing
thread has the pallid bespectacled face and bent back of
a Talmud scholar and every spare moment of his time
seems to be spent reading Hebrew books and Yiddish
periodicals. It is pleasantly startling to see him move
swiftly through continents of ideas and language as he
lifts his head, sees a customer, puts down his tome, and
says to the woman, with a nod of Castilian grace, *"Muy
buenas dias, señora. Puedo ayudarle?"* Or, wandering
through the market, you may find an old tattered lady
wandering too (if she hasn't found room to set up her

orange crate stand outside); she may try to sell you a pair of torn nylons for 25 cents, or one of her stock of a half-dozen desperately ugly kerchiefs, or one of three or four shabby caps. You won't be able to use anything she has to sell and her raggedness may bother you, but talk to her anyway because she's clever and good-natured and has a brilliant young smile, like a shower of flowers.

If the assault of sights and noises hasn't worn you down, walk back to 116th Street and west toward Madison, past the rows of radiant petticoats hanging high and billowy, like Tiepolo clouds, above the clothing shops. Cross Madison toward Fifth and go into *The India Botanical Garden* (on the south side of 116th) and buy yourself a dream book; you never know when it might come in handy. Beyond the *botanica* is a chilling storefront church—the Little Jericho Mission—made of a conglomeration of discarded doors and slats, whitewashed, with no window visible, like a large up-ended white coffin.

At Fifth Avenue you will begin to hear English (this is where English-speaking Harlem blends with Spanish) and it will be a shock. You will realize, if you hadn't before, that you've heard or seen very little English: the women gossip in Spanish, the men drink and argue in Spanish and, as the children pour out of school, they fly and shout in Spanish; even with *"beisbol"* bats in their hands, striving for *"hon rons,"* they live in Spanish. Legal and medical problems are seen to by *abogados, dentistas,* and *medicos,* prescriptions are filled by *farmacias Latinas,* and the dead are buried by *funerarias.* If you know Spanish, by the way, don't feel deflated if your brand doesn't function too well here; the language you learned in school or in Mexico or Spain bears only a root resemblance to that spoken by Puerto Rican New Yorkers. They apparently hate the sound of *s* and eliminate it almost entirely, they are impatient of long words (and even short ones) and cut off syllables ruthlessly; all their sentences are torn through with a reckless clatter. Another quality of Puerto Rican casualness with language is their Elizabethan disdain for spelling: *negocios* is spelt with fanciful play on the positions and numbers of the *c* and *s*, and a litter of assorted stock can be announced as a "sale" or "sail." Sometimes English and Spanish are welded into a purist's horror, such as *"Hacemos deliveres,"* which may prophesy a new dialect or possibly a new language altogether.

ITALIAN HARLEM: BACK ON 116TH STREET

Assuming that you are still between Madison and Fifth on 116th Street, turn around and go east, toward Park Avenue on the north side of the street. It will be Spanish until you pass Park Avenue and into Lexington where, on the corner, there is a bar and grill which is also a *pizzeria;* this announces your entrance to what is left of Italian Harlem. East of Lexington there are still some Spanish record shops and guitar menders and the San Juan Bar and Grill, but across from these is a large old Italian musical-instrument shop and, as Lexington Avenue moves toward Third and Third toward Second, more and more Italian stores and names come into prominence. The grocery counters carry small vats of anchovies in salt. Restaurants serve pizza and *pasta,* and "Il Triunfo" still molds *gelati* and bakes anise-laden cakes, although its competitor on the corner has capitulated to change and now flanks *sfogliatelle* and *panetone* with apple pies and jelly rolls.

Eating in East Harlem may turn out to be a memorable experience, but not necessarily for the food. For a snack, and to satisfy your curiosity, you might have something at the market stalls, or if sitting down has become imperative, have some pizza at the Bar and Grill on Lexington at 116th Street. Or, you might try to make it a little farther east on 116th Street to the *San Juan Restaurant* (167 E. 116th St.), where you can have Spanish sausage and rice, or shrimp creole, or *mofongo,* all modestly priced.

The *Ting Ho* (304 E. 116th St., at Second Ave.) is almost sure proof that Italian Harlem has lost its purely Italian identity; a Chinese restaurant in a foreign neighborhood is usually one of the signs and concomitants of deghettoization. This one is small and ordinary, but new and clean and unique in that, in slow hours, the cook seats himself and an assortment of bowls at one of the tables and proceeds to stuff and wrap dozens of egg rolls for the edification and enlightenment of the customers.

Coppola's (219 E. 116th St.) caters to a neighborhood clientele and its menu is consequently limited to local eating habits, but the locals are knowing, so the food is good of its Sicilian kind, especially the pizza. They seem to use a very superior type of *mozzarella* which does not turn to white rubber bands when it is cooked, but melts to the consistency of a fondue. When you go, find out if the garden is in use; it is a garden only by courtesy of a narrow strip of flowers; shade is improvised by assorted strips of canvas, and the tables are elementary in design —adding up to a faithful reproduction of a Neapolitan *trattoria*.

ONE MORE SUGGESTION: Pick up some hero sandwiches in an Italian grocery and cake in one of the bakeshops, take them to the East River walk (there is a crosswalk over the highway in the vicinity), sit down on a bench and eat as you watch the cars streaming across the branches of the Triborough Bridge and the dowdy little tugs pulling preposterous weights up the river.

A Brooklyn Trio

Brooklyn has nearly everything Manhattan has though more modest in size and number, and might possibly have reached greater extravagance had it not been reduced in 1898 (and with considerable protest) to being merely one of the limbs in the body of Greater New York. It has a fine museum, a good concert hall, a Broadway, a Harlem, a quiet Greenwich Village, a Jewish East Side, a Levant, Italian villages, Scandinavian, Polish, and Hungarian hamlets and, like Manhattan, roving bands of international sailors on its long, busy waterfronts (including Coney Island).

It is hardly reasonable to expect extensive exploration (although Brooklyn deserves it) of a visitor whose eye is glued to the splendors of Manhattan. The variety of Brooklyn should, at least, be tasted, and you might start with three areas not too far from Manhattan, letting the hinterland go for some future visit.

BROOKLYN HEIGHTS (THE MIND)

By car, across the Brooklyn Bridge; just south of the end of bridge; or, by subway, via the Seventh Avenue IRT to Clark Street in Brooklyn (express stop).

This waterfront section is Brooklyn's "Village," not in the role of tourists' spider web, although it contains some less resplendent crafts shops, but as the Village of old brick houses, tired gentility in small hotels, and the presence of art and culture among its tenants.

The interest in culture predates the artists and writers who came rather recently to the old romantic houses which sit on the far shores of the East River; culture and uplift were important products of Brooklyn Heights many years before. Early in the nineteenth century, New England Yankees bought up some of the Dutch farms in the area and began to engage in shipping. They built substantial waterfront houses from which they could watch their clipper ships rounding up the bay and into the river, often to their very gardens which covered the roofs of their warehouses beneath. Like their Newport and Salem cousins, they had cultivated tastes for the silks and carvings of a more exotic world and their houses were often luxurious with the arts of the Orient. They also brought, in time, the busyness of the New England conscience, which led to educational drives, temperance lectures, literary societies, and debates on ethical problems.

One of the temples of uplift was Henry Ward Beecher's Plymouth Church on Orange Street, indelibly associated with the Abolitionist movement which it fostered long before public discussions of the subject were permitted in other cities. Like many powerful religious leaders, Henry Ward Beecher was an imaginative producer and actor, and it was at Plymouth Church that he staged an auction of slave girls to make immediately vivid the horrors of slavery; on his invitation, Thackeray delivered a lecture in the church and Lincoln came to hear a sermon. From this pulpit he whipped up many moral passions (and more terrestrial passions which exploded into a loud and juicy scandal for which, unfortunately, there is no room here).

The high emotion and ferment have evaporated. What remains in the rectangle of Fulton to State Streets, the East River to Clinton Street, are appealing, small houses on quiet old streets named Pineapple, Orange, Cranberry, Poplar, and Willow built by landowners, it is said, who had a New England disinclination to publicize their wealth, unlike their neighbors who were less modest, or very much richer—the Montagues and the Pierreponts—whose names appear on other street signs. On this matter there is a piece of Heights folklore which involves a Miss Middagh who objected to the anonymity of being a fruit or tree. When her name was taken off the street by the local authorities and an impersonal one substituted, she tore out the new sign and put back her own. This was removed and the official one replanted, and back and forth the battle seesawed, until Miss Middagh and her crusading strength won out. Now, between the street of the poplar and the street of the cranberry, stands the street of Miss Middagh.

The streets are fairly homogeneous and you will get something of the total effect by walking northward on Willow Street (off Clark) and winding through the short fruit streets and Middagh, and at its end, south on Hicks Street to Pierrepont, Montague, and Remsen, where some of the more opulent houses still stand. Back of Remsen are little alleys (Hunt's Lane, Grace Court) which are mews of converted stables like Macdougal Alley in Greenwich Village. Still south of these are Willow Street again and Columbia Place, almost entirely filled by an enormous old apartment house which must once have been a thing of forbidding splendor, its dour, heavy brick embroidered with many small turrets and blue ironwork balconies.

You will have seen in your walk houses with outmoded and lovely scrollwork, with decorated doorways, with New Orleans balconies, with mellow gardens and ancient vines, with low, crooked doors and with high, pillared entrances. The best of Brooklyn Heights, though, lies at the foot of Montague Street, where there is a river walk (with benches) which reveals one of the most beautiful views of Manhattan or of any city, for that matter. In the clear, blue light of late afternoon, the skyscrapers appear light and graceful, their colors blending into a soft glow. From their melded bases radiate the straight lines of warehouses and railroad sidings and, farther out, appear the shifting linear patterns of moving ferries and barges which waft across the river and bay the deep sounds of their gravel-throated horn music.

NOTE: Combine with exploration of *Knapp's* (page 238) and lunch at *Seaford's* (93 Henry St.) a large, comfortable relic with decent food at moderate prices.

ATLANTIC AVENUE LEVANT (THE FLESH)

By following Clinton Street southward from Brooklyn Heights, you will shortly reach Atlantic Avenue, which, between Court and Clinton Streets, constitutes the market of the surrounding Syrian, Lebanese, and Egyptian colony. (Turks, Armenians, and Greeks are more likely to have stayed in Manhattan in the East 20's and West 40's.) It is a group that originally settled around Washington Street in lower Manhattan, sustaining itself by establishing small shops and restaurants or by peddling household furnishings from door to door. There are many New Yorkers who still remember the slight, dark man with an exotic accent who brought an enormous pack wrapped in black oilcloth and released from it a flow of treasures—tablecloths embroidered with violent red roses, rippling moonlight on romantic ponds painted on black velvet, thin green and red rugs, Cupid and Psyche in dead-white stone, coarse lace curtains with fringe, and marble bowls surrounded by pigeons which could be lifted out and replaced in their niches. Payment was made in small weekly sums, and they went on forever because rarely was one irresistible object paid for before the customer succumbed to another.

Much of Washington Street was demolished for the construction of the Battery Tunnel, and the shopkeepers and peddlers took their families to Brooklyn, where some

of them opened new shops. Those on Atlantic Avenue—
owned by Alwans, Sahadis, Shalhoubs—are, by and large,
food stores with sections devoted to a mélange of assorted
objects of local and touristic appeal. The food side will
have large sacks of pistachio nuts and sesame seeds, eggplant (dried, stuffed variously, and in brine), vats of
grapeleaves and olives, jars of rose-petal jam, bottles of
flower waters, flat tins of Oriental nut-and-honey confections and, conveniently placed on the counter, a large
jar containing chunks of gum arabic which the neighborhood women use as chewing gum. (It isn't bad, something like white tar flavored with eucalyptus.) The other
side will be the department of kohl, of small, graceful
drums, Syrian lutes and quills for playing them, Arabian
prayer beads of amber or plastic, unfamiliar pastry molds,
lamp shades of punched brass, slippers with flattened
backs and pointed toes, huge copper-covered trays and,
always, a hookah or two.

The area is a very good one for tasting around in; go
hungry, and while you're staring into windows or listening to Arab records in the local music stores, you might
chew on one of the spinach pies or sesame rings baked
in *Alexander's Syrian Bakery* (150 Atlantic Ave.), or the
pastries of *Joseph Shalhoub* at 152 (or, for that matter,
almost anywhere in the neighborhood, since this is a
colony obviously addicted to sweets and every shop carries them). For more substantial eating, have the shish
kebab at the *Pyramids* (185) or the *Eastern Star* (205);
both are simple restaurants from which not too much is
to be expected, but the food is authentically prepared
and quite cheap. Forgo dessert and walk into the ice-
cream parlor of *Fouad Alwan* (189), instead. On week
ends he makes nut-stuffed pancakes and fried honey-nut
balls dipped in syrup to add to his counterful of pastries,
his unusual supply of fruit ices (with recognizable flavors), and a pistachio ice cream which is quite unlike the
expected smooth, green cream. This version is almost all
pistachios, held together by a combination of what seems
to be condensed milk and gum arabic—odd, rich, slightly
rubbery, and quite good. The service is almost non-
existent; you will probably have to go to the counter to

order and pick up your ice cream and then get your own glass of water; this is neither systematized self-service nor xenophobia, more a dreamy indifference to the disturbances of trade.

WILLIAMSBURG (THE SPIRIT)

By car, across the Williamsburg Bridge; then on Broadway in Brooklyn to Keap or Hooper Streets. By subway: BMT Broadway line to Hewes Street (local stop).

The predominant tone of Williamsburg is so anciently Jewish that it is hard to believe that, one hundred years ago, it was a German village with beer gardens, *Turnvereins*, choral societies, and a population large enough to support a small newspaper. There were, even then, a few Jewish families who, the story goes, had to cross the river in rowboats to attend synagogue services in New York. The group increased with the influx of Jewish tailors, tobacconists, and leather dealers who came from Central Europe in the 1860's and 1870's. It was not, however, until the 1880's or later that the great flood of Eastern European Jews, the base of the present colony, poured into Williamsburg from the hamlets and ghettos of Russia, Poland, Rumania, and Hungary. They were a more orthodox and less worldly people than their predecessors, who, by that time, were beginning to move more freely around the city and the country. Joined by some of the more intensely devout of the Lower East Side, they settled into their accustomed modes of the eighteenth-century *stetl*, without the gnawing poverty or the threats of pogroms, but with the same stubborn preservation of the laws and obligations of classic orthodoxy.

These restraints are basically religious, the rules of Kashruth, of Sabbath observances, of holy-day rituals, and of daily prayers; but as if their lives were strengthened by prohibitions, some strictures have been gathered from folklore and superstition, from the ascetic mysticism of legendary rabbis and from centuries of trying to come to terms with constant fear. There are households now in Williamsburg where an English book may not be read on the Sabbath, where a wife is addressed as "Woman" (if addressed at all) except on Friday night and Saturday, when she becomes "Queen"; here live emaciated young Talmudic scholars with study-bent backs and pale indoor skins, who will avoid talking to or touching a woman and, if addressed by a woman, will keep their eyes cast down; there are women here who make long trips to especially kosher shops because they suspect the ritual safeness of what ordinarily passes for kosher among less exacting people.

It all may seem to be dour and difficult, but to sense the pleasurable aspects of this orthodoxy, go to Williamsburg on some early Saturday afternoon when the weather is clear. Little girls in long stockings and dresses with long sleeves (even the very young must be very chaste) and little boys with wisps of side curls emerging from their skullcaps, the pale scholar's face already visible in the childish features, sit on the stoops of the tenements, content to be a smiling audience for the Gentile sprites noisily playing games forbidden to the Jewish children on Saturday. They don't feel deprived; they have been taught to choose being the especially chosen, and this is one of the confirmations of that important fact. From the doorway of the house emerges a large elderly man of regal bearing, followed by several young men who listen to him deferentially. His side curls, not as long as those zealously affected by some of the younger men, are still long enough to symbolize the curls of David, and his long beard makes him one with Abraham. He wears fine black boots, a rich black coat, carries a handsome walking stick, and on his head is a great halo of fox fur, a style of headgear borrowed from the princes of Hasidism (and there were some who lived like Medicis, with their private staffs of artisans and jewelers); they, in turn, had borrowed the style from the Polish landowners of the seventeenth century. Whatever else he is during the unimportant week—a pants presser, the beadle of a poor synagogue, a teacher in the local Hebrew school—he is now a king and savant, a leader of men, and at peace with the world.

Somewhat later, his wife walks out with a married daughter who lives within walking distance (to have ridden would have been a transgression). Mamma had taken her weekly bath the afternoon before, after her floors were scrubbed, the windows washed, and the best table-cloth spread. The remains of the egg-yellow Sabbath twist bread rest on a good plate under a crisp white napkin; in the refrigerator there is a mound of gefulte fish which had been chopped and patted early on Friday; and in the oven there is a mash of carrots, prunes, pota-toes, and meat, which has been simmering slowly since Friday afternoon, to obviate lighting the forbidden fire on Saturday. Mamma shines in her dark silk dress of unfashionable cut and her lively brownish-red wig, ar-ranged in rigid, metallic waves. Her hair had been cut off when she was married, according to ancient tradition, and so was that of her daughter who wears a wig of the same style and color. Since hair as an adornment is con-sidered a temptation, a wig as hair must not adorn either, and therefore the same bright stiff wig inappropriately surrounds a lovely, fresh face and a worn, wrinkled one. Both women may look odd to you, but their carriage is that of queens of a Sabbath house, one of the achieve-ments for which they were born and trained.

As night falls, the walkers, the visitors, and the deco-rous children return to their homes to say a formal fare-well to the Sabbath. They take off their fine clothes and prepare for their strict, mundane week, waiting for God to bring another Sabbath.

5
MUSEUMS

You will notice large gaps in this section, made by the absence of the Metropolitan Museum of Art and its adjunct, The Cloisters, and of the Museum of Modern Art and its neighbor, the Whitney Museum of American Art. Except in their roles as oases (pages 40-41), they have been omitted because they are already great loadstones, while some of the lesser museums deserve and even need greater patronage. In addition to these, it should be kept in mind that the *Public Library* (42nd St. and Fifth Ave.) and the *Grolier Club* (47 E. 60th St.) have frequent, stimulating exhibitions dealing with books; the *Frick Collection*, housed in an imperious mansion at 70th Street and Fifth Avenue, contains magnificent paintings and sculpture; and the *Museum of Primitive Art* (15 W. 54th St.) is a unique institution which encompasses superb examples of art from primitive communities all over the world, those still flourishing and those long departed. Some of the better shops, too, are small museums with price tags; *Bonnier's* (605 Madison Ave.), *Jensen's* (667 Fifth Ave.), some of the antique shops, and the special boutiques in the Fifth Avenue stores are also repositories of the rare and beautiful, and they don't at all mind being viewed as such if you can't afford to buy.

NOTE ON THE MUSEUMS:

Museum of Modern Art, 15 West 53rd Street (Daily 11 to 6; Sunday 1 to 7; Admission)

Museum of Primitive Art, 15 West 54th Street (Tuesday through Sunday 1 to 5; Admission)

Whitney Museum of American Art, 22 West 54th Street (Daily and Sunday 1 to 5; Admission)

Frick Collection, Fifth Avenue and 70th Street (Daily, except Mondays, 10 to 5; Sundays and holidays 1 to 5; Free)

Solomon R. Guggenheim Museum, 7 East 72nd Street until its new Frank Lloyd Wright building on 88th Street and Fifth Avenue is completed (Tuesday through Sunday 10 to 6; Sundays and holidays 12 to 6; Closed Monday; Free)

Museum of Natural History, Central Park West from 77th to 81st Streets (Daily 10 to 5; Sundays and holidays 1 to 5; Free)

> *Metropolitan Museum of Art,* Fifth Avenue and 82nd
> Street (Daily 10 to 5; Sundays and holidays 1 to 5; Free)
> *The Cloisters,* Fort Tryon Park (Daily, except Mondays,
> 10 to 5; Sundays 1 to 5; during summer 1 to 6; Admission)

Museum of the City of New York

Fifth Avenue at 104th Street.
Tuesday through Saturday 10 to 5; Sunday and Holidays 1 to 5;
closed Mondays and Christmas Day. Free.
Lexington IRT to 103rd Street (local); or Fifth Avenue bus
(Nos. 1, 2, 3, or 4).

Old maps and engravings show the city as a lyrical little
place, serene and unprotected, open to the sea and sky.
Many glass-encased miniatures make concrete important
events or scenes in the city's history—the sale of Manhattan,
the inauguration of George Washington, South Street as it
looked in clipper-ship days. Correctly detailed, the miniatures have the stiff old-fashioned quality of pictures in old
history books (apparently still used, if one were to believe
the little boys who run from section to section, shouting
"This picture is in my history book and this one and this
one!").

Among the cases of shoe buckles, cuff links, silver, and
jewelry, is one of watches decorated with examples of the
lost art of watch-paper making. These delicately cut and
colored designs, arranged to be visible when the watch was
opened, speak as clearly of the Romantic and Victorian eras
as do the portraits in the second-floor gallery of theirs. Those
are mainly of prominent early New Yorkers, all of whom
appear to share the same characteristics—sobriety without
nobility, prosperity without style, and no charm at all. They
couldn't all have been like that; it must have been something
inherent in the Colonial portrait style.

The museum reminds us again that New York City was
always an important seaport; in its Marine Gallery on the
second floor, there are models of every kind of vessel that
sailed into the harbor, from the fat little Dutch *Half Moon*
to an overwhelming silhouette, in scale, of the *United States,*
looming like a Leviathan over the other models.

An old-fashioned toy shop has been set up on the third
floor; its shelves hold a wealth of dolls of every size and
degree of fashion, of wooden animals, of puzzles, nostalgia-
drenched trolleys, and Jenny Lind paper dolls. The only
items that seem to have no modern counterpart are the
mechanical penny banks, small monuments of crude inge-

nuity: a coin placed in Uncle Sam's hand drops into his carpetbag, which opens and then shuts on the penny as Uncle wags his whiskers; the penny on Jonah's back goes into the whale's mouth when a lever is pushed. These will very likely stay a thing of the past. What self-respecting child will accept a penny now?

As one might expect, the museum contains a good deal of furniture, costumes, and accessories of various periods from the Dutch through the early twentieth century. These are not nearly as complete (and make no attempt to be) as the rooms in the historic houses (see pages 121-26) but if once over lightly is all you can use of early decor of body and house, this collection should be completely adequate.

An unusual and very interesting service maintained by the museum is a succession of temporary exhibits, all concerned with New York. There have been a series of evocative photos of Ellis Island on display, a group of paintings of New York City covering the last century, and an exhibit devoted to the contribution of the Negro in drama, music, and dance. The "Theatre Gallery" has shown a history of *My Fair Lady* and how she grew from Ovid to von Suppé to W. S. Gilbert to Shaw to Lerner-Loewe, each stage illustrated by appropriate manuscripts and photos. By all means, see the special shows when you go.

The Old Merchant's House

29 East 4th Street.
Tuesday through Saturday 11 to 5; Sunday and Holidays 1 to 5; closed Mondays, Christmas, and all of August.
Admission 50 cents.
Third Avenue bus to 4th Street; or IRT Lexington local to Astor Place.

When it was built, in 1830 by Joseph Brewster (a descendant of a Mayflower Brewster) the Old Merchant's House must have thrown its Georgian shine over an elegant neighborhood. Now it stands on one of the lost streets, flanked by a small warehouse and blearily gazed at by little dusty shops, itself a bit grimy and tired. It is, however, unique and very much worth a visit because, unlike many other historic houses, it contains only the articles accumulated by one family over a century of continuous residence; no "articles of the period," as the brochures state it, were brought in.

A hardware merchant, Seabury Tredwell, bought the house and moved into it in 1835. The family continued to grow in wealth and size and ultimately included five daughters, two of whom received or wrested, in time, Papa's permission to marry. Three stayed at home, letting the years and changes go by as they guarded the purity of their house against innovations, growing old in Jamesian exclusiveness as the city heaved and roared by. In 1933, the last of the Tredwell sisters (Gertrude, who was in her nineties by this time) died, in surroundings very much like those into which she was born. After her death, the house had no inhabitants and little care, and had reached the point of being nearly sold at auction when, in a dramatically close nick of time, a grandnephew bought it and presented it to the city as a museum.

Because of the years of past and present neglect, the Old Merchant's House is musty and dim; its carpets are threadbare, the draperies are dusty, and the walls not so much discolored as de-colored. These symptoms of decay give the house some of its special appeal and make it almost possible to believe the stories which grew like barnacles on the house —stories of clanking ghosts who sit in the Chippendale and Phyfe chairs, sleep in Mama's and Papa's majestically canopied beds, drink smuggled wine (once carried on subterranean paths from the river to the house) from imported glasses, and dress up in the exquisitely delicate gowns and Chantilly lace shawls of the Tredwell ladies.

NOTE: Don't go away if the doorbell isn't answered as soon as you think it should be. The only attendant is the curator, who must conduct each person or group through the three visible floors of the house. She may have to run all the way down from the top floor or up from the basement floor where she lives (which is why you can't see the old kitchen, by the way). 50 cents plus a short wait is little to pay for a view of mummified mercantile splendor and, in addition, a sprightly, informative tour through it led by an engaging young woman. The visit combines well with one to The Cooper Union Museum (*below*) or with either the Slavic walk (page 64) or the Village walk (page 70).

The Cooper Union Museum

Cooper Square, Third and Fourth Avenues, 7th-8th Streets. 10-5 P.M. Daily.

Tuesday and Thursday until 9 from October through April; closed Holidays and on Saturdays from June 1st to September 15th. Free.

IRT Lexington line to Astor Place (local); or Third Avenue bus to 7th Street.

On the fourth floor of an old building whose history, if not its appearance, is imposing, in a neighborhood that has been passed by in the northward rush of the city, resides one of the most lively museums in the city. Its air of quiet bustle and productivity stems from the fact that it is a study institution essentially, its enormous collection available not only to students of Cooper Union but to anyone working or studying in the decorative arts. In the study rooms off the main galleries, a group of art students pores over pictures in the extensive Picture Library, a designer explores the modern possibilities of eighteenth-century wallpaper design, a decorator looks for a freshening of ideas. The objects on view are not glass-encased dead matter, but living elements in a continuous stream of design development.

Founded modestly in 1897 by the granddaughters of Peter Cooper, the museum grew, by the accretion of gifts, into a rich and varied repository of the decorative arts numbering 80,000 items, among them a unique group of Coptic and medieval fabrics and textiles dating back to 1500 B.C. The collection of wallpapers extends through two centuries and many styles, and the collection of drawings, etchings and engravings exemplifying architectural and ornamental design reaches from the fifteenth century to the present day. There are ceramics, metalwork, glass, woodwork, costume accessories, and examples of needlework, all available for study, with or without the amiable assistance of staff members who are specialists in their various fields. For research there is a large reference library and also a classified collection of pictures (three-quarters of a million of them) culled from every conceivable source to make an impressive record of changing tastes in design and the range of imagination in expressing them.

Do you like birdcages? There are many enchanting ones, particularly a Chinese birdcage ornamented with finely carved ivory plaques. Do you incline toward Eastern arts? Look at the Persian calligraphy and the Indian cotton and the block prints. Or better still, just wander in the bounty of the clever displays. Elegant wooden panels of the eighteenth century back a small case holding early Egyptian figurines and a piece of fourth-century tapestry; a demonstration of the use of natural shapes—in this case, a pear—uses an English tea kettle of silver, a French jar of porcelain, a small eighteenth-century enamel bottle, and a fairly modern trophy cup; a wallpaper marked with the angular, tart humor of Saul Steinberg hangs near a massive baroque-classic doorway; an old tapestry hangs stiff and regal near a playful bit of French embroidery; and on and on it goes, endlessly instructive and engaging.

You may have a sense, as you go, of something missing; the picture is pleasantly awry. What you probably miss is the sight of tired, indifferent guards to put the stamp of "Museum" on the place. The guards are unobtrusive here and what help you may need comes eagerly from the experts who dart happily from one study gallery to another, stopping now and then to help a visitor open a wall case or to offer information.

Theodore Roosevelt Museum

28 East 20th Street.
Tuesday through Saturday 10 to 5; Sunday 1 to 5; closed Mondays and on major holidays. Free.
Madison, Fifth, or Lexington Avenue buses bring you close enough.

Unlike the Old Merchant's House, which sustains itself meagerly on your half-dollar and on a kind word from the city, the Theodore Roosevelt Museum has rich relations and shows it. The Roosevelt Memorial Association (Theodore, or Republican, variety) which established the museum in the house where the Roughrider was born, has lovingly gathered every remotely pertinent scrap of material and information concerning him, and has displayed it in well-made, well-lit cases in the pine-paneled basement floor of the house. In addition to small personal effects and some family records, there are numerous cartoons, newspaper clippings, books, letters, and documents, all commemorating incidents of a conspicuously public life. Out of the African safari days come a stuffed lion, mounted heads, a couple of bear and zebra skins, and even a bush jacket worn in the jungle. Roosevelt's cowboy period is marked by the appropriate branding irons and chaps, and the Spanish-American War by other fitting trophies, no single object of especially great interest but the aggregate making an impressively idolatrous whole.

The same devotion that went into garnering and cherishing the collection obviously touched the restored house, which now shines with respectability, past and present. Each crystal drop of the drawing-room chandelier glistens with cleanliness, the silk hangings and puffy chairs are full and prosperous; you know the beds are of the best wood and the sheets of the best linen. As you absorb these mid-nineteenth-century testaments of substantial living, you can almost smell the odors of a full, hearty meal creeping up the stairs—not fancy, but four-square, built around a good solid joint, like a happy Dickens ending.

Pierpont Morgan Library

36th Street between Park and Madison Avenues.
9:30 to 5 except Sundays and Holidays; closed Saturdays in June and July, and altogether in August. (Art section open on Tuesday, Thursday, and Saturday.)

A baronial setting almost unreal in its excess—bronze doors, green and African marble panels, lunettes framed in gold, exquisitely inlaid book shelves, Strozzi chairs and Tuscan *cassoni,* Brussels tapestry, superlative paintings—surrounds an almost equally unbelievable collection of rare books and documents. More vividly than statistics of money earned and spent, the two buildings and their contents give some idea of what it meant to be a Morgan, or a Hadrian, or a Pope Julius II; Morgan had the advantage of a larger old world to shop in.

The range of the collection moves from papyrus sheets from the *Book of the Dead* (ninth-tenth centuries B.C.) through Byzantine holy-picture books, through martyrologies and sacramentaries illuminated by medieval monks, through elegant and worldly *Books of Hours* painted for the great houses of the Middle Ages, through lovely choir books illuminated by minor Duccios. And then one stops for an awed moment before a Gutenberg Bible, an experience comparable to shaking the hand of Chaucer. We continue, after a proper obeisance, through examples of early printing, including a spate of scientific tomes—medical books, herbals, natural science compendia—a rush which may have been waiting for freedom from the judgment of the scriptoria. Of a later date, there are the ornate bejeweled bindings made for royal, though not necessarily literate, houses, and the simpler, much more beautiful books of the East.

The manuscripts and letters show the hands of Dickens, Scott, Keats, Burns, Byron, Balzac, to name a few. These, like the great print collections, are not all always on view, but changing groups are exhibited and, of course, the total is available to scholars. There was displayed recently, for instance, a letter written by Dürer to a patron, not the words and thoughts of genius, but the respectful words of a modest craftsman complaining across the centuries about difficulties in cutting a woodblock for printing.

Museum of Moneys

1254 Sixth Avenue (near 50th Street; Rockefeller Center).
Mondays through Fridays 10 to 5; closed Saturdays, Sundays and Holidays.

The Money Museum (Collection of Chase Manhattan Bank) holds an impressive and worrisome array of what was, is, and possibly may again be, money. It is an informative and troublesome sight. If copper rods, bent spear blades, throwing knives, and rings are African money; if glass beads, banana seeds, fiber armlets, dogs' teeth, tiger claws, fishhooks and fishbones, empty bullet cartridges and musket balls buy other goods as well as each other; if a stone weighing over one hundred pounds and perforated to be carried on a pole by two men is money; if peppercorns and cocoa beans and cheese and tea bricks are money; if silk, soap, cotton, seaweed bread, whiskey, salt, and fish eggs have the power to buy; if an Aztec chopper could be money—what really are the green pieces of paper that sustain us? If a note marked one hundred quintillion Hungarian pengo was worth (in 1946) less than an American penny, why should a note marked eight million, five hundred thousand dollars be worth the United Nations site? There are answers, no doubt, expert and cogent, but it gives one to think—which shouldn't seriously mar anyone's pleasure in a small and very interesting museum.

Museum of Contemporary Crafts

29 West 53rd Street.
Open Monday through Saturday 12 to 6; Sunday 2 to 6. Free.

We have finally achieved a museum in which to show off our national crafts skills, largely through the efforts of the American Craftsmen's Council, whose selling stand is *America House* (page 247).

The museum is not large, as such mammoths go, but it has a breadth of light and air which expands its actual size. The sense of space is enhanced, too, by an imaginative handling of displays: except for very small pieces, the objects are not set in categories, avoiding that dulling tendency by grouping objects of different materials and purpose in one well-designed unit. For instance, a bench with a ceramic top may hold a silver candlestick and a wooden bowl, both of which rest on a piece of hand-loomed cloth. The display arrangements have interesting variety in themselves; sometimes they are square shallow boxes which rest on the floor, others are open glass shelves or closed cases in varying dimensions. A screen may hang free from the ceiling, a rug may be attached to one of the pillars. Nothing sits embedded in museum torpor.

It hardly needs saying that each object exhibited in the changing shows is uniquely designed and skillfully made. If you're one of the many to whom the word "crafts" meant lumpy vases groping for shape, leather bags brutally stitched by a mad surgeon, or earrings of agonized design, Contemporary Crafts will be an imposing revelation.

New York Historical Society

Central Park West at 77th Street.
Open Saturdays, 10 A.M. to 5 P.M., other days, 1 to 5 P.M.; closed Mondays, on major holidays, and August. Free.
Eighth Avenue and Central Park buses to 77th Street; or Eighth Avenue IND subway to 81st Street (local).

The Historical Society does not call itself a museum; it is and it isn't: there are permanent exhibitions of displays pertaining to American history with especial emphasis, of course, on New York, but it also maintains special exhibits which are of interest only to the expert or hobbyist, such as a large roomful of unremarkable paintings by a trustee of the Society, or corridors full of political sketches by a cartoonist who was adept, but monotonous.

Unless these matters have particular appeal for you, pass them by and make for some of the permanent exhibitions. One of the best is the Port of New York Gallery, one end of which is designed as the captain's cabin of an old sailing vessel. At the portholes are small panoramas of New York Harbor as it looked in 1626, 1742, and on up through the years. The atmosphere of a clipper is maintained in the larger hall adjoining the cabin by the suggestion of sail and mast high overhead and the presence of sailing articles of the times—belaying pins, old life preservers, ropes, and strings of cork floats. Over the nautical prints, instruments, beautiful ship models (a very large one of the famous Hudson River steamboat), wheels, binnacles, and an immense eighteenth-century anchor, hangs a portrait of Robert Fulton, brooding and dark, with a Byronic lock on his forehead and the *souffrant* expression of romantic sensibilities outraged; maybe he really looked like that, but it's a difficult head to match with cool engineering genius.

In a case near the back of the hall is a collection of one of our more curious folk arts, scrimshaw articles made by sailors on whaling vessels. Voyages were long and entertainment limited, so some sailors, using whales' teeth and jaw sections, took to carving small objects and figures, many of which show considerable skill and inventiveness.

The flight below the main floor contains three sections of old vehicles, each group surrounded by appropriate prints: one is a group of sleds, varying widely in style from a big cumbersome thing like a primitive bed to an enchanting Victorian belle of a sled, and including a strange tight one-man affair, heavy with carving, made in Holland in the eighteenth century. Another area is devoted to coaches and carriages—a regal painted coach brought from France before the American Revolution, a later and much simpler pony cart for children, and several types of stage and mail coaches. The fire-equipment room is proclaimed by a large wooden figure of an ancient fireman, his face and body vividly strained in alarm. Behind him stand a few fire-fighting machines, light and pretty vehicles decorated with fanciful metalwork and bells to clear the way, obviously and terrifyingly ineffectual in stopping any blaze livelier than a boys' bonfire.

On the upper floors, you might linger over the portraits of local old worthies, or in contemplation of some of the worst portraiture ever perpetrated—rough, graceless paintings of Dutch worthies by men who were obviously underpaid, loathed their sitters, and lacked talent to begin with. It might be better to go right on to the Audubon room, which holds some of his most beautiful prints and has on view the magnificent elephant folio volumes engraved from the original drawings. Or, if crafts interest you more, you might wander through the rooms of American glass—pressed, cut, engraved, milk, "whimsies"—English and American earthenware and china, utensils of pewter and of silver, of pictures in needlework and pictures on glass, of painted boxes and painted wooden Indians, of period rooms and period costumes.

If you're serious about New York history, there will be much to absorb you: galleries of visual history, which include pictures of several impressive Indian chiefs; Henry Hudson's contract with the Dutch East India Company (the ancestors of Wall Street); the commission from Charles III of England, directing his governors to retake New York from the Dutch who, after the initial struggle of 1664, regained the city for a very short period. Among this group of documents is an extraordinarily enlightening map which demonstrates what the New World looked like to the *cognoscenti* of 1600: South America is pretty accurately drawn, firmly and completely enclosed in its familiar shape, but North America's lines falter and fade and spray into unintelligible nothingness as they travel northward above the Hudson Valley.

For the snapper-up of unconsidered trifles: the toy section, whose stars are a large Noah's ark waiting for a small sea of animals supervised by Noah, Ham, Shem, and their wives, and a cluster of stylized roosters with peculiarly fanned-out brilliant tail feathers; a row of cotton and silk kerchiefs of intense patriotism, one bearing the Declaration of Independence, another with portraits of Lincoln and Washington linked by the American eagle, and a third depicting victorious vessels of the War of 1812, in its center a banner shouting "Huzza! Huzza!"; a votive corner dedicated to Jenny Lind, whose programs and sheet music are here, as well as a curiously irreverent assortment of articles decorated with her effigy. Around the corner from Jenny is a bright stream of posters and ads for balloon ascensions, circuses, fairs, auctions, and sober products like soap and insurance, and an announcement of the "First Appearance of a female baseball contest" between the "Female Red Stockings" and the "Female Blue Stockings."

Jewish Museum

92nd Street at Fifth Avenue.
Open Monday through Thursday 1 to 5 P.M., Sundays from 11 to 6; closed Friday and Saturday and Jewish holidays. Free.
Fifth Avenue bus Nos. 1, 2, 3, or 4.

For a change, let's start from the top down, a method which has some logic since it is actually less exhausting.

The top (fourth) floor contains a large diorama of Israel made by New York Jewish children. Of paper, clay, cloth, wood, and paint, they have created a vivid structure crowded with camels and clinics, pipelines and hospitals, trucks and people. Imaginative, brilliantly alive, and not too realistic, it manages to present Israel with more veracity than many painters and photographers have.

The third floor has a section devoted to Jewish life in the early years of American history—paintings and silhouettes of prominent citizens, books, prints, ceremonial objects, and the Torah Ark of the Charleston Synagogue, dating from shortly before the American Revolution, simple and modestly direct, in thoroughly Colonial style. Another room contains relics of Jewish life in late classical times: coins minted by the Romans, seven-branched candelabrum coins of the Maccabees, clay candlesticks, and simple lamps. Painted on the walls of this room are copies of the murals in the third-century Dura Europos Synagogue in Syria, the oldest synagogue yet unearthed. The paintings are of Biblical scenes done in a late Roman style, strongly reminiscent of the Fayyum grave-paintings of Egypt and possibly executed by similarly trained craftsmen. The remainder of the third floor encompasses displays of Jewish folk arts in many materials, essentially ceremonial in purpose, and stemming from such wide-flung areas as Persia, Italy, Germany, and North Africa. Notice especially two moving acts of dedication: a painstakingly elaborate Torah Ark, hand-carved in 1899 by a Jewish cattle dealer in Sioux City, and a wooden Hannukah Menorah made by a boy in a French D.P. camp. It is crude, defiantly large, and awesome.

Among the spice boxes, the Torah headpieces, the pointers, and the precise circumcision sets on the second floor, are a number of large rings, some of them mounted with intricately worked little replicas of synagogues; these were worn by Jewish women for only one week after the wedding ceremony and then replaced by simple, mundane bands—an unmistakable way of saying the honeymoon is over.

Changing shows of arts and crafts occupy the main floor. Limited to ritual and synagogue pieces, the best combine modern fluidity and ancient solemnity, and from the blending there often emerges a beautiful piece which soars beyond the limits of its stated use, into high art.

Several thoughts crowd one another while one browses through the handsome rooms of the Jewish Museum (once the home of the Felix M. Warburgs). One wonders at the multiplicity of objects used in Jewish ceremonial life; one conjectures about how much more there would have been to collect if it weren't for the destruction and uprooting which have been indigenous to Jewish history, and how remarkable it is that so much has been left to be gathered. And one thinks about the many styles of Jewish objects—the Colonial Ark, the German spice boxes modeled on the early *Schloss,* the Roman paintings, the very Italianate objects— which are not only the inevitable concomitants of ceaseless dispersion, but also a testament to the Jew's insistence on staying, a stubbornness which takes on the guise of pliant adaptability.

THE AUDUBON TERRACE GROUP

Cut into Broadway, between 155th and 156th Streets, violating the strict angularity of most of New York City in imitation of the *piazzette* and mews of Europe, is Audubon Terrace. Its first surprise is a huge weather-beaten totem pole whose primitive impact is enhanced by the surprising contrast of a set of neo-classic buildings behind it. These house several societies rather remote from the general public, such as the National Institute of Arts and Letters and the American Geographical Society. However, there are three others, exceedingly interesting to the general public, which fill the rest of the gray stone plaza.

Hispanic Society of America, Museum and Library (Spanish Museum)

Audubon Terrace (Broadway and 155th St.).
10 to 4:30 Tuesday through Saturday; 2 to 5 on Sundays; closed on Holidays (Library open 1 to 4:30 Tuesday through Saturday; closed Sundays and throughout August). Free.
Fifth Avenue bus No. 5 to 155th Street; or IRT Seventh Avenue-Broadway line to 157th Street (express stop).

Most of us compress Spanish culture into a neat little bundle of three painters, two composers, one playwright, and one poet—the bundle decorated by sprigs of flamenco and "Carmen." We tend to neglect the lustrous years of the Arab occupation and much of the grandeur which made and was made by the *Conquistadores*. Here, in more compact form than you can see it in Spain, are selected reminders of those glories.

Judging from the objects of Arab work and influence, they seem to have inhabited an airier, more playful, world than the later Spaniards. The carved ivories, the patterned silks, the lusterware bowls and platters indicate a civilization which was lightly sybaritic and wonderfully intelligent, which not only had mathematics while the rest of Europe was still counting on its fingers, but could bend that knowledge to the creation of enchanting pleasure palaces. If you've never seen them, and would like some idea of what dazzles and charms in the Alhambra, in the Alcazar of Seville, in the Great Mosque of Cordoba, look at a tenth-century ivory box made in the region of Cordoba. In this handful, you will find their controlled luxury of design, their elegant rhythms, their perfect workmanship, and the great delight in the making of the thing itself, apart from concern about its function.

Of Catholic Spain there are great inlaid and gilded sets of drawers and chests covered in velvet and adorned with ornate locks and hinges, types of safes suitable for guarding the treasures bought with Inca gold. At the far side of the court there is a display of immense door knockers suggesting the forbidding fortresses which were the castles of Spain. The church art echoes the proud, self-confident tone of the furniture, except for some small jet figurines of Gothic forthrightness and two early pieces—a Madonna and an Angel, both of the thirteenth century—which are startlingly simple and modern in their stylization and reduction to semiabstract forms.

Later Spanish art is reflected in the paintings, which include a number of El Grecos and a roomful of panels depicting the folk color of various Spanish provinces. These latter are much admired by some people, and considerably less by others.

The library is considered one of the most important of its kind, not only for its size, but for the number of remarkable books and manuscripts it contains. A Mozarabic missal, some very early dictionaries, and examples of antique music have found their way here. Several books printed in the Americas soon after the Conquest are part of the collection, and, of course, thousands of later books dealing with every facet of Spanish and Portuguese history and art.

American Numismatic Society

Audubon Terrace (for directions, see Hispanic Society, page 118).
Tuesday through Saturdays 10 to 5. Free.

The door doesn't swing freely open as in other museums, but ring the bell and you will be admitted by an affable gentleman who'll appear surprised and pleased to see you. There, in almost solitary splendor, you can follow the evolution of American currency, of British coinage from the time of the Romans and Anglo-Saxons to the present day, of the developments of the German thaler as it became various kinds of dollars. In one of the central cases, there is a display of exquisite Siamese porcelain tokens used in gambling, in the shapes of butterflies, fish, birds, and lanterns. Nearby is a group of Italian Renaissance coins, portraits of the Sforzas, the d'Estes and the Medicis, all with the arrogant look that says history and evolution might as well stop with them. The

same look molds the faces of the Malatestas and the Gon-
zagas commemorated on magnificent medals worked by Pisa-
nello and Spinello.

Getting oneself commemorated in metal went on long
before the time of the Renaissance demigods and continued
on long after them; the line runs through Roman senators,
Christian saints, French kings, and modern statesmen, and
also through celebrations of various victories: the lifting of
the Turkish siege of Vienna, the victory at Waterloo, and the
triumphs of the French and American Revolutions.

The Numismatic Society museum is attractively lit and
logically arranged and, since it is sparsely inhabited, has a
quiet repose which makes a welcome break between the
dark, weighty Hispanic Museum and the fascinating clutter
of the Museum of the American Indian.

Museum of the American Indian

Audubon Terrace (for directions see Hispanic Society, page
118). Tuesday through Saturday 1 to 5 P.M.; closed Holidays
and all of July and August. Free.

The Museum's brochure states that only a small portion of
its specimens can be housed in this building; the rest is
available to scholars in a research annex at the outer edges
of the Bronx. The mind recoils from imagining such a collection, once having tried to encompass even the "small" public
portion. The Museum, formerly obscured by poor lighting
and display, is now acquiring a new face—the Hall of
American Indian Ethnology has been beautified and extensive renovations are in process.

What the Prado is to Goya, the Museum of the American
Indian is to the artisans of the Kwakiutls, of the Hopis, of
the Aztecs, and the Iroquois, but many of the extraordinary
objects have no space through which their splendor might
radiate and the eye is often distracted and exhausted by the
crowded plethora of fascinating things, too casually illuminated. It's worth the effort you'll have to make to see this
collection, however.

It is impossible for the nonexpert to evaluate their ethno-
logic importance, but there are a number of grotesques that
should not be missed. At the top of the first flight of stairs
there stands a Kwakiutl doorpost which strongly suggests
a caricature of Daniel Webster in a flight of oratory, teeth
bared and face set in impassioned conviction. Flanking the
entrance to one of the Latin-American exhibits hang two

large evil-colored masks with lizards, snakes, frogs, and many-legged bugs crawling around the mouths and eyes. These were placed in the dance plazas during certain cere-monies. (Was it to ward off evil spirits? Or to serve as *memento mori* when the mescal flowed too freely? Or were they Tarascan Halloween pumpkins? The answer can be found out, of course, but this kind of nonscientific conjecture is often more rewarding for the layman.) Another startling group is a set of *Pipil* dolls from El Salvador which seem to be caricatures of the *Conquistadores,* nasty and funny. The upper faces are delicate white and pink, the lower cheeks and jaws painted a strong, dark blue, apparently to indicate beards which must have appeared strange and murky to Indians. The faces are pancake flat, as if the Indian artist were especially impressed by the contrast to his own highly contoured face, the bright blue eyes are fringed with long thick lashes, flamboyant curves of black paint make the care-ful symmetry of the mustaches. Various possibilities float through the mind: Were the Indians enchanted by the flower cheeks and maidenly eyelashes? Or were they repelled by the hairy eyes and the matted jaws and chins? Did they think of these creatures as masculine women or feminine men, or did they so fear the Spaniards that they had to reduce them to insipid dolls? Or, did they make them gods for their difference, as some Mexican Indians worship a blonde, fair-cheeked Mary bedecked in shiny North American rayon?

These objects described are meant to serve as inviting rarities, selected out of an enormously imposing collection, including beautiful Kachina dolls, exquisite Peruvian feather-work, Chilean silver, golden ornaments from Panama, stone images from Mexico, and countless baskets, tools, and cere-monial objects of diversified Indian cultures. The collection makes one of the great museums; it should be treated with more respect and care by a rich city.

EVEN FARTHER UPTOWN

The Jumel Mansion

West 161st Street and Edgecombe Avenue.
11 to 5; closed Monday. Free.
Fifth Avenue bus 2 or 3 to 162nd Street; or IND Eighth Avenue to 163rd Street (AA local).

The Jumel Mansion (also known as the Morris-Jumel) stands like a minor Acropolis topping the highest crest of the city, a fitting situation for a house which sheltered eminences of political, social, and military life in early New York. The plot of land, with a commanding view (then) of both rivers and the hills and islands beyond, was first deeded to a Dutch farmer. It subsequently passed through a number of hands and, in 1765, was bought by Roger Morris, a wealthy young Englishman who was looking for a summer retreat in which to escape the heat of Stone Street and was no doubt attracted by the advertisement which offered a house, a large barn, an unusually prolific orchard, and two rivers for fishing and clamming. The Morrises (she was a member of the lordly Philipse family) built the present mansion and renamed the estate "Mount Morris."

Shortly afterward, however, the American Revolution violated their bucolic pleasures and ultimately the Tory Morrises had to return to England. The house then became military headquarters for General Heath and later for George Washington, who retreated to the area after the Battle of Long Island, using the mansion as headquarters. Following Washington's removal, the mansion was taken over by British officers and troops who remained through the seven years of the occupation. Neglected and damaged through the years of military occupancy, the house faded from splendor and became a tavern and later a farmhouse.

Then came the ebullient Madame Jumel, one of the first in a long line of New York fancy ladies, a bit crude and flamboyant, but one must remember that she functioned in what was still an outpost of civilization. Betsy was an ambitious career girl who left the workhouse very early to live and work in more profitable houses. By the time she was eighteen (and a mother) she was ready for travel abroad. This she arranged with the utmost economy: she traveled as the guest of the captain. After a profitable time, she reintroduced herself to New York City as a Frenchwoman, complete with wardrobe, accent, mannerisms, and touched with the pathetic charm of invented widowhood.

She was entertained and entertaining, enjoying many gay friendships, though few with women, until Stephen Jumel came along. He had been a rich plantation owner in the West Indies who had come to New York to rebuild his fortunes, which he did quickly and steadily. Although he maintained her in high style, Betsy wanted respectability and a surer hold on the Jumel wealth. Subscribing always to *toujours l'audace,* she staged a deathbed scene, it was said, during which she gaspingly begged to be allowed to die

respectable. Jumel succumbed and his wife recovered sufficiently to plan and execute a more formal wedding and gala
reception from which the solid burghers stayed away in conspicuous numbers. They stayed as insistently away when she
invited them to the newly refurbished Morris Mansion, which
Jumel bought her in 1810 and stocked with luxurious furnishings.

The house that topped the city didn't allay Mme Jumel's
restlessness or insatiable ambition and she launched upon
another trip through France where she soon became involved in Bonapartist plots (whether amatory, political, or
both doesn't seem to be certain). The Jumels were therefore
invited out of France, but not before they had procured
some of Napoleon's furniture to grace their mansion.

Stephen Jumel died in 1832. Betsy, by this time near sixty
and as rich as she had ever hoped to be, cast her eye on
Aaron Burr, who had grown poor, out of favor, and seventy-
eight years old. They were married, soon fought and separated, instituting flavorful divorce proceedings including ac-
cusations of adultery, which Burr, at least, found flattering.
The short, noisy, vituperative marriage would seem an incon-
gruously vigorous dance for two elderly people if it didn't
involve these particular two, who may have decayed but
never became elderly.

The Jumel fortune was scattered by Madame's reckless
hands; when she died there was just enough of it left to be
consumed by litigation. She was ninety when she died, proving something or other about the wages of sin. Her house
was sold and resold and, by 1903, was slated for demolition.
After considerable petitioning by the citizenry, the city
bought it; it is still city property, its contents cared for by
a group founded by the Daughters of the American Revolution.

The mansion is an extraordinarily handsome building of
mid-Georgian design, somewhat unusual in that it has a
two-storied portico at the front, a style which was not generally used until later. The rooms are gracefully proportioned
and furnished with late eighteenth-century and early nineteenth-century pieces, some of which were bought by the
Jumels and others gathered from authentic sources or copied
from period designs. On the main floor is the tea room in
which Burr and Mme Jumel were married, and across the
hall from it is a courtly formal dining room. Toward the
back is a large octagonal room (also an unusually early
example of this style) which served as library to the Morrises,

as headquarters for Washington, and, later, as the drawing room of the Jumels.

At the top of the stairs, to the right, there is a little room, the powder room, from which our current euphemism possibly derives its name although the original was used, literally, as a place where gentlemen's wigs were powdered. The rest of the upper floor is occupied by an ornate Empire bedroom furnished by the Jumels and, through a narrow hallway, the small rear room in which Washington slept and worked; it is not an attractive room, but the presence of an ingenious camp cot which Washington used gives the man and his period great immediacy.

Coming back into the main upper hall, you will pass a small office, crammed with books and photographs, one of them of the Chateau Chambord of the Loire. It was once owned by the family of the good-looking, white-haired gentleman who may be sitting at a desk in the room. Stop to talk with him; he is Mr. Henry Harrison de Frise, the Curator of the Morris-Jumel Mansion, very well informed about the history of New York and generous about sharing it with interested visitors.

Dyckman House

Broadway at 204th Street.
Open every day, 10 to 5, except Monday. Free.
IND Subway (Eighth Avenue) to 204th Street.

Infinitely more modest than the Jumel Mansion or Van Cortlandt House (*see below*), the Dyckman House more closely represents the ordinary style of living in New York in the eighteenth century. It is the only farmhouse of the period still in existence in Manhattan, small, simple, the rooms tight and the ceilings low. Although the Dyckmans were prosperous enough for cutglass decanters and substantial four-poster beds, the house has an aura of serious work and little play, the furnishings and ornaments respectable rather than imaginative. It is possibly this lack of show that adds to its atmosphere of authenticity.

The kitchen is the most stimulating room: the many caldrons, pothooks, irons, skillets, and ovens bring echoes and shadows of bustling women in big skirts, bending over sizzling pans and steaming kettles.

Van Cortlandt House Museum

Van Cortlandt Park, Bronx.
Weekdays, 10:30 to 4:30; Sunday and Monday 2 to 4:30; closed in February.

Free Thursday, Friday, and Saturday; 25 cents other days.
IRT Broadway line to Van Cortlandt Park (end of line).

The Van Cortlandt House was built in 1748 and reflects, in
its Dutch and English elements, the combination of Dutch
and English wealth which produced it. Frederick Van Cortlandt, who built it, was the descendant of an influential Dutch
family and had married a member of the family of the Lord
of the Manor of Philipse. The house itself, set in the large
estate which is now Van Cortlandt Park, was the core of a
completely self-sustained economic and social unit, like a
medieval village; food was provided by the crops and animals raised by slaves, clothing by the women who spun and
wove the home-grown flax, while skilled laborers and artisans
planned and built. The decades modified its original living
design greatly, of course, but the descendants of the family
used the house for one hundred and fifty years until, in 1889,
the estate was deeded to the city and made a public park.

The exterior of the house is solid and assured, its only
mannerism being a set of gargoyle-like keystones above the
windows; these echo a contemporary Dutch style, although
the house is mainly Georgian. The interior is a set of spacious
rooms full of well-arranged furnishings of Dutch, English,
and American origin: there is a lovely English spinet and
some very handsome Chippendale pieces in the parlor; the
dining room contains a mixture of English and American
furniture and English china as well as curtains of English
crewelwork. The Exhibition Room holds a remarkable collection of Dutch delftware, some fine old brass, and a large
display of Colonial glass, including three bottles which may
possibly be the only existing ones made on Manhattan
Island (about four blocks west of where Macy's now stands,
to be more precise). Some of the glasses have dispropor-
tionately heavy bases, a device which cut down the break-
age in taverns and clubs, particularly when spirits rose and
spilled over into vigorous table-banging as a mode of applause (then called "firing") in response to toasts.

The bedrooms upstairs also contain some rare and good
pieces of furniture of the period, particularly two imposing
old beds, whose size, height, covering, and draperies seem
to surround sleep with solemn, ritualistic importance. Another bedroom, Dutch in style, contains a bed which is more
a sleeping closet, to be entered by a small aperture whose
doors close, keeping the sleeper protected from the abhor-
rent night air, from the interference of light and, in its dour
imitation of a large coffin, from life itself.

Although the whole house is interesting and the furnishings an important collection of seventeenth- and eighteenth-century and early nineteenth-century articles, the most appealing rooms are the two least formal, the nursery and the kitchen. The nursery, which is on the third floor, has been arranged as if the children who occupy it had just gone out for a short while. The dolls sit quite casually in the little chairs and the small four-poster bed, the tea table, and the minute tea set look as if they were imminently to be used and then put back into the lovely eighteenth-century dollhouse. The kitchen is a lively, orderly gathering of Dutch, Flemish, and English kitchenware—pewter and brass, peels and waffle irons, a candle maker, cake boards, a spinning wheel, and a robust variety of pots, pans, kettles, and caldrons—surrounding an enormous, and undoubtedly efficient, fireplace.

Brooklyn Museum

Weekdays 10 to 5; Sunday and Holidays 1 to 5; closed Christmas. Free.

IRT Broadway line to Brooklyn Museum Station (express stop).

In a number of ways Brooklyn's Museum is reminiscent of the small, good museums that dot New England, swathed in an aura of old culture and sure, independent taste.

It is not really small, having a good variety of sections with extensive exhibits in some of them. Here, as in other museums, preliminary selections should be made; you can't see it all in one visit. An illustrated chart, costing 5 cents clearly indicates where you will find what, including restrooms and telephones, and if you collect commemorative pieces of paper, it makes an attractive souvenir.

The first floor allows space for changing exhibits—recently a display celebrating the seventy-fifth anniversary of the opening of the Brooklyn Bridge, an event which inspired an impressive amount of poetry and painting; the poetry didn't show, but there were some fine and remarkably diversified paintings, along with prints, and photographs, and even engineers' charts. The bulk of the main floor is, however, occupied (except for the space used by the Gallery Shop—page 260) by an imposing collection of primitive art from the Latin-American countries, Africa, and the Pacific Islands principally, not too cumbersomely labeled with explanatory matter concerning the styles, purposes, and materials involved in making the various objects. These halls produce a number of surprises for many of us who equate primitivism with crudity: an exquisite South-American headdress made of painstakingly matched feathers in subtle colors; the carefully beaten and shaped gold ornaments of Central America; the incredible lacy architecture of Uxmal and Palenque; and the precise, sophisticated abstraction of a Pacific Islands doorjamb, designed to hold the spirit of a protective ancestor. Nor is there any coarseness in the masks from Ceylon or the aristocratic Javanese shadow-play puppets. The cruder things of religion and war have their own fearsome beauty: stern totems of carved ancestral figures painted in dull earth colors, tall monolithic Death-god figures and grotesque masks of many kinds, used to instill terror and awe.

Incidentally, if you have never seen an authentic shrunken head, there is one here (better than those in Times Square), and also what might easily be the largest punchbowl in the world—of wood, and used for ceremonies in the Admiralty Islands, it could easily accommodate the makings of a high time for a large bibulous village, and probably does. Oriental Arts occupy most of the second floor: jade, paintings, and bronzes from China, with an especially good selection of pottery and some interesting tomb pillars which are startlingly primitive against the rest of the very urbane Chinese art. The Japanese section has a rich assortment of prints and scrolls, pottery, and a few serene and graceful pieces of wood sculpture. India is represented by cotton hangings and bronze heads, as well as by some figurines and plaques of old bas-relief; and on nearby walls are glowing Turkish textiles, Syrian tiles, and lordly Arab robes. Less conspicuous, but very much worth looking for are some beautiful pages of Persian books, the calligraphy as sinuously perfect as the miniature illustrations and the total page a remarkably felicitous piece of design.

Try not to give up at this point because, one flight up, is one of the best Egyptian collections to be seen. The strong sculpture and the brilliant mummy cases let themselves be directly known, but search out some of the wonderful smaller things, like the very earliest pieces of Egyptian sculpture known, two simple female figures, their arms and bodies curved in lovely dance gestures. Or find the faïence rings of sure design and great delicacy; or the ivory figure of Thoth, about one and one-half inches tall and withal large and majestic; or a wooden jackal, long and elegant, his tail straight down in a vertical thrust; or a pair of ivory clappers in the shape of a pair of fine, gracefully curved hands; or the many cosmetic boxes imaginatively carved in animal forms.

REMINDER ONE: If weather permits, save some time and energy for the adjoining *Botanic Gardens,* which are delightful.

REMINDER TWO: The museum has a very good shop for inexpensive gifts (see page 260).

Staten Island Historical Society

Tuesdays through Saturdays, 2-5; Sundays 2-6; closed Mondays. Free.
Via Staten Island Ferry from Manhattan (see page 37); then via bus or car—ask directions at Staten Island ferry terminal.

In Richmond, Staten Island, a very short distance off Arthur Kill Road into Center Street, stands the Staten Island Historical Society's headquarters. It is an altogether engaging place, not too large, and containing a little of every aspect of life and history in Staten Island, without dull, overloaded concentration in any area. The large main room downstairs has a section set up as an old general store, complete with ornate tin canisters for spices and tea, a huge coffee grinder, and apothecary bottles and drawers with Latin labels in handsome calligraphy. The shelves hold candy boxes, cosmetics, liniments, and hair and machine oil; the glass case on the counter shows a mélange of baby bottles, superlong hairpins, laces, ribbons, braids, and passementerie. Flanking the shelves and counter stand stolid kerosene vats and cracker barrels. Off in one corner sits the decayed splendor of a red plush barber's chair accompanied by a rack of shaving mugs, each in its individual cubby, each bearing the owner's name and most decorated with exuberant floral designs or the heads of sleek, blooded horses. A wooden Indian surveys the spread of domestic implements from the spinning wheel and the large crude loom to an ur-washing machine and a variety of irons, little round-bottomed ones for fluting and ruffles and big awkward steam irons for heavy trousers.

The balcony which rings the large room brings in more threads to enrich the fabric; here are the businessman's pocket scales for weighing coins, the physician's instruments for bleeding and his surgical kit (including a murderous cleaver), the dentist's crude instruments, and—in a lighter section—toy trains in a rococo station and a beautiful doll carriage with high, delicate wheels, gracefully curved springs, and fine corduroy upholstery, surmounted by the extravagant burst of a white lace umbrella.

6

EATING AND DINING

There are two sets of facts you should know about the advice given here. The first is that the price designations which appear with each restaurant should be translated as: *modest*—up to $2.25 for a dinner; *moderate*—up to $5.00; *expensive*—anything above. The second is that many restaurants are closed through summer week ends and for several weeks during the summer; it is advisable to phone before you go. Also, "open Sundays" often means dinners only.

And then there is a third, "a fact of life"; the rent and, consequently, the prices in a restaurant go up, the chef's wife leaves him, the headwaiter has dental trouble, the proprietor can't cope, and the pleasure promised turns sour. For such possibilities, apologies beforehand and a hope that yours is not one of these days of doom.

A Pause in the Day's Occupation

Dining in the sense of leisured, festive eating, garnished with decor and service, will be dealt with farther on. Here we should like to consider the luncheonette, the place for purveying lunches (which would also include the chains such as Stouffer's, Schrafft's and Childs', but these latter are too large, too anonymous, too famous, and sometimes too flavorless to consider here). The New York City luncheonette, whether it is called a "Coffee House" or "Louie's," is personal, crowded, and reeking of flavor.

They vary widely, from those which occupy a slice of a shop, just large enough to contain eight stools, a counter, a coffee urn, a refrigerator and stove, to vast establishments with three or four large sets of stools-and-counter, a balcony with tables, and a monstrous growth of artificial jungle leaves trailing from the balcony railing. Informality is what they all have in common. No headwaiter will usher you in or thank you out, no waiter will hover, no waiter-in-training will refill your water glass or give you a second pat of butter. You'll have to battle your way *alone*.

We'll set the scene: It is one o'clock and you're hungry. On a side street in midtown you've spotted a luncheonette, whose undecorated window gives only its name and the day's menu. You push your way through a group just emerging, past the cashier's desk. On your left as you enter there is likely to be a glut of boys waiting to take lunch orders out to the surrounding offices. Beyond this small mob is the genie who frantically fills and seals coffee jars and wraps sandwiches delivered to him with loud announcements by a distant assistant (with speed and sureness, he also pours milk, cuts pie, mixes sodas, ladles soup—less like a man than a perspiring octopus). You move along to survey the possibilities of a seat and food. In the back, a cul-de-sac of steamy animation, there are no seats, so you walk to the front counter, which is barnacled by a solid wall of backs, each head bent over its trough. There is only one thing to do—it is rude and could be annoying if New Yorkers were not so thoroughly inured to it (also, *you* will shortly be the victim of the same act). As you make your way down the counter, examine each plate. If it contains a salad or spaghetti or soup, there's more to come, so search on. When you see a near-finished piece of pie, or a cup of coffee tilted fairly high, make your move. Take a stand behind the tilter and don't budge. You have a situation calling for some delicacy: How close can you stand without annoying your enthroned predecessor or tripping him as he slides off the stool? And yet, how politely far can you stand without running the risk of having someone, fleet and slippery, straddle the seat before you can get to it? It is a problem that requires neat judgment and sharp alertness, but it can be handled, and the triumph is worth the effort.

Once settled, you feel the breeze of a menu being waved in front of your face. Grab it before it disappears, and study—if the counterman lets you—the rather astonishing list. In the larger luncheonettes the menu reflects (more than anyplace except the subway) the really international quality of the city. You'll find Italian spaghetti, Hungarian goulash, Spanish omelette, Rumanian-Jewish pastrami, Southern fried chicken, and Chinese spareribs among the hamburgers and tuna-fish salads. These more exotic menus prevail mainly in midtown, where the clientele has mixed and pampered tastes, but there are more and more dishes which have lost their stamp of origin and are becoming indispensably New York City items. For instance, Irish saloons, German *Bierstuben* and Spanish-American "greasy spoons" all display signs advertising hot pastrami; and Chinese egg rolls nest cosily near hot Italian sausages on the feast day of St. Gennaro (see page 331). There is a very small candy-newspaper-lunch shop near Union Square which apparently caters to Puerto Ricans. On its windows is often chalked "Pasteles—dumplings" and "Pastelillos—knishes," by-passing the English language entirely and adopting not only the Yiddish dish, but the Yiddish word for it, just as menus in Chinese restaurants list dumpling soup as "kreplach" soup, assuming that this would be understandable to a major portion of the clientele, and it is.

No matter what its size or menu, the luncheonette is almost always an unbuttoned, relaxed place. It is a refuge from the office and from home, and its intimacy has the additional charm of indifference. If a habitué tells the counterman, "You gave me last night's coffee. Whatsa matter, you can't afford fresh coffee every day?" the counterman is not inclined to fire him as his boss might, or sulk as his wife would, but casually answers, "Gowan, it's the bad taste in your mouth; you got a lousy disposition today." Each one has let off steam and no one carries off injury. The customer, it is understood, has the right to be sullen, taciturn, tired, disgruntled, or gay and loquacious. The man behind the counter has the same rights and the thick air rings with bustle, bawd, and the swift exchange of insult. It can be an enriching half-hour and instructive in the speech and humor of a large segment of New York, if you have the nerve to keep your seat that long.

The greatest concentration of luncheonettes is, naturally, in the side streets between Lexington Avenue and Sixth, between 34th and 48th Streets. If you are a searcher for the most profound of any kind of experience, look for those whose countermen are pale and spare, with water-logged skins and washed-out eyes, the

effects of very slow drowning in coffee-urn steam and
hot dishwater; these are the men with the best-oiled
tongues and most freewheeling personalities.

Although a good number of coffee houses (those that
designate themselves *"espresso"*) won't shine as long as
the sun does, there are some which provide short luncheon menus attached to lists of Italian, Austrian, and Turkish coffee. A small village of coffee houses with elaborate
coffee-blasting machines have settled on 56th Street between Fifth and Sixth Avenues. Two of the oldest settlers
are the *Coffee Mill* (46 W. 56th St.) and *Orsini's* (at 43),
both still highly favored, though the charge for *avant-
garde* artwork in the first and Roman almost-antiques in
the latter brings the cost of a simple lunch a bit higher
than it might be. Greenwich Village, too, has some early-
rising coffee houses among its too many (page 313).
(There was a time when an empty store was taken over
by derelicts or gypsies. Now someone rushes in a few
tables and chairs—preferably of the old ice-cream-parlor
variety, too narrow and too hard—and a can of white-
wash for the walls, purple for the façade, a shuddering
mobile to hang, a worn-out dress mannequin to place at
the door, *et voila!* a coffee house.)

In the East Midtown area, there are: *The Isle of Capri*
(1028 Third Ave. at 61st St.), which serves decent Neapolitan dishes and drinks like *orzata* and *tamarindo,* as
well as Italian styles of coffee; the *House of Hamburg*
(1116 Second Ave. at 59th St.), decorated with everything, including Spanish moss; *Serendipity* (225 E. 60th
St.—page 313), which serves light lunches and coffee in
back of its extravagantly chic shop; on Second Avenue,
near 53rd Street, conveniently near the Design Center
(page 247), a small, pleasant place called *Back Street,*
which serves modest lunches and Italian coffee.

As a genre apart, there are the many Automats and
cafeterias in all sorts of moods and colors, from dour
and indifferent to light and pretty, with fresh flowers
between well-arranged platters, like good smorgasbord
tables. One or two of them (like *Hector's* at 1491, 1506,
and 1627 Broadway) add the refinement of a spigot of
charged water, known locally as "seltzer," a specific for

heartburn. The **Belmore** (407 Fourth Ave. at 28th St.) and the six **Waldorf** cafeterias around town believe firmly in thick sandwiches and plenty of whipped cream on desserts. (Like the **Horn & Hardart Automats**—see page 192—the Belmore is an especial favorite with taxi drivers.) A full-course cafeteria dinner may amount to as much as a moderate-priced restaurant meal but the breakfast and dinner specials featured by many cafeterias are good, generous values.

NOTE: A shrewd way of eating well and not too expensively is to have your large meal in the middle of the day when most good restaurants serve dinners (disguised as luncheons) at considerably less cost than they do at night.

"De Haut En Bas" Cuisine: French Restaurants

The great temples of French cuisine like the Pavillon, the Côte Basque, Chambord, Brussels, Chateaubriand, Café Chauveron, Maud Chez Elle, and Voisin are serious, elegant, quiet places (with reservations absolutely essential) dedicated to elevating tasting, chewing, and swallowing to a high aesthetic experience, which it is in these places and at a cost (about what it would cost to ingest comparable poundage in chopped dollar bills).

Once in a while the accustomed hushed atmosphere of these places is shattered by a party of unlimited, bibulous expense-accounters or by some extraordinary event such as the one happily remembered by a lucky few: the night Voisin's went lovingly mad. It was the night before the restaurant was moved from its former quarters to make way for the inevitable skyscraper. A new location had not yet been definitely arranged for and some of the devout had gathered for a possible last supper. The air was heady with sentiment before impending doom and polite restraints quickly melted and disappeared; customers ordered and ate recklessly and the waiters kept stuffing them solicitously, racing the hors d'oeuvres cart as if it were an emergency car, heaping plates again, again, and topping the great gorging with double and triple desserts—confections of meringue, chocolate, creams, cocoanut, marrons—for free, while spreading smiles and compliments with an equal end-of-the-world profligacy. It was a magnificent wallowing.

> NOTE: Most of the city's French restaurants are located in the dense rectangle of midtown from Second Avenue to Eighth Avenue. However, a few listed below are somewhat out of the center and it might be well to note their distance from theaters and shops, etc., when you make your day's plans.

L'Armorique

> Second Avenue at 54th Street; Reservations, PL 3-3787.
> Dinners only; closed Mondays. *Expensive.*

As soon as you're seated you'll be accosted by a beaming, well-fed man in a large chef's hat who will suggest dishes and describe their preparation; he is the owner and chef and a leftover Celtic bard who is best inspired by two seafood dishes: *quennelles* and lobster Armorique. You are there as the Breton fisherman leaves his humble cottage in the frosty morn to seine in the gleaming fish. With the chef-poet, you carefully bone and skin the fish, regretfully grind its tender flesh, mix it with herbs, shape it into little patties, and slip it into a boiling brew of wine and magic. What emerges is an Olympic version of gefulte fish. The adventure with the lobster is equally dramatic, involving intense claw-cracking, shell-emptying, shell-restuffing, and delicate prayerful infusions of the lobster meat with cream and anisette, or is it Pernod?

Since the prices are fairly high, it must be assumed that there is some charge for the dramatic recitations, but the tormented lobster does have a rare and lovely flavor, as do some of the less histrionically derived dishes, like the beautifully sauced steak, the wine-doused chicken, and the luxuriant desserts.

Le Valois

> 45 East 58th Street; Reservations, MU 8-7630.
> Closed Sundays. *Expensive;* DC.

In addition to rich hollandaise on artichokes and excellent burnished duck with olive or cherry sauce, Le Valois serves up a surprise in the form of its doorman—or doorgirl. In a costume of Third Man coat, dark stockings, and sneakers, with a heavy doorman's hat pressing heavily on her blonde fringe, she is a gamin who assorts oddly with the highly dignified interior.

Le Marmiton

41 East 49th Street; MU 8-1232
Closed Sundays. *Moderate;* DC.

Busy with editors and publishers darting from table to table, exchanging handshakes and gossip. They are a small tribe as the size of New York businesses go, but friendly and marvelously verbal, which accounts for the cheerful noise and bustle at lunchtime. They seem to come back for dinner, too, because the atmosphere lasts into the evening. Try not to become too distracted; the hors d'oeuvres, the sea-food dishes, the guinea hen with wild rice, and the duck in tangerine sauce deserve concentration.

Charles

452 Sixth Avenue (between 10th and 11th Sts.); GR 7-3300.
Closed Sundays. *Moderate to Expensive;* DC.

Confident, stately, and subdued, Charles has been minding its own serious business for almost half a century while the rest of the Village whirled through periods of tea rooms, candle-lit basements, borsch-cum-personality *boîtes,* and hamburger dispensaries. This is one of those rare, completely trustworthy restaurants where you can follow the waiter's suggestion (without feeling that his favorite is what the kitchen has too much of) with the sure expectation that it will be of fine quality, expertly cooked and pleasantly served.

Pierre's

52 East 53rd Street; EL 5-4074.
Moderate to Expensive; DC.

Small, crowded, lively, and not excessively dignified. Great splashes of personality and determined charm from waiters and other customers may threaten to inundate you if you're feeling recessive, but don't mind; turn your attention to the excellent lobster bisque, the rich sweetbreads, the frogs' legs, and the *coupe au marron,* which is unique in that it is studded with an open-handed quantity of marrons.

La Toque Blanche

359 East 50th Street (near First Ave.); Reservations, PL 5-3552.
Open Sundays. *Moderate.*

In the classic arrangement of the basement restaurant, this one is a few steps down, presents first its bar, flanked by several small tables, and then spreads into a not-too-large,

MERIDIAN BOOKS, INC.

MERIDIAN BOOKS / LIVING AGE BOOKS

17 Union Square, New York 3, N.Y. ORegon 5-9220

12 E. 22 St.   NY 10

Enclosed for Review:

MG 18

Publication Date:

Please send us two copies of your review when it appears. In this way we may ascertain your continued interest in our publications and keep your name on the review list. Those books which you are unable to review, please be so kind as to return.

but crowded, dining room. The waiters are thus given opportunities for some fine stretching and balancing as they skirt one another's loaded trays, an effort which doesn't impair their good humor at all.

Some of the best of French regional dishes appear here and smell and taste authentically of French country kitchens. The paté is full-bodied and peppery, the *champignons à la grecque* start off oddly bland and end up in a strong Mediterranean flavor. The rural *gigot d'agneau* is patiently marinated and the proper shade of pink, the tripe is really in the style of Normandy, the frogs' legs have the odor of Provence, and that great poor-man's dish, *cassoulet*, might just have been brought forth from a kitchen in Périgueux, hot, hearty, and reckless of calories.

If all this doesn't arouse your nostalgia for France, try the coffee *filtré* for 25 cents above the cost of the dinner; it will be the same indescribably jolting experience French coffee always is—penance for eating too much and too well.

Café St. Denis

11 East 53rd Street; EL 5-8032.
Closed Sundays. *Expensive.*

In spite of the dim lighting and the weighty setting, the mood is light, possibly the effect of a strong Provençal influence which affects the dining room as well as the kitchen. The lobster Thermidor is stiff with sherry and the beef dishes heated with spice; no suspicion of a careful Parisian hand here, but of its hearty kind the food is delectable.

Café Argenteuil

253 East 52nd Street (near Second Ave.); PL 3-9273.
Closed Sundays. *Moderate.*

A nice, quiet place, gently decorated in French Provincial style, which serves especially well Provençal specialties like *quiche Lorraine,* bouillabaisse, a good country paté, clams, and mussels. They won't be rushed and it may be rather difficult to get across town to the theater, so don't count on the *Argenteuil* (or other East Side restaurants, for that matter) for hurried pre-theater dining.

La Potinière

60 West 55th Street; Reservations, CI 5-6764.
Open Sundays. *Moderate; DC.*

Possibly it is the buoyant sketches of Paris on the walls or the radiant faces of one or two young waiters, but this is one

138

of the few restaurants which can be both large and gay at the same time. The chef sends out creamy crepes of crab-meat as appetizers and then follows them with medallions of veal or beef in suave sauces, succulent poultry, and festive desserts. (The original Poinière, at number 47, across the street, is now the annex for dining later, up to midnight.)

Le Moal

942 Third Avenue (near 56th Street); Reservations MU 8-8860. Open Sundays. *Moderate;* DC.

The move, some years ago, from red-checkered tablecloths and haphazard service across the street, to the present status of wood panels, oil paintings, and careful service hasn't impaired the quality of the food or the generosity of the portions. The paté and *moules Ravigotte* should be seriously considered as openers and, as main course, the *moules mari-niéres* (many and strongly laced with white wine), the tripe or *poulet* in any number of well-devised styles.

Le Veau d'Or and Au Canari d'Or

Le Veau: 129 East 60th Street; TE 8-8133.
Au Canari: 134 East 61st Street; TE 8-7987.
Both closed Sundays. *Moderate.*

The back-to-back "d'Ors" are quite similar in their excellent cuisine and affable ambience. Both serve the classic French specialties—paté, beef Bordelaise, snails, and *escalope de veau* unpretentiously and well.

L'Auberge de France

58 West 56th Street; JU 6-7788.
Open Sundays. *Moderate.*

The proprietor and staff (with no noticeable exception) talk an engaging mixture of French and English, which should encourage you to try returning your something-like-French. There is no doubt, however, of which language the cooking is done in: it is unmistakably country French—*cassoulet,* sausage in crust, veal in cream, calf's brain—consumed by shiny-faced patrons in a lively little room which manages also to encompass a bright canopied bar.

Henry IV

823 Lexington Avenue (63rd Street); TE 8-2138.
Open Sundays. *Modest to Moderate.*

Something like the Village restaurants of years ago—below the street, darkish, candlelit, with checkered tablecloths. The dishes are standard French and pleasant to eat among pink-cheeked college girls in outsize sweaters timidly stepping, with their boys, out of the culinary world of the hamburger.

Larré's

50 West 56th Street; CI 7-8980.
Closed Sundays. *Modest to Moderate.*

Casual, simple and rambling, with a respectable list of established favorites like *coq au vin,* onion soup, and frog's legs.

Café Brittany

807 Ninth Avenue (near 52nd St.); CI 7-9566.
Open Sundays at 6 P.M. *Modest.*

Once upon a time the Café Brittany was a large, dim saloon, wallpapered in the wrathful designs found in second-class French hotels. The bar was large and zinc and attended by a brisk, robust barmaid, at her best when the French Merchant Marine docked. At those times the quiet saloon exploded with arguments which ebbed down, at about one o'clock in the morning, to two or three melancholy voices softly weaving songs of the Auvergne or the Breton coast. In those days, the only nonalcoholic refreshments were a coarse *paté maison,* cheese with French bread, and an odd replica of coffee. Now the old spacious somnolence has been brightened and crowded with tables, with little room for French mariners, boisterous or melancholy; but the cuisine, in its greatly expanded repertory, is still solid French rural: home-style paté, calf's brains, *escalope de veau, coq au vin,* and scallops Provençal (highly commendable if you like garlic). Try to go on a weekday; on week ends the Brittany belongs to young intellectuals.

Gerbe d'Or

365 West 50th Street (east of Ninth Ave.); CO 5-6980.
Dinner only; closed Sundays. *Modest.*

In two small adjoining stores, *monsieur et madame* (he the chef, she the waitress, but he the cashier) have set up an unassuming little restaurant very much like the one they may have had in an unfashionable quarter of Nice, and they comport themselves appropriately. She is dark, small, tired, and offhand; he is the voluble member, in and out of the kitchen to discuss, describe, recommend, and complain a little. As in all Provençal cooking, garlic and wine are basic here, but *monsieur* plays them with some subtlety, as in the clams *Monegasque* and the *poulet Nicoise.*

Paris-Brest

738 Ninth Avenue (near 50th St.); CI 7-9143.
Closed Sundays. *Modest.*

A minute matriarchy, which consists of the proprietress-barmaid-cashier and one very busy waitress trying to navigate in the few inches of space left between the tables. Pass the paté by (its quality is unstable) and start with the mussels and pickled onions appetizer or the mackerel in wine. For entrée; either the chicken Brest or the duck *Bigarade,* neither of which is "*haute*" but in good bourgeois style.

Fleur de Lis

141 West 69th Street; TR 4-9060.
Open Sundays. *Modest.*

The Fleur de Lis' entrance used to be dark and nicely inconspicuous like that of a speakeasy. A front of flat shine now masks the old dimness, but the interior and the food haven't, fortunately, undergone much change. The menu still lists the middle-class French classics—fresh asparagus vinaigrette in season, *tête de veau,* brains in black butter, *tripe à la mode de Caen,* frogs' legs, snails, and omelettes—in addition to a few Italian and American mainstays. But stay with the French dishes (you can get spaghetti and hamburger as good or better elsewhere)—they are decently prepared, served by genial waitresses and, besides, are more appropriate to the decor.

Au Petit Paris

116 Lexington Avenue; MU 4-4294.
Closed Sundays. *Modest.*

This might just conceivably be Paris, but it would be the Paris of the *Porte d'Italie* or the neighborhood of the *Marché au Puces;* no frills, a sturdy plain bar, a too-low ceiling, and a handwritten menu mimeographed into near illegibility. At the extraordinarily low prices asked for complete dinners —*paté maison,* onion soup, chicken *sauté chasseur* and Camembert cheese, for instance—neither the decor nor the cuisine can be very exalted, but the food is completely satisfactory and particularly cheap for French cooking, which often comes high in New York.

Romans and Their Countrymen: Italian Restaurants

In speaking of certain Italian restaurants in New York, people will sometimes compare them enthusiastically with the Pappagallo, Fagiano's, Giannini's. But the comparisons are a bit stretched; we haven't the same produce to work with, nor the eating habits, nor the ennobling antique reputations, nor the marvelously courteous waiters. We do have some reasonable American facsimiles of good restaurants in Italy, like the San Marino, Romeo Salta, and the Mercurio, which do fine things with *scampi*, veal in several styles, and greens. They are well appointed and well attended, so you will probably need a reservation as well as money, though not an exorbitant amount.

The following restaurants (other than the extravaganza that is the Forum of the Twelve Caesars) are more obscure, cheaper, and in their different ways, wholly admirable.

MIDTOWN

Forum of the Twelve Caesars

57 West 48th Street; phone for reservations, PL 7-3450.
Expensive.

The theme is, of course, Rome; not only Imperial Rome, but Rome of the Renaissance, of the French Empires, of romantic painting, and the never-never land of modern decorators. Over the bust of Bacchus which dominates the bar hangs a chandelier of linked Roman torches and one wall of the bar is a mosaic panel depicting things Roman—a section of aqueduct, shielded warriors, and the ubiquitous wolf who suckled Romulus and Remus. The Twelve Caesars stare down from the other walls of the bar in dusky bronze and appear again in huge oil paintings (pale, popeyed, and sneering) hung against the rich red fabric of the dining-room walls. Bacchus also reappears, smiling up from the magnificent copper and brass service places, from the cover of the formidable menu, and from the seal which binds its sash of Tyrian purple.

The menu itself—as print design, as prose, and as invitation to culinary delights and curios—is a work of high imagination evoking the far-flung Roman Empire and its great appetites with phrases like "Belgic Paté with Wild Boar, Sauce of Damascus Plums," or dishes called "Sylvan," "Lucanian" and "Apician," or goose "Germanicus" and partridge "Brittanicus," or a heady piling up of excess: "Pheasant of the Golden House on a Silver Shield of Gilded Plumage Roasted with an Exquisite Sauce." Since these are a very small sampling of a menu which is the very best of current restaurant prose, allow ample time for reading as well as for examining the little salt dish borne by silver elephants and the wine servers like helmets or Scythian bows, and for dipping into the generous bowls of mixed olives from Italy, Spain, and the Levant. And you'll need time to study the succession of the Twelve Caesars printed on a card the waiter will hand you.

Gorgeous, extravagant, lush, lusty, educational, entertaining, with delectable dishes of towering names flambéed with the pyromania of Nero, the Forum is no place for pre-theater gulping nor careful purse-watching. While you're sipping your coffee from its outsize cup, incidentally, you might play the Forum game, which is quite simple: it consists of adding possible items to the menu, such as "Tears of Dido" cocktail, "*Tranche* of braised Brutus," "Gracchi on Toast," "Breast of Messalina *à la bonne femme.*" The management, apparently imaginative and playful, might be charmed by your suggestions.

Giovanni's

66 East 55th Street; PL 3-1230.
Closed Sundays. *Expensive.*

A small bar downstairs and two rooms upstairs, almost violently alive with Italian bonhomie. You will be charmed by a plain waiter—middle-aged, bespectacled, and withal a tempter—into eating more than you need or want. The more resistant customers are handled by the hypnotic dark eyes under a glittering baldness, the noble Roman nose, and the silken Iago baritone of Signore Giovanni himself. Though you may be tempted, you won't be wronged: the *osso bucco* with marrow bone, mushrooms, and sherry is remarkable; so is the breast of chicken crusted with cheese and the house specialty—a paté of clam in chopped aspic. Although the small menu lists a number of $5.00 dinners, the price will somehow come to more. Under "desserts" there should be a listing: "Charm—$2.00" and no one would mind.

Del Pezzo

33 West 47th Street; JU 6-9705.
Closed Sundays. *Moderate.*

One rarely goes *into* an Italian restaurant; it is either *down* a few stairs or *up* a flight or two. Del Pezzo is both up and down. It is in a small old house squeezed in by office and factory buildings, but still faintly echoing older, gracious days. The entrance, a few steps down, opens onto a long unused bar, a telephone booth, and a flight of stairs. Follow the sounds of cutlery upstairs to the dining room, and while you're waiting for the *spiedino* or the shrimps *marinara*, notice the heavy ceilings and the darkened elaborations of turn-of-the-century style.

Whatever you choose will not be elusively subtle (Italian cooking rarely is) but the food at Del Pezzo's avoids the excesses of Naples and Palermo, staying closer to the moderations of Rome.

Barbetta's

321 West 46th Street; CI 6-9171.
Closed Mondays. *Moderate.*

Conspicuously close to the theater district as it is, large enough to accommodate a generous number of diners, and established over forty years, Barbetta's is periodically "discovered" by food and restaurant connoisseurs. This does not seem to affect the prices, the faithful customers, the quiet patience of the waiters, or the quality of the food. The cuisine is mainly northern Italian, which means that the use of garlic and tomato sauce is sparing and *pastas* appear as a relatively minor part of the menu. The antipasto is abundant and handsomely arranged, and the veal dishes, the calf's liver *Veneziana* (cooked with onions and wine), and the *risotto* are as good as you'll find in Florence, or better. For dessert, have the pears in wine or the creamy, hot *zabaglione* or the staggering *zuppa inglese,* which is an imposing mound of rum-soaked cake completely imbedded in whipped cream. Why this baroque structure is called "English soup" is a minor linguistic mystery or a lost culinary joke.

Barbetta's has no dinner menu, so the cost of your dinner would be dictated by your choice of dishes, but none are expensive.

Torino Caffee

309 East 59th Street (near Second Ave.); MU 8-9718.
Closed Sundays; dancing on Friday and Saturday nights. *Modest to Moderate.*

Large, dark, uncrowded, and quiet on most nights, the Torino bursts into song on Friday and Saturday nights, at an increase in price. On Thursdays there is occasional decorous piano music, nothing that will interfere with your conversation or the sense of repose, a rarity in Italian restaurants. Whatever night you go, however, order the house specialty appetizer, a dish of raw vegetables—peppers, celery, finochio, lettuce—which you dip into a vat of oil kept hot on the table. It will keep you quite busy for a while and it tastes surprisingly good.

Gino's

780 Lexington Avenue (near 60th St.); TE 8-9827.
Open Sundays. *Moderate.*

The menu follows the traditional courses, with inclinations toward the north of Italy. Order anything; the kitchen treats it all with imagination and respect, the waiters serve it with enthusiasm, and the salads are likely to contain Italian greens you may not meet elsewhere.

Luigino's

147 West 48th Street; JU 6-9617.
Open every night. *Modest.*

Pizza and spaghetti in what might be a *trattoria* in Naples (except that they favor pizza less than we do); the booths are inelegant, the tables bare wood, and a wilderness of affectionate photos smile down from the walls; there are large community tables at which all sorts of strangers are plumped down with each other in *festa* informality, and some of the younger waiters stand and stare in comatose delight at any low-necked female bosom. This potpourri of *joie de vivre, pasta,* and sex has the added charm of costing very little.

La Strada

134 West 46th Street; JU 2-9646.
Open every night. *Moderate.*

Resist immoderate consumption of the beautiful bread. Save room for the rich, large meal to follow: hot hors d'oeuvres of shrimps, baked clams and peppers, veal stuffed or drenched in outspoken sauces, confections of *pasta*-cheese-tomatoes. The salads, as in most Italian restaurants, are zesty, and the desserts (if you're still breathing) worth the ensuing sensation of being dangerously explosive.

Via Veneto

56 West 56th Street; CI 5-9869.
Open Sundays and also for coffee after the theater. *Moderate.*

You may find the Sforza wallpaper a bit overwhelming in so small a restaurant, but pay it no mind and dive, instead, into the *fettucini a la Alfredo* which, as in Rome, is whirled about at your table (except that no one here is old enough to dare copy Alfredo's large, well-trained mustaches) and tastes almost as good. You may have to select among the *piccata* of veal, the *saltimbocca,* or the cheese-covered breast of chicken as you might pick a horse to bet on, by closing your eyes and sticking a pin into the menu; the difference from horse-racing is that you'll do well no matter what the selection. For dessert, have the unusual cheese cake or *semi-freddo,* a cold *zabaglione.*

Capri

233 West 52nd Street; CO 5-9654.
Open Sundays. *Moderate.*

The Capri is mellow and unpretentious and its waiters seriously intent on serving you well and with dignity as in a good restaurant in Catania or Messina. The front room has a burnished look, made by the soft lights and the glow of bottles on the high-stacked corner bar. If that room is full, you'll be conducted through the kitchen (whose white surfaces are softened by large floral decals) and into a smaller back room which bears two murals of the Italian restaurant school—large, literal, and often littoral, richer in nostalgia than talent, and nevertheless quite appealing.

The servings are Sicilian in both style and size; *ziti a la Siciliana* is a heroic dish, for instance, as is the *linguini* with *calamaretti,* either of which can be followed by the smooth, light *zabaglione* to make a satisfactory meal. Or you might order a half-portion of the *pasta* and go on to the chicken *oreganata* or the clams and shrimps *a la Roberto,* but in any case watch out for the whole cloves of garlic which, like slices of lemon and capers, are strewn through many southern Italian dishes, creating hazards for the more self-conscious.

La Scala

142 West 54th Street; Reservations, CI 5-1575.
Open Sundays. *Moderate; DC.*

If the contradiction of rubbing shoulders with Joe Di Maggio
while the recorded voice of Tebaldi sobs *"mai più, mai più"*
doesn't jar you, La Scala has much to offer. The elbow-rub-
bing is almost literal; La Scala is popular and not very spacious and it's best to make a reservation if you have scheduled
plans. The waiter will make insistent suggestions while you
try to read the menu. Fold it and succumb. He'll probably
order for you the hot antipasto, Italian-style chicken fricas-
see, and small pieces of veal cooked in wine. Unless he's
outraged your sense of independence, you'll approve of his
choice.

Marchi's

251 East 31st Street (near Second Ave.); Reservations,
MU 4-9843.
Open every night; dinners only. *Moderate.*

Marchi's is about as unpublic as a restaurant can be and still
be hospitable. No sign calls from the street, luncheon is never
served, and there is rarely available space unless it has been
reserved. (Here it is *important* to make a reservation because,
since it is outside the restaurant belt, the alternatives are to
travel some distance, nursing disappointment and hunger, or
settle in a dismal coffeepot around the corner.) No menu is
offered for the simple reason that the customer doesn't
select his dinner—though he may choose his wine—but eats
in the style of a guest or a boarder. The cooking is that of
the extreme north of Italy, where the vari-shaped *pastas* are
not essentials of cooking. Consequently the serving of *pasta*
will be very modest compared to the farinaceous sea served
in other Italian restaurants, but it is designed to be followed
by a long array of dishes—fish and veal interspersed with
mushrooms, beans, cooked greens, and salad—the delectable
parade ending up in fanfares of crisp, light coils of sugared
pastry, a specialty of the house.

LITTLE ITALY

Angelo's

146 Mulberry Street (near Grand St.); CA 6-8527.
Open Sundays. *Moderate.*

Don't be misled by the dingy, somnolent tenements surrounding Angelo's. If you insist on stuffed artichoke when it's out

of season and lobster *Fra Diavolo*, the bill will surprise you, but if you wander in the more earthy terrains of spaghetti in a variety of sauces, or squid, or the hearty soups, it won't be painful.

Grotta Azzurra

387 Broome Street; CA 6-9283.
Closed Mondays. *Moderate.*

The low-ceilinged Grotta is finished in a rough, bumpy plaster painted blue in a wistful suggestion of the Wonder of Capri. There is nothing suggestive, however, about the food which loudly shouts "Napoli!" and, like the streets of Naples, is highly colored and flavored, redolent of oregano, garlic, and olive oil.

GREENWICH VILLAGE

The Village is full of Italian restaurants, some with opera-singing waiters, some with small gardens in back, and others in which the back is used by the local *boccie* players. The musical restaurants are well-advertised and almost inescapable; the stiller ones can be found by roaming Macdougal, Thompson, Sullivan, and Bleecker Streets. There are only two guarantees which can be offered with these: the *pasta* will be good and the prices low. Those that follow are surer things.

Mary's

42 Bedford Street (just off Seventh Ave.); CH 2-9588.
Open Sundays. *Moderate.*

Mary is a small, round, brisk woman who runs her restaurant with a firm maternal hand, enhancing the atmosphere of eating in a private home. The restaurant actually occupies the two lower floors of a small house very much like its inconspicuous neighbors. The basement floor holds no more than four or five tables, but affords a view of the absurdly small kitchen and the chef magically managing a confusion of pots and food. Upstairs consists of a small room (one-family size) and a larger one sporting a high-manteled fireplace as a reminder of its former status as a living room. Go easy, if you have the moral stamina, on the dark Italian bread which will be set before you. You should be able to accommodate large icy shrimps in a heady sauce or baked mussels or clams as appetizers; or spaghetti in clam or meat sauce, or the deep minestrone, followed by any one of the veal dishes Mary might suggest. (There is no menu.) If you've brought the required appetite and attitude, you should last through the dessert of Neapolitan pastry.

Rocco's

181 Thompson Street; GR 3-9267.
Closed Tuesdays. *Moderate.*

To the accompaniment of garlic toast (just ask for it), have the baked clams or the hot stuffed artichoke, and then go on to veal cooked in white wine and heaped with mushrooms, spaghetti in clam sauce, or *zuppa di pesce*. Rest awhile over a glass of Orvieto or Ruffino Chianti; then, with renewed strength, attack the pastry tray which may still bear a flattened triangular horn made of thin ribbons of dough, a little like strudel and a little like toasted cocoanut, stuffed with sweetened *ricotta*. Its curious, bland taste combines well with the strong Italian coffee.

Grand Ticino

228 Thompson Street (near W. 3rd St.); GR 3-8876.
Closed Sundays. *Modest.*

This simple, large basement (whose pool tables once bumped into a number of good poets) has been a Village favorite for over thirty years. Its prices haven't changed too drastically over that span of time; it is still possible to eat well, though simply (a dinner of spaghetti, *ossi bucco*, and coffee, for instance) for under $2.00.

Renato Restaurant

21 Vandam Street; AL 5-9899.
Closed Sundays. *Moderate.*

In an old house in the southernmost part of the Village, once part of the estate of John Adams. Both *pasta* and garlic appear but are not star-featured. The minestrone and mussels *marinara* are old reliables, along with variations on veal themes. If you go in the late spring or summer, try for a table in the large, attractive garden.

Luigi's

432 Sixth Avenue (between 9th and 10th Sts.); GR 3-1528.
Open Sundays. *Moderate;* DC.

Handsome and unspectacular, with no Sicilian flourishes or Roman grandeur, Luigi's is quiet, seasoned, and civilized, with north-Italian specialties.

Sixty-Eight

59 Fifth Avenue (near 13th St.); AL 5-8744.
Open Sundays. *Moderate;* DC.

The name commemorates the old address across the street,
if you're wondering what it means. Wood paneled upstairs
and down, hung with caricatures touchingly decade-before-
last. The tone of welcome is established by the bar immediately at the entrance, lovingly festooned with old customers contentedly floating away the time before they can
sit down to the homemade *tagliarini,* the trout, the mussels,
and the *scampi,* the latter denuded for them if the bar has
blurred co-ordination.

Chinese

For the simple reason that most of the Chinese people
who originally settled in New York came from the
Canton area of China, the great majority of Chinese
restaurants serve Canton-style dishes. In recent years,
however, northern Chinese cooking (also called "Peking," "Shanghai," "Mandarin") has become increasingly
popular. It is more subtle and varied, in its American
versions at least, than the Cantonese, less burdened with
garlic and the green of scallions. In the listings below,
specific mention will be made of restaurants which serve
in this latter style and a few dishes will be described.

CHINATOWN

Chinatown's restaurants are of almost equal quality and
price, varying mainly in size and decor; all serve Cantonese food (the old familiars), and all are open on Sundays.

Wah Kee

16 Doyer Street (which grows out of Pell St., which, in turn,
sprouts from Mott).

In times of great rush (usually weekends) when the two
basement rooms are full, "the back" of this absolute favorite
of the connoisseurs is used; in addition to overflow customers,
it sometimes houses one of the neighborhood disreputables
whom the soft-hearted waiters won't throw out. "The back"
is reached by sidling past a gallery of silent cooks tamping

down tanks of steaming rice and swiftly cleaving through chickens and ducks with huge blades. It contains several small tables surrounded by stacks of canned goods, bags of rice and spices, and hanging overhead, like grotesque lanterns, lacquered ducks burnished with syrups and time. The storehouse smells and the very dead birds bother some people; others love it. In any case, you won't be left indifferent.

The menu is very much like that in other Cantonese restaurants, which means most of those in New York, with the difference that the egg rolls contain less dough and more shrimp, the pork is rather like that described by Charles Lamb, and the vegetables younger and sprightlier. Whatever else you order, include a dish of chicken with walnuts and the shrimp with Chinese vegetables.

Other Chinatown stand-bys include:

Yat Bun Sing's (16 Mott St.) is a simple place and consistently satisfactory.

The Chinese Rathskeller (45 Mott St.), in spite of its hybridized name, serves an undeviating list of the classic favorites—Cantonese lobster, egg rolls, barbecued spareribs, shrimps in lobster sauce, and so on.

The Port Arthur (7 Mott St.) is a vast place still sporting a few palatial decorations of a brighter day.

The Rice Bowl (44 Mott St.) is more worldly than some of its neighbors, with a slick little bar and cocktail-lounge lighting.

Lee's (36 Pell St.) is reputed to be the oldest restaurant in the area and still a favorite for a Sunday brunch of dumplings and/or more solid fare.

Bo-Bo's (20½ Pell St.) is crowded and lively, touched with a little Bohemianism.

MIDTOWN

Such statistics are hard to come by, but it is possible that Hong Kong possesses fewer Chinese restaurants than does midtown Manhattan. Most of them are good, a few not so good and a few superb; the great majority serve the style of food which stems from Canton, via Chinatown. The menus encompass what is most commonly considered "Chinese," including those favorites of doubtful parentage, chow mein and chop suey. (All open Sundays.)

Ruby Foo's Den (240 W. 52nd St., CO 5-0705; DC) and *The House of Chan* (7th Ave at 52nd St.; PL 7-4470; DC) are both, as you probably know, opulent temples housing large crowds of the faithful who keep coming week after week and year after year. *Moderate* to *Expensive*, depending upon your capacities.

Freeman-Chum

142 East 53rd Street; PL 5-9889.
Moderate; DC.

An old reliable for Won-ton soup, spareribs, and shrimps in lobster sauce, with a special talent for fish, Chinese style.

Lum Fong

150 West 52nd Street; CI 5-8563.
Moderate; DC.

The uptown branch of a Chinatown favorite (220 Canal Street), long established and still fully authentic. Have the lobster and the beef-and-vegetable combinations.

Q. Lung

125 West 49th Street; CO 5-4572.
Moderate.

Should you want a very early breakfast of egg rolls, roast pork, and snow peas, you can get it here, providing you arrive before 5:30 A.M. Not to be overlooked for more ordinary meals and hours, however.

The Gold Coin

994 Second Avenue (53rd St.); PL 8-1251.
Moderate to Expensive.

There is a rumor that the chef can and will whip up an imitation of anything you might have eaten in a minute hamlet on the Yangtze. The rumor is colorful but unverified, and you might as well stay with the light, subtle sweet-and-sour shrimp.

Ho-Ho Restaurant (Northern and Cantonese)

789 Seventh Avenue (51st-52nd Sts.); CI 6-3278.
Open every day until 4 A.M.; *Moderate.*

Cantonese dishes form the bulk of the menu, but there are some very satisfactory dishes in northern style available. Ask your waiter about the "Mandarin" listings if you're not familiar with this style. Being in the Broadway area and ambitiously decorated, the Ho-Ho's prices will be a little higher than they are in less central places, but still not excessive.

Sun Luck (Northern and Cantonese)

143 West 49th Street (Sixth-Seventh Aves.); PL 7-6962.
Open until 4 A.M., *Moderate;* DC.

An encyclopedic menu offers an embarrassment of riches and probable bewilderment. You'll be safe with the Cantonese favorites, but it would be better to try some of the rarer dishes like the shrimp balls and the Peking duck, which is eaten as a series of courses elaborated with crepes, scallions, and sauces, or one of the black-bean sauce dishes.

HERE AND THERE

The Shanghai Cafe (Northern)

3217 Broadway (just above 125th St.); MO 2-1990.
Open until 10 P.M. every day. *Modest to Moderate.*

Although it moved to larger quarters a few years ago, the Shanghai is still ridiculously small for its reputation. It is not conveniently located, it has no style, and what little spare space there is for the waiters to squeeze through is almost consumed by loaded coatracks. (Fortunately, the waiters are thin, except for one who is fast burning himself down in violent arguments with the chef.) Should you come at an ordinary dining hour you're likely to find yourself on a long line which trails into the street. Should you come late, you'll find the service suddenly stopped: the waiters have gathered their bottles of beer and food and are sitting at dinner. Dinner over, they will roll out huge vats of garbage from the kitchen, past your table, to let them rest at the front door.

Reservations are made for six or more; if you haven't been able to beg or borrow enough people, you're for the line unless you arrange to eat before 6:30 P.M. or after 8:00 P.M. A large party is, of course, most rewarding since it offers opportunities for trying many more kinds of dishes, even though they appear in one overwhelming wave of food, necessitating frantic reaching and passing and covering and uncovering of many bowls—if the waiter remembers to bring covers.

The clatter, the crowding, and the market-place informality hardly permit gracious dining, but you'll eat unbelievably well. Start with the ten-ingredient soup (by actual careful count, more than ten) and then go on to fried dumplings and shrimp balls and any or all of the following: sweet-and-sour bass cooked in a syrup of Oriental nectars; a chicken mousse called "velvet"; spicy pork in black-bean sauce; "Happy Family," which consists of everything around plus abalone and any sudden inspiration of the chef; the ugly and delectable black Chinese mushrooms; thin, elusive, shiny noodles; the beef in oyster sauce.

For as little as $2.50 one can be a poor man's Lucullus and gather a conversation piece as well, the clientele and some of the waiters being often as fascinating as the menu.

If, with careful planning, you still haven't been able to get into the Shanghai, you might try the *Tien Tsin* across the street (569 W. 125th St.). It has been growing and practicing on the Shanghai overflow and now produces thoroughly palatable dishes in the same style.

The Great Shanghai (Northern)

2685 Broadway (102-103rd Sts.); UN 4-5906.
IRT Seventh Avenue to 103rd Street or Broadway bus.
Open every day until 1:30 A.M. *Modest to Moderate.*

Compared to its boisterous uptown counterpart, the Great Shanghai is quiet and ladylike, possibly because it is run by a woman, Mrs. Sheila Chang. The unprepossessing set of booths at the entrance lead to two spacious, comfortable rooms in the back. Reservations are accepted for four or more, or you can wait at the small bar and enjoy the other customers (who often look like a committee of the U.N.) and the pretty hostesses in their tight, slit skirts and fitted, high-collared jackets of Chinese silk.

Although three menus are offered—American (the usual staples), Cantonese, and the Shanghai—it is the latter which lists the unusual dishes featured here. For appetizer, you might start with "porcupines" (chopped pork and vegetables rolled in cold cooked rice) and shrimp toast (hardly altogether authentic, but very good nevertheless). Next, the sweet-and-sour soup, followed by sizzling rice with a shrimp or meat mixture. With it, as contrast, you might order the pork in brown sauce and chicken cooked with mushrooms and peanuts. Or you might disregard this advice and consult the manageress, who is an attractive person and an expert's expert.

The same management operates **Shanghai East,** 1059 Third Avenue (62nd-63rd Sts.).

Sing Wu (Northern and Cantonese)
123 Second Avenue (7th St.); GR 5-7540.
Open daily, including Sunday, until 11:30 P.M.; Saturdays
until 1:30 A.M. *Moderate.*

Comparatively new, oddly placed in the Polish sausage and
Jewish sour-cream belt, and running among three menus—
American, Cantonese, and Shanghai—this promises to become one of the popular dispensers of fried dumplings and
ten-ingredient soup. Not only is it close to a good number of
off-Broadway theaters, but the shrimp toast is heaped high,
the dumplings packed full, and the waiters listen if you ask
them to bring only a couple of dishes at a time when your
party is large and the simultaneous plenitude of large Chinese meals apt to confuse.

The sweet-and-sour fish (in a sauce of fruits, ginger, several
mysteries, and minute shrimp) is something to try even if
you don't like it. The chicken and peanuts in a spicy sauce
may be more your style, or the shrimp balls. Remember not
to order soup if you have sizzling shrimp; it floats in a
delicate soup of its own.

Mandarin House (Northern and Cantonese)
133-35 West 13th Street (Sixth-Seventh Aves.); WA 9-0551.
Open Sundays through Thursdays until midnight; Fridays and
Saturdays until 1 A.M. *Moderate.*

Complete dinners in either northern or southern style are
available for approximately $3.00 to $4.00. By ordering à la
carte, you can mix styles as, for instance, dumplings followed
by lobster Cantonese, or you can take a wild fling, with dried
tiger lilies, bamboo shoots, and shredded pork in an omelette.
If you go in the summertime, ask to be seated in the garden.

"Denizens of the Deep"

Sweets
Corner of Fulton Street and South Street (Take IRT or BMT
line or Broadway bus to Fulton St. and walk east).
Closed Saturdays and Sundays. *Moderate.*

The great ancient of them all, Sweets, is held in awe for its
age, its food, and its no-nonsense integrity. No one arrives
fashionably late, because the doors are firmly closed a little
before eight. Few customers are boisterous because this is a

serious place to be approached as one might a historic monument, which it is; customers accustomed to tripping confidently into the more splendid of the city's places, walk up the steps (until recently visibly worn by over a hundred years of feet, but now redone) quietly and with dignity. No one goes drunk to Sweets or gets drunk there; it would be as unthinkable as visiting Ralph Waldo Emerson with a snootful. The first Mr. Sweet started his restaurant, then part of a hotel, in 1845, to serve the local spice and fish merchants and the captains off the ships which came to anchor at South Street. The gentry from farther uptown discovered its excellences and joined the downtown faithful, some of whom ate every lunch of their working lives in Sweets. The years have caused changes of ownership, but not of principle: the fish is still the freshest obtainable, the cooking simple and perfect, and the elderly waiters, a number of whom have been there over thirty years, still speak and serve with antique grace. Barring grudging changes in the lighting, not much has changed in Sweets for many years; the stamped metal walls are of a vintage popular generations ago, and so are the huge, cumbersome sideboards.

Sweets has the reputation, tenaciously upheld and well deserved, for being one of the best sea-food restaurants anywhere, if not *the* best, so that anything you order will be extraordinary, but be sure to have a cup of one of the sea-food soups and something lowly, like the finnan haddie, to find out how fine a dish it can be when treated with deference.

Gage and Tollner

374 Fulton Street, Brooklyn; TR 5-5181.
Via IND Eighth Ave. Subway to Jay Street, or IRT Lexington line to Borough Hall.
Closed Sundays. *Moderate.*

Brooklyn's companion piece to Sweets, near it in venerability and repute, and more self-conscious. It fusses about its old lighting fixtures, the antique fans on the ceiling, and its polished old wood—and justly, because they are rare and attractive. Some of the waiters are of the same courtly-mannered vintage as the men at Sweets, even in the harrying challenge of a Saturday rush.

Choose whatever appeals to you from the long menu; the standards remain consistently high over the years.

THIRD AVENUE

Third Avenue from 14th Street to 79th is sea-food row, with concentrations at the main crosstown streets, 14th, 23rd, 34th, etc. They are rarely burdened by decor—a stuffed fish, a loop of fish net, a sign extolling the maiden freshness of the fish served, is as far as most of them go. You can't go too far wrong in any of them, but there are, of course, some with more extensive and imaginative menus than others.

King of the Sea

879 Third Avenue (near 53rd St.); EL 5-9309.
Open Sundays. *Moderate;* DC.

Its generous size can't always hold the throngs that press through its doors. If you manage to storm the gates, order the king crab legs, which are magnificent.

Oscar's Salt of the Sea

1155 Third Avenue (near 68th St.); TR 9-1199.
Closed Sundays. *Moderate.*

Informal, crowded, noisy, and very good. The mastermind, Oscar, is a slim, slangy man who has a good store of quips and stories with which to placate waiting, hungry customers. Have the baked Imperial crab or one of the fancier shrimp dishes.

Should you find yourself in their vicinity, overtaken by a need for sea food, the following less extrovert places will do very well, too:

Fisherman's Net, 493 Third Avenue (33-34th Sts.); Open Sundays; MU 4-8911; DC.

Harvey's Seafood House, 509 Third Avenue (34-35th Sts.); Open Sundays; MU 3-7587; DC.

Fin'n Claw, 1394 Third Avenue (near 79th St.); Open Sundays; RH 4-9047.

GREENWICH VILLAGE

Sea-Fare

41 West 8th Street; AL 4-5640.
Open Sundays. *Moderate.*

What was once a small, bare-wooden-tabled fish house, moved across the street a year or two ago and burgeoned into munificence, replete with sculptured decorations and a caged waterfall. The prices and menu have also moved into more opulent brackets, though not wildly. The lemon sole was a favorite in the simpler days, and still is; or order the bouillabaisse.

Lobster Roll

411 Bleecker Street (near Bank St.); OR 4-9456.
Closed Sundays. *Moderate.*

A small, quiet place, tastefully designed. The waiters are polite and efficient, but the kitchen won't be rushed. However, you won't regret having waited for the lobster sautéed in garlicked butter or the shrimp in dill sauce.

ELSEWHERE IN MIDTOWN

The Lobster

145 West 45th Street (between Sixth Ave. and Broadway); JU 2-0400.
Closed Sundays. *Moderate;* DC.

The fatherly waiters are long accustomed to getting people out on time for theater performances; just tell your waiter when you have to leave and he'll do the rest. The cheaper of the two shore dinners is a good buy, particularly if you have the lobster.

Paddy's Clam House

215 West 34th Street (near Penn Station); CH 4-9123.
Open Sundays. *Modest to Moderate.*

One of the venerables, and still highly respected; plain, the decoration limited to a fresh coat of paint now and then—with pleasantly plain prices.

Sea-Fare

1033 First Avenue (just south of 57th St.); PL 9-4176.
Open Sundays. *Moderate.*

Of the same ownership and gorgeousness as the branch in the Village. Unless you can't stand curry at all, try the seafood curries; if not, the baked oysters.

Neptune's Corner

1217 Sixth Avenue (at 48th St.).
Open Sundays. *Moderate;* CO 5-4430.

Lush à la Newburg arrangements, generous sea-food salads, and big staring lobsters in a setting of Broadway rococo; the range of desserts is wider than most sea-food houses offer. If one of the party is a dissenter, there's shishkebab, lamb kampana, and lamb barbecue Oriental, as well as the sea food.

Oyster Bar

(Lower level, Grand Central Station); CI 6-5800.
Open Sundays. *Modest.*

The menu does list other items beside the oyster stew, but for many people the Oyster Bar means only the almost legendary oyster stew.

NOTE: The above, except Sweets, serve quite late.

BY THE SEA

The following are far out of bus or reasonable taxi range; they can be reached by subway in long involved trips that won't leave you disposed for pleasure. If you hire a car or are provident enough to own a friend who owns one, a sea-food dinner and a walk on the waterfront can make a pleasant summer evening.

At City Island (east of the upper Bronx; follow AAA maps of city and vicinity):

Thwaite's Inn, 536 City Island Avenue; Open Sundays; CI 8-1023; DC.

Lobster Box, 34 City Island Avenue; Open Sundays; CI 8-1952.

There are others, not quite as showy, along the one main street of City Island. They all have this in common though: menus featuring tremendous shore dinners of five, six, or more courses, attractively priced and stultifying if you're not accustomed to great bouts of ingestion. *All Moderate.*

Sheepshead Bay (at the southern end of Brooklyn, not far from Coney Island; follow AAA maps of city) has several restaurants. The most famous is *Lundys* (open Sundays), which—in spite of being closed for several years—is back as big and crowded as ever with the same immense sea-food dinners and gigantic portions. *Moderate.*

Good Red Meat

For no discernible reason, East 45th Street is the steak corner in New York City's bazaar of restaurants. They bear similarity to each other, differing mainly in details of decor and table arrangement. The patrons they share among them also have a certain homogeneity—breezy, confident, verbal, and sleek, with Broadway overtones. The menus, in most cases, are pared down to broiled meats and some sea-food dishes, with a few appetizers and desserts to round out a dinner. All are *Expensive*.

Scribe's, 209 East 45th Street; MU 2-9400; Closed Sundays; DC.

Danny's Hide-a-Way, 151 East 45th Street; YU 6-5350; Open Sundays.

Pen and Pencil, 205 East 45th Street; MU 2-8660; Open Sundays; DC.

Press Box, 139 East 45th Street; PL 3-3352; Closed Saturday and Sunday; DC.

Editorial, 155 East 45th Street; MU 2-9378; Closed Saturday; DC.

Christ Cella

160 East 46th Street; OX 7-2479.
Closed Sundays. *Expensive.*

One of the first steak houses in this area, and still venerated. In spite of the disturbingly spiritual name, it is heartily and successfully devoted to the flesh.

In the same neighborhood, near 45th Street on Second Avenue (837) is *The Palm* (closed Sundays). Two long, narrow rooms, decorated *con amore* with almost anything that strikes the proprietor's fancy, it has cheerfully casual service and very good food. You will, of course, go there for the beef and lobster, but anything on the menu will prove a good choice. *Expensive.*

Cavanagh's

260 West 23rd Street (between Seventh and Eighth Aves.); Reservations, AL 5-1100.
Open Sundays. *Moderate to Expensive;* DC.

Out of the center of things, but not difficult to get to; large, lordly, old and highly esteemed by the Henry-the-Eighths among us. Full-measure drinks, weighty portions, and a hand-some list of hearty foods on which steaks, great roasts, chops, and famous stews take prominence, although the sea-food is equally choice. On St. Patrick's Day the menu might as well be written in Gaelic.

Old Homestead

56 Ninth Avenue (between 14th and 15th Sts.); CH 2-9040.
Open Sundays. *Moderate;* DC.

In the wholesale meat section and founded for and by the local merchants a long time ago; in fact, the oldest steak house in the city. The fact that these vigorous and knowing trencherman still crowd the small old shrine should be recommendation enough. Combines well with a walk in the Village, which is a short distance south.

Manny Wolf's Chop House

49th Street at Third Avenue; EL 5-1240.
Open Sundays. *Moderate to Expensive;* DC.

Big and convivial, with a well-rounded clientele (separately and together). Although the kitchen concentrates on abbatoirs full of beef, the menu carries a few popular American-Jewish items, among them gefulte fish and that potent elixir, chicken soup.

BROADWAY AREA

Broadway Joe's

315 West 46th Street; CI 6-6513.
Closed Sundays. *Moderate.*

The menu is basic, short enough to be recited by the manager, and obviates the necessity for making choices. The heart of the matter here is steak, in several cuts and sizes, served with baked potato and salad. Quite close to almost all Broadway theaters, Broadway Joe's is equally convenient for dinner before or after a performance.

Keen's English Chop House

72 West 36th Street (near Sixth Ave.); WI 7-3636.
Closed Sundays. *Moderate to Expensive;* DC.

Its staid, beamed interior, and the stately service surrounding its roast beef and famous mutton chops (a rarity in these parts) has made Keen's a tourist attraction for many years. In spite of that, the quality of its meats and the polite Anglo-Saxon reserve of its waiters remains uncorrupted.

Gallagher's Steak House

228 West 52nd Street (between Broadway and Eighth Ave.);
CI 5-5336.
Open Sundays except July and August. *Expensive;* DC.

Old-fashioned dignity and high polish, behind a handsome
façade which makes a strong contrast with the Broadway
razzle-dazzle around it; the drinks and portions are seriously
sized.

VILLAGE

Even Greenwich Village, which leans to the Continental
and hamburgers in its food tastes, must have its occasional steak. The need is filled by:

Peter's Backyard

64 West 10th Street (near Sixth Ave.); GR 3-4476.
Open Sundays. *Moderate to Expensive;* DC.

Steaks and chops charcoal-broiled at a huge hearth, giving
that wholesome primitive feeling to the busy proceedings.

The Steak Joint

58 Greenwich Avenue (near Seventh Ave.); CH 2-0010.
Open Sundays. *Moderate to Expensive;* DC.

Popular and bustling, a far cry from the retiring spinster of
a tearoom which occupied the site many years ago.

CHEAPER BUT NOT NECESSARILY TOUGH

A number of places in the city serve steak at considerably less than the usual high prices. These listed below
are for the school which considers $3.00 to $8.00 for a
slab of meat, which any careful child could cook, a high
price. The meat served is not cut from the scions of bulls
whose lustful glance at a cow costs several thousand
dollars; their proletarian cousins yield these very palatable cuts. All are *Moderate:*

Albert's, 42 East 11th Street; Open Sundays.
Maisel Restaurants (see page 192); Open Sundays (all
branches); DC.
Walsh's, 24th Street at First Avenue; Open Sundays; DC.
The Old Garden, 15 West 29th Street; closed Sundays.

THE BRONX

If you become tired of peanuts during a trip to the Bronx Zoo and too hungry to wait to get downtown, go east on 180th Street to *Dominick's,* just west of Third Avenue. Good shrimp cocktails and French-fried onions introduce a variety of beef cuts. The neighborhood trails off sadly into a no man's land and the restaurant can stand a little refurbishing, but there's the comfort of knowing that should you have a sudden seizure, the best of Bronx medical skill is likely to be sitting all around you. *Moderate.*

LATE BEEF

For chomping on beef late at night, to the rhythms of good jazz. Be prepared to pay for entertainment.

The Composer, 68 West 58th Street, PL 9-6683; DC.

The Embers, 161 East 54th Street, PL 9-3228; DC.

The Roundtable, 151 East 50th Street, PL 8-0310; DC.

Hickory House, 144 West 52nd Street, JU 6-1150; DC.

Sour Cream and Pickles

Twenty years ago and more, Second Avenue below 14th Street was the Via Veneto, the rue de la Paix, the Broadway and the Fifth Avenue of the Jewish intellectual and older Bohemian (the youngsters has already discovered Greenwich Village). What is now the Phoenix Theatre, at the corner of 12th Street, was the Yiddish Art Theatre, which produced a stimulating variety of folk dramas, problem plays, Shakespearean tragedies, and experimental European plays. Farther down the street, one could see the Habimah Players, who acted in Hebrew, or the Vilna Troupe, a famous repertory theater whose avant-garde productions were carefully observed by the whole theater world. Other theaters featured gay, fleshy musicals, or tear-jerkers based on their greatest of tragedies—the good Jewish son playing footsie with a *shiksa.* The playwrights, poets, journalists, and publishers lived and worked here, too, and in the evening would gather at one of the local cafes for a glass of tea and indefatigable discussion charged with seriousness and insult. The low mutter of dispute rose to a roar when the theater people made their entrances—and they were entrances in the old theatrical style, flourished with romantic hat brims, velvet-collared cloaks, and expressions of profound, complex thoughts and rare pain. Their midnight mecca was the Cafe Royal, now defunct and irreplaceable because the clientele was irreplaceable. Where is one to find a poet who can carry on hours of conversation—politics, gossip, sex, or philosophy—in rhymed couplets and in Yiddish? Or the dark-voiced actresses in red velvet restlessly dancing a set of theatrical poses, embroidering their gestured speech with elegant, incorrect French and Russian?

All the lovely, gaudy people are gone, and so are the theaters and the flashy shops and the intellectual noise. (The off-Broadway theater is burgeoning in this area, but the actors and *régisseurs* sleep, feed, and shed their social luster elsewhere.) What is left are a few restaurants and the formidable Jewish cuisine. This is a compound of central and eastern European "poor dishes" with variations arising from removal in time and distance from their origins. Jewish food is a set of very definite statements, no elusive subtleties, no soupçons, each application of sauce or flavoring done lavishly and each portion lavish. Like the southern Italian, Jewish cooking rests solidly on dough in a fanciful number of forms; big balls, little bows, broad noodles, thin noodles, small squares, and smaller dots. These appear in soups, are mixed with buckwheat, baked with eggs and raisins, buried in sour cream, stuffed with meat and boiled, stuffed with cheese and fried, or simply drowned in chicken fat or butter. The greatest dough creations are, however, the breads, which run the gamut from the light feminine Sabbath *challeh* to the grainy, virile pumpernickel, which the old-timers still call "soldier's bread." In between range the rye breads, spiced with seeds or bits of onions, and the rolls, of which the most famous is the bagel. It might be the faintly comic name, or its resemblance to a stone doughnut or the triumph won in tearing through its lacquered, stubborn surface, but for some reason the bagel has become as indigenous to New York as pizza pie, and its widening habitat even more extensive. Connoisseurs and basic eaters let the blintzes and *varnishkes* go and, for about thirty cents, will make a lunch of coffee and butter to go with the heap of rolls set before them, engulfing a half-dozen or more while the waiter tries to look indifferent.

Before the plunge into specific restaurants, it might be well to explain that, because of the complications entailed in kosher cooking and eating, the older restaurants maintain a separation of categories, some devoted to meat dishes and others to dishes made with butter, cheese, milk—generally lumped as "dairy." Sometimes, cream slips into the coffee in the meat restaurants, but never when they announce themselves as "kosher"; then you drink your coffee black or struggle with tea in an unbearably hot glass.

DAIRY RESTAURANTS

Ratner's

111 Second Avenue (near 6th St.); GR 3-7374.
Open night and day except for the Jewish Holidays (variable days in the fall and spring). *Modest.*

One of the significant dough emporia, redecorated in recent years and its former haphazardness muffled in Broadway decor. The waiters haven't succumbed, though, and are as valiantly chummy as before, slapping the brimming plates down with the old vigor. If your waiter approves (for an explanation, see page 26), order the borsch with sour cream (and cold potato, if you like), then the gefulte fish with violent red horseradish. Your heatened palate can then be cooled by the sour cream heaped on blintzes of cheese or berries, or a substantial serving of cheesecake combined with strawberries or cherries.

A Ratner relative runs a restaurant at 138 Delancey Street, farther south, also recently refurbished and carrying pretty much the same range of life-giving soups, *kreplach,* and great gouts of cake.

Rapoport's

93 Second Avenue (between 5th and 6th Sts.); GR 7-9338.
Open twenty-four hours a day except during Jewish Holidays. *Modest.*

It is smaller and simpler than Ratner's, but has the same seductive baskets of rolls, and the large portions carried by rivers of sour cream.

Steinberg's

2270 Broadway (between 81st and 82nd Sts.); EN 2-2030.
Open Sundays. *Moderate.*

Under the blazing Latin color of upper Broadway, there is still much of the tone of Second Avenue. Steinberg's has helped maintain it for many years with the time-honored pickled herring-borsch-cheesecake menu and affectionate, erratic waiters.

Farmfood Restaurants

104 West 40th Street (near Sixth Ave.); and 142 West 49th Street (between Sixth and Seventh Aves.).
Open Sundays. *Modest.*

Although these are really dairy restaurants in the Second Avenue style, the psychological approach of waiters and clientele is different: Second Avenue is for eating; Farmfood is for health, suggesting fresh air, purity, and abstention from corrupting meat. The menu is inclined towards Health Salads and plates of combined vegetables very simply boiled. To suggest a core of solidity in their meals, for those who need it, and to prove a vegetarian point, there are "steaks" of nuts and health foods, shaped into unreasonable facsimiles. Don't let the excessive greenery disturb you; the fish and soups are good and so are the blintzes and the prices.

MEAT RESTAURANTS

There are several classics in this group, sharing similarity in the characterful service and the abundant plate-fuls, as well as in the range of dishes. Some serve chicken fat to put on your bread, but you will have to ask for it. And some of those not marked "Kosher" will even give you (on request) butter for your bread and cream for your coffee.

Moskowitz and Lupowitz

40 Second Avenue (2nd St.); OR 4-0362.
Open Sundays. *Moderate;* DC.

For many years seriously dedicated to savoury *mushk* steak, solidly stuffed derma, meats and poultry smothered in heady Rumanian vapors and hearty voices.

Phil Gluckstern's

209 West 48th Street (near Broadway); CI 6-3960.
Open Sundays. *Moderate;* DC.

Really kosher; not a whisper of milk products. The gleaming chicken soup (with *kreplach* or *knedlach*) is as resplendent as the decor; the gefulte fish is highly approved of by the gefulte-fish connoisseurship, which is as numerous and argumentative a tribe as the Martini experts. Or if your mother, like a million others, was the *best* fish chopper and patter and you can love no other, have the cabbage, stuffed with seasoned ground meat, or the pot roast.

Lou G. Siegel's

209 West 38th Street (near Broadway); WI 7-1262.
Closed Saturdays, Open Sundays.

You may achieve pleasantly cheap satiety by watching the other trencherman engulf huge delicatessen sandwiches and hills of goulash. In the heart of the garment industry and best at lunch for eavesdropping on the executives (to pick up vital information of "Whither the lapel?"). Kosher.

Japanese

Saito

70 West 55th Street (in Hotel Devon); JU 2-7809.
Closed Sundays. *Moderate to Expensive;* DC.

Oriental tact gives you the opportunity of meeting the challenges of Japanese dining in three possible ways: you can stay on the surface by going only as far as the tempura bar, near the entrance, and sampling fried shrimp, fish, or vegetables, served piece by piece as it emerges from the oil bowl. If you want to explore further, there is a large dining room, where you can have fish, raw or broiled, or the mélange of sukiyaki while seated at an Occidental table with your long Occidental legs hanging from an Occidental chair seat. Or plunge (after removing your shoes) into one of the several Japanese-style rooms, small and pretty, with grasscloth walls in subdued colors, neutral mats on the floors, and silent sliding doors. (This might possibly be the key to the hushed quality of Japanese decor.) Having negotiated the embarrassment of removing your shoes publicly (reminiscent of childhood dreams in which you went to the movies in a too-short undershirt), you descend to the low floor cushion, which rests near the suitably low table. Crossed-legged is obviously the way to do it, but getting down—women should not make the attempt in narrow-skirted dresses—is not easy and staying that way through a long, formal feast even more difficult. You'll find yourself quite busy arranging and re-arranging your legs, tangling with the desperately mobile limbs of your partners as you all search for your absent cir-culation.

While this sub-table business goes on, there is much to enjoy—the hot cloths for hand-washing, resting in lovely curved trays; the pretty waitresses who guide you through the meal in soft little bursts of near-English, their stiff kimonos and obis whispering as they kneel to serve you; the lovely dishes and trays used, the graceful, minute sake vases and cups, the exquisite relish arrangements and, of course, the food, whose charms please more deeply than the eye. If you must, by all means have the sukiyaki. But if you can resist the lure of having your food cooked before your eyes, try some of the more interesting dishes, like *sashami* (raw fish), *chawan-mushi* (egg, seafood, and custard in broth), or *yakinasu* (toasted eggplant with a strange sauce). In ordering a set dinner, it's a good idea to find out what the courses are—one dinner is made up of several varieties of fish, treated in widely different ways, it's true, but somewhat monotonous, unless you're addicted to fish. The other din-ners are more reasonably balanced.

Miyako

> 20 West 56th Street (near Fifth Ave.); CO 5-3177.
> Closed Mondays. *Moderate.*

The ample space in three floors of a converted house make for pleasant uncrowded dining; several dinners emphasizing different combinations of tempura and sukiyaki, simply but prettily served.

Fuji

> 238 West 56th Street (near Broadway); CI 5-8594.
> Closed Tuesdays. *Moderate.*

The decor is a little less abstemious, somewhat gayer and less restrained than usual in Japanese restaurants, and the lighting leans to the Occidental romantic. If you'd like to wander from the usual sukiyaki and tempura, the waiters will be pleased to introduce you to more novel fare.

Scandinavian

Red Brick

212 East 53rd Street (between Second and Third Aves.); EL 5-8273.
Open Sundays. *Modest.*

The most soft-spoken of the smorgasbord places in Midtown; like a Wisconsin church supper with a generous arrangement of the simpler Swedish dishes. Smorgasbord, soup, dessert, and coffee add up to a fine inexpensive supper. Other dinners—Swedish meatballs, stuffed cabbage, duck—equally wholesome in style and price.

Gripsholm

324 East 57th Street (between First and Second Aves.); PL 9-6260.
Open Sundays. *Moderate;* DC.

A queenly array of smorgasbord on castles of ice. Don't let the refined decor inhibit you from going back for more and more of the opulent spread, particularly if you're having only smorgasbord and dessert for dinner.

Three Crowns

12 East 54th Street; PL 3-9692.
Open Sundays. *Moderate;* DC.

Cool, quiet, and darkly mirrored; a slightly glacial atmosphere suitable to thoughts of fjords and ingestion of Swedish meatballs, cold salmon, and *gjetost*. The hots, the colds, the sweets, the sours, are invitingly arranged and pleasurable to inspect on a once-around tour before you begin to heap your plate.

Stockholm

151 West 51st Street (near Broadway); CI 6-6560.
Open Sundays. *Moderate;* DC.

A little more hectic, with less of the usual Scandinavian calm (probably some of the noise and nerviness of nearby Broadway flowing through the doors) and often quite crowded because of its proximity to theaters; nevertheless, a companionable and open-handed restaurant.

German

The distinction between German cooking and the cuisine of Central Europe (pages 170-75) is often limited to the translation of food names from the German into the Czech or Hungarian, or vice versa. A *sauerbraten* is a *sauerbraten,* even if there are six ways of saying it. Of course, Viennese restaurants (which have been included under Central Europe) might insist that they are properly the creators of German cuisine, but Vienna is classically uncertain of where it belongs. The one thing that is certain is that Viennese cooking in New York is indistinguishable from German. Where German restaurants may run to beer steins and boar's heads on the walls, the Austrian ones tend towards violin music or mementoes of Old Vienna.

Luchow's

110 East 14th Street; GR 7-4860.
Closed Mondays; open until midnight. *Expensive.*

One of the most skillfully merchandised restaurants in New York, *Luchow's* still retains its classic dignity and imperturbable façade. With seemingly endless rooms, styled in the decor of the 1880's, it gives the impression of a Hapsburg banquet hall. It is justly famous for its various wursts, *Wiener schnitzel,* and boiled beef. Its seasonal festivals on behalf of venison, bock beer, and May wine—in addition to being admirable salesmanship—make available the finest of Rhine and Moselle wines as well as the best of German dark beers. Reservations are advised for lunch when the tumult can be overwhelming.

Old Town Bar and Restaurant

45 East 18th Street; GR 7-9794.
Closed Sundays; only bar on Saturdays. *Modest.*

Straight-forward and unpretentious, with nineteenth-century booths and glass-work and a bar that looks inviting, the Old Town serves good, solid, traditional German fare (with an occasional nod to the Irish for corned beef and cabbage).

Joe King's Rathskeller

190 Third Avenue (on 17th St.).
Dinner until 1 A.M. *Moderate.*

Although the atmosphere and the ample food are what one might expect in an authentic *rathskeller,* the patronage on weekends is roistering American collegians who down endless steins of beer and roar out college songs in imitation of a Heidelberg they'd love to know.

Klube's

158 East 23rd Street; GR 5-4143.
Closed Sundays. *Moderate.*

Excellent goulash with *spatzle,* homemade strudels, and the roll call of predictable German dishes provide the substance for the comfortable, leisurely, and pleasing atmosphere of Klube's. The daily specials introduce a welcome element of chance.

Blue Ribbon Restaurant and Cafe

145 West 44th Street; JU 2-4898.
Closed Sunday; open until midnight. *Moderate.*

The characteristic German combination of seriousness and controlled jollity marks the atmosphere of the Blue Ribbon. With innumerable small nooks and rooms giving the sense of privacy, the Blue Ribbon serves from an enormous menu, including at least six different kinds of *schnitzels,* the eternal *sauerbraten,* German pancakes, and homemade pastries.

Jager House

1251 Lexington Avenue; RH 4-3820.
Daily until 1 A.M. *Moderate;* DC.

The decorations in the main dining room are a struggle of contradictions, modern and cheerful, while authentic and traditional. The result is what one might expect a German tourists' shop to come up with by way of furniture and bric-a-brac. The food is excellent, however. If you wish to avoid a continuous medley of Bach, Beethoven, and the pops from a zither-piano combo, try eating in the handsome bar to the side of the main dining room.

Central European and Slavic

Serving local trade, as they do, the smaller Hungarian, Czech, Ukrainian, and Austrian restaurants act as clubs for their regular patrons, often rooming-house bachelors or husbands whose families are still in Europe. Foreign-language newspapers are available, messages are taken and given, and the refuge of one's own language and food supplied, and it's all very cheap.

These restaurants are particularly appealing on rainy nights; the regulars stay longer and engage the unbusy waiters in bilingual banter. The cooks (often women) bring their kerchiefed heads and big-bellied aprons out of the kitchen and, with the owners and the rest of the help, gossip and sing to the schmaltzy tunes of the juke-box. If the restaurant is thoroughly free of outlander Americans, they may essay a few hops of the czardas or turn swiftly in a Viennese waltz.

Park Garden

279 East 10th Street (near Avenue A); SP 7-0133.
Closed Tuesdays. *Modest.*

In the multiplicity of New York restaurants, it is impossible to pick *the* cheapest, but the Park Garden may be *it*. Pared down to pure function, except for the blue-and-red paint on the walls, the room gives the effect of being an extension of the kitchen, quite probably because the food and service are that of an immigrant kitchen. The waiter is a large, gentle man with a mildly paternal interest in your order, and the food is very simple and generously heaped. The almost solid cabbage soups, potato soups, and borsch brim over the edges of the large bowls, and one order of *pirogy* is many of them swimming in a yellow pool of butter; these are stuffed with potatoes or cheese, boiled or fried. On week ends, the special delicacy is calves' foot jelly served with horseradish, and stuffed cabbage is almost always on the menu. Almost as basic as food can be, it is very good of its peasant kind, not too far from the Second Avenue theaters—and a dollar will buy you a dinner.

Polish National Home Restaurant

19 St. Marks Place (between Second and Third Aves.); OR 4-2585.
Open Sundays. *Modest.*

The duck is crisp and innocent of the damp debris too often called *à l'orange* simply because some orange peel has been thrown into a doubtful brew. The justly famous Polish sausage is usually served two ways: a big portion with hot sauerkraut or a smaller one with sauerkraut blended with bits of meat and fowl in a savory sauce. Neither is a memo-rable dish, but the honest flavors are a relief from some of the more expensive, pallid fare around.

Situated right in one of the densest off-Broadway theater areas, the Polish National Home Restaurant has the ad-ditional advantage of rarely being crowded, so that you can be sure of being served and of getting into the theater on time without anxious nudging and harried gulping. At seven or seven-thirty there might not be any meat dumplings left (the local clientele engulf them early), but there will still be cheese dumplings, cheese pancakes, and always the mainstay, the Polish sausage.

If you have a few minutes to spare, wander into the rooms adjacent to and above the restaurant. You'll find, probably, a meeting of the local Democratic Club (conducted in Polish) or a ballet class consisting of the local fair, high-cheeked girls.

Bohemian National Hall

321 East 73rd Street (between First and Second Aves.); BU 8-6211.
Open Sundays. *Moderate.*

The food is similar in range and treatment to that in other Central European restaurants; the setting and atmosphere are, however, considerably different. A conspicuous neon sign leads to a large building fronted by heavy smooth columns. If you enter at the left, you will find a cool, dark roomy bar, once a lively *Bierstube*, but now a quiet place for peaceful ruminating—unless the television is blatting out hits and runs. On the way from the bar to the restaurant, look into a central back room where a soccer club may be practicing or the Jan Hus Settlement House Ladies' Auxiliary bustling through a bazaar.

Beyond, you will find the restaurant, wood-paneled and decorated with dimmed medallions of stylized peasant design, but that is all that's peasant; the polite service, the crisp white tablecloths and, especially, the clientele, reflect a middle-class solidity not as stolid as the German nor as self-consciously "charming" as the Austrian. The greater number of the women happily tucking away bread dumplings, roast duck, pork, and combinations of sliced lung and heart in cream (*haslets*) are fair, fat, and forty, obviously undisturbed by their unfashionable shapes and still meltingly responsive to the strains of Viennese waltzes played a little out of kilter by two musicians who wander in during the supper hours.

Zsuzsi

1564 First Avenue (between 81st and 82nd Sts.); UN 1-9363.
Open Sundays. *Modest.*

Apparently having some difficulty describing itself or the scope of its ambitions, this little place decided on the "Hungarian Little Espresso, Luncheonette, Restaurant"—

and it is all three as well as the local neighborhood cafe. Here the Hungarian papers may be read, a political argument quickly stirred up, or a date made with one of the receptive-looking girls who linger long over coffee.

No useful amount of English is spoken by the waiter, but pointing to items on the menu works well enough. Picking dessert is a little more involved. The menu isn't informative and it is best to walk over to the cake cabinet and put a finger staunchly on what you want as the waiter watches narrowly and thinks his private Magyar thoughts. The food is tasty, filling, and cheap: noodles with poppy seeds or walnuts make a good lunch for little; goulash soup (exactly what it is, soup with chunks of goulash meat and potatoes in it) for under a dollar; cabbage with meat balls, stuffed cabbage, and pork dishes. Or try it at night for coffee and strudel.

Meyer's

1574 Second Avenue (between 81st and 82nd Sts.); TR 9-9845.
Open Sundays. *Modest.*

Undisturbed by decor, you can have Wiener *backhuhn,* *schnitzel* with *spätzle,* or chicken *paprikash,* with dessert and coffee, for about what it would cost to cook it at home. Appetizers are 20 to 25 cents extra, and *politchinta* for dessert will raise the dinner cost by all of 15 cents.

Gay Vienna

1611 Second Avenue (between 82nd and 83rd Sts.); RE 4-9552.
Open Sundays. *Moderate.*

Wood-paneled and bestrewn with beer steins and red-checked tablecloths. This resolutely *gemütlich* atmosphere is thickened by zither music in the evening and the endless gush of beer from the bar. *Schnitzel,* chicken, and pork in the Central European manner.

Beseda Czech Restaurant

339 East 75th Street (near First Ave.); RH 4-9896.
Open Sundays. *Modest.*

Small and simple, the only decorations being the yellow-checked tablecloths (under plastic covers) and the coat hooks symmetrically placed along the walls. If you talk Czech you will immediately be a blood-brother. But even without such claims to intimacy, you can enjoy the crisp duck or the huge Czech liver sausage, both served with bread dumplings and sauerkraut speckled with caraway seeds.

Hungarian Sokol Hall

420 East 71st Street (between First and York Aves.); RE 7-9272.
Open Sundays. *Modest.*

The tone is set by the place settings: the silver and napkin cradled in a soup plate, in Central European country fashion. As in most of these places, the duck is crisp and brown, but there are a few specialties you might prefer, like Bohemian style sauerbraten, beef with dill sauce, or the goulash. If it is available, order the spinach, whose green flavor is sharpened with onion and goose fat.

Mrs. Rose Terhes' Old Hungary

1327 Second Avenue (near 69th St.); YU 8-2143.
Open every day 11 A.M. to midnight. *Moderate.*

Fairly new and too American to be as *gemütlich* as some of the others, it still has the old-country habit of enormous portions. For comparatively little, you can try to engulf a large dinner—chicken paprika, roast goose, duck or goulash.

Budapest

1481 Second Avenue (near 77th St.); RH 4-9169.
Open Sundays. *Modest to Moderate.*

Plain and good, all the way from the chicken soup through the strudel by way of Magyar classics, all doled out lavishly.

Blaue Donau

301 East 81st Street (near Second Ave.); RH 4-9841.
Open Sundays. *Modest.*

A tiny saloon which serves enormous bowlsful of hearty soups and huge stretches of *Wiener schnitzel*. The waitress is an amiable woman and whoever cooks and lays out the servings must be amiable also.

If none of the above appeal to you, try any one of the places with Hungarian names strung along 79th Street east of Second Avenue. They are intimate in proportion and atmosphere, the menus are small, the portions are large, and they are inexpensive.

Vorst's

127 Columbus Avenue (65th St.); TR 4-8760.
Open Sundays. *Moderate.*

Hearty, busy, pleasantly middle-class, and situated nearer Midtown. The menu, though essentially Central European, extends through a wide range of sea food and steaks as well.

Middle Eastern

Differences exist among the various national cuisines that make up the "Middle Eastern" category. Yet the similarities are very great. Lamb is basic to cooking according to Armenian, Lebanese, Syrian, and Turkish styles; so are rice and eggplant. Other vegetables appear in varying combinations, and onions, nuts, and honey put in frequent appearances. The quota of olive oil usually varies according to the country of origin. In general, the Syrian cuisine is apt to be more delicate and subtle, the Greek often considerably less so, with the Armenian and Turkish occupying midway points. In the lists that follow, the grouping is on a national basis.

GREEK

Hellas Cafe
143 West 44th Street (near Broadway); JU 2-1845.
Open Sundays. *Modest.*

Quiet, even a little *triste*, with monosyllabic waiters. If you can eat the full-course dinner, of the lamb-eggplant-rice-in-generous-splashes-of-oil variety, during the luncheon hours, this is a worthy place to know because the full works come to about a dollar or so during that time.

Pantheon
689 Eighth Avenue (near 43rd St.); JU 6-9672.
Open Sundays. *Modest.*

Long established and well liked, a mainstay of the Greek business colony which still persists in Paddy's Market, a few blocks away. The Greek version of shishkebab (pretty much like Armenian or Russian or Israeli) is always safe, or venture into one of the chopped lamb-eggplant combinations.

New Byzantion
308 West 42nd Street (near Eighth Ave.); LO 3-9581.
Closed Tuesdays. *Modest to Moderate.*

If you stay long enough, the restaurant will turn into a Greek nightclub, like its compatriots in the West 20's (see page 307). One male singer who appears fairly regularly has a style highly esteemed by the cognoscenti of the *Greek Daily Herald*, who should know.

LEBANESE

The Sheik

132 Lexington Avenue (near 28th St.).
Closed Sunday. *Modest.*

The Sheik has a peripatetic and glamorous history—and a
long one as restaurant longevity is measured in New York.
It was first established in 1913 on Washington Street, which
was for many years the primary Arab-speaking enclave of
the city and suitably placed (near the waterfront and the
tip of the island) to serve as a refuge for Arab-speaking
seamen and merchants. The story goes that John Barrymore,
an habitué, objected to the stern simplicity of the family
name on the window and suggested that the restaurant be
renamed "The Sheik." And so it remained, through moves
from Washington Street to Fifth Avenue, then to Second Avenue, and finally to Lexington.

The menu, in proper Arabic manner, opens from right to
left and consists of several long columns in English and
Arabic. It is an immutable list of the full repertoire; that
which is available on any particular day is indicated by an
accompanying price—no price, no dish. Almost always available, however, and very much worth trying are the appetizers—sesame-seed mashes mixed with chickpeas (*hoomus*),
or eggplant (*baba gannouge*), or Egyptian broad beans.
Then you might have the baked *kibbee,* which is almost a
national dish and consists of ground, spiced lamb with
cracked wheat, onions, spices, pieces of lamb, and pine nuts,
all baked in a large flat pan and cut into serving portions;
or you might prefer the eggplant baked with lamb, or skewered chopped lamb. Should there be meat pies available
when you visit, by all means have them or anything else
the polished, affable Messrs. Kirdahy might suggest.

ARMENIAN

Balkan Armenian

129 East 27th Street; MU 9-7925.
Closed Sunday. *Modest to Moderate.*

Although the food is as authentically Middle Eastern as in
the neighboring restaurants, the Balkan seems zippier and
has more American go-getter ebullience. Possibly, it is the
presence of a bar (which most of the others don't have) or

the careful, loving explanations printed on the menu, or the enterprise which lies in a booklet of full-colored photographs of various dishes, to help you if the prose isn't graphic enough.

The two favorite appetizers are grape leaves stuffed with spiced rice, currants, onions, and pine nuts; and mussels treated pretty much the same way. For a party of four or more, Mr. Berberian has devised a handsome mixed tray of these two plus eggplant, artichokes, and a bean salad. Cold *tanabour,* a soup which neither Heinz, Campbell's, nor mother ever made, is a stimulating experience with which to follow the appetizers. If you've had shishkebab the day before as *shashlik* or skewered something or other (this is one of those dishes which—like egg rolls, pastrami, and spaghetti—are becoming all-American foods), have the eggplant stuffed with lamb, onions, or nuts; or the lamb and tomatoes served on rice. The desserts are small and very sweet; the favorite is *baklava,* but the other concentrations of nuts, honey, and pastry are equally rich, especially *ekmek kadayiff,* which overstates its richness with an added dollop of cream.

Sayat Nova

91 Charles Street (Greenwich Village); OR 5-7364.
Closed Sundays. *Modest to Moderate.*

In keeping with the Village tenet that the direct statement is never the interesting one, to get to the Sayat Nova you must go down a flight of stairs that leads into a short alleyway, accept the surprise of two minute fountains spraying through the cement, and enter a Schiaparelli pink door. The interior doesn't quite match the outside, but the menu card has style and the cooking odors that cling to the low ceiling are full of promise. Lamb, lamb, and lamb—skewered, pattied, diced, ground; stuffed into eggplants, tomatoes, squash—make up the entree list, as on other Moslem-influenced menus, but they are well and imaginatively prepared. The hors d'oeuvres run the usual gamut, too, except for a larger variety of bean salads than usual. Should you want to avoid the honey-nut mashes which are the standard desserts, you can order fruit compote or *bagh baghag,* whose truculent sound will bring you plain old ice cream.

NOTE: Never, never, make the mistake of ordering "Turkish" coffee in an Armenian restaurant; call it "Armenian" or "Oriental."

Arpenik's Armenian Restaurant

139 East 27th Street; OR 9-0924.
Open Sundays. *Modest.*

Although the name, menu, and some of the customers are
Armenian, Arpenik's somewhat resembles the students' restaurants which may still exist in the university quarter of
Paris. It must be the proprietress—she is brisk and efficient
(which, once in a while, drives her to ordering your meal
from the kitchen before you've read the menu) and at the
same time informal and friendly, stopping for snatches of
conversation with old customers while she manipulates a
battery of laden shishkebab skewers. One looks for a high
stool, fronting a *caisse*, to complete the picture. The restaurant itself is the simplest one in a generally unpretentious
group—a few tables, a few booths, a few photographs of
an Armenian festival, an announcement or two of the forth-
coming show or concert of a patron, but the atmosphere is
easy and relaxed, the food is good, and the prices are comfortable indeed for this day and age.

SYRIAN

Mecca

6 East 30th Street (one flight up); MU 4-8586.
Closed Mondays and summer months. *Modest.*

The Mecca is the largest and oldest Syrian restaurant in the
United States, and there are more than you'd think. This one
is large and rather plain, adorned with surprising formal
dark-red wallpaper and an old piano which stands mutely
to one side of the long room. Mr. Khouri, the proprietor, is
also the cook and baker, and a gifted one; he prepares the
hummus bitaheeny and *baba ghannouge,* which open the
dinner, as well as the various combinations of lamb, vegetables, and cracked wheat, which make the main courses—
breast of lamb stuffed with rice, pine nuts, and *laban* (yoghurt), skewered shishkebab and *kifta kabab,* the classic
kibby, babab hindy, and *dahood pasha.*

Not to be missed if they're around are the small spinach
pies and meat pies and other delicacies not listed on the
menu; just ask Mr. Khouri. Given a day's notice, he will also
whip up a Moroccan *couscous* or Egyptian *milhoukhia,* as
well as the pies, but remember to leave room for his magnificent cakes which stand in large round tins near the cash
register. Unlike ours, they contain little flour and aren't
baked for height or prettiness, but are marvelous-tasting

mashes of nuts, preserved fruits, cocoanut, and honey. You may go to the counter, inspect, and pick your dessert, but it's dangerous; very few people have come away with an abstemious choice of only one slice. To go with these heaps of nuts and honey, try the Syrian coffee, plain, or with cardamom seed if you enjoy spice flavors or with rose petals in it, for feeling like an Oriental potentate.

Regrettably, Mr. Khouri's hospitality is not available to summer visitors or to New Yorkers stuck in the city during the hot months.

Spanish and Latin-American

Here's how to cope with a Spanish restaurant: go late, at nine or later, if you can hold out. Although some of these restaurants are conveniently near the Broadway area, the service is too uncertain and the indigenous customers don't gather until time for the second act. Latin-American waiters in Mexico, Cuba, and Puerto Rico as well as in the United States often seem to have an odd onset of nerves when a customer is seated. They rush, dart, fly by your table, occasionally dropping a napkin or a basket of bread, but can't seem to land long enough to take a complete order or answer a question; you'll have to do it piecemeal, as they run. The Spanish-speaking customers just yell, or catch and fix a waiter by using a strong arm and an authoritative voice. This leads to an argument, the customer extending his speech through a detailed and precise order of what he wants, how big it must be, how long it must cook, and how it should be trimmed. The waiter says it isn't possible and anyhow no self-respecting man eats like that and, having established that he is a man of independence, retreats to the kitchen and orders exactly what was requested. It takes some time arriving, however.

In the meantime, the noise is augmented by comments from the other tables, meant to catalyze the argument into an uproar. This failing, the customers go from table to table, having a drink with one group of friends, meat with others, and brandy with still others, creating a restlessness which is friendly and pleasant in a confusing way.

West 14th Street between Seventh and Eighth Avenues is to Spaniards what East 79th Street is to Hungarians, the traditional "home away from home." The restaurants are quite inexpensive and, Spanish cuisine being what it is, rather like each other in range. The stellar production is always *paella;* then come the rice and shrimp or sausage or chicken; the rest is various uninspired treatments of meat or chicken, with a grand finale of *flan,* which is caramelized custard pudding. The **Oviedo** at 202 West 14th Street, mainly a bar with a few tables behind the grillwork (they almost all use a piece or two of Sevillian-style grillwork as leitmotif) hardly considers itself a restaurant, but it will feed you decently. Above a remarkable shop called the Casa Moneo (see page 242), is **La Bilbaina** (at number 218), a smallish pleasant room in a not-too-converted apartment. Across the street (at 245) is the **Trocadero Valencia,** a little fancier, but restful and still cheap. For *paella,* Spain's prize dish (essentially a poor man's mélange of rice and bits of mixed things, and inferior to some of the Andalusian sea-food stews which seem not to have reached these shores), you might investigate several Village restaurants—the **Sevilla** (closed Mondays) at 62 Charles Street; **El Charro** (closed Sundays) at 4 Charles Street; or **El Faro,** 823 Greenwich Street, not far from Hudson, small and cherished by a few local enthusiasts (open Sundays). Any one of these will do if you want to try a Spanish meal resembling those available in the majority of Spain's restaurants.

There are a few restaurants whose bored cooks experiment, and successfully. **Granados** (125 Macdougal Street), not as cheap as the others, serves a few extraordinary dishes among the stand-bys, and a proud, pungent salad dressing quite unlike any other. The **Jai-Alai** (82 Bank Street), which goes back to the time when Maxwell Bodenheim earned his drinking by reciting his poems in the local clubs, is still an oddly distinguished little place and still very inexpensive, with a few Basque novelties to vary the Spanish menu (open Sundays).

Farther uptown, the basic Spanish listings take on a Cuban, Venezuelan, Mexican, and Puerto Rican color:

Fornos

236 West 52nd Street (between Broadway and Eighth Ave.); CI 7-9420.
Open Sundays. *Modest to Moderate.*

One of the first in the Broadway area to introduce Mexican *mole, enchiladas,* and *arroz con chorizos,* and now something of a classic in this category, stable and respectable. Traditional Spanish dishes, as well.

La Barraca

253 West 51st Street (between Broadway and Eighth Ave.); JU 6-9055.
Open Sundays. *Moderate.*

Island beans-and-rice mixtures and fried bananas incline this one more to the Americas, as does the piano player who has a large repertoire of tunes about deep passion and inconsolable lost love.

Liborio

884 Eighth Avenue (between 53rd and 54th Sts.); JU 2-6188.
Open Sundays. *Moderate.*

More or less Pan-American; basically Spanish, of course, with a touch of Mexican, Cuban, and southward. Music most nights, varying from solo flamenco guitarists to ensembles.

Xochitl Mexican Restaurant

146 West 46th Street (near Broadway); PL 7-1325.
Open Sundays. *Moderate.*

When you lift your eyes from the dog sleeping on the bar in front, do it carefully; the walls are dizzyingly painted in longitudinal stripes of every conceivable color, as if a huge Saltillo serape were wrapped around the room. As a general introduction to Mexican foods, order the combination dish of *enchiladas, tacos,* and *tamales,* or *tostadas,* and if your palate shrieks in protest, soothe it with the excellent Mexican beer.

Fundador

117 West 47th Street (near Sixth Ave.); JU 6-9363.
Open Sundays; service until 1 P.M. *Moderate.*

Ask for some Venezuelan corn biscuits, which look discouragingly pale and heavy, but are not; they're very good for melting butter in or dunking into sauce. The *tamale* fancier might try the Venezuelan variety or stay with the Mexican in a combination with *tacos* and *enchiladas*. Spain is represented by *arroz con pollo, bacalao,* a very good *paella,* and several treatments of *merluza* (which, in Spain, is hake, specifically, but here in New York describes haddock, red snapper, bass, or almost any fish which can be served in a slice). Squid in its own ink, if you like it, is very often on the menu, and also *ropa vieja*—"old clothes," an appealingly honest description of shredded beef in a pungent tomato and onion sauce.

"Continental"

This often means an international roving in cuisine or that an Italian restaurant has gone up a notch. It has moved eastward, expanded its wine cellar, reupholstered its benches in dark, plushy fabrics (like old railroad carriages), tacked up old-gold Renaissance wall sconces, and hired a headwaiter who learned his French from a Swiss waiter in Florence. The menu is likely to list French and Frenchified Italian specialties and such American safeties as soft-shell crabs, lobster Newburg, and steaks. If not always remarkable, this group is always reliable for better-than-average cooking, proving a New York axiom to be fairly true: some of the best French chefs are Italian.

Laurent

111 East 56th Street (near Lexington Ave.), PL 3-2729.
Open Sundays. *Expensive;* DC.

In addition to the excellence of its food, the Laurent is an odd mixture of formal, almost regal decor (darkest Tudor) and chumminess. It may be the low-ceilinged acoustics which make the livelier customers seem boisterous and which cause the sotto voce conclaves of the waiters to rise like a Babel of French, Italian, and tongues. Sharpen your French and Italian for some of the waiters' comments on the diabolic drives of the customers and then assuage the insult to your kind which the superb crabmeat au gratin and the mocha cake.

Gaston

48 East 49th Street; PL 5-4285.
Closed Saturdays and Sundays. *Expensive;* DC.

Paté and mussels with your drinks, and the balm of polite, attentive service. The menu is citified French and north Italian, spurning the coarser regional tripes, *cassoulets,* and most *pastas.* Have the *scampi,* the best item in a distinguished list.

In Boboli

1591 Second Avenue (82nd St.); TR 9-3777.
Open late and on Sundays; closed Mondays. *Expensive;* DC.

With a menu that mixes frogs' legs, veal *trifolata,* and caviar in *blini,* with a name borrowed from Florentine gardens, with a location in the *hasenpfeffer* heart of Yorkville (to which it dedicates a neighborly dish like *Wiener schnitzel*), and an identity which has not yet determined whether it is a dinner restaurant, supper club, or both, In Boboli emerges as a place of oddly mixed pleasures and patrons.

Most evenings, the patrons are a well-heeled group who listen politely to the entertainers, but one early Sunday evening you may find a large robust family of Hungarians celebrating a family event. When the lady fiddler and pianist strike up a czardas, Grandma and Grandpa rise, lift their hands to each other's shoulders, and break into a lively dance, unhampered by the discreet decor or the embarrassed smiles of the surrounding Anglos. In a corner, a short fat man with a damp red neck removes his monocle to read the menu and orders steak in authentic rough English. The violin begins to throb and quiver gypsy tunes, and the fat man closes his eyes and sings with it in Hungarian, swaying and beating his breast to destroy the deep nostalgic pain. On all this excess, the *maître,* dark and suave like George London as Scarpia, glances with an iron smile.

In Boboli will undoubtedly be whipped into a more reserved shape in time; that would be a loss, even if the food stays as good as it is.

Quo Vadis

26 East 63rd Street (near Madison Ave.); Reservations, TE 8-0590.
Closed Sundays. *Expensive;* DC.

Not quite in the "temple" class, but almost. The ambience is graceful and worldly, the paté a smooth blend of complexities, the meats and poultry elegantly dressed in herbs and spices, and the waiters highly civilized.

Brevoort Restaurant

1 East 8th Street (at Fifth Ave.); AL 4-4303.
Open Sundays. *Expensive;* DC.

Where the old Brevoort Hotel used to stand with nineteenth-century dignity, a new apartment house has been erected. Among its many modern features is what might be called a multi-continental restaurant—serving, among others, American, French, Italian, Hungarian, Russian, Indian food. Among interesting sea-food possibilities are the Long Island flounder stuffed with Maryland crabmeat and oysters *finelli.* Don't be troubled by the interlingual descriptions; in spite of them, the Indian curry and the Long Island duckling retain their authenticity.

Cafe Nicholson

146 East 57th Street; EL 5-6769.
Dinners only (opening for luncheon probably during 1959); Closed Sundays. *Expensive.*

Amid the styled elegances of a bygone era—Edwardian decor and an often Edwardian clientele—Cafe Nicholson serves a classically simple dinner. There is no menu, few choices, two fine wines, and a fixed dinner price of $8.00. But the filet mignon and individual chocolate soufflés are hard to match. Figure $5.00 is for the food and $3.00 for the privilege of getting a table.

Pablo's

232 East 58th Street; EL 5-8685.
Dinners only, open Sundays. *Moderate;* DC.

A party of four can eat, simultaneously, if they are amiably inclined toward each other, in Javanese, Spanish, Armenian, and Italian.

Fedora's

239 West 4th Street (Village); CH 2-9691. Closed Tuesdays. *Modest to Moderate.*

Barbecued spareribs, Florentine baked prawns, shishkebab, Indian curry, steaks, fruity Villagers.

The Cookery

8th Street at University Place (one block east of Fifth Ave.); OR 4-4450.
Open until 1 A.M., including Sundays. *Modest to Moderate.*

On the eastern fringe of the Village and used for Sunday
brunches, for continental outdoor cafe-sitting (in season),
for late snacks, for extensions of N.Y.U. seminars and, at
bottom, an amusingly decorated hamburger joint. The kitchen
cuts a wide, imaginative swath with weekly specialties im-
probably called Texas *Pot au Feu, La Hachua, Poulet Este-
ven, Poh Loh Kai,* Chicken *en Capilotade,* etc. Regularly, one
can have oriental *Rumaki* or *Teriyaki* or reach for familiarity
toward a platter of lox, whitefish, and cream cheese (with
trimmings), or rush back to the safety of a hamburger. Old-
fashioned banana splits and utterly enormous sundaes, too—
there's one that costs $9 and can keep a whole tableful of
young people busy indefinitely.

The Teheran

45 West 44th Street (near Sixth Ave.); MU 2-6588.
Closed Sundays. *Moderate;* DC.

The exotic marriage of Persian and Italian cuisine produces
a curious menu: *pasta* cheek by jowl with stuffed grape
leaves, sour cream vying with tomato paste, and shishkebab
with veal cutlet *parmigiana.* If neither Persian nor Italian
food seems appealing, the kitchen is prepared to wander into
Russian beef Stroganoff, Indian shrimp curry, and even
simple American steaks, chops, and chicken.

The *caponata* and the lemon soup are very good openings
to a dinner which could include *tchillow* with *sultanee kebab*
(unless a raw egg yoke staring out of a bed of rice seems
too challenging), or onion stuffed with meat and nuts and
baked in a sauce of sour cream and wine; then go on to
baklava or Italian rum cake. *Caveat:* the cold *zabaglione* is
not what you might expect it to be; it seems to be mainly a
small glassful of chilled whipped cream and edible, if that's
what you'd like, but not the heady mixture of egg and Mar-
sala wine usually called by this name.

Quite crowded at lunch, less so at dinnertime, and a free
glass of crème de menthe on ice as farewell.

A Miscellany

Nom Wah Tea Parlor

13 Doyer Street (Chinatown).
Open 11 to 3 every day, including Sunday. *Modest.*

It is best to go for lunch to the Nom Wah not too long after
noon since the seemingly inexhaustible supply of dumplings

does ultimately give out. It is a roomy, plain place with a counter, booths, numerous small tables, no menus, and no questions asked—unless you sit at the counter; this indicates that you want only a very small snack and you name the kind of dumpling you'd like. At the tables, though, a waitress brings several little dishes of dumplings, one or two for each person, almost as soon as you are seated. Some are fish patties, some are little hobo-bags of shining dough which enfold shrimps and vegetables, some are frilled dough cases holding chopped pork or beef mixtures; some are square, some round, and others oblong. As one set of dishes is emptied, it is shoved to the side of the table to be counted later and the dishes keep coming until you ask for dessert dumplings (peanut butter, preserves, fruits) or call a halt altogether. The accumulation of dishes is then counted as in a French café and the cost of dumplings not eaten carefully deducted.

The monotony of dumplings, although they are astonishingly varied, can be relieved by ordering some cubed meat which is about the only dish not priced per piece. Whether you afford yourself the luxury of meat or not, the cost of an interesting and filling lunch will be agreeably negligible.

PLANNING NOTE: Combine with Chinatown-Bowery walk or lower East Side walk.

DUMPLING NOTE: Mott Street has many little dumpling and tea shops squeezed among and almost obscured by the showier shops and restaurants. Most of them are counter-and-stool affairs with a rather limited repertoire of dumplings, and you may have some communication difficulties. Try *"Har kow"* for shrimp pasties and *"Soo mai"* for meat-and-vegetable dumplings; it may work.

Manganaro's

488 Ninth Avenue (near 38th St.).
Closed Sundays. *Modest.*

The European worker's lunch of bread-plus-something has gone through our traditional mode of immigrant progress in the United States and taken on a glamorous name and opulence. Though it is still mainly bread, the "plus" has developed great variety and complexity—to the point where Manganaro's lists over thirty kinds of hero sandwiches, and will extend this list to any combination you might devise.

Manganaro's is a large Italian grocery, established in Paddy's Market (see page 73) for about fifty years. Its ceilings still bear clusters of salamis and hams and bundles of round cheese and long cheese. Around the walls are ranged the expected *pastas* and olive-oil cans, but they seem to serve mainly as backdrop for the busy sandwich traffic. All along the strip of counter that runs the considerable length of the store are stations of bread, Italian delicatessen, cheese, and the ubiquitous peppers, arranged for the rush "take-out" trade. By some unstated but strong rule, the "in-eaters" go to the farthest counter, in the back, where coffee and soft drinks are also available. Nearby are three kitchen tables in a tight row where (although there is a new luncheonette, Manganaro-owned and Manganaro-stocked, next door) the old customers prefer to eat. They sit in two rows along the tables, facing each other and rarely talking; the business at hand is eating, eating earnestly and quickly, the hats they wear rocking back and forth with the strong movement of their jaws, like anchored rowboats in a storm.

Some service, appropriately informal and rapid, is available in a small room over the back of the store, led to by a stairway near the rear tables. It has small tables and an odd assortment of chairs; it is quickly crowded and quickly emptied. Often, by one-thirty in the afternoon, the room is altogether empty and animated by a mummified haste, like Pompeii: the napkins just being carelessly crumpled, the pop bottles just pulled away from sucking lips, the chairs just now swiftly pushed back from the table.

You can take your sandwich out, to eat during the noon-time recorded concert in Bryant Park (page 293), but the best way to savor the store and the sandwiches is to order an audacious combination (the Manganaro boys love to play along with your greed) and sit down among the silent, hatted men. It may be one of those days on which a black, round grating cheese has been rolled under your table for storage; you can use it as a foot rest if there aren't already too many feet on it.

Taj Mahal

201 East 34th Street (near Third Ave.); MU 4-9895.
Open Sundays. *Moderate.*

Pretty and small, its ceiling draped in large billows of red and yellow cotton, clusters of glass lanterns and walls paneled with Moorish archways (it might sound excessively decorated, but it isn't), the Taj Mahal is an engaging place to satisfy a taste for curry and the culinary embroidery that surrounds it—*pekoras, papadums, samosas, dahl,* mangoes, chutney, fried onions, and raisins, and, of course, saffron rice. Finish with the rose-petal ice cream—really authentic rose petals.

There are dishes other than curries—chicken in Indian, Pakistani, and Russian styles, and the inevitable steaks and chops, but these take a fairly long time to make, possibly because they are unexpected blows which throw the little, busy kitchen into great confusion. The service is somewhat erratic—sometimes slow, sometimes too fast, occasionally forgetful—but always polite and gentle.

Karachi

144 West 46th Street (upstairs; near Broadway); CI 5-9643. Open Sundays. *Modest to Moderate.*

Though resolutely Pakistani, which you mustn't forget, the food is served by French waitresses who guide you through the meal in charming, inappropriate accents. The curries are not very hot, but if you like, a hot sauce is served separately. The menu lists several dinners of which the de luxe offers the greatest variety of shapes, colors, and tastes. Peppery little split-pea pasties accompany the soup, and with any one of the ensuing curries comes a variety of relishes, mango, meat pies, *dahl,* and *poories,* surrounding a pile of rice dotted with raisins and nuts. The desserts, to use an art-gallery word, are "interesting."

Philippine Garden

455 Second Avenue (near 26th St.); MU 4-9625. Open Sundays. *Modest.*

Modest stretches of bamboo and an incredible vine or two serve to suggest, somehow, a believable atmosphere. The flavors are remotely Chinese, with enough difference, though, to make a distinctly separate cuisine. As in Chinese restaurants, the menu lists combination and family dinners. However you order, try to include the huge shrimp stuffed with beef and scallions, the *bistik tagalog* (especially treated steak), Philippine egg roll, and the chicken stuffed with a potpourri of well-blended objects like raisins, sausage, eggs, olives, and ground meats.

Chalet Suisse

45 West 52nd Street (near Sixth Ave.); CI 5-9781. Closed Sundays. *Moderate.*

If your tastes run to such concentrations, you can make a complete meal of cheese dishes here—a ramequin of hot cheese or cheese-and-onion pie to begin with, cheese fondue as entree, and Swiss apple tart with cheese for dessert. One is not doomed to cheese, however; you may start with *escargots* and continue with a very well-prepared *saltimbocca*, but the best choice is the fondue *Bourguignonne*. This dish combines the charms of doing it yourself and the memories of rainy afternoons in childhood when much of the day was spent in making confections of water, mustard, sugar, flour, spices, and anything else your mother would let you have a bit of. The Chalet Suisse version of this early pleasure consists of a pot of hot oil, a plate of raw beef cut into cubes, and a semicircle of sauces and accompaniments. You spear a piece of beef with a long fork, cook it to your taste, and then dip it into any, all, or inventive mixtures of the sauces. Beside healthy, creative play, you'll have the pleasure of tasting many good dishes in one.

Gilhuly Brothers

729 Eighth Avenue (46th St.); JU 2-9507.
Dinner served until 2 A.M. Closed Sundays. *Moderate.*

Opened before the turn of the century (quite an age as time is measured in this city) Gilhuly's is as matter-of-fact and unchic as some of the Madison Square Garden negotiators who eat there. The menu is simple Irish-American, innocent of surprises or culinary mysteries; the steaks and chops, the Dublin stew, the Irish bacon and eggs are honest, manly foods whose flavor is enhanced by the glow from the burnished old wood of the bar and that lovely smell of a respectable old saloon. Corned beef and cabbage on Tuesdays, Thursdays, and Saturdays.

Russian Tea Room

150 West 57th Street (near Carnegie Hall); CO 5-0947.
Open Sundays. *Moderate; DC.*

Not listed with the Central European-Slavic group because it is of quite another caste. Although the standard Russian repertoire is available and expert here—calf's-foot jelly, fat *piroshki* with the borsch, beef Stroganoff, and cutlets with Imperial Russian names—the prime ingredient is temperament. Its patrons are primarily musicians and music-lovers involved with Carnegie Hall next door, ballerinas who work and practice in the neighborhood, and middle-aged European actors and intellectuals still seeking the radiance of the old Cafe Royal (page 163). The noise, when the assembled egos try to drown each other out, is incredible and, normally, you would be warned off the crowded hours (dinner and after a concert), but the noisy extrovert times are by far the best.

Mme. Romaine de Lyon

133 East 56th Street (near Lexington Ave.); PL 8-2422.
Closed Sundays; lunch only on Saturdays. *Moderate.*

In a space not too much larger than a frying pan, Mme. Romaine whips up (by hand) a variety of superb omelettes, ranging from just egg to one gemmed with paté. Nothing else is served but salads, desserts, and coffee, which fill out a fine lunch or light dinner.

Absinthe House

103 West 48th Street (Sixth Ave.); CO 5-6571.
Closed Sundays. *Moderate.*

The mélange of French, Spanish, West Indian, and plain Southern that makes New Orleans cuisine is carefully and well duplicated here, with special attention to sea-food dishes. Have the crayfish bisque and any or all versions of the shrimp.

East of Suez

308 East 58th Street (near Second Ave.); PL 9-4340.
Dinners only; open Sundays. *Moderate.*

Just where the street empties into an approach to the 59th Street Bridge, you will find an old house whose window blinds are blow-ups of photos of the Orient and whose door bears a wooden plaque of Oriental carving. The interior is a dim series of hushed rooms which smell of sandalwood and the pages of Somerset Maugham, and from the back of the back of them emerge delectable Oriental dinners—Mandarin Chinese, Javanese, and Indian—introduced and explained by the courtly, gently spoken couple who are the proprietors, and delicately served by the graceful waiters. Whether you have the *rijstafel* (which looks something like the tympani section of an orchestra when it is all served, with the large dish of rice in the center and the smaller bowls of shrimp and rice, chicken curry, mixed vegetables, and condiments surrounding it) or the curry dinner with its complexities of tastes, or the Chinese dishes, you will probably be tasting as near authentic Oriental food as New York affords, or so the atmosphere makes it seem.

7

CHILDREN, FEEDING AND
ENTERTAINING OF

Feeding

Everyone knows that cuisine is wasted on children, as are elegant service, discreet lights, and artistic murals. The culinary world of the American child would seem to be composed almost exclusively of peanut butter, beef (chopped or in a slab), spaghetti, pizza, ice cream, and hot dogs. A few adventurers may succumb to the more popular Chinese dishes, like spareribs and chow mein, but the rest cleave stubbornly to the classics. For these primitive chompers, there are satisfying and economical places, in addition to the omnipresent luncheonettes and hamburger bars, spaghetti houses, and pizza stands.

The Arthur Maisel chain (DC) runs efficient, bright restaurants located in easily accessible spots in the Midtown area, differentiated from each other by sonorous state names—the *Floridian*, the *Virginian*, etc. They concentrate on steaks in varied lengths and density and cream-drenched desserts, all moderately priced. See the Manhattan phone book, under *Maisel*, for the locations.

At hours other than lunchtime (when the physical and emotional hazards are overwhelming), cafeterias and Automats (see pages 133-34) are good, offering the charms of exploration and selection, plus the pleasurable challenge of balancing a loaded tray and—in Automats —the fascinations of automation activated by one's own independent handful of nickels.

For an inexpensive collection of their favorite delicacies and a *tranche de vie Times Square*, take the children to *Grant's* on 42nd Street, just west of Broadway; they may bump into people whose like they may never see elsewhere and may possibly never forget.

Entertaining

Brooklyn Children's Museum

185 Brooklyn Avenue (between Park Pl. and St. Mark's Ave.). IRT Seventh Avenue ("New Lots") subway to Kingston Avenue Station; walk four blocks north on Kingston to Park Place and then left one block. Weekdays 10 to 5; Sundays and Holidays 1 to 5; Bower Park Building, closed Sundays, Mondays, and Holidays. Summers—open Monday through Friday only.

The Children's Museum is the largest and oldest institution entirely devoted to the interests and capacities of children. The labels are simple and sparse, well within a child's impatient limit, the cases are simply arranged and uncrowded, and so placed that they are at a comfortable child's-eye level. It functions in two rangy old houses whose once-bright paint sets off myriads of finger smudges low on the walls. There is no hush-hush in stately halls here; the mingled sounds of giggles, of exclamations of surprise and delight, of the light bounce of running feet on stairs, of the murmur of scuffling over who gets first try at some magic button, lighten the museum air.

In the Bower Park Building, a child may push buttons to light up peephole displays demonstrating phenomena of light and color; he may hear his own voice as it sounds on a telephone, or match his wits with an electronic "Tic-Tac-Toe" game which (you had better warn your child) always wins or draws. He can examine various old models of telephones or stand amazed before the small sea of 472 separate parts that make up the modern phone he so casually uses. The upper floor contains models of Indian habitat groups, changing groups of costumes and crafts of foreign countries, and usually, a demonstration of some particular artistic skill. The one on carving, as an example, involves whittling, clay and metal etching, and carved objects of ivory and stone, with the rare addition of an Egyptian ostrich shell elaborately incised and minute Chinese nut-carvings, almost microscopically small and fine.

The other building (St. Mark's Avenue Building) is, like the first, set in a green lawn—large for the city—and is devoted more to aspects of the natural sciences familiar and useful to the city child. Tanks of guppies and goldfish carry placards asking and answering questions about feeding and breeding of fish—the kind of queries likely to occur to a child with a small, inexpensive aquarium. Beyond the fish is a small zoo of animals which, at times, can be handled, and all of which have temperaments suitable to handling— a disarmed skunk, a perpetually startled kinkajou, a racoon, white mice, guinea pigs, chinchillas, and two fat rabbits. The displays of birds (stuffed) are very intelligently categorized and labeled by their modes of life—differentiated as "scratching" birds, or "wading" birds, or "perching," or "pecking."

Near the very modest snack bar on the main floor there is an equally modest shop which sells toys from all over the world, some simplified science books, star charts, and boxes of stone samples, most of them inexpensive and easily absorbed in the usual child's allowance.

NOTE FOR NEW YORKERS: The museum has an active club schedule for children: science projects worked on in groups and individually; a craft club which makes all sorts of objects to carry home in triumph; a pet club for the junior zoologist, where he may buy overstock cheaply; a doll club in which the girls learn to make costumes as well as dolls; a bird club for the city ornithologist; and, of course, there is a literary club which issues a "Museum Gazette"—any of which might be worth trying on your television-enmeshed young. There are also special programs for handicapped and emotionally disturbed children.

Junior Museum of Metropolitan Museum of Art

Fifth Avenue at 82nd Street. Fifth Avenue bus (2, 3, 4) to Museum: Lexington IRT Subway to 86th Street; walk west three blocks to Fifth, then south. Free. Open 10 to 5 weekdays; 1 to 5 Sundays and Holidays.

An elegant supplement to the Brooklyn Children's Museum (above), the Junior Museum on Manhattan's upper Fifth Avenue concentrates on art and history and, having the vast resources of the Museum to work with, produces some handsome and informative displays. They change, of course, but one typical program which dealt mainly with the Age of Discovery included a portrait of Elizabeth I, an ornate Elizabethan jacket and, when a button was pressed, the sound of a lute emerged from the case and wrapped the whole exhibit in authenticity.

A large map of the world was studded with little ships; when one pressed the "Magellan" or "Columbus" or "Marco Polo" buttons, these lit up progressively to mark the particular route of each explorer. There were articles from the Spain of the *conquistadores,* the guns and swords which forced the conquest, and material and artifacts of the peoples they conquered. Ship models of the time, the navigational instruments used, armor, and pictures all made a more concrete world than textbooks do. China, India, and Bali— the sought-for spice countries whose existence inspired exploration—were brought to vividness by small cases of examples of their arts, with set-in viewers giving glimpses of their temples. Bali also had its musical push button, which caused to float forth the light perfume of gamelang music.

The Junior Museum has a lunchroom and a large, light

library, open all the Museum hours; it does not lend books but its sizable collection is available to all children for reading in the library.

NOTE FOR NEW YORKERS: The Museum holds Saturday art classes (different hours for different age groups) for the children of members of the Museum. Membership is not expensive, affords certain privileges and a steady stream of beautifully designed announcements, brochures, and bulletins, adding color and tone to the ordinary drab run of mail.

SPECIAL INTERESTS

Since children's interests and temperaments vary, fortunately, a bit more than do their tastes in food and dress, this listing is designed, roughly, to indicate those places which will prove rewarding to some particular child. No child, of course, lives in any one category exclusively, but the knowing parent can make suitable selections from the abundant possibilities. Some of the museums listed are more fully described elsewhere but, with a few exceptions they are too large for a single visit; so it seems best to select specific sections to match individual enthusiasms. All places mentioned are free except where otherwise noted.

HISTORY

Metropolitan Museum of Art (see page 107), Egyptian section, costume and furniture sections.

Brooklyn Museum (see page 126). Extensive materials on ancient cultures and primitive arts.

Museum of the City of New York (see page 107).

AMERICAN INDIANS

Museum of Natural History, main floor (see page 106). Remarkable habitat groups with life-size models, houses, implements, and crafts of the Navajos, Hopis, Tlingits, Eskimos, etc.

Museum of the American Indian (see page 120). Since this is *all* American Indian, there is no telling you where to start or stop; your own judgment or your offspring's limits of energy and temper will undoubtedly guide you.

For the older child, the following may hold considerable interest:

The Cloisters (page 40)
The New York Historical Society (page 114)

NATURAL SCIENCES

The Museum of Natural History (page 106) is, as you know, one of the greatest in this category and formidably large and full. The best thing to do is pick up a brochure at the museum and select what you and your child would most like to see. Having decided, check directions with a guide and march directly. Avoid little alcoves that may catch the corner of your eye; they are the openings to fascinating, exhausting labyrinths, and you'll never get to see what you really wanted to.

The **Bronx Zoo** (page 197) and the **Central Park Zoo** (page 198) both have much to offer the serious young natural scientist; meanwhile his little sister (and his parents) can watch the same animals for simple enjoyment. Since the heavens are becoming, in this post-Einstein age, quite as wild and fascinating as a zoo, it is possibly reassuring to see them in captivity at the **Hayden Planetarium** (Central Park W. at 81st St. Check performance times by calling TR 3-1300. Generally scheduled at 2, 3:30, and 8:30; extra performances on weekends and holidays).

SHIPS

Visiting is permitted on many ships, especially transatlantic passenger ships where, within two or three hours of departure, you may get a visitor's pass for a nominal sum and go aboard. To find out which ships are in and preparing for departure, look for the daily shipping news listings in the New York *Times* and *Herald Tribune*. U.S. Navy vessels may also be boarded on occasion; check with headquarters, RE 2-9100, for current rules.

Ships exhibit, **Museum of the City of New York** (page 107).

Staten Island Ferry ride, starting at the tip of Manhattan (South Ferry) to Staten Island and back is justly famous; pleasant, cheap, and affording magnificent views of the city as well as sea and ships. (See also page 37.)

Marine Museum of the Seaman's Church Institute (25 South St. Open weekdays 10:30 to 6; Saturdays, Sundays, and Holidays 11 to 4. Broadway bus or Seventh Ave. IRT to South Ferry; BMT subway to Whitehall St.; Lexington IRT to Bowling Green). Ships, models of every country, period, and purpose—Royal Siamese barge, Irish currach, Portuguese seaweed boat, Maori canoe, Ceylon outrigger, Brazilian fishing raft, ancient Nile barge, Roman galley, Ghana fishing boats, as well as meticulously made models of the *Kon-Tiki* raft, the *Half Moon,* the *Bounty,* and U.S. Navy models. Worth the long trip if your boy is seriously interested in ships and ships' models. He might also be very much interested in the marine-supply shops (some of them very old) on and around South Street. (See Rims of Waters Walk, page 52.)

TOYS AND DOLLS

The Museum of the City of New York (page 107) and the **New York Historical Society** (page 114) have famous exhibits of toys and dolls of many colorful eras in New York's history.

TRAINS AND FIRE ENGINES

Lionel Trains Showroom, 15 West 26th Street. Monday through Friday, 9 A.M. to 5 P.M.

Museum of the City of New York, third floor (see page 107). Old toy trains, trucks, trolleys, and fire engines.

Gilbert Hall of Science, 1 West 25th Street. Mondays through Saturdays, 9:30 through 5 P.M. Model trains displayed. Also, large motor-driven erector structures.

Home Insurance Company Fire Museum, 59 Maiden Lane. Mondays through Fridays; by appointment only; call WH 3-2200. Historic display of fire-fighting apparatus; variety of model engines.

Fire Department Museum, 104 Duane Street. Monday through Friday, 9 A.M. to 3 P.M. Equipment and fire-prevention movie.

Pennsylvania Terminal tour, Seventh Avenue at 33rd Street. For arrangements phone PE 6-6000.

Grand Central Terminal tours, 42nd Street at Vanderbilt Ave. Call MU 9-5400.

New York Historical Society (see page 114). Old engines, coaches, and sleighs.

ZOOS

Bronx Zoo

East and north of Westchester Avenue and 177th Street, Bronx. Open daily from 10 to dusk. Admission 10¢ on Tuesday, Wednesday, Thursday; free on other days.
IRT subway (either Lexington or Seventh Ave. lines) to 177th St.

Wherever possible use the miniature World's Fair vehicles that ply between various points in the park. They are strings of colorful little open buses which whip and swerve from side to side like drunken caterpillars. Children enjoy riding them and they serve well to diminish the suffering of hot, tired feet. (Children may also do some riding—for fun, if not for point-to-point transportation—of less mechanical beasts, like ponies and camels.)

As in the Museum of Natural History, a conference for selection should be held on a bench conveniently near the entrance. For some totemic reason, all children want to see the seals and the elephants. Having resigned yourself to these, you might then suggest the impressive "African Plains," a wide veldt on which assorted lions, ostriches, peacocks, and African deer roam freely together, separated from you only by inconspicuous moats. Or visit the "Great Apes House," where, in good weather, the gorillas and orangs glower and spit from their rocky yards, while the chimpanzees cavort in show-off glee. For the junior aesthete, there is the "Jewel Room" in the bird section, where beautifully colored little birds swoop and dart in brightly lit cases embedded in a totally darkened room; the effect is utterly lovely. For the child who likes the rare and exotic, there is the platypus (if it has survived—they do badly in captivity); the big, rare, and utterly murderous taipan (an Australian snake not housed by any other American zoo); the sea snake that comes up to breathe periodically; the kinkajous; the sloths; and the large birds with unlikely plumes and ribald calls. Just possibly, by the time this goes to press, the State Department may have relaxed its trade regulations to admit one Communist panda, languishing in Peiping though all the free world's zoos yearn for him. (P.S. The State Department didn't permit his entry. No panda.)

Your more serious scientist might like to spend some time in the "Question House," where he will get answers to questions that the cage placards don't answer, and for the very young child for whom animals are still to cuddle there is the Children's Zoo (open April through September), where, among traditional storybook settings, children may play with mice, ducks, lambs, and small pigs. There is a small entrance charge and any childless adult who wants to play with the animals will have to borrow a child, because no unaccompanied grown-up is permitted to enter—a neat and just reversal of the usual order of things.

Central Park Zoo

Inside entrance to Central Park at Fifth Avenue and 66th Street. Open daily until dusk. Free.

A playful miniature of a zoo, pretty and small, and completely adequate if your children are satisfied with a more limited collection of animals, including such oddities as a tiglon (the offspring of a tiger and a lion) and a tapir who rooms with a sheep. They might also enjoy the fact that there is a carousel not too far from the pony rides and great quantities of popcorn and peanuts at every crosswalk.

ASSORTED FUN

There is an abundance of children's entertainments in the city, ranging in cost from nothing to $2.00, and rarely that much. The bulk of showings fall on Saturdays, the Easter vacation, and the Christmas vacation, but there are films and performances scheduled for Sundays and occasional weekday afternoons.

The week-end and holiday cornucopia includes puppet shows, folk-song and dance festivals, plays based on traditional stories, original plays, and musical plays— some to participate in and some at which to sit politely. There are concerts, dance demonstrations, and live Indian shows in schools, churches, and settlement houses, as well as concert halls and off-Broadway theaters. The *YMHA* (92nd St. and Lexington Ave.) and the *Henry Street Playhouse* (466 Grand St.) have particularly lively schedules, the latter at only 10 cents per child per performance and 60 cents for adults. For what is going on specifically when you want it, see the newspapers. The New York *Times* lists an especially complete (as might be expected) calendar of events for children on Wednesdays. Also consult "A Weekly Guide to Leisure Time in New York" in the Saturday *World-Telegram and Sun; Cue* and *The New Yorker* are also useful.

The Brooklyn Children's Museum (page 192) has a crowded Saturday schedule (free) starting at 11 and continuing until about 5 P.M., with programs arranged for various age groups—films, story hours, science demonstrations, a live animal show, talks on different cultures, and even a chess hour. From July 1 to September 15, the museum is open only Mondays through Fridays with a daily program of three movie showings (at 11, 2, and 4), a story hour at 11:30, and a science demonstration at 3. Incidentally, the directors ask that *groups* call the Education Department (PR 4-2900) before they visit so that proper arrangements can be made: the halls and stairways are narrow and pandemonium too easy.

The Museum of the City of New York (page 107) has free film showings at 11 A.M. and 1:30 P.M. on Saturdays, in a general alternation of films for children of 8 to 14, and others from the 4 to 8 group; usually, the younger children are also entertained with a story and toy demonstration from the museum's collection. Call LE 4-1672 for program data.

The Brooklyn Museum (page 126) shows travel films and comedies on Saturday afternoons. Call NE 8-5000 for information.

Junior Museum of Metropolitan Museum of Art (page 194) offers free art-history lectures at 11 A.M. on Saturdays for children and parents, and films, usually on history and art, on Sundays at 1:30 P.M. It might be best not to take very young children. TR 9-5500.

At 2 P.M. on Saturdays, the *Museum of Natural History* (page 195) shows science and ethnology films; the *New York Botanical Garden* in Bronx Park (too long a trip unless you combine it with a walk through the gardens) shows travelogues at 3:30 P.M. These, also, are not for young children.

Story hours for young children are frequently held on Saturday mornings and weekdays at branches of the *New York Public Library* (OX 5-4200).

If you're planning to stay for some length of time and have bored-on-Sunday children, you might investigate *Cinema 16's* subscription series of five programs, spaced at three-week intervals. The selected films are shown late on Sunday mornings and are suitable for four- to eight-year-olds. Call MU 9-7288.

OUTDOORS

Unless yours is an extremely hardy family, you'll avoid outdoor entertainment in New York's late fall and winter, except to gape at the enchanting Christmas windows on Fifth Avenue. It seems unreasonable, otherwise, to get too far from our nice stultifying steam heat, but if you must, take your children ice-skating at the *Wollman Memorial Rink* in Central Park (near the Fifth Ave. entrance at 64th St.). Admission for children up to fourteen is free on Saturday, vacation, and holiday mornings (not Sunday) from 10 A.M. to noon; at other times the prices range from 10 cents for children and 25 cents for adults, up to a dollar for fancy skating. Since there is a rather complicated schedule through the day and evening, with certain hours devoted to figure-skating, speed-skating, etc., it would probably be a good idea to call the Department of Parks (RE 4-1000) for price and time information. Incidentally, instructors are on hand for lessons, and a snack bar for the hot comfort of coffee.

There is also the world-famous skating rink in Rockefeller Plaza, a little more conveniently located and infinitely more exotic in its tall funnel of skyscrapers, but more expensive, too. (For information, call CI 6-5800 during regular business hours, or CI 6-5810 at other times.)

Should there be a snowfall and should you have a friend who keeps a sled in New York, you might take your children coasting on the slopes of Central Park.

During the kindlier seasons: If your children can brook no more sightseeing, you can let them loose (with a pocketful of change) among the dizzying blandishments of Coney Island or Palisades Amusement Park or Rockaway's Playland or Rye Playland. As you know, the cost of cotton candy and frankfurters and roller-coaster rides has gone up along with everything else, and the expense after the longish trip (the return trip will seem even longer, lengthened by exhaustion and bellyache) may not be exactly your idea of a pleasant vacation day. Cheaper and easier appeasement can be found in the city parks, particularly Central Park, in the warmer months (all free).

If you *must* provide an older child with an amusement-park type of experience, an unreasonable but convenient facsimile of Coney Island can be achieved in the amusement arcades along Broadway and on 42nd Street in the Times Square area. The authentic touch of sand in the shoes will be missing and the centers, though large, can't encompass Ferris wheels. But the neighborhoods abound in hot dogs, soft drinks, pizza, and candy. Thus properly freighted, your child can disport himself among distorting mirrors, pinball games, ski ball, bucking mechanical horses, tests of strength, and shooting galleries. You may have to be forceful about keeping him away from the hand-painted ties and gag dish towels which he will undoubtedly find enchanting. And if he stands transfixed before the dirty-joke postcards and the scatological souvenirs, asking to have them explained, and you're having a confused time of it, remember Ring Lardner's solution: " 'Shut up!' I explained carefully."

The Institute of Magic at 741 Eighth Avenue (between 46th and 47th Sts.) is a rewarding place to take a boy interested in tricks and magic. It is run by a former vaudeville magician who enjoys talking about the old days and the parlous new ones when magicians are much more rarely seen. He gives lessons in magic and frequently on-the-spot demonstrations for people who seem genuinely interested. A visit may cost the price of a game or puzzle—apparently there isn't enough money in purely professional equipment—but you could see some good tricks done or hear technical discussions between proprietor and clients, exploring the subtle properties that make one collapsible rubber pineapple superior to another.

FOR THE VERY YOUNG

Carousel rides in Central Park (about parallel to 65th St. in the middle of the park) and in Prospect Park in Brooklyn (at Flatbush Ave. near Empire Blvd. entrance).

Pony rides, near Central Park Zoo (close to 64th St. and Fifth Ave.). Also playgrounds of slides, swings, and see-saws line the western edge of Central Park (opposite the 70 and 80 streets; Eighth Ave. bus), and the park strips west of Riverside Drive (Fifth Ave. bus #5).

Story hours are held at the Hans Christian Andersen Memorial (Conservatory Lake at West 72nd Street in Central Park) on Saturdays and Wednesdays at 11 A.M., from the middle of June through early September; also on the lawn of the New York Historical Society (page 114) on Fridays in the summertime (Call TR 4-3400 for hours).

Marionette shows tour the five boroughs from the middle of June through August; some performances in Central Park (west of the Shakespeare Gardens, near West 80th Street; Eighth Ave. bus or IND subway to 79th St.). Call RE 4-1000 for dates and places, and also for information about children's concerts held in the city's parks.

FOR OLDER CHILDREN

Boating at 72nd Street and at 110th Street in Central Park. (The Fifth Avenue bus #1, 2, 3, or 4 will take you to either.) Model yachts tested and raced afternoons and weekends at Conservatory Lake (74th Street at Fifth; Fifth Avenue bus 1, 2, 3, 4).

Boat trip around Manhattan (page 47)

Folk Festivals, song and dance (page 295-97)

Square dancing (page 297)

Parades, fiestas, public celebrations (consult the calendar, beginning on page 317)

Frederick's Cowboy Shop (page 244)

The Butterfly Shop (page 246)

Shackman's (page 244)

Third Avenue bus ride (page 48)

8

BARGAINS

Shopping in New York can be swimming in a river of gold or choking on the bones of frustration, depending on your temperament and bank account. For that reason, you are offered here a group of shops (and bargain counters) which cover a varied, though by no means exhaustive, range. Whether you can't or won't buy in them, those described should afford the pleasure of an extra dimension—a visit to a general store in a foreign town; wandering in a small, eclectic museum; meeting a rare personality; finding the extraordinary in an ordinary category; examining things you have never seen before and whose existence you never suspected.

KEEP IN MIND: Unless otherwise noted, store hours can be assumed to be 10 A.M. to 5 P.M.; many open earlier and close later, but that is the safe spread. A few small object and antique shops open a little later, and there's hardly any point at all to shopping in the Village before noon.

For comparable objects, prices are apt to be considerably higher on and around Madison and Fifth Avenues than they are in less choice areas.

Many department stores are open on Thursday nights and some on Monday evenings; they are almost all of them closed on Saturdays through the summer and this is true of smaller shops as well.

Inexpensive souvenirs to take home can be found in the foreign shops. For instance, old Chinese eggs, in Chinese groceries (page 57); goose-feather pastry brushes at Weiss's (page 257); prayer beads from the Atlantic Avenue shops (page 100); Greek honey, Turkish candy, and rose-petal jelly from the same sources or Paddy's Market (page 73); a few betel nuts from Trinacria (page 232). Or, you might look at Shackman's fun and games (page 244), or carry off one of "I, Michael's" (page 211) flourishes of prose.

Clothing

Loehmann's

Bedford Avenue at Sterling Place, Brooklyn (IRT Express to Franklin Ave., then ask for proper walking directions—about three blocks from station). Open 9:30 to 9:00 P.M., Monday through Saturday.

Quite possibly, Loehmann's is not the best-decorated shop in the world, but it is easily the *most*-decorated, in a mixed style which can only be pallidly described as "Very Fancy." The windows sport grillwork and black columns with spiral gold encrustations, shadows of imitations of imitation Bernini, and above the windows, painted golden sunbursts and golden peacocks. Inside, the endless crowded racks of women's clothing are hemmed in by marble lions, Neo-Gothic *prie-dieus,* zebra-cloth couches, fat plaster angels, exuberant candelabra, and French screens dripping dusty fruits and flowers. The cashiers sit in grillwork cages (the grillwork shaped into peacock tails) and are surrounded by more twisted columns. Some years ago, the broad marble staircase was guarded by a life-size blackamoor in turban and Turkish knee-pants who stared at the seminaked ladies (plaster and flesh) with the shocked eye of the exophthalmic.

The sight of the large, staring boy must have been too much for the ladies, or vice versa. At any rate, he is no longer there, but the ladies are, and still darting (not the plaster girls) between racks, pushing back dress after dress, efficiently searching for the miracle dress, unencumbered by anything but underwear, shoes, and pocketbooks. There are no dressing rooms; your own coat and dress are dumped on an ornate couch fronting a gilt-trimmed mirror and you're free to wander. No one will tell you how many tidbits you may taste; you can stagger to your corner of the couch heaped to the ears with dresses and have an all-day orgy of trying on. Sometimes one of the saleswomen will appoint herself your duenna and make a real effort to find something for you and, having found it, will encourage you with conspiratorial whispers and incantations about its noble designer and the low shameful price to which it has been reduced.

The store is roughly divided into departments by price: the street floor carries the least expensive articles, as low as $10 for an attractive dress and $20 for a topcoat; at the top of the marble staircase is a huge roomful of moderate-priced clothing. Near the back of the long wall upstairs stand several covered racks which hold showy, gala clothes—cloth-of-gold dresses, velvet evening coats trimmed with lush furs, handmade marvels—reduced in price from fantastic to unbelievable, but a respectful look will cost you nothing. You might take a look, too, at the clothing in the small room at the very front of the upper floor; these are "name" designers' creations, not cheap but considerably cheaper than they would be on Madison or Fifth Avenues.

When you've become confused and exhausted, sit down on one of the rococo couches and look around you. Nearby is a portly woman with her daughter in tow; like a mother bird teaching her fledgling to fly, she is carefully training her daughter in dress-buying: how a well-made dress looks on the inside, how the seams should be finished, where to look for a designer's initials, and which designers to revere. Not far from the mirror stands a woman (A), whose rapacious eyes are glued to another (B), who is trying on a dress she (A) must absolutely have. A third woman (C), standing nearby, the same gleam in her eye, must have it, too. Will B go off with the dress and, if she doesn't, which of the two crows will be first to swoop down from the limb and capture the prize? There are many such dramas of suspense going on, and if none presents itself in your vicinity, you can enjoy the limitless varieties of bras, girdles, slips, and the female shapes they contain.

> **PRACTICAL NOTE:** Don't go when you need something specific immediately. Loehmann's is for general bargain-hunting; you can't count on finding any particular dress at any particular time. Also, remember that no returns are permitted, nor deliveries or alterations made, and there is no system of charges or credits. Carry valid identification (charge plates or driver's license) if you intend to pay by check.

Klein's

Union Square (East Side IRT to 14th St., which is the southern limit of the Square; Lexington or Madison bus to 14th St.).

The easiest dodge to use about Klein's is that it is indescribable, and it very nearly is. It sprawls across the south side of Union Square, as much monument and repository of legend as emporium (mainly clothing, although it has recently edged into other fields). You've undoubtedly heard of the French original picked up for $30 and the Italian silk sweater for $1.99; and, on the darker side, of the dresses bought to wear at weddings and funerals (by participants including the principal ones) and then returned, and of the thefts—women donning four or five dresses, one on top of the other, and then sauntering out in their voluminous coats. Certainly the stories of the thefts had their bases in actual incidents, and blinkered tenacity has rewarded some women with rare buys, but the other stories sound like the whispering campaigns of competition and not to be taken seriously.

In shopping for clothing at Klein's you might find your Cinderella dress easily, or you might claw your way through thousands of ghastly errors with no reward, or having finally confronted the great dress, find that it has been mangled by rough handling. The dressing rooms are large enclosures, often supervised by the gimlet eyes of women sitting high above the floor, searching for larceny; the rooms smell a little like the subway and, like the subway, contain crowded varieties of human flesh, except that at Klein's there is less clothing to afford a minimal bit of privacy.

However, don't let these drawbacks deter you; by all means go, if you've never been, but go in the spirit of hunting for buried treasure, with a willingness to endure discomfort for the promise of great reward. You may be one of the lucky ones who can get to a counter when Klein's stampedes the city by advertising mink stoles or genuine pearls at Woolworth prices. It can be rough, but not deadly, an *experience* charged with color and primitive drive—if you can stay in condition to appreciate it.

NOTE: See the "Practical Note" about Loehmann's on page 208; the same general conditions apply to Klein's, except that returns are permitted on most categories of merchandise (5-day limit).

Ohrbach's

34th Street, between Fifth and Sixth Avenues.
Open Monday and Thursday until 8:30 P.M.

The bargains may not be what they were when Ohrbach's was on Union Square where the rent was cheaper and the competing presence of Klein's across the Square kept the prices flat down; but they still exist.

The dressing rooms are little cubbies in a communal room, leaving at least one side of you vulnerable to glances and comments. Each customer is allowed to try only four dresses at a time, necessitating dressing and undressing for each additional foray in the racks. As at Klein's, there is no delivery or pick-up service and you have to wait on line at a cashier's desk to pay for your purchases. These inconveniences, of course, serve to make substantial cuts in prices, from which you profit.

When you go, try to avoid the 11-to-2 rush, if you can: the abounding bargain tables are then strongly attacked by experienced hunters who make Ohrbach's their lunchtime retreat; they know these grab-bag tables often hold the best special purchases.

The haphazard, "Find what you want" service improves considerably in Ohrbach's two high-priced departments, the "Oval Room" for dresses and the "Gray Room" for suits and coats for women. Both are little enclaves of elegance and service where, for moderate prices, you can buy copies of extravagantly high styles. Whether it's high style or ordinary kitchen variety of clothing you want, though, you'll do well here, especially for gloves, bags, costume jewelry, and children's and women's clothing.

Lane's

14th Street at Fifth Avenue.

The calm, modern exterior seems to belie the bustling activity inside, crammed full of inexpensive clothing. By general consensus, the best buys seem to be simple children's clothing, women's sportswear (inexpensive slacks, blouses, shorts), and sample-size clothing, found in the section called "Peach Lane."

RESALE CLOTHING

Neither thrift shops nor dress shops proper, these institutions, whose capital is Madison Avenue in the Eighties, perform a unique set of functions. Mrs. Q., who has made a purchasing error realized too late for return; Mrs. X., who bought a tight dress to diet into and never quite made it; Mrs. Y., whose rare husband says, "That old thing again?" after the second appearance of a dress; Mrs. Z., who was the victim of an inept fitter—all try to recoup some of their losses here. They send the articles (which must be good in condition and quality) to the resale shops to be held on consignment at an agreed-upon price and handling percentage.

The stores have a surprising similarity, physically: most are one flight up, in rambling converted apartments, neat but not burdened with an excess of the amenities. The salespeople have the leisured sales approach and affability of many antique dealers; and, like antique dealers, offer provenance, designers' names, and original prices as if they were handling rare objects. These awed attitudes are occasionally justified by the presence of magnificent things at inconsequential cost, especially the more spectacular varieties of evening clothes, which arrive via the television and night-club routes, where the costume turnover must necessarily be dizzying.

Of course, these are second-hand stores essentially, but quite high-class and a great boon to all the champagne-taste, beer-pocket women who must make one grand splash on some ceremonial occasions, or who need the comfort of looking richer than they are. If the idea of wearing second-hand clothing makes you feel uncomfortable, the following rationalizations might help: some of the resold clothing has never been worn; new clothing in other shops is tried on by many people and, consequently, could be considered at least *a little* worn; all the clothing has been carefully cleaned. Or, these rationalizations failing, you could make believe your sister gave the dress to you.

> NOTE FOR NEW YORKERS: Fairly constant customers whose sizes and tastes have become familiar to the personnel are apprized by phone of new and suitable treasures when they arrive, a service which not only cuts down searching time, but gives the whole negotiation the expensive cachet of personal service.

Aywon Resale Dress Shop (1065 Madison Ave.) offers the luxury of two chairs and a public ashtray. This shop seems to concentrate on simpler, more frequently usable clothing; the price range is commensurately low.

Bagatelle (1043 Madison Ave.) burgeons with lace, beads, spangles, and gorgeous excesses of silk, spraying from the racks like colored fountains. But don't be dazzled into forgetting the more sober racks of modest dresses, which are also worth looking through.

Michael of Resale Associates (1041 Madison Ave.). Michael's current advertising brochure starts with "I, Michael, have a real need!" and this desperate cry for help is followed by high-flying prose which soars through names of Olympic designers and descriptions of stratospheric sellers and buyers —brokers' wives, golden debutantes, untouchably elegant models, lady psychiatrists—who, after a "completely feminine holiday in Rome" swathed in breath-taking Italian creations, must relinquish their "ethereal" gowns to reality (apparently they become males or neuters when they're back in New York, if we are to believe Michael). And we mustn't forget the "adorable, improbable poof of a Countess," the Queen bee who lightens her load at Michael's.

The romanticism that inclines Michael to such purple prose also sometimes leads him to a purchase suitable to a Valentino movie—and possibly of the same vintage—like a sweeping, painted velvet cape, hooded, gold stamped, and perfect for Nita Naldi oozing into a torrid love scene. But, by and large, the shop carries a well-balanced mixture of clothing, from beautiful evening ensembles, through neat little wool suits, to nicely styled cottons. Incidentally, when you go, try to pick up one of the advertising brochures; the prose may have curled into even fancier arabesques.

Wardrobes from Hollywood (64 E. 34th St.). The transmutation which occurs when the little beggar girl becomes a princess as she dons the royal magic cloak may just possibly happen to you when you wear one of these "Hollywood dresses," advertised as coming from the fount of our latter-day fairy tales. There is no guarantee that you will turn into Ava Gardner if you shop among the extravagances here, but you might enjoy trying.

Second Act, upstairs at 1046 Madison Avenue (80th St.), spreads over a rangy set of rooms—one for infants, one for girls, one for boys, and the end room for teen-agers' clothing; there is, in addition, a small section for maternity clothes. Because of the waywardness of children's growth and the cornucopias which grandparents are, the large stock contains many new and near-new articles, particularly in infants' sizes. The party dresses for teen-agers and the hand-embroidered, belaced and beruffled smaller dresses, which usually cost a great deal and are rarely worn, are especially worth looking through. Mrs. MacLeod, the proprietress, is cordial and very helpful; just tell her what you are looking for and she'll gladly pull out some suitable fancy.

Second Act performs one other valuable service: on opposite sides of the entrance corridor are hung two bulletin boards, one marked "Wanted" and the other "For Sale," listing bicycles, cribs, baby carriages, strollers, small pianos, desks, electric trains, and canaries. Thus (for a percentage fee) you can get rid of outgrown clutter or pick up, inexpensively, some temporary necessity. And, if you need an increased size of ice skates or roller skates, Mrs. MacLeod has gleaming piles of them, in varied sizes and in thoroughly usable condition.

Encore (1132 Madison Ave.) has done so well with the re-sale of women's clothes and furs that they have opened another shop, for women *and men* (550 Third Ave., near 36th St.). Other than the sad racks in Spanish Harlem, the Bowery, and the thrift shops, this seems to be the only resale shop for men's clothing at present.

RESALE FURS

Though the turnover is slower and the camaraderie of steady customer and salesperson lacking, the fur-resale houses function pretty much as the dress shops do. They require a more knowing and careful eye, however, and a firmer restraint of impulse buying.

Foremost is the famous *Ritz Thrift Shop* (107 W. 57th St.), owned by the brother of "I, Michael" and given to the same silken whisper of rich names, but in more subdued hyperbole. Mr. Raphael Kaye, the proprietor, a man whose natural courtliness is aided by the fact that his height forces a gracious bend to his body when he talks to smaller people, is of the third generation of a fur-resale family. The present shop is fifteen years old and has established a solid reputation for the variety and quality of its furs, its willingness to make adjustments or refunds, and its unhurried, polite service.

The comfortable chairs and couches, the oil paintings (non-vintage) on the walls, and the Oriental-type rug suggest, if they do not quite reach, elegance. Best of all, there is no clutter of visible racks: the coats, stoles, jackets, and fur pieces remain politely concealed until asked for. The range of coats goes from about $200 for lesser animals to $20,000 for a rare sable, but the core of the business is its $500 mink, of which there is, at all times, a supply of two to three hundred to choose from. Their original owners, by the way, don't beat a path to the Ritz Thrift Shop; the department stores and furriers arrange the resale of the coats for them and credit their accounts, preserving for them anonymity and distance from the harsh breath of trade.

The Ritz Thrift Shop is the king of them all, but there are less resplendent resale-fur shops where you might also find seal for the price of rabbit:

Carnegie Thrift Resale Shop, 903 Seventh Avenue

Lang's Thrift Shop, 73 West 46th Street

Sertner's Thrift Shop, 28 West 46th Street

Simone's Furs, 169 West 57th Street

Mary's Thrift Shop, 142 West 57th Street

Also, the thrift shops mentioned (pages 219-20) have fur pieces for sale from time to time.

CLOTHING—SAMPLES AND OVERSTOCK

With the exception of Loehmann's and Klein's, most of the shops which sell women's sample clothing or manufacturers' remainders (both purchased and sold at reduced rates), are rather small, crowded with pipe-stem racks, and inclined to disorder. The disorder is mainly the fault of eager customers who select and discard at a frenzied pace, in great fear of overlooking the one perfect gem or of having it grabbed away. If you're not stunned by the avid atmosphere, and if you have an experienced hand and eye, seasoned through much bargain-hunting, these are good little mines to dig in:

Bolton's, 1180 Madison Avenue (near 86th St.)

Shapiro's, 1244 Madison Avenue (near 90th St.) and 2328 Broadway (near 84th St.)

Children's Sample Center, 1138 Madison Avenue (between 84th and 85th Sts.)

Dressy clothing for children in attractive designs at moderate prices. Stock is not extensive in each type and size, but there are rewarding surprises.

Assorted Accessories for Body and Mind

SAMPLE HATS—WOMEN'S

Marcelle and Bess, 1420 Sixth Avenue (near 59th St.). Nicely designed and made; under $15.00.

JEWELRY

The angle of Canal Street and the Bowery houses a string of jewelry shops which often yield good values to an astute eye. The Third Avenue bus will take you there; or you can use either the BMT or Lexington IRT to the Canal Street station, then walk east.

POCKETBOOKS

The Handbag Outlet Shop, in a basement on the south side of 14th Street between Seventh and Eighth Avenues (nearer Eighth), has a large stock at good prices.

The Bargain Basement, 143 Orchard Street, and *Robin's* (at 141) are grab-bags which include some odd confections in wood and plastics as well as fine, classic styles.

Fine and Klein, 131 Orchard Street. Good assortment of evening bags as well as tailored pocketbooks.

SHOES—MEN'S AND WOMEN'S

Bloom's

311 Sixth Avenue (IND subway, Sixth or Eighth Ave. lines, to Washington Sq.—W. 4th St.).

Old enough to have sold shoes to the original Provincetown Players—assuming they could afford shoes—and solid enough to have withstood the excavation for the Independent Subway beneath it, Bloom's still stands, unimposing and easy as ever. Spiced with the exotic touch of Arab pantofles, Navaho boots, and Hellenic sandals, the stock consists mainly of inexpensive sports shoes and Bloom's specialty—buffalo-hide sandals whose cork-lined soles make a light tread. No one presses a sale at Bloom's, no one lectures on podiatry. Buying is anachronistically simple here: shoes are supposed to fit and their looks please. And, many models are considerably cheaper here than elsewhere.

The basement at *Ohrbach's* (see page 209) is particularly good for inexpensive flat sandals, sneakers, etc. Women's sample-size shoes here and on the third floor. Also try *Miller's Outlet,* 167 West 46th Street (at Broadway).

The chain stores on 34th Street, between Fifth and Sixth Avenues, and on 14th Street, near Fourth Avenue, have shoes which, in Dorothy Parker's phrase, are "cheap, conspicuous, and charming." Delancey Street, off Orchard, has several men's shoe shops which sell at "downtown" prices.

TIES

Just south of Houston, on Allen Street, a long row of little shops sell nothing but ties, some at wholesale, but most at retail. Nothing you might want to give Cary Grant, but quite pleasing at the prices.

FABRICS (*Upholstery and drapery mainly*)

Mill-end shops on 45th Street between Fifth and Sixth Avenues. Small yard-goods stores on 14th Street near Sixth Avenue. Lower East Side—lines of shops on each side of Broome between Allen and Forsythe, and on Grand Street between Allen and Forsythe. Also *Kochman's*, 152 Lexington Avenue (between 29th and 30th).

FABRICS (*Dress*)

Hester Street: *Harry Snyder* at 70 and *Jerry Brown* at 85 have beautiful imported dress and suit fabrics. Jerry Brown is a designer *manqué*—with sure taste and an unsure, but enthusiastic, vocabulary; listen between his linguistic lapses, his ideas on fashion are worth the effort. Also explore Eldridge Street, from Delancey to East Broadway. *Village Fabrics Shop* (37 E. 8th St., near University Pl.) usually comes up with an engaging item or two.

HOSIERY AND UNDERWEAR

Woolworth's as a general stand-by. Also Grand Street, between Allen and Orchard, whose wholesale shops sometimes sell at retail.

MEN'S CLOTHING

Good work clothing and work shoes can be found in many of the Army and Navy stores (see classified telephone book for addresses) and in waterfront shops near the Hudson and lower East River.

TOYS

Try *Reiss Bros.* (54 E. 59th St.), *Michael's* (555 Amsterdam Ave., at 87th St.), and the discount houses (see pages 225-26).

RECORDS

Goody's (main store at 235 W. 49th St.; Annex at 250, across the street). With rare exceptions, every record in

Sam Goody's market is reduced (most record departments in the city are now meeting if not occasionally underselling Goody's), and with rare exceptions every record purchaser in New York and environs makes his way there, especially on Saturdays. If you can't shop any other day, get a catalogue instead and order by mail, unless you're exceptionally sturdy. There are no listening booths, so that you will have to test the quality of your records at home and, if you want to return them, the listening will cost you 50 cents off the refund price; in most cases, you'll still be ahead of the usual retail costs. Open until 8 P.M., Monday through Saturday.

The Record Hunter, 507 Fifth Avenue (between 42nd and 43rd Sts.); DC. The frequent sales here, sometimes based on imaginative arbitrary devices like all the works of "M" composers—Mendelssohn, Milhaud, and Monteverdi—one day, and the "S" another, make it possible to take advantage of one record bargain or another whenever you go. Open until 8 P.M. Monday through Friday; Saturday until 7 P.M.

A block or two north of 42nd Street along Sixth Avenue, there are a number of record shops which carry a large variety of records, although not necessarily what you might be looking for, at cut rates. Try *The Record Haven* (1143 Sixth Ave.) and *Geiger's "Record Counter"* (1149a Sixth Ave.), which also has collector's items. Try also a smaller shop at 1131 Sixth Avenue for odd bargains in jazz or folk music. All open late, some until near midnight.

BOOKS

New York's used book center is Fourth Avenue between 14th Street and 9th Street; some specialize, some are omnivorous; some are neatly arranged; some are like dumping grounds; and any one of them might yield the one book you've been searching for.

NOTE: "Used Book Alley" is close to a number of other interesting areas. Its lower limit (9th St.) is within sight of Cooper Union, for example, and the Old Merchants House is nearby. Several of the walks described in Chapter 2—Greenwich Village, Slavic, and others—can be readily combined with your Fourth Avenue explorations depending on your time and energy.

The thrift shops sometimes carry small displays of books, often old juveniles—Louisa May Alcott and pre-jet adventures of the Rover Boys. Once in a while, though, someone heedlessly throws a first edition into the stack. Don't count on it, but remember to look through the book shelves if you're a bibliophile and also a thrift-shop hunter.

The Times Square area contains a number of good, busy book shops with debased prices.

Marboro Books sell immense quantities of books and prints at reduced prices. They have four stores in Manhattan, all open until midnight: 56 West 8th Street (Village), 47 West 42nd Street (Times Square); 144 West 57th Street (near Carnegie Hall); and 8 East 59th Street (near Fifth Ave.). *Metropolitan Book Store* (38 E. 23rd St.), *Metropolitan Book Shop* (1133 Sixth Ave.) and *Concord Books* (1501 Broadway, next to Paramount Theater) also have frequent book closeouts with profit for all.

FURNITURE

Bon Marche, 26th East 14th Street (one flight up). What might be a dour loft is lightened by varicolored stripes of crepe paper, vaguely suggesting cafe canopies and maypoles. They breeze over a collection of furniture, marble table tops, lamps, and attractive ceramic accessories in good contemporary designs and at exceedingly comfortable prices, about one-third less than usual.

Should you be in town immediately after an election and want reduced-price office furniture, go to *Regan's* at 270 Madison Avenue (39th St.). They resell desks, tables, cabinets, chairs, and lamps used in temporary campaign offices; in a lukewarm campaign their condition stays near pristine and the prices are always good, hot election or cool.

The very simplest furniture—kitchen chairs, high chairs, small end tables, chests of drawers for repainting—can be found at the *Salvation Army Shop* on First Avenue, between 63rd and 64th Streets, and in the second-hand stores on Third Avenue in the 90's.

POTTERY, GLASS, CHINA

The Pottery Barn, 231 Tenth Avenue (near 24th St.). One of the oldest of this group, with large, well-arranged displays of china, glassware, ceramics, stainless steel, and decorative utensils, imported and domestic; most of the wares are new, although there are a few "slight seconds" (as they are known in the trade) available. The prices are held below those for comparable objects in the usual retail shops; and although they might not be as low as other outlet shops, the remarkable range and variety make up for the small difference.

Other similar, though smaller, shops:

Pottery of All Nations, 108 Seventh Avenue South (Sheridan Sq., above Riker's).

Pottery Bazaar, 21 East 8th Street (between Fifth Ave. and University Pl., one flight up).

Pottery Center, 1135 First Avenue. Good for odds and ends.

Chinalier, 37 Greenwich Avenue (one block west of Sixth Ave., near 8th St.). Seconds in china; some glass.

THRIFT SHOPS

Although they issue commands in the hard tones of Lady Macbeth—"No one with shopping bag admitted!" "No credit!" "No checks!" "No returns!"—thrift shops are really the mad Ophelias of the city, wearing tattered, discolored furs, trailing bits of lace, dusty mantillas set awry on their dusty heads and, in their dirt-stained fingers, old fans whose silk webs are long dead. The appurtenances of living clustered around them are also distrait: the cups have no companion saucers, the spoons are separated from their forks and knives, a tureen is bereft of its lid, and a bag of its lining. And the windows are proper stage sets for this disorder, displaying celluloid kewpie dolls holding false flowers of ardent color, and a faded *traje de luces* still glinting faintly of swords and gallantry.

The thrift shops huddle together (maybe for mutual protection) on Third Avenue in the West 70's and 80's. There are some in other areas, but these are the center. Many of them are maintained by various philanthropic bodies which collect clothing and objects to be resold for charity proceeds. It takes patience and enormous drive to search the thrift shops, the kind of determination required for actually finding a needle in a haystack. For the shrewd and imaginative evaluator, however, for the woman who doesn't mind imperfections and the nuisance of repairs, there are remarkable things to be found once in a while, like French gowns, fine evening bags, and old and rare books.

Godmothers' League, 1224 Third Avenue

Irvington House Thrift Shop, 1230 Third Avenue

National Jewish Hospital at Denver, 1281 Third Avenue

Lots for Little, 1343 Third Avenue

Girl's Club of N.Y., 1405 Third Avenue

Memorial Cancer Center, 1410 Third Avenue

Stuyvesant Square Thrift Shop, Third Avenue at 80th Street

Spence Chapin Corner Shop, 1065 Lexington Avenue

Nearly New Thrift Shop, Ninth Avenue at 53rd Street

THE BODY BEAUTIFUL?

He or she who would brave Klein's and the thrift shops for bargains won't mind the wild uncertainties of a barber-college haircut or a beauty-school permanent.

The *Atlas Barber School* cuts hair for about 40 cents and shaves for about 30, the ministrations given (they all assure you) by advanced and even talented students. Atlas' main branch is at 209 East 14th Street; the others are all on Third Avenue—at 12th, 22nd, and 20th Streets.

Or, for even more dangerous living, try the Bowery barber schools: *Central Barber School* at 200½ Bowery and *Vaughn Barber School* at 46.

Beauty-culture schools require no appointments, except possibly for permanents. All you need do is call, find out when classes are held, and offer yourself as guinea pig; the cost to you will be little more than the price of materials and whatever lacerations your vanity might suffer. Manicures range from 25 cents to 50 cents, shampoo and sets from 50 cents to $1.00, and permanents from $2.50 to $5.00.

Taking your head in your own hands, you might call:

Vogue School of Beauty Culture, 1263 Broadway (near 32nd St.), MU 4-6427.

Banford Academy of Beauty Culture, 165 West 46th Street (near Broadway), PL 7-0933.

Marinello, 157 West 43rd Street, CO 5-3896.

Wilfred Academy, 1657 Broadway (51st St.), CO 5-1122.

One or two of the schools specialize: **Lillian Shaw Hair Coloring School,** whose proprietress and principal claims the distinction of having invented the silver-blonde dye, offers nothing but hair coloring by somewhat experienced beauticians who are taking their graduate degrees here (117 E. 30th St., OR 9-2585). **Ingrid's Beauty School** (34 W. 13th St., CH 2-5224) specializes in hair design, so, in exchange for inexpensive services, you relinquish the choice of a hair style; they decide (on esoteric standards set by hairdressers' societies) what your type is, and you had best agree.

Auctions

CUSTOMS HOUSE AUCTIONS

On the third Thursday of March, June, September and December (unless it falls on a holiday and the sale is postponed), the United States Customs holds auctions of three kinds of matter: unclaimed merchandise, simply neglected or lacking identifying labels, which has already been held for one year; "abandoned" merchandise which had been left by the purchaser because it was unsatisfactory on arrival and by this act of abandonment he saves the cost of duties; near-smuggled objects confiscated from seamen. The first two categories are of interest mainly to dealers because they are often very large lots of goods unusable to private persons (like a gross of imported sweaters or a warehouseful of desks), but the third category yields interesting small pieces which are usually sold at the pre-Christmas auction. On Monday and Tuesday preceding the sale, the goods are on exhibition from 9 to 4, and detailed catalogues are distributed. On Wednesday the objects are repacked and, on Thursday, the purchaser bids from the notes in his catalogue—the articles are no longer on view. For this reason—to protect themselves and to prevent the purchase of pigs in pokes and the nuisance of ensuing complaint—all persons who appear at the actual auction but have not seen the exhibition are asked to leave.

To get on the mailing list, write your request to the Deputy Collector, Storage and Sales Section, 201 Varick Street, New York 14. If you don't appear at a sale (you needn't buy) after two notices are sent, you will be crossed off the list and will have to apply again. Should there be any confusion about the date of a sale, or other questions you want to ask, phone WA 4-3000. The exhibition and sales are held at the Varick Street address, just south of the Houston Street station (local) of the Seventh Avenue IRT.

POST OFFICE AUCTIONS

On the first or second Tuesday of March, June, September, and December, the U.S. Post Office runs its auctions of strayed, dislocated, and damaged goods. These have, about two weeks previously, been advertised in every post office in the city. As in some of the other government auctions, nothing is visible on the actual day of sale; the material is displayed on the Monday before, and catalogues distributed for marking and price notes. The range of goods varies, again, from small bits of jewelry to large lots of damaged radios (on which the P.O. has paid insurance and would like to recover a little something), from an elegant fitted case to a tumbled heap of men's clothing.

POLICE DEPARTMENT AUCTION SALES

Anything, literally anything, can turn up in the lost-and-found sections of a police department serving 8,000,000 people of myriad interests, necessities, and degrees of absent-mindedness. Public sales of these articles take place two or three times a year. Write the Property Clerk's Office at 400 Broome Street for the catalogue of the next sale or, when you're in town, call CA 6-2000 on the off-chance that a sale might be going on during your visit.

AUCTION GALLERIES

Parke-Bernet Galleries

980 Madison Avenue (near 77th St.)

No sales during summer; frequent throughout the rest of the year. Pick up or write for monthly bulletin, or watch newspapers for dates.

To list Parke-Bernet under "Auctions" is to confuse a bird of paradise with a parakeet, but it *is* an auction house (with what an air!) that deals mainly in household furnishings, with frequent sales, also, of jewels, furs, art, and rare books. Almost all of the furniture offered is antique, some of it with scintillant names like *poudreuse* and *bonheur du jour* which might frighten off the inexpert, but there are lovely pieces with more mundane names which can be had cheaply. Cheaply, that is, unless the dealers, who attend all Parke-Bernet auctions religiously, beat one out. However, they often let the more modest pieces go, reserving their efforts and money for special articles which happen to be in high decorating fashion, so your chances for a simple table and chair aren't too bad.

It is rarely possible to display a large, heterogeneous mixture of furniture as a set of arranged rooms, but Parke-Bernet tries, and often succeeds in placing the pieces in reasonable, pleasing groups, giving some notion of how they might or should look in a room. The rooms are spacious and well lit, and amiable for browsing; but the greatest Parke-Bernet charm lies in its core of steady clientele. The Galleries seem to be a way of life for a number of middle-class, middle-aged Americanized Europeans, mainly women, who know good china, good furniture, and good silver, and who are shrewd about their value. French, German, and Spanish emerge from little parties of women in dark tailored suits, their face veils pulled tight over heavily powdered faces and eyes blackened in UFA style. They are reserved and serious during the actual auctions, studying their catalogues with the intensity of horse players over dope sheets, letting the young (there are many young New Yorkers whose apartments are almost completely Parke-Bernet furnished) carry the excitement.

The Europeans, the young American couples, the dealers sitting in a guarded, frozen row like an Egyptian frieze, the darting eyes of the attendants as they catch and fix bids, the rueful, scolding tone of the auctioneer when he doesn't like the pusillanimous bidding, the unbelievable designs and purposes of some of the objects, all add up to a fine entertaining show and worth watching whether you come away with Marie Antoinette's bed for $100 or just a catalogue.

Provident Loan Society, Auction and Exhibition Room, 346 Fourth Avenue (25th St.). Four times a year—in March,

June, September, and December—the Provident Loan Society auctions off unredeemed articles, pledged for loans more than a year earlier.

On its street floor, in cases considerately marked with price categories ($5 to $10, $10 to $25, and up to $1,000 and over), are displayed the watches, jewelry, stamps, flatware, silver services, and coins. Larger articles, such as fur coats, radios, guns, cameras, musical instruments, and sewing machines are on the floor above. All the articles may be seen two or three days before the sale and you can get the estimated price of any particular object that catches your fancy simply by asking one of the men who stand behind the counters. Dates of both exhibition and auction sale appear in the newspapers, or you may ask to be put on the mailing list for announcements by writing the Auction Sale Department of the Provident Loan Society.

These scrupulously, almost puritanically cautious auctions, without flourish or fanfare, are watched by the cognoscenti, and you might find yourself rubbing famous elbows as you wait for the bidding to start on the antique watch you covet.

University Place, in Greenwich Village, and the side streets running east from lower Fifth Avenue have a concentration of auction houses and uptown there is a dispersed, but worthwhile, contingent.

Winegarden's and *Schlesinger,* both at 12 East 12th Street

Pollack's, 58 East 13th Street

Lawner's, 81 University Place

Coleman Auction Galleries, 324 East 59th Street

Savoy Art and Auction Galleries, 5 East 59th Street

Plaza Art Galleries, 406 East 79th Street

Birnbaum Auction Galleries, 750 Broadway

Arthur Ross, 699 Second Avenue

Tobias, Fischer, 71 West 45th Street

NOTE: The Sunday papers usually list the sales schedules of larger auction galleries; for the smaller ones, and for more immediate information, it might be best to phone. Always be sure you understand the terms of an auction sale before you bid; the auction catalog will usually contain the relevant information.

WARNING: Stay away from the Times Square auction houses. Or, if you go, treat it strictly as a spectator sport.

Discount Houses

While the female contingent of lunchtime shoppers heads for department and specialty shops, the men pour into the discount houses. Originally, most of them featured household appliances, radios, and cameras mainly, sold on a vague "membership" arrangement (consisting of an easily obtained card) to avoid "fair-trade" pact restrictions, which hampered the sale of certain articles at reduced prices. With the recent relaxation of these restraints, the club façade has been dropped and the range of stock widened (clothing, toys, garden tools, gifts, etc.), so that they now function as miniature department stores whose prices are often lower than the general going scale. Most New Yorkers still use them mainly, however, for buying large appliances and photographic supplies.

Korvette's operates a chain of discount houses, with three in Manhattan: At 147 East 44th Street (entrance also on 45th) is their three-story department store, the newest in the city and air-conditioned, which carries a complete line of all sorts of apparel, appliances, records, jewelry, etc. Loudspeakers announce the whereabouts of special bargains, and the responding lemming-like rushes of groups of local typists, shopping on their lunch hours, is a small New York curio. 24 West 48th Street emphasizes hard goods—appliances, toys, kitchenware, etc. At 42 West 48th Street are mainly apparel and accessories for men and women. (Children's clothing is sold in the 44th St. branch and in the very large Korvette store at Fulton and Lawrence Sts. in Brooklyn.)

Other popular discount houses include *Master's* (66 W. 48th St., between Fifth and Sixth Aves.), *Charles Appliances, Inc.* (38 Union Sq., near Klein's), and *Klein's* itself, where appliance, toy, jewelry, watch, and similar departments operate substantially as specialized discount houses. It should not be assumed, however, that price-conscious department stores, confronted with competition, will not (if they do not already) meet discount prices.

REMINDER: For the often very considerable price advantages of shopping in discount houses, one forgoes many accustomed retail-store services. Normally, discount houses sell on a cash-and-carry basis, without frills, and with little time for leisurely customer-salesman consultation. In some cases, too, manufacturers' warranties or service agreements are affected by discount purchase; ask about this aspect if it is an important consideration.

THE BOTTOM OF THE BARREL

For 98-cent children's dresses, 47-cent nylons, shoes at $1.50 a pair, and bras at 50 cents, the logical places are the markets:

Park Avenue, 110th to 116th Streets.

Orchard Street, from Houston down to Grand.

Essex Street, at Delancey.

First Avenue, at 10th Street.

Very cheap men's clothing can be found on the Bowery, in the shops and stalls of Orchard Street, and in a row of shops on Bayard Street (off the Bowery).

THE VERY BOTTOM

Not that you want any today, but tomorrow is uncertain:

Day-old baked goods—*Dugan's* (571 Ninth Ave.).

Day-old cooked foods—*Horn and Hardart* (577 Ninth Ave.).

Fish heads—*Park Avenue Market* (110th St.).

Shark meat—*Lenox Avenue Fish Shop* (136th Street).

Unclaimed laundry (blouses, uniforms, shirts, cotton dresses)—726 Ninth Avenue.

Unclaimed shoes—shoe repair shop on Park Avenue at 121st Street (children's, 50 cents; men's and women's, about $1.50); also 726 and 787 Ninth Avenue.

OTHER BARRELS

The thrift tables in the center section of Macy's main floor carry different combinations of anything (perfumes, towels, playclothes, and rompers) each day. Don't make a special trip, but look for the tables when you go. Small, temporary stores on 14th Street, which feature changing groups of overstock, often have good small appliances, socks, toys and wallets; also on Sixth Avenue off 14th Street. Shop carefully. Sometime, when you happen to be in a large subway station (34th Street or 42nd Street on any line), examine some of the small subterranean shops; they show prints, costume jewelry (especially at the northeast entrance of 86th and Lexington), books, groceries, and fabrics (see West 40th St. entrance of Times Square IRT).

Inexpensive flowers can be bought in the smaller shops of the wholesale flower market (see page 316), after the florists have made their purchases, noon or later.

Every once in a while, the city's zoos find themselves with an excess hippo, a contingent of llamas, a pride of lions, or an old gnu. If you're interested in making such a purchase, call the Department of Parks for information (RE 4-1000).

Egyptian antiquities in sizable numbers were sold off not long ago in a clearance held by the Metropolitan Museum of Art; earlier, they held auctions to make space and money, and since the sales have been successful, they very likely will go on. Watch the papers or call the Museum (TR 9-5500) if you want to be the curator of your own collection.

The New York Public Library (42nd and Fifth) and the Morgan Library (36th Street at Madison) sell attractive greeting cards of rare design at low, nonprofit prices.

9

SHOPS:
THE TERRESTRIAL CITY

Foods

Chinese Food Fair

20 East Broadway (Open every day, including Sundays).

At some point during your stay in New York you will inevitably make the pilgrimage to Chinatown to eat (page 149), to look at the imitation opium pipes and the backscratchers (made mainly in Japan), to examine the moribund old mission on Doyer Street, or to peer at the city's oldest drugstore, Olliffe's, on the Bowery (reputed to sell leeches, but that was a long time ago). You will probably stay within the traditional borders of Chinatown with the Bowery as one of the boundaries. However, Chinatown has flowed across the Bowery into the old Jewish East Side, and in the newer area there are two supermarkets to supplement the many food shops on Mott Street. One, the Far East Supermarket (5 Division St.), is antiseptic and orderly, with a good supply of Chinese groceries and a stalwart row of efficient shopping wagons waiting at the front of the store.

The other, The Chinese Food Fair, at 20 East Broadway, is another matter. It is certainly clean, but not with cold glisten; and it is orderly enough, but not rigidly so. Its paramount charm (other than the presence of varicolored bean curds, water chestnuts fresh and canned, seaweed, old eggs, many sizes of dried mushrooms, dehydrated octopus, lily root, dried duck's gizzards, medicinal herbs, and so forth) are the children of the family who work in the store on weekends. The boys and their friends clamber up and down the shelves arranging cans with the solemn joy of self-importance, while a lovely serious adolescent sister takes over the more important work of price-stamping vats of soy sauce. The hostess and public relations genius of the family is nine-year-old Virginia, who is made of bouncy springs, a tremendous smile, and a tight little head encased in a battery of pincurls. She'll guide you through the shop as if it were her favorite toy box—and it very likely is. Like the little boys who leap on your car in Mexican and Spanish towns, she has great poise and delicate, quick awareness, a combination which makes the very best guides and hostesses.

Rohr's Coffee Roasting Establishment

1492 Second Avenue (near 78th St.).

The word "establishment"—set in fat gold lettering on a dark red band over its door—evokes the time of the shop's founding, sixty-one years ago, when household shopping meant several leisured visits to small specialized stores, now engulfed and eclipsed by the omnivorous supermarkets. In a city where nothing endures but the persistent need for change, sixty-one years is a very long time.

The interior of Rohr's echoes the anachronistic charm of the fancy old-fashioned lettering outside. Just inside the door, barred yet eminently visible, like an old caged tiger, stands the massive still-like coffee roaster as it stood when the shop first opened. The mocha from Yemen and the coffee from Java, like the Russian Samovar tea and the Green Gunpowder tea and the fermented Smoky Souchang, are housed in suitably exotic old tea canisters of red and gold, ornamented with Chinese symbols. Beside the canisters and the roaster there is little else in the store except large open sacks of unroasted coffee resting against the back wall, fabled place names stamped on their burlap, and the suggestive atmosphere—aromatic and quiet, left-behind and patiently persisting.

Atlas Importing

1109 Second Avenue (near 58th St.).

An old spice shop whose owners (and their own sole employees) are a vigorous mother and daughter. Like other owners of small, unique businesses, they enjoy showing and discussing their rare possessions.

The names of the spices are often as heady as the odors that push through the store to the stale outside air and hang on the two windows, which show neat arrangements of mung beans, Egyptian lentils, corn silk, vervain, mullein leaves, Irish moss, and blue cohosh. Covering the walls and counters inside are sacks and boxes full of Egyptian henna, wormwood, malva flowers, barley coffee, boldo leaves, clover tops, and an infinity of other seeds, flours, grains, and spices, whose exotic looks and names might have emerged from a medieval herbarium.

Allerton Fruit Shop

546 Madison Avenue (near 54th St.).

A boxlike store, so small that, standing in the middle, one can read the labels on all the cans. The foods range from the unusual but still palatable (like genuine Parma violets crystallized), to the demented (like a can of oysters in the shell which you *must* not eat—they have been treated with something sickening, if not deadly—but open only in the hopes of finding a cultured pearl). No statistics are available

on how many cans average one pearl; it's definitely a horse-
player's purchase.

Although it is called a fruit shop, there isn't much fruit in
view, but you can get kangaroo-tail soup, reindeer steak in
wine, venison steak with chestnuts, shark-fin soup, partridge
stuffed with *foie gras* and cooked in port, barbecued snake
meat, iguana meat, alligator soup, and for a fitting end,
Greek chiclets made of gum arabic.

Cheese Unlimited

1263 Lexington Avenue (85th St.).

Almost anytime on a fair day, the corner of 85th Street and
Lexington is looped by a queue emerging from Mr. Sol
Chackam's universe of cheeses; the store is small and the
cheeses and devotees many. Both cheese and customers are
equally varied in national origin and degrees of elegance:
a Greek baker waiting for a piece of white, firm Mazithra
is followed in line by a refugee baron trying to decide between a *pont l'Evêque* or a *Carré de l'Est*.

Pressed between mounds of cheese and importunate customers, Mr. Chackam, resplendent in white apron and
trousers and a large chef's hat, navigates with pleasure and
equanimity, answering questions, advising, and dispensing
slivers of cheese for sampling—a bit of Kajmak from Turkey,
or Scottish Dunlap, or Gethsemane Trappist cheese from
Kentucky, or Rumanian *brindza*, or Halloumi from Cyprus, or
a hard, sharp cheese from Iceland. Israel is represented by
a Caskaval, Poland by a Warsawski Syr, and Lithuania by
Rutka Matki, a coarse farmer cheese dotted with colorful
spots of fermented relish, and Finland by an Edam-type
cheese. Of course, there are wheels, wedges, and loaves of
French, Italian, Dutch, English, German, and Scandinavian
cheeses of every kind—and to drain all possibilities, canapé
cheese pastes, smoked cheeses, cheeses in wines, diet cheeses,
kosher cheeses, and a special Belgian yoghurt.

Trinacria

415 Third Avenue (near 29th St.).

Trinacria is listed prosaically in the Red Book under "Im-
porters, General," and "Grocers, Wholesale." It might more
accurately be: "Purveyors of Pots, Pans, Soujouk, Betel Nuts,
Papadums, Hero Sandwiches, Meat Balls and Peppers, Pome-
granate Seeds, and Polenta"; also, hospitality and enticing
odors.

The best time to go is around noon, although it may take

a little pushing to get in because, just inside the door, Mrs. Romano is dispensing hero sandwiches of hot veal and peppers, of Italian meat balls, or peppers and egg; next to her, Mr. Bono and Mr. Angelo are busy with the cold sandwiches of *prosciutto*, salami, and cheese; a small crowd of customers, eating heroic chunks of bread and waiting to take others out, toss pleasantries in several languages back and forth across the counter with the sandwich-makers.

Having ordered your sandwich (you've picked out your own bread from a box near the door), there are two things you can do with it: go back in the narrow first aisle until you are stopped by a row of three-hundred-pound Provolones. Just before you reach them, beyond the dried apricots and the piñon nuts and the glazed fruits, you will find a small piece of counter space, limited by a can of dried currants on one side and a jar of cashew nuts on the other. This is the dining room, dignified by a box of paper napkins and the presence of other diners. Or, munching and dripping as you go, you can wander through the tight aisles and inspect the unbelievable stock. The shop was once an Italian grocery, of which the present-day boxes of garlic and noodles and the long loaves of bread are echoes; more recently, translated romantic yearnings and the stimulating presence of the U.N. not too far away have made it one of the truly international food shops in the city. There are *fava* beans from Turkey; *pasteles criollos* from Puerto Rico; anything at all from Italy, including Montecatini salts; flower waters from Syria; couscous from Morocco; ginger from China; English biscuits and syrup for making toffee; canned frog's legs from France; lemon pickle and betel nuts from India.

Besides being a noontime restaurant and an imported foods trove, Trinacria has a housewares department, which is located on the ceiling; coffee-makers and molds, graters and mashers, enamel pans, beer steins, garlic presses, and sprays of baskets sprout from the ceiling like mangrove roots. There hardly seems to be room for another package of slim breadsticks, but if Mr. Bono hears of baked piranha being packaged along the Amazon, some will soon appear between the *frijoles* and the Bombay duck.

Soupçon

203 East 61st Street (east of Third Ave.).

The two small rooms and kitchen are swathed in enticing cooking odors, pleasing airs to accompany gazing at lovely French copper and china (old and new) and well-fashioned pewter, or for selecting one of the many attractive cocktail and hors d'oeuvres trays or one of the rose-tree vases.

Appealing as these things are, the emphasis at Soupçon is on their prepared foods, made with choice ingredients, no preservatives, and always in small quantities so that nothing stales. The lists include several cocktail spreads, a group of sauces and dressings, a dozen or so soups, and some preserves. These are not in the A & P price range, but they are unusually good preparations, and if you can afford this sort of kitchen shopping, the price should be inconsequential. Should you, by the way, need to send a bon voyage basket, look at the French string bag containing tricolor packages and sporting tricolor carnations—simple and imaginative, an "in the know" sort of gift.

Oriental Food Shop

1302 Amsterdam Avenue (124th St.).
IRT Broadway line to 125th Street or Eighth Avenue-Amsterdam bus.

Unless you have a burning interest in Oriental foods, this shop is too far out of the way to be visited for itself alone, but interesting enough to combine with a Harlem trip or an early dinner at the Shanghai Cafe (page 152) or, for that matter, any trip to the upper West Side of Manhattan.

Bright, new, and dazzling white, this small supermarket carries only Oriental foods—mainly Japanese now, but some Korean and some Hawaiian—and the proprietors are developing a Chinese section to serve the large Chinese colony in the neighborhood. Japanese foods as we know them—the meat and vegetables and soy sauce for sukiyaki, the rices, rice cakes, and varieties of tea—fill the neat shelves, but there are countless kinds of food, many of them flown in from Los Angeles and Hawaii, which are unfamiliar to the non-connoisseur. For instance: minute fish and marine worms preserved in pastes of salt, soy, and sugar (it *does* taste peculiar the first time); seafood in brine in the style of the Philippines; fiery hot pickle commonly eaten in Korea; sliced salmon in sake mash; barracuda steamed and pulverized and sold from a loaf; there is fresh bean curd and fried cakes of it; seaweed in several forms; spaghetti of incredible delicacy; tea cakes in bright colors and traditional shapes ready for steaming and eating; and a confection which painstakingly imitates a bunch of Gargantuan grapes. They are balls of plastic, tastefully arranged with artificial leaves, and filled with a kind of thin grape jelly; they are pierced with a pin and the jelly sucked out of them. Both the making and the eating seem like a good deal of bother, but it is novel, almost as novel as the Japanese cocktail sausage made of tuna fish, which took five years of a biochemist's time to develop (it's difficult to know why).

The Oriental Food Shop also sells well-priced Japanese cooking utensils, Oriental cookbooks, and a few souvenir novelties. Foods can be ordered by mail from a printed list, and if you like and can afford the large gesture, you can order a Hawaiian poi on a week's notice to be flown in for you from the West Coast.

Kalustyan

407 Third Avenue (28th St.).

Mr. Kalustyan's shop combines the highly spiced exoticisms of Near Eastern food and the austere purity of health foods —offering high, tasty living and the cures for it simultaneously. Thus, lively Greek cheeses can be balanced by bland natural nut-butters, the preserved fish of Turkey (*lakerda*) quietened by healthful dollops of wheat-germ oil, while non-fattening rice acts as penance for the excess of sweet, rich *baklava*.

Both eating and curing departments, which are well intermingled, consist of sacks and jars of odd and curious substances—at least to an American ignorant of the properties of health foods and the subtleties of Eastern cooking: soya granules, strings of dried okra, Greek lemon jam, chick-pea flour, St. John's bread, wild onions in oil and vinegar, rose water, quinine bark, star anise, fenugreek and sumach berries, and sweets made of sesame seeds, of grape jelly and nuts, and of various fruit jellies dusted with sugar.

Selling seems to be divided between two men. One, a pleasant, tall elderly gentleman, who has no particular interest in the health foods, sells them as he'll sell anything else you might ask for. Mr. Kalustyan, on the other hand, has made the health foods his special domain and the health-food customers his particular concern. It is entertaining and instructive to see him, slender and elegant, put together fine measures of wheat-germ oil, soy granules, and other life-giving ingredients, explaining throughout this act of alchemy the vitamin contents and specific properties of each substance, and ending the lecture with a vivid personal testimonial to the bounty which lies in the mixture.

Blum's

700 Fifth Avenue (55th St.).

Were Madame Pompadour to have changed careers she might have opened a candy shop like Blum's—satiny rococo, suggesting perfumed pink-and-white dalliance. Some of the prices are also French Court: $145 for two-and-one-half pounds of chocolates (possibly myrrh and frankincense infused) in an exquisite Limoges box, and a shade less for assortments in Italian boxes of painted wood and antique metal. If you are not of the mood or purse for such an extravagant gift, buy chocolates of the same superlative quality in lesser boxes. These run down the scale to about $2.00 per pound and stop there; no chewing gum, no penny candy.

Le Buffet Français

1048 Third Avenue (62nd St.).
Open until 7 P.M., Monday through Saturday.

Related by ownership to Cheese Unlimited (page 232) and possessed of the same high style—here concentrated in what is substantially a huge glass-windowed refrigerator containing prepared French dishes, and topped by tricolor awnings. Always on tap are several types of paté, magnificent galantines (which can be ordered whole or bought by the slice and in varying quantity and variety—depending on the demands of the weather), sea-food and meat aspics, and elusive sauces. Prices are fairly high, much higher than if you concocted these delicacies yourself—but could you?

Old Denmark

135 East 57th Street (near Lexington Ave.).

A respectable number of New York hostesses solve hors d'oeuvres and Sunday supper problems by buying a brick of paté and a pile of smoked-salmon slices at Old Denmark and let it go at that; both are cheaper than the French and Nova Scotia varieties and almost equally good. For more lavish spreads, try the mushroom salads and the lobster and crabmeat salads, the cheeses, and one or two of the practically imperishable cakes. The cautious buyer might try sampling the prepared foods by having lunch at the one table (for a slender four) in the place.

For the absolutely superlative in range of imports, rarity, variety, elegance, and price, investigate:

Charles, 340 Madison Avenue; DC.

Vendôme, 15 East 48th Street; DC.

Maison Glass, 52 East 58th Street.

Ellen Gray, 712 Madison Avenue (caviar).

Fraser Morris, 872 Madison Avenue; DC.

Martin's Fruit Shop, 1042 Madison Avenue.

Other food shops are mentioned in several walks on pages 45-103, and don't overlook the Scandinavian food shops on Third Avenue: the delicatessen at the corner of 58th Street, *Nyborg and Nelson* at 51st Street, *Scandinavian Delicacies* between 64th and 65th Streets, and the *Swedish Kondis Bakery* (204 East 58th St., near Third), which makes flat, heart-shaped cakes bearing flowers and messages in the bright colors and naive designs of Swedish toys.

Old and Middle-aged Antiques, Objets, and Things

The following section (running south to north) deals with objects of several kinds—genuine antiques, oldish things fading into rarity, and international and domestic oddities which you might consider for gifts or souvenirs or hoard as your own. And if none of these shops yield anything that tempts you, the department stores all stock a large variety of objects. Fifth Avenue and Madison Avenue and the streets which surround them—the 40's, 50's, and 60's—also shine with attractive objects. A few of the choice emporia, for example, are *Jensen's* (667 Fifth Avenue), *Bonnier's* (605 Fifth Avenue), *Plummer's* (734 Fifth Avenue), *Piazza Montici* (19 East 55th Street), and *Venini Glass* (125 East 55th Street).

Always, too, there's the large, haphazard boutique called Greenwich Village; and the broad alley of antiques, enticing junk, and things of the limbo in between, on Second and Third Avenues from 40th Street into the 60's.

An effulgence of "objet"erias, recently sprouted in the 50's and 60's east of Third Avenue, has perfected a fascinating and irritating trick of psychology and snobbism. It consists of taking a discarded thing (let's say an old-fashioned dressmaker's dummy or a vase of cumbersome cut glass), recently old and never loved, displaying it in surroundings of verve and chic, and covering it with an illusion of beauty and desirability. Then comes the one-upmanship of taste: "If we, who are so dazzlingly advanced and awesomely tasteful, like it, it's smart" and any niggling doubt on your part is frightened away by shrill cries of "It's so mad! So utterly gay!" Any dissenters are automatically labeled dull, sane, and somber. Since this is such an embarrassing class to be in, few bleats of protest are heard.

The foregoing shouldn't, however, deter you from snooping in these entertaining shops; just don't take them as seriously as they'd like and then go on to other shops in the neighborhood where you will find attractive sets of things less self-consciously cherished.

Knapp's

Three almost contiguous stores on Fulton Street from Pineapple Street to Clark, in Brooklyn. (Via Seventh Ave. IRT to Clark St., Brooklyn, or IND Eighth Ave. to High St., Brooklyn.)

It may hardly seem worth troubling about Knapp's since the shops are open only Friday, Saturday, and Monday— and closed those rare days, too, when Mr. Knapp goes on long European shopping trips (phone TR 5-4563 before-hand) but it is a remarkable place for the "snapper-up of unconsidered trifles." Although there are no immutable rules or even habits at Knapp's, the corner store (Fulton and Pine-apple) seems to be the depot of larger objects, such as octagonal chests of myriad drawers for the *very* orderly, brass beds with mother-of-pearl inlay, an old thirsty beer dispenser, a painted Currier and Ives sleigh, and assorted masses of neoclassicism but, in general, the three shops are joined heaps of impassioned acquisitiveness. What is available, Mr. Knapp buys, but he buys more of what was recently in fashion. Ships' lanterns? He has dozens of them. Apothecary jars? He must have rifled every Spanish drugstore in the summer of 1958; there are rows and rows of jars. One of the stores has a basement thick with dank cellar smell and swollen with kettles, pots, basins, and pans of copper. There is at least a little of everything at Knapp's except drugs, liquor, and groceries; the curious assortment is entertaining to walk through. The prices run through mysterious fluctuations which are dictated, say the habitués—a number of

Brooklynites spend many of their Saturdays here—by how Mr. Knapp feels on any given day.

Eagle Bag and Burlap Co.

12 Fulton Street (downtown, reached by Broadway bus or IRT Seventh Ave. subway—both to Fulton St., then walking east). Open to 8:30 P.M., Monday through Friday; Saturday, 11 to 6.

There is neither bag nor burlap in sight; they have been relegated to unseen corners of the old four-story building, which was once the headquarters for a volunteer fire company. The weatherbeaten sign remains, nevertheless, hanging dully against the silver fire escapes and window frames. The reason for this decor, says Mr. Louis Cohen, the proprietor, is not so much for its beauty—although he likes the startling effect on dim Fulton Street—as for its practicality: the paint is luminous and its merciless light would immediately show up any marauder. A burglar might think twice about entering, in any case, if he had an idea of the hazards, other than legal, of entry here. He might break his leg on a huge Chinese chest of camphorwood, he might be impaled on an African assagai, he might rouse the neighborhood by dislodging a thousand things that jangle, clatter, crash, clang, and thump; the very multiplicity and variety of objects make effective burglar alarms.

Mr. Cohen began pushing burlap and bags aside when he started an informal lively trade with individual sailors many years ago. He bought a Persian rug from one and ivory figurines from another and, as his purchasing became more catholic, from more formal sources, cramming his building full. Although his aggregate stock is enormous, there is no way of telling when Mr. Cohen will be bullish in any category. He may have several good African primitives in one week and no others for a year. One month he may have stacks of Chinese boxes, inlaid and brass bound, which soon disappear and are not replaced for a long time. If you can pick your way over, under, through and by the crowded sections, you may find a rarity hidden in the efflorescences of tourist drums, smooth African sculpture, temple bells, and queues of ivory elephants.

Mr. Cohen is not a gallery-trained connoisseur by any means, but he has picked up a substantial amount of information over the years and his prices are eminently fair, often considerably cheaper than comparable items elsewhere in the city. As a matter of fact, other dealers go down to comparison-shop, to buy pieces, and simply to argue, "How can you sell so cheap? We have to sell it for twice as much uptown!" The rejoinder, after Mr. Cohen has uprooted the stump of cigar which grows from his lips, is, "Alright, so move downtown."

Basket Bazaar

133 West 3rd Street (Greenwich Village, east of Sixth Ave.). Open noon to 7 P.M., Monday through Saturday.

Ann Mayrson, whose talents include appearing patrician while glued to the World Series on a violent radio, picks her baskets and straw accessories meticulously, careful of design and workmanship. There are standing baskets and hanging baskets, fish traps and bread baskets, a crescent-moon bird cage and woven coat hangers. Straw monkeys come from Hong Kong, fly swatters from Japan, and straw lace things from Italy. Look, also, at some lovely bamboo-framed mirrors, a long narrow bamboo vase-holder, all sorts of coasters and mats and a Scotch market basket large enough to cradle Gargantua.

Jon's Scandinavian Shop

181 West 4th Street (Village, between Sixth and Seventh Ave.).

Down into a cellar and up a flight of stairs, an extensive collection of Scandinavian pottery, linen, toys, vases, posters, ashtrays, and pitchers in controlled, usable Northern taste —and, as contrast, a flash of Latin heat from a stray Spanish wineskin.

Mary Muller

66 Greenwich Avenue (Village, between Sixth and Seventh Aves.).

Reed-Karen Antique Shop

49 Greenwich Avenue.

Both shops specialize in Americana. Mary Muller will likely have more small objects like old bottles, glassware, and toys; whereas Reed-Karen runs to hobby horses and grandfather clocks. The "Reed" of the latter establishment is the folk singer, Susan Reed, during the other half of her professional life.

Little Portugal

15 Christopher Street (near Greenwich Ave., close to Sixth Ave. and Eighth Sts.).

An unusual and lovely group of craft works, including white pitchers and platters with blue floral designs, lustrous pewter-toned pottery, deep-hued woolen blankets and throws, handsome woolen shirts, and huge, delicately ornamented candles.

Piñata Party

129 Macdougal Street (off southwest corner of Washington Sq. Park).

Open 1:30 to 10:30, Monday through Thursday; 1:30 to midnight, Friday and Saturday.

The biggest *piñata* on record, spilling gifts which might frighten the most stolid child; a back room, for instance, is dramatically half-lit and full of Pre-Columbian savagery—masks, spears, skins, skulls, and unmouthed teeth. Among the milder objects scattered through the rambling shop-museum are Andean knit face masks (a good idea for a Lakes winter even if they do make you look like Lon Chaney in "The Phantom of the Opera"), ear-lapped Peruvian wool caps which suit a few choice adults and all children, enormous fur slippers which might make efficient floor waxers if wearing them proves awkward, crude and beautiful fur rugs, hand-loomed textile bags, primitive jewelry, and a hundred other oddities, some repellent, some attractive, and all provocative.

Si Como No

118 Macdougal Street.

A small basement not quite dark enough to hide a number of unusual Mexican objects. You won't find the omnipresent Mexican hat ashtrays here or book ends laden with dozing Mexicans; you will find good masks, claywork candelabra, and pottery in traditional designs from the few obscure regions which have not yet become souvenir mills.

Merrill Ames

41 East 8th Street (near University Pl.).

A startling contrast to most Village stores where vigorous heaping stands for arranging. Here the decorative accessories and household objects—pottery, glass, vases, matches, and baskets are beautifully placed in relationship to each other, with good areas of calm space around them.

Village Antiques Mart

89 University Place (between 11th and 12th Sts.).

Open noon to 9 P.M.

Everything, anything—good, questionable, and indifferent—in a number of groups extensive enough to cover many categories and grades of quality; certainly worth a visit if you're interested in a variety of antiques. In one of the auction centers (see page 224).

The Casa Moneo

218 West 14th Street (west of Seventh Ave.).

In space not much larger than an ordinary grocery store, the owners have, in crowded order, garnered almost everything available from Spain and Latin-American countries, a sort of counterconquest. The red front opens on two windows crammed with Cuban records, Spanish tambourines, Mexican canned goods, bottles of Puerto Rican syrups, Basque *alpargatas,* and jars of Yerba maté. Three steps down and inside one finds row on row of Spanish olives and oil, sardines, eels, squid in its own ink, anchovies, fruit pastes, and boxes of Spanish nut candy. From Mexico come chiles, canned *enchiladas, tamales, tortillas,* sauces to put over them, and several kinds of *molé,* the Mexican sauce too complex to describe. Beyond this area is the authentically grocery section. On a small counter standing before a glass-fronted refrigerator case, the proprietors weigh out fresh Spanish sausage, sweet or hot, black Colombian or Puerto Rican coffees, slabs of dried cod, chunks of cheese, and thin slices of delicious Iberian ham.

Beyond the grocery department, Casa Moneo becomes transfigured; it is now a miniature bookshop with periodicals and paperbacks in Spanish and a fascinating display of post cards. The religious post cards are usually tinted in vapid, vague pinks and blues, except where enthusiasm has deepened the faces to shocking pink, turning the benign calm into incipient apoplexy. It is no surprise to find post cards featuring the fateful face of Manolete, but there is a piquancy in finding his costume embroidered in bright silk thread and the glitter of his jeweled shoulders represented by two little sequins. Another group of cards has pictures of loving couples on them, the hair and cheeks tinted with treacle and the girls' dresses embroidered in fluorescent silks; the picture itself can be flipped away from the card to reveal a tender, soulful love poem.

The same basic sentiments, now fleshed in melodies and rhythm, emerge much more insistent and *macho* from the *merengues* and sambas and *zarzuelas* which sound from the record shop that the Casa Moneo turns into at its deepest end.

In scattered cases that make the shop a maze to walk through, sit the filigrees and Aztec-style designs of Mexican silver, Toledo blades, and the gold-and-black geometry of

Toledo trinkets; Spanish wine sacks, serapes, castanets, fans; casseroles large enough for a town banquet of *paella;* dolls and perfumes from Spain; *maracas* from Cuba. Where there is an inch of space and no appropriate Hispanic product to fill it, the romantic souls of the owners put an inexpensive Japanese object, a small piece of Indian brass, and even Russian caviar and French truffles.

Bazar Français
666 Sixth Avenue (near 20th St.).

Merely to shop here for household objects makes some women feel like fine French cooks (and possibly actually improves their performances at the stove). It is an old store of firm reputation and undisputed authority, crammed with fine knives, omelette skillets, *bain maries,* heavy casseroles, and efficient corkscrews. There is very little attempt at artistic arrangements or neatly designed displays; no time for frippery in this serious place, which provides the tools of a serious art.

Isidore Grossman
139 West 22nd Street (near Sixth Ave.), CH 3-2513.

A dim vestibule and several long unrelenting flights of narrow stairs without the grace of a turn lead to a well-locked door. After an alternation of ringing and pounding, the door is opened, Mr. Grossman's spectacles glisten at you and his apron wafts small clouds of chalk dust and wood chips as you enter the loft-studio-workshop. By inclination a sculptor who creates complex, ashen structures laden with symbols of fertility and decay, Mr. Grossman must also earn a living, and this he does in a particular niche he has cut out for himself. Should the Museum of Primitive Art need to have a mask mounted, or a collector the proper base for a head of Buddha, they will very likely trudge up the interminable stairs and deliver the treasure to the judgment and skill of the maestro. It will await its turn in a dusty mélange of Maori disks, busy Sivas, fragments of Gothic altar screens, and sculptures of outraged steel—all of which inspire voluble opinions from the ready Mr. Grossman. There is no visible work bench or table (although some reasonable facsimile of such must exist in some obscure corner) and notes, addresses, and telephone numbers are written on a section of dusty wall first rubbed clean by one of the Grossman fists. But in spite of the Collier brothers disorder, the work emerges beautifully done and in impeccable taste. (Price: subject to whim.)

The Butterfly Shop

77 Madison Avenue (28th St.).

Even for the person to whom a butterfly means only the lift
and grace of summer, The Butterfly Shop is a pleasant place
to snoop. The shop is worn, but the dim, tired interior sets
off the luster of the kaleidoscopic butterfly cases, adding
glow to the luminous blue-greens, lavenders, and yellows of
the butterflies' wings.

Among the endless cases of butterflies—little and big,
pretty and magnificent, with stripes on their wings, with
arabesques, with eyes, dotted, flat-colored—and moths,
there are boxes of pinned scarabs and beetles in rich dark
tones like bits of precious stone, and boxes of praying man-
tises and spiders, their long legs tensed and waiting.

The insect and butterfly, dead and pure, are not all there
is here; earrings, cuff links, and pendants are devised of
butterflies' wings and small still lifes, consisting of butterflies
and grasses and flowers simply mounted. About the oddest
appearance of the beautiful deep blue-green of one species is
in a set of holy pictures, copies of Renaissance paintings, in
which the sections in blue have been cut out and replaced
by the blue of the butterfly, a discord in textures and a confusion of purposes which may possibly meet some tastes and
not others.

Round the World Basket and Gift Shop, Inc.

444 Third Avenue (near 31st St.).

The name is large for so small a shop, but it's not a mis-
nomer and the middle-aged couple from the Bronx who own
it take pride in the international flavor of their stock and
run the foreign names off with considerable pleasure. Especially attractive are the bamboo bird cages, the lantern-like
hanging baskets from which to trail ivy, and the international
collection of straw toys.

Shackman's

2 West 35th Street (at Fifth Ave.).

A light, amiable supermarket of small toys, tricks, and nice
nonsense in an astonishing range. Neatly set out on counters
where you may inspect and play with them—in seemly mod-
eration—are small dolls that stand or loll or conceal smaller
replicas of themselves or encase coloring pencils; miniature
cars, trains, kitchen utensils; party favors, tricks, puzzles, and
elusive little teasers for wearing away time and patience.

Hobby House

103 West 44th St. (near Sixth Ave.).

Small and wildly unneat (even for a place of this kind), the Hobby House is devoted mainly to the harder facts of recent history: guns, swords, coins, flasks, epaulets, and military decorations. A glass case holds some of the firearms and coins, but the fire helmets may be lying along with severed sections of armor and epaulets in buckets on the floor. Turn from the after-the-battle atmosphere and immerse yourself in the pile of ancient newspapers lying around, somewhere. These might give you a different glimpse of American history, presented as hot news rather than the careful distillate which seeps into history books. You might also be soothed by the trumpetings of bad news day after day, decade after decade —and here you are, still.

Nelson's Folly

860 Second Avenue (46th St.).
Open 10 to 7 P.M., Monday through Saturday.

Mr. Nelson Cowell's "folly" is hardly that at all; he has assembled a remarkably eclectic collection and an equally eclectic, faithful clientele, feats rarely accomplished by folly.

The thing he hasn't, or hasn't had, or won't have tomorrow, you could hardly name. Old Paisley shawls and patchwork blankets lie heaped on an old chest; Oriental ewers serve as vases for clumps of peacock feathers, which sway like painted clumps of swamp weed; little tables hold boxes of beads, ornaments, old stereo viewers, and obsolete coffee grinders. Inlaid cabinets conceal drawers of buttons, watches, and buckles. One window shows a fine group of ships' models (if the house has any specialties, this is the one) and the other window contains old pistols and rifles.

At any time, the large shop—somehow airy in spite of the enticing stuffing—is likely to be loaded with huge carnival masks or Italian puppets in Japanese style. You might want to buy one of the old pieces of rug which cover the floor or take home with you Mr. or Mrs. Cowell (or both); in their separate ways, they are persons of impact.

Abraham Belinsky

873 Second Avenue (between 46th and 47th Sts.).

Among the pieces of antique glass and silver which Mr. Belinsky polishes with care and patience, you will find a good, small collection of Hebriaca: old pointers, menorahs, ceremonial beakers and platters, Torah scrolls and arks and prayer books. There are often other objects around—Latin texts, antique copper and pewter trays, possibly a seventeenth-century mortar and some early German prints, but Mr. Belinsky is most quickly roused to discussion by the synagogue art about which he is well informed and enthusiastically communicative.

Frederick's Cowboy Shop

815 Eighth Avenue (opposite Madison Square Garden).
Open until 9 P.M. except on Wednesday and Saturday, when closed at 7.

Santa Fé on Eighth Avenue: from rustic natural-wood counters and shelves gleam massive silver buckles, arrogant stirrups, turquoise-studded Navaho jewelry and businesslike knives. Stacks of fringed leather jackets, fancy shirts, and tight cowboy pants crowd the shelves, along with ten-gallon hats, whips, and moccasins. Near the door, as if to lure with a strong whiff of a shop's flavor, hangs a cluster of saddles, holsters, and gunbelts, most of them highly ornamented and overstated. The overstatement is what undoubtedly attracts the photographers who rent this equipment and the visiting rodeo people who supplement their wardrobes here.

The bulk of the nonprofessional customers (and the most devoted ones) consists of the dudes whose mesquite and cactus grow in Westchester, and the boys whose dazzled eyes paint Western self-portraits—tall in the saddle, taciturn but alert, unsmiling but kindly, their invincible guns eager for the bad men in the black hats—as the atmosphere mesmerizes them. You couldn't do much more for a boy (unless he insists on a private rocket ship) than bring him here to shop.

America House

32 East 52nd Street (near Madison).

In a sense, the salesroom for the Museum of Contemporary Crafts (see page 113); founded earlier than the Museum, by the same people. More crowded and less solicitously displayed than in the Museum, the pieces still represent a well-rounded collection of craft objects currently made in the United States, in silver, enamel, glass, fabrics, wood, and jewelry. The objects are, generally, honest, sober things, but once in a while a daft note is struck, as by a mobile recently displayed—a large, sensitively balanced spoon made of irregularly meshed metal with brilliant chunks of crude stone entrapped in the mesh, swaying in the air, glittering down at the stolid wares below.

Design Center for Interiors

415 East 53rd Street (east of First Ave.).
Open 11:30 to 5:30, Monday through Saturday; to 9 P.M. on Wednesdays.

To anyone interested in shopping for modern furniture, floor or wall coverings, lamps, fabrics, or decorative objects, a visit to the Design Center can be of great value. As in the similar exhibitions in London, Copenhagen, and Milan, it is possible to see many admirably arranged groups of furnishing articles and panoramic displays of developing trends devised by leading people in the fields of decorating and designing. The single most important section to the potential shopper is the Information Bureau, which supplies pertinent information: the price of an article, its designer's name, the colors available, the manufacturer's address, shops which sell it or decorators through whom it can be bought.

Rita Ford

907 Third Avenue (54th-55th St.).
Open 10 to 6, Monday through Saturday.

Although Mrs. Ford hopes to sell off some of her miscellaneous antiques or shunt them aside, if necessary, to make room for a growing collection of old and rare musical instruments, the apples of her enthusiastic eye are the music boxes. En masse, they reveal surprising differences to the non-expert; some small machines tinkle with the anemic, sad sweetness of a Wordsworth Lucy, others rattle and roar in a beery recklessness; there are boxes that make flat little melodies in undeviating mechanical rhythms, and some that suggest the dynamics and subtler blends of tone approaching real music.

Even though the sounds offer incomplete musical experiences except to the yearners for that mystical "more innocent time," the mechanisms themselves are greatly entertaining. For instance, a Swiss chalet which, fed coins like a juke box, produces a zesty clatter with its fat music roll, drums played by Chinesey musicians, castanets and cymbals that seem to propel themselves, and—in front of the whole busy show—three minute dancing girls. Even more overwhelming is the German beer-garden box dating from about 1890. Almost the size of an armoire, the doors ornamented with a rural scene of pure *kitsch,* it too is activated by coins. The response is of vast largesse: the roller emits big metallic sounds, the piano hammers bang away at the upright strings, the cymbals clash, the xylophone clacks, the drums boom, and the triangle pings—all good and loud.

The quieter treasures are beautiful inlaid boxes, made with the care and delicacy of fine old furniture; these, of course, emit appropriately elegant sounds.

Other types of music boxes, in which the importance of sound is diminished, are the automatons, dolls which perform specific repeated acts in synchronization with concealed sound mechanisms. To the thin strains of the waltz from *Faust,* Mephisto plucks at a lute, rolls his lustrous eyes, and opens his red lips in song; a cross-legged Arab sips coffee and smokes a hookah accompanied by the unimpassioned trickle of an old popular song.

Before you are completely carried away by Mrs. Ford's passion for her boxes and lose your covetous head over these wonderful toys, remember that the most beautiful and complex run high, several hundred to two thousand dollars.

Helena Penrose

931 Third Avenue (55th St.).

Miss Penrose is considered, in the hard judgment of her peers and neighbors, absolutely the most knowing, the possessor of the strictest standards, and the best collector of Americana and American primitives of the eighteenth and the early nineteenth centuries.

The bulk of the viewable parts of her collection rests in a large basement area below the entrance. It is always unsafe to describe specific objects in this sort of establishment, but as a general guide, here are some things you might find: a huge primitive rocker made of a root and branches of a birch tree, a wonder of imagination and rude construction rather than comfort; a male figure carved by an untutored local sculptor or signmaker about a century ago. Unrefined and perfect, it is as shocking and imposing as a work of art should be. In addition, Miss Penrose has rare antique toys (she once sold a complete antique toy store as well as an apothecary's shop), stately cigar-store Indians, barber poles, scarecrows, store signs, boxes, figureheads, and furniture made by fine craftsmen and careful, courageous householders who worked empirically and surprisingly well.

A few adjoining rooms are paneled in authentic woods. One is set up as a taproom with a large fireplace, a table bearing two dozen beautifully made Lake Michigan snipe, and on the walls eight animated watercolors relating an elopement. The second room is a living room of sorts, with authentic period windows and elegant furniture. The third room makes a fine setting for a movie or a nightmare: forbidding cigar-store figures, large gilded lions, carousel giraffes, and frenzied figureheads leap frighteningly out of the dim, low-ceilinged gloom as the door opens on them.

Miss Penrose will not appraise antiques but does serve as an authenticator, and so jealously guarded is the reputation of her shop that articles are sold with the understanding that they are to be returned at the full purchase price if their authenticity is only breathed on adversely.

La Cuisinière

133 East 55th Street (near Lexington Ave.; one flight up).

The walls glisten with heavy copper pans from France and Italy; a handsome sideboard displays antique plates and bric-a-brac; molds, cookie cutters, parsley baskets (a midget lettuce basket), and bowls of appealing color and design look up from the well-arranged table. A good place for dish towels of advanced design and potholders of distinction.

Antique Porcelain Co., Inc.

48 East 57th Street (near Madison Ave.).

If you are an antique porcelain fancier ("fancier" is too light a word; at these prices it has to be an obsession) this would be one of the places for you. It is elegantly forbidding, the objects displayed in locked cases or concealed in a safe and guarded over by young women with intimidating British accents and the vocabularies of experts. However, if you're badly in need of dishes, you might look at the famous Meissen Swan service, which contains 1200 to 1400 pieces in magnificent lustrous white, each plate embossed with a swan design and carrying, as its one piece of color, a royal coat of arms. A small platter costs about $2,400, a simple plate about $1,250, and a chop platter $10,000. Of course, it *is* unique and not available at Macy's. For the smaller apartment there is a more modest Limoges set, fifteenth-century, of enamel on copper. This is *not* unique, since the Victoria and Albert Museum in London has another like it.

Simpler, more easily portable purchases may be made—a Chelsea owl dating from the middle of the eighteenth century (at $29,000); an exquisitely shaped and colored pineapple tureen, the only one of its kind ($8,500); a small box wrought of four kinds of gold ($27,000); an antique Spanish pendant, one of the baubles of the royal family ($175,000). A tasteful hostess gift, the kind sent by British bloods to their hosts, would be one of the Chelsea "toys"—small porcelain charms, some converted into seals and the larger ones into perfume bottles. They are perfect, enchanting, and modestly priced ($100 to $750). In a small case by itself is a Sevres bowl of a high white glaze, with a pinkish knob on the bottom and resting on a support of three rams' heads. On closer examination, the bowl turns out to be a breast, whose small pink nipple is stamped with the crest and crown of Marie Antoinette. For $21,000 it is undoubtedly the best buy—a conversation piece, a symbol of an age, a spur to the imagination.

Pan American Shop

822 Lexington Avenue (near 63rd St.).

Playful and colorful, like many of the Mexican objects it houses, this would be a good place to buy something for that mythical monster—the friend who has everything. Possibly he just doesn't have a tin bird cage painted shocking pink, silly and lovely. If he does, try him with a stolid, puritanic mermaid of Oaxacan clay or a Peruvian poncho. His wife might respond to a *quexquematl* or a coarse, brilliant *rebozo* from Mitla. Should these fail, buy some yards of beautiful hand-woven materials from Guatemala or Mexico and suggest they make their own gifts.

George Karger Antiques

1145½ Second Avenue (near 60th St.).

Once a traveler, photographer, always and still an inveterate collector, Mr. Karger, a round man with beguiling bounce, has now settled down to selling and renting (to TV and advertising photographers) his collections. A general description of the Karger treasures could be his own phrase: "offbeat accessories," a definition which runs off a little at the ill-defined edges unless weathervanes, duck decoys, Naughty-Nelly bootjacks, and a large tin hat once used as a shop sign may be considered accessories, and they might be at that.

Among the many, two or three kinds of articles seem to take dominance by superiority of numbers: old shop signs, marine articles, and old games and gambling devices. Some of this last group are of the period of recent-sliding-into-past, like a chuck-a-luck cage or an old version of the fruit-and-bell wheel, or a keno device; some are quite old, a gambling wheel used in coffee houses, for instance. To accompany these iniquities, there are old playing cards.

Be prepared to be told that this or that is not for sale. It is never a question of personal animus or of holding out for a price; Mr. Karger simply can't part with some of his things, particularly one or two gambling devices. He may possibly rent them to you, though.

A. L. Brandon

852 Lexington Avenue (near 65th St.).

This is the Mecca of the people who call, "Backward, turn backward, o Time, in your flight"—of those who send old-fashioned cards crowded with birds, flowers, and fair-haired children, and who love old playbills and posters of the turn of the century, extravagantly sentimental and simple-minded, in roaring colors.

These are, however, only a portion of the stock, which consists also of paper ornaments: strips of paper lace; of scallops and tassels; of flower bouquet designs; of roses, horses, bowers, kittens, and birds; of minute silver knives and forks (still paper); and of shiny letters of the alphabet. Flocks of angels can be taken apart to be mounted in ornate silver-paper frames. The store is small and busy, often crowded with patient lovers of minutiae, seriously searching out the ingredients of pleasurable, useless projects, an engaging contrast to the rest of the purposeful city.

Juergens

1100 Third Avenue (64th-65th St.).
Open 10 to 5, Monday through Saturday; closed February and March.

Possibly the only way to describe Mr. Juergen's unclassifiable private museum, housed in a small store and its cellar, is simply to mention a small portion of objects available within a short period:

For the necrophilic, skulls in various stages of decomposition, shrunken heads, head-hunters' trophy heads and the baskets in which to carry them with ease and refinement; a glass box containing a wax doll lying on a luxurious couch, surrounded by fringed silk, flowers, and little angels—a souvenir of a dead child, made to be carried in a funeral procession or kept on a French mantel.

Less-developed tastes might be satisfied with a Mandarin wedding headdress in very thin metal and adorned with minute florets and strings of beads, or an imposing Naga headdress or American Indian costume of skin and beads, or a mask from New Ireland, a wooden Dogon mask, a Congo mask of brass, a gold mask from pre-Columbian Peru, or ancient pottery from Mexico and South America and clay pipes from Africa. Of cloths, there are rare Coptic pieces, ancient Peruvian cloth, regal old saris, heavily embroidered Serbian costumes, tapa cloth, bark cloth, and ecclesiastical cloths. There are Egyptian antiquities and Chinese; a pile of Javanese puppets; African stools; baskets from India and Polynesia; a gamelang instrument and an African xylophone; commemorative bits of pottery; a huge Arabian water jug; a fine group of Congo knives; shields from the Solomon Islands, Australia, and Assam; icons; two very beautiful carved bamboo door posts from China; East Indian playing cards; an old digitorium; a primitive sterilizer which sprayed carbolic acid too freely; and, infinitely, et cetera.

If this sort of thing means anything at all to you, or if you are looking for the absolutely most unusual gift, by all means go. Try to remember, when you do, that Mr. Juergens, a gentle, cultivated man, is hard of hearing. This should present no problems; just speak distinctly and not too fast.

The Irish Book Shop

876 Lexington Avenue (near 65th St.).

The Irish Book Shop is quiet and genteel, gently looked after by two exquisitely spoken Irish ladies, one of whom is knowing and the other beautifully polite. Their wares are good examples of Irish crafts—briar pipes; Irish linens; woolen stoles and steamer rugs in subtle, muted tones; poplin ties; and delicate, pearly Belleek China. In racks and on the walls are hand-colored prints and poems inspired by Irish scenes, and folk sayings decorated with the coiled, interlaced designs of the Book of Kells. The cherished Connemara marble is displayed in ashtrays and boxes of simple design.

If you're passionately Irish (and there probably is no other way to be Irish), you will be delighted to find your family coat of arms available for purchase here, and also an ancestral map of Ireland which lists most of the Gaelic families and traces their lines of descent. The Irish Book Shop also carries books on Irish literature, folklore, and history; Irish genealogies; works of Irish authors generally; and Gaelic primers and study books, as well as the annual volumes of the Irish Text Society, in English and Gaelic.

If you have no burning interest in things Irish and no Irish friends for whom to buy gifts, stop by anyhow, if it's convenient, to hear English as it should be spoken and rarely is.

Robert Abels

860 Lexington Avenue (65th St.).

To an inhabitant of the atomic world, the Abels collection has a rare innocence; it speaks of a time when combat was direct and uncomplicated, one man against one man, and no ominous trail of impersonal death as an aftermath of battle. The studded maces and long war axes, the graceful swords and arquebuses, the wheel locks and the flintlocks, made their simple, final statements and that was that. The modes of protections, too, have naivete; what gases and vapors can a shield bar, or a porous coat of chain mail, or even a coat of armor so heavy and tightly jointed that the knight encased in it had to be hoisted to the back of his horse?

Never completely removed from warfare, there are, however, some things here to look at and buy (assuming you're a collector and can afford it) which wear enough of the aesthetic to blur their essential purpose: magnificently ornamented sword sheaths, exquisitely carved and inlaid pistols, finely detailed miniature armor, and a steel horse-mask of a clean, noble design which would suit perfectly the wall of a large, modern room.

Or, if your tastes run to purer, simpler sadism, you might consider a pair of thumbscrews.

Vivienne Colle

211 East 66th Street (between Second and Third Aves.).

Fancy and whim are the prime ingredients of the objects Vivienne Colle designs or makes (with the help—she insists —of Benjamin, her tiny poodle). The being and seeming of their things are rarely the same: a pair of children's mittens seems to be a set of girl-and-boy puppets, or vice versa; a black felt hand with red fingernails and a paste diamond on one finger conceals a tape measure and could act as a pin cushion. A section of patchwork quilt turns into a skirt; another skirt is a field of fat appliquéd strawberries; plain blue jeans are lifted into fantasy by the laying on of cloth labels, watermelon slices, fish, and fruits. And what was born a nice quiet sweater now gives off the sound of Indian bells.

As pleased with other people's whimsey as with her own, Vivienne Colle likes to design sentimental, commemorative gestures. For instance, if your husband had a huge poker win and shared it with you, she might make you a skirt with

moneybags as pockets and lined with a print of playing cards,
to please him. A good part of the pleasure of designing it
with her (and, maybe, Benjamin) will be the untrammeled
conversation, darting from Benjamin's habits to psychother-
apy, from the eternal verities to the charms of a pair of realistic eyes painted on a cup, from the color of a piece of
ribbon to the problems of alcoholism.

Prices are difficult to gauge because there are no similar
objects to compare with; judged as clothing, they are rather
high, as works of imagination, not very.

Grapevine Antiques

1331 Second Avenue (70th St.).

The Grapevine is devoted mainly to Americana in the
stricter sense of that classification, American antiques that
date from before 1880. Other than some pretty little German
calling cards of the nineteenth century, almost all the neat
display consists of American furniture, china, pictures, and
homespuns in shawls and rugs. The objects are placed as
they might be in a small museum, appropriate to each other
and in nice balance; and the owner, Mr. Calvert—grave,
polite, and expert—carries with him the same aura of quiet
and order, giving more the impression of curator than owner.

M. Drexel

1294 Third Avenue (near 74th St.).

Not quite rarefied and selective enough to be an antique
shop nor omnivorous enough to be an emporium, Drexel's
falls somewhere between both categories or shuttles between
them. Some days the window may carry a magnificent pair
of Japanese Emperor and Empress dolls, quite old, dressed
in exquisite copies of ceremonial robes; shortly after, there
will be a display of nothing impressive. But the shop is worth
looking into, if only to gaze at the handsome acting couple
who run it, assuming that they have not gone back to the
stage or Hollywood.

Helen Cole

963 Lexington Avenue (70th St.).

Gentle gags and pretty trivia are the main occupation of the
street-floor store. This is the place to buy such small conversation pieces as mink-tailed dusters, little individual fire
extinguishers (for pyromaniacs who can't resist the impulse
but don't want to do too much damage), plastic paper-

weights with real quarters and dimes imbedded in them, thread spools ringed with pearls and capped by minute flowers, wine cork de-drippers, and small music boxes which are the bases for caricature figures. Not all the objects are playful; among the featherweights there are some very attractive boxes and trays, mats in unusual colors, and impressive candle holders.

The imposing upper story is dedicated to magnificent structures of artificial fruits and flowers in trees, towers, wreaths, cornucopias, and espaliers—imaginative, widely varied, expensive, and lovely.

Americana Shop

1320 Third Avenue (near 75th St.).

"Americana" has the unkempt, promising look of a pleasant household attic, not so crowded as to be confusing, nor so logically arranged as to erase surprise. What any antique shop may have from day to day is unpredictable, but generally the range of objects here dates from the later decades of the nineteenth century through the early twentieth, and there are almost always boxes of various materials, toys, homemade paintings of a certain hideous charm, and fat letters off old storefronts.

Mr. Grossman, the proprietor, has a passion for old signs, some of which he keeps in the back (which is very much like the front, except that someone has forgotten to take down a piece of wall). With luck you may find a piece of display art which scorned the meagerly functional and trumpeted its mission with mother-of-pearl inlay, gilt, and banners and arabesques of floral ornament. Two of the more imposing specialties of the house are Thonet bentwood chairs and rockers and a collection of Tiffany vases. A third specialty is the geniality of Mr. Grossman, who spends a good portion of his day rushing for containers of coffee for his friends and customers, a distinction which dissolves rapidly in the flow of coffee and conversation.

Mattie Haskins' Irish Record Shop

1332 Third Avenue (near 76th St.).

More sentimental and folksy than its confrere on Lexington Avenue, this shop leans toward shillelaghs and the rebel faces of Michael Collins and Terence McSwiney on picture postcards. Clay pipes, tins of Irish tobacco and snuff, boxes of Irish chocolates, canisters of Irish tea, John McCormack records, and sheet music which yearns for Kathleen and

Mavourneen make a pure Gaelic distillate which may have been captured in the perfume called "Blarney Kiss."

At almost any hour, one can hear, mingled with the strains of an old recorded ballad, the dewy accents of the salespeople as they discuss their tea: Shall we have it now? Has the water boiled? Has it steeped enough? And one by one they disappear into the back of the store which has (not surprisingly) been designed as an Irish cottage, complete with window boxes full of artificial flowers and a shaggy dog lying across its front door.

As redolent and pure as the rest of the articles is the literature sold: religious matter; a wide variety of works on Irish genealogy and history; booklets on fortune-telling through cards; copies of *Old Moore's Almanac,* featuring importantly a list of the fairs of Ireland. Like the first statement of a leitmotif, there stands, outside the door, a rack full of newspapers from Limerick, Donegal, Derry, Tipperary, Ulster, Connacht, Kerry, and Sligo, three or four weeks old, it is true, but still authentic voices from the Ould Sod.

French & Company, Inc.

978 Madison Avenue (77th St.).

The storehouse of the Metropolitan Museum of Art and Hearst's San Simeon have not been renovated, but French & Company, their rival, has been. In recently modernized quarters (this means the frayed elegance of the nineteenth century has been transformed into pristine nineteenth-century elegance), French dispenses Gobelin tapestries, medieval armor, antique furniture, and comparable immensities which few can afford, but many can enjoy looking at.

The White Stove

249 East 77th Street (between Second and Third Aves.).

A cheerful sort of bedlam, full of the extravagance of surrealism and none of its terror. Old-fashioned sleds float near the ceiling, old shutters loom in unexpected places, kitchen alarm clocks and ornate mantel monsters proclaim wildly different times, in agreement only in that each is wrong, and like a varicolored ribbon tying them all together, wind rows and rows of old paperbacked books.

If you can squeeze your way through the clutter and the white potbellied stove and the lady decorators, you might find almost anything, including a boxful of old canceled checks in many unbelievable sums backed by imposing names. They won't buy you much, but think of the prestige.

Lar

1034 Lexington Avenue (near 74th St.).

There is a sign in the door which says "Please come in and just look around." The proprietors really mean it, offering you a polite greeting, and then a happy respite from salesmanship. The shop is small, but so well arranged that the amazing diversity of objects stays in harmonious balance, while each object maintains its separate attractiveness.

The purchasing at Lar has been controlled by good taste and that only, with no attempt to out-shock or out-chic, even in its most unusual things; rugs made of Mexican coyote fur or goat fur may seem strange, but they are chastely designed and escape completely the wild aura of the exotic. No period, nation, or price range is especially emphasized, although Lar shows nothing extraordinarily expensive, and a number of prices are pleasantly low. A recent variety of objects included an Indian printing block, two hundred years old, and modern Scandinavian pottery; a modern rug from Israel and a piece of eighteenth-century Chinese embroidery; Mexican branding irons and a Balinese mask; an Oriental whale-oil lamp and a Chilean blanket. Most of the objects are one of a kind or not readily duplicated. The stock may be completely different by the time you go, but it will assuredly be handsome, and maybe there will still be available an ingenious little Chinese box in which you can carry your opium.

There is another Lar store at 28 East 49th Street, which is between Fifth and Madison Avenues, in the neighborhood of St. Patrick's Cathedral and the Rockefeller Center buildings.

Paprikas Weiss

1504 Second Avenue (near 79th St.).

The name is the lure and function of this shop for a good number of housekeepers for whom paprika in neat little tins is merely red dust. At Weiss's they can get it sweet, semi-sweet, or hot, and packed that very day.

From a large, square bin which fronts the door, the Middle European *hausfrau* can squeeze, heft, examine, discard, and then choose a Hungarian salami (now manufactured in Holland), and from a decorative display of dozens of kinds of ladles, find the exactly right one. If she plans to bake, she buys heavy, stiff *lekvar*, ready-made *strudel* sheets, chooses the nuts and poppy seeds and has them freshly ground, and then selects a goose-feather pastry brush for glazing the cake.

Even under the safe assumption that most travelers wouldn't want to stop for a bout of *strudel*-making, Paprikas Weiss should be explored in its role of miniature Middle European market, with a section devoted to Gugelhupf forms, liter measures, and gram scales; a section of spices and herb tea; and one of nuts and candy. Czech frankfurters, hams, pickles, and Carlsbad *oblatten* jostle Hungarian acacia honey and tins of Hungarian goose-livers.

To the left of the entrance, in the nostalgia corner, stands a rack of Hungarian records—czardas, Gypsy ballads, and marches. Near them hang a few embroidered peasant blouses, the remnants of a once-brilliant and popular folk art, and challis headkerchiefs in the traditional flower patterns still worn here by older Polish and Czech women. To counter the nostalgia, there is a conspicuously placed and lively collection of international cookbooks, ranging all the way from Jewish, through related varieties of Central European, to East Indian and Chinese.

Mr. Edward Weiss, the son of the proprietor ("Paprikas"?), is well-informed about the various products he sells and very pleasant about answering foolish questions, when he's not too occupied weighing out *lekvar* or gnarled Hungarian sausage.

Museum Shop (*Museum of Natural History*)

79th Street at Central Park West (see page 106 for hours and directions).

Handicrafts from Africa and Asia, reproductions of pre-Columbian jewelry, nature books and records, rock specimens, shells, and educational toys, many of them not available elsewhere and all meticulously priced.

Anne Benjamin

1398 Third Avenue (between 79th and 80th Sts.).

A flea market of American objects, mainly turn-of-the-century —mounds of them, heaps of them, hanging from the shelves, from the ceilings, bursting out of closets, weighing down shelves, trailing off hangers; objects containing objects; wash bowls and urns perched on old garden furniture, Franklin stoves laden with patchwork quilts and brass bathroom fixtures; brass eagles and old picture frames staring down from overhead beams and ancient lace umbrellas sprouting from old vases. To the nonexpert the effect is a little overwhelming; to the purchaser on a dedicated search it should prove a promising place—particularly to anyone interested in old dolls and toys and lacy greeting cards damp with sentiment.

H. Roth and Son

1577 First Avenue (80th St.).

Beside the mainstays of poppy seeds, *lekvar*, paprika, and the dried fruits, roots, berries, and grains which make up a large part of Hungarian cooking and dosing, Roth's have seemingly appointed themselves the suppliers of primitive farm tools to the Middle European section. Where a man can use a large scythe or a full-curved sickle in the tight terrain of the East 80's is a minor mystery, but there they are, gleaming out oddly and purposefully into the field of First Avenue, waiting to be used by an old First Avenue peasant, smoking one of Roth's fancy pipes with a two-foot cherry-wood stem.

Globe-Trotter Antiques

1046 Madison Avenue (near 80th St.).

Save this one, if you can, for a rainy day when business is slow and talk can be undisturbed. Mrs. Potter, the owner, has a cordial, responsive face and enjoys talking about dogs, objects, and people, all with an expression of charmed surprise. Scorning specialization, Mrs. Potter has amassed an assortment of rings, bracelets, earrings, hatpins, dance cards, crystal, glass, beer steins, pewter, and dissociated chessmen from many countries and many periods, and ranging widely in price.

For the antique lover who cannot afford a fine "Blanc de Chine" Siva or a Nuremberg rooster of rock crystal and silver, there is a $3.00 window of constantly-changing articles—old costume jewelry (but not old enough to be antique), odd hair ornaments, a lighter, little bottles, a small evening bag —anything which hasn't sold at five or six dollars, or something saved for thirty or forty years which didn't reach great value and won't, or simply something Mrs. Potter can't bear to look at any more. They might make unusual gifts.

Metropolitan Museum of Art Shops

82nd Street at Fifth Avenue (see page 107 for hours and directions).

There are actually three shops. The first, to the immediate left of the entrance, carries an extensive collection of art books (some small and less expensive than you might expect) and prints. The second, a circular counter in the main hall, handles jewelry reproductions of some of the museum's pieces: a small Roman horse, stylized Luristan animals, heavy earrings, bizarre and beautiful, bracelets crude but by no means primitive. Some of them are surprisingly cheap (well under $5.00) and others, of course, go higher, but the prices are never excessive for such unique and carefully made pieces. Also in the main halls, along the side, is a set of cases exhibiting an enormous variety of Christmas and greeting cards, ranging in price from five cents for a simple old wood-cut to ten times that for elaborately mounted Oriental prints. The card shop is one in which you *must* do your Christmas shopping early; after Thanksgiving it becomes difficult, and almost impossible on week ends.

Northland Gifts

1232 Lexington Avenue (83rd-84th Sts.).

A little out of the usual ways, but worth looking for if you're fond of Scandinavian utensils, pottery, handwork, and decorative objects. As in most Scandinavian shops (it must be the interreaction of temperament and design) the bowls and pitchers and vases are arranged in an orderly, pleasing manner with little drama; prices, also, are undramatically sensible.

The Gallery Shop—Brooklyn Museum

(See page 126 for directions and hours.)

Echoing the Brooklyn Museum's primacy in the field of primitive and folk arts, The Gallery Shop, which is part of the Museum, maintains a well-selected collection of contemporary folk art from over thirty countries, attractively arranged and comfortably priced. For inconsequential sums one can buy dolls and toys from Germany, Mexico, Sweden, India, Denmark, Japan, Peru, and even the United States, the dolls ranging in style from urbane Japanese dancer dolls to the round little velvet ball with faces that the Navahos make.

As decorative pieces, there are Chinese teakwood ornaments, Korean brass bowls, Indian hand-blocked cloth, forceful Eskimo carvings, and some of the Eastern dolls which are too beautiful and frail for ruthless handling by children. Among the loveliest of the objects are two from Yugoslavia—a carved wooden shepherd's cup and a one-stringed instrument, also of carved wood, accompanied by a bow whose line has great dash (these are available in several sizes)—and a collection of Japanese prints, carefully made in the ancient wood-block technique and reproducing with extraordinary fidelity masterpieces of Japanese print-making.

Possibly the rarest pieces, and inexpensive considering their rarity, are clay Karaja figurines brought from the jungles of Brazil by a complex combination of every kind of transportation except skis. They are simple and engaging human figures, brightened by a judicious use of color: women working, fishermen, and exultant athletes.

The more utilitarian objects, meticulously chosen for their pleasing design and modest price, make highly acceptable gifts, as do the many pieces of jewelry—some made by modern craftsmen of Mexico, Iran, and Yugoslavia, some by American Navahos, and some made here after the designs of ancient worlds: earrings and cuff links after Greek, Renaissance, and pre-Columbian designs; pendants in the Egyptian mode and in the style of Central American gold ornaments.

Also available for sale is a good collection of inexpensive art books and cards and, for free, a catalogue from which you may, at some future time, order by mail.

Women's Clothing

There is a type of women's clothing in New York which has the "New York look" to some out-of-towners. To uptown New Yorkers it has the "Village look"; to the Village it has the "Provincetown look." It is the international-art-colony look (expensive edition) that speaks of Taos, Woodstock, Saint-Tropez, and, possibly, Safad. The characteristics are extremes of color, either passionate or dimmed to muteness, combined in startling juxtapositions, and a pervasive asexuality in design, an insistent denial of female lumps and bumps. Blouses are rarely fitted, and sweaters are large and loose to keep breasts obscure; slacks are cut for concave thighs, and waists are rarely defined because that might also define hips and behinds. And though their designers scorn fully equipped girls, there is no profit in scorning these clothes, because they do play dazzling games with colors and fabrics and invent wonderfully entertaining and tricky accessories.

Some of these shops that feature such fashions also stock men's "leisure clothes" in addition to gifts and small household items of unusual design and color. As one might expect of such citadels of taste and imagination, the stores are interestingly arranged and so are the windows and the personnel.

Robert Leader

146 East 54th Street (near Third Ave.).

Mr. Leader is as happy a proprietor as you'll find anywhere but in a liquor store during the Christmas holidays. He likes his customers, the clothing he sells (some of which he designs), and the lush fabrics and patterns, with a special affection for the more frantic creations, whether or not they sell. Besides the good will and jollity, he dispenses much good-looking clothing in the anti-Gina mode mainly, with a few tight-bodiced exceptions thrown in.

Jax

15 East 57th Street (east of Fifth Ave.).

The clothing here has both the restraints and flights of modern jazz and of classic abstract art—beautiful, cool, and intellectual; what you might get if Mondrian or Mies van der Rohe were designing clothes.

Ellen Herbert

44 East 52nd Street (near Madison Ave.; upstairs).
Tuesdays and Thursday, 11 to 7; Mondays, Wednesdays, Fridays, 11 to 6; Saturdays, 12 to 6.

Ellen Herbert has a sharp eye for color and design, responsiveness to the bold gestures of Italian and French clothes, and a clientele whose tastes match hers. They are mainly theater and television people, which accounts for the odd shop hours and for the uniquely dramatic quality of most of her clothes and accessories; and, since these are very often to be worn in public appearances, the suits, dresses, and coats are one of a kind.

She has a small, carefully selected group of French suits, and blouses and dresses of French materials in classic models and in current styles. "Fantasia Italiana" wafts through much of the stock: dashing sweaters in unexpected colors, velveteen pajamas in the colors of the Palio of Siena, blouses in startling and beautiful patterns. (Alterations on all these are done well and quickly.)

In the heaped hodgepodge of the apartment-shop lie, hang, and trail imported gloves, bags, boxes, cuff links, mounds of handsome junk jewelry, stoles, handkerchiefs, and dolls, through which you can wander (but carefully, since there is always some box dangerously underfoot) as you sip from the mug of coffee hospitably proffered by the house as soon as you enter.

Not for the timid purse or ego.

Women's Haberdashers

554 Madison Avenue (55th St.); also Carlton House, 680 Madison Avenue.

The designer here has the distinction of being the only American asked to show his styles to Elizabeth II of England and, it is reported, one model from this source was bought by eight (well, maybe six) members of the royal family. The assembled royal females thus dressed wouldn't necessarily be as dreary a sight as you might imagine because, using simple basic styles of meticulous cut, the workroom plays infinite variations on good themes, using extraordinarily lovely and unique materials. The imported fabrics are worked into ensembles of dress-coat, suit-coat, and skirt-coat, any of which may be purchased separately.

The prices can be frightening if your financial level is department-store basement, but these clothes stay trustworthy and loyal practically forever. The salesroom is airy and soothing in color, the saleswomen are attractive, knowing women with high-style accents, and the clientele has the lovely smell of good grooming and money.

Tomas

609 Madison Avenue (near 58th St.).

Ropy, magnificent sweaters for men and women, startling cuff links, a steady parade of shirts and blouses in juicy colors, and stimulating oddities scattered around.

Chequer

816 Third Avenue (near 50th St.).

An unusually handsome shop where imagination has been bridled just enough by a sense of order. The sparsely and tastefully dressed window is backed by a quiet version of a Mediterranean bead curtain and the interior is a clever arrangement of black and red on white, hence the name. The clothing and accessories for men and women are meticulously chosen, in limited ranges of design but cut in a great variety of fabrics and color. In addition, Chequer makes it a point to show some good, chaste jewelry, many glistening yards of beads, and a selection of international ornaments— silk flower balls from Japan, Burmese lacquer and gold-leaf boxes, African trade cloth, bamboo wind chimes, toy horses from India, and Tarot cards—any of which make fine gifts for those friends who are dreamers of far-off places.

Parisette

411 Fifth Avenue (37th St.).

French and Italian sweaters, gloves, bags, and scarves; also imported and domestic suits, blouses, skirts, and coats. Although the selections are not extensive, they are almost invariably choice and quite reasonably priced. This is one of the few places where the word "import" doesn't necessarily mean the loss of *all* your spending money.

Fava-San

139 East 61st Street (near Lexington Ave.; one flight up).

Out of a minute workroom and a not-much-larger show room, come some beautiful coats, suits, and dresses, designed, with appropriate dash, in the avant-garde French or Italian manner. Unfortunately, there is little that you can take away with you; orders usually take ten days to two weeks to fill. If you have the time to wait, these are worth waiting for and very decently priced for the workmanship, fabric, and creativeness that go into them.

Marthe Alice Schweitzer

755 Madison Avenue (near 65th St.).

Not for the tweedy type or the woman who lives in sensible shirtwaist dresses; the heavy silks and stiff brocades in elegant evening styles are for *infantas* and subtle *femmes fatales*, suggesting crown jewels and court intrigue. The prices of some of these confections should come as no surprise.

À La Carte

780 Madison Avenue (between 66th and 67th Sts.).

If one were to take a gifted child with a highly developed color sense and a good deal of imagination and let her loose in a museum of rare fabrics with a doll to drape she might come up with an À La Carte collection. Cut and styling are of no great consequence here; the interest lies in combinations of colors, fabrics, and ornaments, which are always extraordinary and almost always successful. For instance, a blouse may be pale blue, its cummerbund orange, and the skirt beneath it pink with large appliqués of gold; a monochrome dress may have an apron of embroidered Chinese silk panels. The decor is suitably surprising, with a leaning to amusing turn-of-the-century monstrosities—a gilded corset-display figure, high-buttoned boots, and old toys. Prepare to spend.

GREENWICH VILLAGE

The Village has a number of clothing shops, particularly on 4th and 8th Streets and Greenwich Avenue, which feature both casual wear and sportswear (interestingly enough, the least *sportif* segment of New York's population is addicted to the most aggressively sporty clothing) some of which is wildly exaggerated and some of it just exaggerated enough to make for comment but not unwearability. The following merit some time and the effort of walking an extra block or two when you make the Village tour (page 70).

Et Cetera
29 West 8th Street (smaller shop at 177 W. 4th).

One of the few places for high style in sizes 6, 7, and 8. Only a few basic styles—with variations in collar and pocket arrangements—appear in the dresses, suits, and coats, but the styling is imaginative and executed in unusual fabrics and colors.

The End
118 Macdougal Street

A basement shop with an incomprehensible name might suggest an atmosphere too *outré* for usable clothing. However, the dresses, blouses, and shorts are sanely good-looking; the same is true of the intelligent, amiable girl who runs the shop and does some of the designing.

Hanlan's
51 Greenwich Avenue

Bright, inventive ideas in separates, and not expensive. Where clothing doesn't crowd the shop, there are groups of accessories of the same engaging type.

Career and Campus
56 East 8th Street

Dresses, skirts, blouses, sweaters, and accessories in young styles in a sizable and inexpensive variety.

Sarin
40 University Place

Distinctively styled blouses, sweaters, scarves, and other accessories; not cheap, but then you wouldn't expect them to be.

Top and Bottom Shop
164 West 4th Street

The very explicit name introduces, of course, sweaters, skirts, slacks, and other tops and bottoms of good quality in a wide range of styles and fabrics, at moderate prices.

NOTE: Village shops tend to open late—some as late as noon—and to stay open late. Many are closed Mondays.

Men's Clothing

The Goliath-David misproportion of space devoted to women's clothing and men's clothing is based on the supposition that a man's tour is not wrapped around a core of shopping as a woman's frequently is. Also, there are fewer men's shops numerically and, usually, their bland satisfactory character (except for size) is very much like that of the shops at home.

It is a matter of general knowledge that most department stores have good men's shops (particularly *Saks Fifth Avenue* at Fifth Ave. and 49th St.) and that there is a fabled, mold-making *Brooks Brothers* (346 Madison Ave., at 44th St.); a fabulous *Sulka* (405 Park Ave., at 54th St.); a quiet, aristocratic *Knize* (24 E. 56th St.); an *Abercrombie and Fitch* (the lodge of the great hunters and fishermen at 45th St. and Madison Ave.); a *Kaiser's* (408 Sixth Ave.) which brings handsome sobriety back to Greenwich Village clothing; and a *Nica-Rattner* (696 Fifth Ave.) for solid British tweeds and Burberry's. Many other shops of lesser, but thoroughly respectable stature, line Madison and Fifth Avenues between 42nd and 57th Streets.

The flair and elegance slowly seeping into the clothing of the American male take some of their quality from such accessories as are available at:

Dominique France (53 E. 52nd St.), specialists in smooth, soft silks in dressing gowns, ties, and shirts from France.

Battaglia (45 E. 50th St.), whose sweaters are hand-made and dashing, and whose sports coats properly belong on the backs of Italian movie stars and aspirants to that class.

Alexander Shields (484 Park Avenue), whose international stock is chosen with the care lavished on fine *objets*.

John Northman (11 E. 5th St.), with fine ready-to-wear but more absorbed in making good monogrammed shirts and beautiful dressing gowns to your order.

NOTE: The prices of the preceding four match the height of their styles.

Men's Town and Country (594 Lexington Avenue) and *Casual-Aire* (7 Greenwich Avenue in the Village, and at 665 Lexington Avenue) offer collegiate elegance and the illusion of eternal youth at moderate prices. Seek out, also, *Tomas* and *Chequer* (for both, see page 263) for men's accessories, and for Italian and English shoes *Lefcourt* (400 Madison Ave.) has an imaginative assortment.

You may not know the stranger shores of the men's accessory world, though. Watch, sometime when you're walking in the upper East 40's and 50's, for shops of exquisite refinement and rare decor, often so elaborate as to hide altogether items of vulgar trade: in a canopied store window, elegantly decorated with small pieces of modern sculpture and arrangements of parasols and unique toys, you may discern very short bathing trunks, open at the sides and laced, little shapely *lederhosen*, bravely colored shirts and ties, and sybaritic lounging clothes. Similar shops appear in considerable number in the Village and one or two are blossoming on upper Madison Avenue, replete with delicate chic and affectation.

Jewelry—Ancient, Old, Modern, Avant-Garde

People with money for burning need not be told about *Van Cleef and Arpels* (744 Fifth Ave.), *Cartier's* (Fifth Ave. at 52nd St.), *Black, Starr and Gorham* (594 Fifth Ave.), *Mario Buccellati* (703 Fifth Ave.), or *Tiffany's* (whose irresistibly ravishing windows, facing Fifth Avenue and 57th Street, lured a couple of jewel thieves into succumbing not long ago—uncaught, so far); people hanging lower on fortune's wheel might content themselves quite well by buying their baubles in one of the lesser palaces mentioned below.

Greenwich Village earnestly works at making and/or selling jewelry in little shops (or half-shops) strung along Macdougal Street, West 8th Street, and especially

West 4th Street. On the latter (the south side, between Sixth Ave. and Bedford) you will probably pass by a shop with impenetrably dusty windows and an unused, locked look; that would be *Carrie's*, an old, good shop, stubbornly unchanged and unneatened through the years, disdainful of the artsy-craftsy shoots going up around it. (Don't go before noon; even then it might be closed.) A bit farther west, at 184, is *Margaret Moore's*, as bright and modern as Carrie's is not, glittering with fascinating beads and semiprecious stones strung and mounted in a number of pleasing ways. Macdougal Street houses the studios where silver is tormented into unreasonable shapes, but you may like it, even en masse.

Among the paper lanterns, hamburgers, sadistic greeting cards, and convulsive lamps on 8th Street (between Fifth and Sixth Aves.) you will find three outstanding jewelry shops, totally different from each other:

Wedding Rings (at 50 W. 8th St.) is the historian of this group. Its special interest is old rings and copies of old rings with ceremonial meanings, particularly matrimonial. This is where you would find copies of ancient Greek and Roman rings, rings of the Renaissance, and Hebrew rings of three centuries, among many others from various places and times.

Paul A. Lobel (at 33 W. 8th St.; one flight up). In a light, cool area which breathes a calm that is unusual for this frantic neighborhood, Mr. Lobel has placed a counter and suspended several display cases to show his imaginative yet classically controlled modern jewelry and figures, some in gold, though most are of silver. The same respect for the essential, fluid line that goes into his sculpture and caricatures in silver (look for a six-handed conductor and an Indian who is also a tepee, if they haven't already been sold) is maintained in the jewelry which is never cluttered or outrageous, but consistently well-designed and carefully executed.

Sam Kramer (29 W. 8th St.; one flight up). Where Mr. Lobel's field is imagination bridled, the neighboring Mr. Kramer's is imagination unbridled; the former is clean shaven and undramatic looking, the latter has dark hair and full dark beard, drooping sad eyes, a drink in his hand, a wire through one pierced ear lobe; 33 is a free and open place, 29 is dark and dense. The Kramer credo is to startle (himself, too) and he succeeds by using extraordinary materials in curious contexts flowing into undisciplined shapes. Glass eyes will stare up at you out of silver massed in the forms of pathology; angry, distorted anatomical forms, studded with what might be gallstones, leap at you from the crowded cases; you might find a ring made around a tooth, a piece of ore, an insect's carapace or a legitimate jewel. The idea of these objects as jewelry may be shocking, but try to stay and stare long enough to find that they are, at the least, venturesome and occasionally beautiful.

OTHER VILLAGE JEWELERS

Objects Big and Small (48 Greenwich Ave.). In the mass of casually assorted things, you may find attractive inexpensive pieces of old jewelry.

Julien Goodenow (18 Christopher St.). Chaste, discreet designs in good, reliable metals.

Village Jewel Box (31 E. 8th St.). An immense collection of earrings in a wide range of styles and prices.

THIRD AVENUE ANTIQUE JEWELRY (40TH TO 65TH STREETS)

Martin's, at 64th Street.

Cole Galleries, 929 Third Avenue (near 56th St.).

Michael Hoffman, 917 Third Avenue (near 55th St.).

B. Harris and Sons (25 East 48th St.) is one of a number of attractive and reputable jewelry shops located on and around Madison Avenue between 47th and 62nd Streets. A rewarding stroll if you're seriously interested in expensive glitter.

Roman Gold

137 East 56th Street.

Italian, golden, in styles that look like large, assured Roman or Milanese matrons.

Two antique button stores have converted much of their accumulations into unusual cuff links and earrings, or will convert buttons still in their pristine state for you:

Lucia Lundene

On the east side of Third Avenue between 46th and 47th Sts.

Inspired by the promptings of her husband—who is a violin instructor and looks absolutely right for the role—and after a quick appraisal of the seriousness of a customer's interest,

Mrs. Lundene will drag out cigar box after cigar box full of buttons of Dresden china, of tortoise shells, of cut steel, of nineteenth-century French enamels, of ivory, of water colors on ivory (Russian), of hallmarked English silver, of the Japanese Satsuma period, signed and unsigned. When she isn't wrapping and unwrapping rare buttons, Mrs. Lundene makes lovely strings of all kinds of beads in tasteful combinations: crystal interspersed with black beads, twisted Czech beads spaced by Chinese jade, among a large number of others priced from $5.00 to about $20.00.

Old Buttons (*Frick's*)

50 East 56th Street (near Madison Ave.).

For a price it is possible to buy a set of men's coat buttons made of covered and mounted water colors on paper, dating back to 1790. Or, you might like a set of grisaille cuff links, or an arrangement of beetles under glass as cuff links, or some heavy silver pieces which once adorned the suit of a matador in eighteenth-century Spain. Less odd or unique and still worth your attention is the large collection of cuff links and earrings in the window and in cases along the walls, and the heaps of unusual buttons which will be disclosed if you express some specific need. (See what happens, for instance, when you ask for something as simple as a large, black button.)

For ancient and primitive jewelry try *Juergen's* (page 251), *Belinsky* (page 245), *Piñata Party* (page 241), the shops of the *Museum of Natural History* (page 258) and of the *Metropolitan Museum of Art* (page 259), and *Carlebach Gallery* (page 284). See also *Jewelry Exchange* (page 79) and "Bargains" (page 214). On Fifth Avenue, *B. Altman's* and *Jensen's* both have sections of old jewelry, the latter particularly good.

Materials

Far Eastern Fabrics

171 Madison Avenue (33rd-34th Sts., one flight up).

Xanadu and Samarkand whisper from the beautiful Oriental damasks, brocades, hand-blocked silks, and brilliant cottons stacked high on the shelves of this shop. From Thailand come silks of lovely blocks of color and batiked cotton sarongs, heavy silk napkins, and mats. Hong Kong sends carefully made robes and pajamas, and although modern China doesn't yield much now, there are a few antique court robes, restored to their ancient, expensive magnificence.

The major portion of material and objects come from India: priceless robes of gold, exquisite saris (some of them museum pieces), an unusual assortment of wild tussah silks, an endless array of Madras patterns and of mirror embroideries. Among the rarer treasures are antique shawls in the finest of tapestry weaves and Kashmiri ring shawls, meltingly soft to the touch and delicate enough for their considerable width to be pulled through a finger ring.

Tacked to the walls, crowding the entranceway, and obscuring the window, is a curious mélange of objects, some old, some new, folk art and hieratic temple art, sacred objects and toys. In one corner, for instance, there may stand a regal Siamese umbrella built in two tiers; and near it, three staring figures in archaic immobility, made in fairly recent times by a sect in Nepal which couldn't possibly know it was echoing Egyptian and pre-Hellenic sculpture modes. Votive lamps obscure temple toys and bronze goddesses painted on round wall plaques gaze down on stone fragments of temple friezes. Some of these objects are suspected of being quite old, but the proprietors cannot authenticate them, so you will have to bring your own expertise as guide.

Tilletts

170 East 80th Street (between Third and Lexington).

Behind a large window set in black, craggy stones and beyond an ornate late-Victorian entrance, Tilletts displays some of its famous materials. Some of it is already made up in shirts, skirts, ties, dresses, beach coats, and mats, and some articles of clothing can be ordered. The styles are limited but handsome; it is the materials themselves which are exciting—designs in hot, unexpected combinations of colors or in muted, dusty tones. Patterns are large and dashing or exquisitely detailed like old prints, or suggestive, floating free forms. They are not cheap, but beautiful and distinctively Tilletts.

NOTE: See also "Bargains" (page 216).

10

SHOPS:

THE CELESTIAL CITY

Bookshops

To the bibliophile all bookshops are interesting, whether they have the dignified spaciousness of Scribner's or consist of two sagging shelves outside a third-hand furniture store. And, as all bibliophiles know, bookshop owners and their employees, like antique dealers and chefs, are a special breed. The temptation is to describe them all fully—books, shops, and owners—but space precludes such immoderation, so that the most workable arrangement is to describe a few unique shops and indicate the special qualities of others, with the understanding that space and worth are not necessarily always commensurate. It should be added that there are dozens of large and small general and personal bookshops throughout the city where this book and thousands of other cloth or paperback titles can be found or ordered.

PAPERBACK BOOKS

Greenwich Village is our greatest engulfer of better paper books; they crowd cigarettes and chewing gum out of the stationers' and cigar stores and have taken over almost entirely one drugstore.

Sheridan Square Chemists (the name gives the address) has four windows; three of them display paper books while one leaves a little room for perfume. The store has all the usual appurtenances of a drugstore but they become increasingly hard to find. You have to make your way through walls of books to reach the lunch counter; Vaseline, absorbent cotton, and toilet water hide behind poetry and drama; getting a prescription filled requires first wading through philosophy (an idea that has its uses). There are, as you can see, potentials for confusion and difficulty; go anyway, if you can.

The Paperbook Gallery is or are two shops. One, a bit like a short, fat tunnel can be reached through West 4th Street at West 10th Street, or West 10th Street at Seventh Avenue (you'd have to see it to find out just how that works). Its uptown side has two or three small outdoor tables in a minuscule plaza, possibly designed for the most civilized kind of browsing. The second shop (90 West 3rd Street), is burdened with only one door for ingress and egress, but the stock of books is equally extensive and also exclusively paperbacked, the young men as agreeable about giving all sorts of information about the Village (we notice here, too, a common Village phenomenon—every shopkeeper a local guide), and open as late: until midnight Monday through Thursday, until 2 A.M. on Friday and Saturday.

Paperbacks are everywhere, as you can't help knowing, but what you might not know is that *Lamston's*, a 5, 10, 25 cent, and $1.69 variety store at 477 Madison Avenue has a surprisingly full selection. Equally improbable is this latter-day dime-store's very location—right in the heart of the fabled gray-flannel-suit district, just a few doors from Columbia Broadcasting System's national headquarters. No mention of midtown sources for paperbacks is complete without directing you to the largest emporium of all, the basement of *Brentano's* (586 Fifth Ave.).

NOTE: Many of the general and specialized bookstores listed below have selections of paperbacks as well as hardbound books. In addition, the four **Marboro** bookstores and the other bargain sources listed on page 217 have wide assortments of paperbacks.

GENERAL BOOKSTORES WITH A PERSONAL ACCENT

Gotham Book Mart
41 West 47th Street (between Fifth and Sixth Aves.).

A bookshop with an unusually touching respect for authors; photos and sketches of them appear on the walls, and it is here that many intellectually Olympian cocktail parties have taken place. Here, too, is where the little privately printed sheaves of poems and advanced criticism are conspicuously displayed and large areas devoted to publications in several languages dealing with art, literature, the dance, and films.

The fact that the magazines, as well as the ample collection of books on these subjects and others, are stacked precariously on the floor, on tables, and in a legendary cellar (which is said to contain, still, dozens of unopened bundles of the long-defunct little magazine, *transition*) doesn't diminish the aura of respect, but rather enhances it in an absent-minded professor-of-arts-and-literature way.

Eighth Street Bookshop
32 West 8th Street.

In addition to a remarkably comprehensive basement paperback department, the Eighth Street Bookshop has the particular distinction of having one of the most thorough stocks of scholarly and generally hard-to-find books (perhaps second only to the famed *Scribner's* on Fifth Avenue). This, in addition to the usual complement of general books, and the personal attention of a most agreeable staff of attendants, makes it worthy of a serious browser's attention.

The Golden Griffin

611 Madison Avenue.

One of the very few (if not the only) Continental bookshops in the city. "Continental" here means airy displays—everything open to the eye—elegance, and modern, handsome appointments. It also (and this is its business) offers a personal selection of general books, fine imported art books, and a generous array of French and Swiss books and periodicals.

East and West Shop

132 East 61st Street (near Lexington Ave.; one flight up).

Miss Weed (who lived and worked in the Orient for seven years) and Mrs. Zeimer will eagerly give you tourist guidance about the Middle and Far East, including what to wear, and will sell you books explaining the mores and manners of Malayans and Pakistanis so that you can keep the social wheels oiled. They will suggest books on the arts and crafts, the literature and histories of Eastern countries for either general background or expert study. For the really ambitious or UNESCO émigrés, they provide primers in Hindi, Gujerati, Swahili, and Urdu, in addition to native literature in some of the Eastern languages and out-of-print books on matters of the Orient or Near East. They will also try to find such books for you if they don't have them.

Should you go, look into the print and framing section at the back of the shop. Its walls are hung with lovely Oriental and European prints, fine old Chinese rice-paper paintings, and a few beguiling travelers' fans of the nineteenth century.

Wittenborn's

1018 Madison Avenue (between 78th and 79th).

George Wittenborn is one of those people who seem to live in two places at once; his eyes are both sharp and diffuse, his acumen is coupled with vagueness, his manner is very personal even while he isn't quite altogether there. There is nothing wrong with him except that he and his amiable, many-tongued employees are slowly losing ground (literally) to the art books, the art publications, the posters, the shelves, and the walls of original art which threaten to engulf them. Everything screams "No room! No room!" Magnificent posters crowd each other off the walls and cling to the ceiling, the piles of books keep expanding, the aisles grow tighter and the customers more numerous.

It might be possible to build ramps or establish courses in levitation so that customers could browse in layers. Mr. Wittenborn's solution is to buy no more books and begin giving them away—or so he says when he becomes tightly wedged into a corner. Push your way in anyhow if you can be at all interested in an extraordinary gathering, in many languages, of books and magazines on art, architecture, and design, and of some remarkable posters and obscure avant-garde pamphlets which may nowhere else or ever again accost your eye.

Barnes and Noble, Inc.
Fifth Avenue at 18th Street.

A highly respected institution, whose existence spells safety for students searching for textbooks; the stock of textbooks, trade books (in and out of print), and paperbacks, is enormous. The department of rare and out-of-print books is upstairs, happily away from the distraught youngsters looking for College Review booklets. If they confuse you a bit, find Elsa Lichtenstein, the female Solon of the Downstairs, who will quickly and pleasantly unravel you and your book problem.

SPECIALIZED BOOKSTORES
(AND OUT-OF-PRINT BOOKS)

The Hungarian Book Shop
1613 First Avenue (near 83rd St.).

Yearning to read *Az Andaui Hid* by James A. Michener? It is available at the Hungarian Book Store, as are other translations into Hungarian, second-hand books in Hungarian (not too many of the new publications can be imported), picture postcards of Budapest, and sixteenth- and seventeenth-century Hungarian engravings and maps. The limited size of the dusty interiors expands and brightens as Mr. Tibor Tudvardy, the proprietor, talks enthusiastically of establishing a book-publishing firm, of supplying Detroit and Cleveland and Chicago with Hungarian books, of being advisor for the New York Public Library in his capacity as expert and owner of the largest Hungarian bookshop in the United States. In among these activities, Mr. Tudvardy somehow finds the time to publish a handsome magazine which contains both Hungarian and English reading matter on matters Hungarian.

Russian National Book Store

317 East 14th Street (between First and Second Aves.).

White as the driven snow or an old Parisian cab driver, stubbornly dismissing the Revolution and the passage of time, the Russian National Book Store serves up ancient glory and dreams of restored monarchy to its small circle of true believers.

The dusty stock of books—some old, some recently published here and in Europe—is relegated to an obscure set of shelves partially hidden by a section of false wall. The low-ceilinged, main room is crammed with chromos, strings of postcards, and strips of paper decorations, their innocent peasant colors setting off dour photographs of the Romanoffs and demonic portraits of Russian poets. At the back of the grotto-like room is a thick display of religious objects, dark red and dark gold, and religious prints of the Madonna and Child, dressed in heavily encrusted gowns, their awesome faces stiff with Byzantine disdain.

The most impressive product of the shop is the cluster of old men of military bearing and wardrobes of seedy elegance who come to inspect the White Russian papers published in this country, or to buy Russian tea or a set of nested toys, or one of the rough *loofa* sponges used to put bite into a Russian bath. They come mainly to keep each other and themselves warm and alive, members of a moribund club whose membership and luster are fast dwindling.

E. Weyhe

794 Lexington Avenue (near 62nd St.).

Behind a façade that suggests another country and another time, Weyhe's has been amassing new, used, and rare books on art and architecture, an equally impressive collection of prints, and a connoisseur following. The atmosphere is of serious quiet and noble age, which is a fine air for peaceful browsing.

Orientalia

11 East 12th Street.

Books on Eastern thought; scholarly and free of frivolous occult fringes.

Robert Brunner

63 Fourth Avenue.

In Used-Book Alley (page 217), but differing from the others in that it specializes (and it is the only shop in the city that does) exclusively in psychology, psychoanalysis, and other matters concerning our overburdened psyches.

Schulte's

80 Fourth Avenue.

The largest shop in the famous alley. Its stock is general with an unusually extensive theology section.

Jaker Biegeleisen

152 East Broadway (lower East Side).

Mr. Biegeleisen is a specialist's specialist in Hebraica. Although he carries a general stock of Hebrew books (as do the other Jewish book dealers who abound in his neighborhood), Mr. Biegeleisen concentrates on books which came out of the Hasidic mystic movement which once thrived in Eastern Europe and now flourishes in remote corners of the city (see Williamsburg, page 102).

Other Jewish bookshops you might find interesting are: **Behrman's Jewish Book House** (1261 Broadway) and **Bloch Publishing Company** (31 W. 31st St.).

Paraclete Book Center

146 East 74th Street.

A well-mannered, well-arranged bookshop which stocks hard-bound and paperback books of Catholic interest.

Other Catholic bookshops are: **The Guild Studios** (148 E. 32nd St.) and **The Irish Book Shop** (page 252).

Inspiration House

129 West 56th Street.

The transfer from a Madison Avenue loft to stylish new quarters has served to extend even further what had seemed quite a searching range: hypnotism, yoga, occult, tarot secrets, and other obscure corners of belief.

Samuel Weiser

117 Fourth Avenue.

Back to that row again, but now in the occult department. Mr. Weiser has an all-embracing tolerance; his centrally located, impartial bulletin board will tell you where to find a yoga lecture or help through color affinities, astrology, or entrail reading; an ad signed "Mesmer" or "Svengali" would surprise no one here.

Salloch

142 Seventh Avenue

A beautiful, informal living room and gallery house a good collection of specialists' and out-of-print books.

Ideal Book Store

1125 Amsterdam Avenue

Informal, too, but hardly beautiful; the energies that might have gone into beautifying have instead been channeled into garnering learned and comprehensive collections in sociology, history, philosophy, and almost everything else of intellectual weight.

Martin's Book Shop

162 West 4th Street

Fine out-of-print books laved in a steady stream of good recorded music.

Philip C. Duschnes

757 Madison Avenue

The specialties narrow to incunabula, first editions, and autographs.

Other good shops in this field are **Walter Schatzki** (127 E. 56th St.) and **William H. Schab** (602 Madison Ave.).

The Seven Bookhunters

142 West 18th Street

If their excellent stock of out-of-print books doesn't include the one you want, all seven sleuths will start tracking it down elsewhere. If a book is really difficult to find, they may ask about $1.00 (per book) for their services, but their tracking is usually fruitful and worth the charge.

Abrahams Magazine Service

56 East 13th Street

Complete runs of likely and unlikely magazines, some dating back into the last century. There is also a very efficient search service. Besides Abrahams there are several shops on Sixth Avenue in the 40's which have sizable stacks of old magazines featuring Laura La Plante and Barbara La Marr in diaphanous veiling; they also carry more respectable if less stimulating back numbers.

OTHER BOOK SOURCES

Bargains in books are dealt with on page 216, and "Etcetera" (on pages 337-38) lists foreign-language and related specialty bookshops. Also, it should be remembered that current books are available in the book departments of *Macy's*, *Bloomingdale's*, *Altman's*, *Gimbel's*, *Stern's*, and *Abraham & Straus* and, of course, there are the *Doubleday Shops* (the phone directory lists branches; DC), *Marboro Books* (see page 217), *Brentano's* (586 Fifth Ave.), *Scribner's* (597 Fifth Ave.) and the *Chaucer Head Bookshop* (38 E. 57th St.).

Art

The mutability of art exhibitions precludes very specific description, but you will find below groups which specialize in certain art areas. For casual window-shopping, 57th Street just east and west of Fifth Avenue, and Madison Avenue from 59th to 81st are best, and you may find more paintings that you care to cope with in coffee shops, restaurants, and inevitably, every enclosure in the Village.

Some of the interesting galleries for modern American and European paintings (most of them have shows of contemporary sculpture from time to time and all of them have a few pieces of sculpture to show from the back room if you ask) are:

Betty Parsons, 15 East 57th Street

Sidney Janis, 15 East 57th Street

Catherine Viviano, 42 East 57 Street

Stable Gallery, 924 Seventh Avenue (American)

Tibor De Nagy, 24 East 67th Street

World House, 987 Madison Avenue

Grace Borgenicht Gallery, 1018 Madison Avenue

Sam Kootz, 1018 Madison Avenue

Sculpture Center, 167 East 69th Street (the only sculpture specialist)

CLASSICS (RECENT AND OLDER)

Knoedler, 14 East 57th Street
Wildenstein, 16 East 64th Street
Perls, 1016 Madison Avenue
Rosenberg, 20 East 79th Street
Duveen Bros. Inc., 18 East 79th Street

NOTE: The Sunday *Times* and the Saturday *World-Telegram and Sun* lists current exhibits and many galleries distribute copies of the monthly bulletin issued by the American Federation of Arts, "The Art Gallery," which includes a comprehensive calendar. Many galleries are closed during the summer, and they tend to have highly individual hours (from 11 to 5, including Saturdays, is generally safe).

The journey to inner cores of emotion and outer boundaries of experimentation are made by a group of small galleries in the new eastern extension of the Village (page 67).

Brata, 89 East 10th Street
Tanager, 90 East 10th Street
Camino, 92 East 10th Street
March, 95 East 10th Street
James, 70 East 12th Street (several flights up)
Fleischman, 227 East 10th Street

NOTE: A visit to these can be combined with a trip to the Cooper Union Museum (page 109) or with the Slavic walk (page 64).

Window displays as art can often be seen at *Tiffany's* (57th St. at Fifth Ave.), *Bonnier's* (603 Madison Ave.), *Bonwit's* (56th at Fifth), and the many Christmas windows along Fifth Avenue, particularly *Lord and Taylor's,* which you may have to stand on a long line to see.

PRIMITIVE ART

Life has become so bewilderingly complicated for us fortunate contemporaries of the atom bomb that we yearn back to the innocence of folk songs, square dancing, and primitive art. As this interest in primitive art has burgeoned so have fakes (talented Mexican boys, for instance, can chip out a beautiful idol in a short time, scrape it, rub dirt into it, bury it, and then sell it to a dealer in fakes who often palms it off as genuine). To protect yourself (assuming you are a collector) do your buying at reputable galleries and even then, since the most knowledgeable experts can make mistakes, ask for certification guaranteeing authenticity and specifying (wherever possible) the approximate date of origin.

Segy Gallery

708 Lexington Avenue

A gallery which handles African art exclusively, founded by Mr. Ladislas Segy, a scholarly Hungarian who is richly, complexly verbal about his pieces. The discourses run the gamut of cultural fashions, from Freud through existentialism and to whatever new movement is showing its coy toe through the door. It is possible that this sort of indoor sport may make you a bit restive, but it is still one of the finest galleries of its kind.

Little Gallery

68 Greenwich Avenue

"Tiny" is the more accurately descriptive word. In its meager space you may find excellent primitive pieces at very reasonable prices from various sources and, always, other stimulating objects.

J. J. Klejman

982 Madison Avenue

Transplanted from Warsaw, where John Klejman had developed one of the finest galleries for primitive art and contemporary painting, the present gallery has a magnificent blind on the first floor (Chinese vases, Mediterranean majolica, occasional Judaic objects, Romanesque and Renaissance statues, Buddhas, French and English furniture). Downstairs are the primitive arts: one of the greatest collections of absolutely first-rate African, South Seas, Pre-Columbian, some Northwest Coast American Indian figures, masks, and other tribal objects. Also Hittite, Etruscan, Iberic, and pre-Hellenic objects downstairs and in the back room upstairs. Prices range from modest to astronomic depending upon size, age, culture, and rarity of the piece.

Delacorte Gallery
822 Madison Avenue

Coptic fabrics and objects; pre-Columbian, ethnological objects from interior South America; Kachina dolls. Excellent values in decorative primitive art objects, nicely lit and shown.

Carlebach Gallery
1040 Madison Avenue (at 79th St.)

The range is as broad as possible. Carlebach has had some great Etruscan objects and a superb collection of old, rare, bizarre chess sets. Look, also, at the primitive jewelry in this most lavish of art shops.

Aaron Furman
46 East 80th Street

Superb pre-Columbian and African objects. Aaron Furman and his charming wife know a great deal about cultures of the pre-Columbian Americas and their taste and judgment are quite reliable.

André Emmerich
17 East 77th Street

André Emmerich's recently constructed gallery is eminently modern—white walls, glass, comfort, and privacy in which to make the fateful decision about some priceless Peruvian gold piece; pre-Columbian objects of high quality, occasional discards from great North American Indian collections, shows of modern American painters (Adolph Gottlieb for one).

SPECIALTY ARTS

William Bowie
342 East 56th Street

Using a good deal of imagination and inventiveness, Mr. Bowie demonstrates what can be done with lowly sponges, natural and cellulose. They are dyed magnificent colors, cut and mounted as beautiful vari-textured mosaics. Similarly lovely objects are made of stained glass—table tops of rich-toned pieces perfectly balanced for color, and glowing mobiles. As if these weren't accomplishments enough, Mr. Bowie is also working in metal sculpture and in time will undoubtedly have an extensive group to show, and almost certainly it will be good.

The Art Fair

615 Columbus Avenue (90th St.; one flight up). Closed July and August; also Mondays. Other months: Tuesdays through Sundays noon to 6.

Not strictly a gallery because there are no exhibitions nor a definite stable of painters to show, the Art Fair has in its two smallish rooms an orderly clutter of paintings by, if not the "greats," certainly the "goods," and a number of them very good. The paintings are limited to Americans though the print section includes some Europeans, also.

Because Art Fair functions on a smaller percentage than does Madison Avenue and pays much less rent, it can act as sort of outlet shop for painters who may have other gallery affiliations but need a quick and possibly more modest sale than the other galleries can make; the accumulated advantages in price become ours.

Mad Mogi

28th Street at Broadway

This is one of the "what is it?" places. The large, numerous signs shrilling from every bit of available space create an air of frenetic activity, with little real activity going on. One sign names the emporium the "Montmartre of Broadway," and another informs that "Through These Portals Pass the Greatest Lovers of Art," and in each window, Mogi's signs beg for offers of barter; make him any offer at all for genuine hand-painted pictures or oil reproductions of photos. He has been made and accepted some curious offers, to judge from the cargo of synthetic shrunken heads heaped in a window not long ago and for sale at $2.50 apiece. Near them sits a dazed artist, laboriously painting away at a meticulously inept landscape.

In addition to being the St. Francis of starving painters, Mogi is a dealer in prints and an art educator. He will put a painting in a conspicuous place in front of the shop and attach to it the lesson for the day or week: "This is a cubist painting. You gotta look at it cross-eyed."

RECORDS

Schneider's

109 West 83rd Street (near Columbus Ave.)

The basement in which Mr. Schneider sits, surveys, and catalogues, surrounded by tight shelves of records, is open

Monday, Tuesday, and Thursday evenings, all day Saturday, and alternate Sundays. Look for a slanting sign in gold on black which says "Schneider, Lawyer—Abogado"; this is Mr. Schneider's work when he is not immersed in his 450,000 records.

The cellar is not a general record shop and Mr. Schneider will tell you so in firm tones. He is essentially a collector who buys records made before 1940 (consequently, no long-playing records) and sells what duplicates he has. If you're looking for "our song," popular in 1927, or a recording of "Yes, We Have No Bananas," he'll probably have one to sell you. A catalogue of records for sale is in preparation, but until its completion you'd better have specific titles in mind.

FOR CONTEMPORARY RECORDS: See *Goody's* (page 216) and *The Record Hunter* (page 217). Special sources (by language or topic) are included under "Records" in the classified list ("Etcetera") on pages 345-46.

11
INNOCENT AND
LESS INNOCENT
MERRIMENT

Entertainment: Free and Cheap

THEATERS

Apart from amateur groups which sometimes produce plays in churches and settlement houses, there are pre-professional groups whose work necessarily involves the presence of an audience, and blanket invitations are extended to fairly regularly scheduled performances through the season.

These are advertised as "free"—a word which, as in philosophy, has variable meanings. From one point of view, the performances can be considered free: there are no tickets to buy and no reserved seats. But there is usually a box on a desk and a sign which says *"Contributions"* or *"Donations"* or, more forthrightly, *"Donations 75 cents."* Should you adhere to the letter of the ad and march right to a seat, you may or may not be tapped on the shoulder and have the sign pointed out to you. It takes extraordinary strength to say, "I was invited; you need me more than I need you and, anyhow, if I'm to make a contribution I'll choose my cause." Everyone pays, to no one's surprise, but the cost is little and, in one way or another, there is usually sufficient reward.

The school-theaters have another characteristic in common, the high priest. He is director, savant, and prophet of glorious vision, playing the different stops of charm with considerable skill—now suave, now sincere, now Continental, now folksy—as he makes his introductory statement of principles and purpose and delicately enlists your support. It's an admirably skillful and persuasive bit of work and, what's more, you *will* find your sympathies enlisted.

> NOTE: The various actors' workshops in the City are often peripatetic; location and longevity are uncertainties. It would be wise to telephone and verify time and address before building an evening around a performance.

Actors' Lab

110 East 59th Street; Wednesday and Friday at 8:30 P.M.; TR 7-7910.

As you leave the elevator (maximum 7 persons) on the third

floor, the first thing you see is a conspicuous listing of the nine Bahai principles. Awed by these cosmic strophes and concepts, you approach the desk outside the auditorium and respond with docility to the sign which suggests *"Donations 75 cents."*

The donation is well spent; first there is art to look at while muted thumps of preparation come from the curtained stage: a huge painting in the colors of mud and dried blood of a Breughel-like "Dance of Death," and the other, even larger, a very lively seascape (this is possibly the "Dance of Life") of lilting waves and sprays lifting ships and a sea-god of the City of New York into a dreamy blue haze; bordering the dream is an alarming array of large eels, turtles, strangling weeds, and Portuguese men-of-war, painted in a forbidding brown.

It's hard to draw the entranced eye away from these wonders, but audience-staring also has its rewards. It ranges from high-school-age to near-doddering, from Klein's-dressed to Bergdorf's, from comics to Buber, from the doting relatives to couples who've exhausted all the other ways of killing an evening; the conglomerate whole makes a good, responsive audience. And there is much to be responsive to: the plays offered are one-acters by the very best names—Tennessee Williams, Chekhov, Shaw—and the acting is sometimes surprisingly perceptive and moving, beyond the minimal demands of "professional." For a change of training pace, the group does improvisations on newspaper themes offered by the audience. Since these are performed intermittently, it might be best to call and find out when they are scheduled.

Actors Repertory Theatre Workshop

498 Third Avenue (33rd-34th Sts.); Friday and Saturday at 8:30 P.M.; OR 9-7594.

Here again you will meet the donation gambit, a little more difficult this time because no sum is stated, and the girl at the entrance desk is likely to be one of the most appealing students, if not the prettiest. The A.R.T. is an acting school whose classes are held weekday evenings (Saturdays for teen-agers) and whose students write plays, usually one-acters, which they also perform.

Like most of these places, the A.R.T. operates on a combination of shoestring and high hopes. It occupies a loft in an unimpressive business building, and its lobby is a minute hall mainly devoted to a huge red Coca-Cola machine, but one can use the stairs going to the next floor as an auxiliary lobby. The size of the lobby and the fact that there seems to be no backstage area creates difficulties: the performers gather near the machine and on the stairs to rest and talk; enchanting to watch—graceful, mobile, and twittering, like a branchful of tropical birds—they effectively inhibit the exchange of critical comment, pro or con, and thus cut off one of the major joys of theatergoing.

The auditorium is small and unadorned, sporting a sizable revolving stage and rather crude lighting devices, but the plays—and, often enough, the performances—outshine their ambience. Modern classics like Elmer Rice's angular, expressionist *Adding Machine* and the later, more humanistic *Winterset* of Maxwell Anderson form the beginnings of what is hoped to be a varied repertory, affording both actors and audiences a range of style and period not commonly available. And even if you're not interested in the great play of thirty years ago which can, admittedly, be as old-fashioned as Pinero, there is always the surprise and excitement of seeing a young man with an anonymous name, daubed with inexpert make-up, grow before your skeptical eye to the commanding size of a fine actor.

New York Shakespeare Festival

Central Park near Belvedere Tower in summer. Full program through July and August (except Mondays) planned, fervently worked and hoped for, but subject to vicissitudes. Heckscher Theatre at 1230 Fifth Avenue for winter season—same uncertain conditions as above (call SA 2-4008 for current schedules).

Heckscher Theatre—any Fifth Avenue bus, except 5 or 15, to 105th St.

Central Park Theatre—Eighth Avenue bus to 81st Street entrance, walk east (there are signs to follow); or Fifth Avenue bus (any but 5 or 15) to 79th Street entrance, then walk directly westward.

The Shakespeare Festival, inaugurated in 1957, exists in a curiously ambivalent situation: it has won almost every local theater award, critics have sung loud hosannas and audiences eagerly queue up on long lines to attend performances, but the company still must plan uncertainly from season to season and week to week for lack of funds. The fault seems to lie with two stubborn bodies: the City of New York, which looks on a free Shakespeare theater as a questionable good, and the management of the Festival, which proudly insists that no charge at all be made—between them it is touch and go for old William. However, the City has unbent sufficiently to let the Department of Parks build a new outdoor stage in the park and to supply light and sound mechanisms, among other necessities; the management yielded to its need for a fatter purse by asking for donations, although there is still no admission price.

Like Homer, this remarkable theater nods once in a while. Not all the acting is superb nor all the sets resplendent; the seats are not for sybarites and you'll have to rush your dinner to get on line by 7:30 for a good seat—and it will all be worth it if you want inventive, imaginative theater for nothing, or for as much as your gratitude dictates.

MUSIC

Amato Opera Theatre

159 Bleecker Street (Greenwich Village). Advance reservations necessary—phone GR 7-2844.

As a showcase for young, undiscovered singing talent, the Amato Theatre is the most tenacious of its kind; we have small opera companies which blossom and fade almost in the same breath, but the Amato with its rudimentary equipment in its old theater goes on year after year as an opera training field.

Two types of performances are given: the classic Italian mainstays like *Aida* and *Tosca* performed almost entire, with costumes and sets (these are free, plus the usual donation); the other type is something Mr. Amato calls an "operalogue," offered only occasionally and sometimes featuring an opera missing from the standard repertory. These performances (Sunday matinees) are accompanied by coffee and cake, if you get there early enough to consume them, and cost $1.00. They also give Mr. Amato's versatility its widest scope. A short, slender, dynamic man, he makes a pleasant welcoming speech, runs through a short history of the opera, recites the names of his cast (there are no programs), introduces the pianist who must imitate an orchestra, and then plunges with great enthusiasm into the opera proper.

The stage lights go on to reveal an elementary suggestion of a set, rather like large nursery-school blocks used for playing house, and some characters in cloaks connoting rather than constituting costumes. Mr. Amato reads the story of the opera in some detail, pausing for the cast to sing the telling arias and ensemble music. He cues, he prompts, he sings off-stage and supporting voices, he joins in the choruses, and conducts with enough vim and sweep to carry a full orchestra and *Aida*-size chorus through a triumphant performance at La Scala.

What if a tremolo widens into a frightening chasm, or a quintet falls apart like a broken egg, or the proper pitch is desperately sought and not quite reached? No opera company is free from such mishaps and you will, at the Amato, often hear good singing in excellent diction, in addition to the pleasure of watching its ringmaster at work.

MUSIC—OUTDOORS

Stadium Concerts

Lewisohn Stadium, City College; Convent Avenue to Amsterdam, 138 to 139th Streets (AD 4-5800). Five nights a week, 8:30, late June through August. 50 cents (get there early for these) to $1.20 for unreserved seats. $2.40 for reserved seats; $3.00 per person for table reserved for 8. Fifth Avenue bus (#3), get off at 138th Street on Convent Avenue; or West Side IRT local to 135th Street, walk east one long block to Amsterdam. On nights when the weather is dubious tune in, on the hour, to Station WNYC or call the station for information (WH 3-3600).

For over forty years, the Stadium Concerts have been the musical teething rings of young New Yorkers; 25 cents (the price has gone up now) bought a seat high on the side of the amphitheater and the first magnificent assault of the Beethoven *Ninth*. This was accompanied by gentle, aesthetic necking and the anticipation of a ride, later on, to Washington Square on the open top of a double-decker bus (gone, and a great loss). The combination might be the best way to teach music appreciation; certainly many middle-aged New Yorkers who spent their summers in the city will vouch for the method.

Necking on the stone seats isn't, of course, required; the bulk of an audience of 18,000 or more simply go to hear the classics performed by major artists. The bulk of the music is symphonic, with emphasis on concerti, but there are occasional operas in concert form, aria recitals, dance programs, jazz programs, and one very popular annual—the George Gershwin concert, devoted to his music alone. Your favorite passage may be shattered by a sudden squall, by a flight of jet planes through the air or the urgent clamor of the fire department, but the faithful have come to consider such interruptions an intrinsic part of the whole experience.

Salmaggi Opera

Triboro Stadium, Randall's Island. Seats $2.00 and $2.50. East Side IRT to 125th Street (express stop), then taxicab or Randall's Island bus from 125th Street.

Our own Baths of Caracalla, featuring Italian opera on a sporadic summer week-end program—watch the newspapers for dates. The jewel of the series is an *Aida* replete with nymphs, ballet, animals, wrestlers, and the rest of the traditional gorgeous exaggeration with which this opera is stuffed.

Bryant Park Concerts

Behind the Central Branch of the Public Library, at 42nd Street and Fifth Avenue, Monday through Friday, 12 noon to 2 P.M. from the middle of June through the middle of September.

Recordings from the extensive collection of the library—the obscure old, the very new; operas, chamber music, instrumentalists, choral works; uncompromisingly highbrow and meticulously chosen for quality and variety. Some of the best musical programming in the city, indoors or out, paid for or free.

Even if you aren't an ardent music lover, pick up a sandwich and container of coffee in one of the luncheonettes nearby, dig into a wire refuse basket for a discarded newspaper to sit on, and take a respite from sightseeing and shopping. *Free.*

Harlem Meer Concerts

Upper end of Central Park, the Harlem Meer (110th St., and Fifth Ave.—Fifth Ave. bus Nos. 1, 2, 3, or 4, to 110th St.).

On Tuesday evenings in the summertime (confirm with the Department of Parks, RE 4-1000) much of Spanish Harlem —the little quick flirtatious girls, the boys in the bright jackets, the baby carriages, the paper bags full of *pasteles*— pours out to listen to a Latin-American band. The lake is Noguchi-shaped and the band stands on a cement apron which reaches into it. From the boathouse across the lake and from the sides of the lake come rowboats, some illumined by flashlights, like large insects lured and gathered in a great fan-shaped movement toward the group of red-coated male Loreleis. On the surrounding rocks and grass, the small, high-heeled feet twist in related rhythms while the boys' hands softly clap out the drum beats. *Free.*

Washington Square Concerts

Fifth Avenue bus (marked "Washington Square") to end of line. For alternate routes, see page 326.

Greenwich Village holds its village-green concerts (chamber-music, mostly) in Washington Square Park, partially sponsored by local enterprises. They have been held on Monday nights in August, but it would be wise to make sure via the newspapers or the Park Department (RE 4-1000). The fare is mixed and often esoteric for standard tastes, concentrating on neglected works (sometimes neglected for ample cause) and new works, which rarely get adequate attention. These are about the intellectual peak of New York's live summer music (with some serious contenders coming up in other parks) digging out little-known Italian Baroque composers and young composers of the arid, knit-one, purl-two school of modern music, who also deserve and get a hearing. *Free.*

Evenings-by-the-River

East River Park Amphitheater; east end of Grand Street. July and August (8:30); check newspapers for programs and dates. Lexington Avenue IRT to Union Square (14th Street). On 14th Street take "D" bus going eastward to last stop (Houston near River). Walk south to Grand Street and enter the park.

Symphony, chamber music, opera, and jazz in a small, neighborhood park. A little out of the way, but very much worth going to. The Delancey Street Bridge cuts black filigree out of the summer sky, the bustling little tugboats on the river scatter red, yellow, and blue lights into the dark trees and the children—Italian, Puerto Rican, Jewish—add to the music the soft sucking noises of bottles and lollipops. *Free.*

Central Park Mall Concerts

From the end of May through the middle of September. Central Park Center Drive at 72nd Street. Any Fifth Avenue bus (except 5 or 15) to 72nd Street; or Eighth Avenue bus to 72nd.

The Goldman Band, a venerable and highly esteemed institution, plays on Sunday, Monday, Wednesday, and Friday nights (8:30); opera, jazz festivals, symphonic music, barbershop quartets and assorted soloists fill in other nights. Sunday newspapers carry listings or call the Department of Parks (RE 4-1000). A very pleasant way to spend a summer evening, but don't spoil it by lingering in the park afterward; the park at night is as hazardous as it is beautiful. *Free.*

Battery Park Band Concerts

Tuesdays at noon, from the end of June to early September. East or West Side IRT (local) to South Ferry.

Uncomplicated *oom-pa-pa* in a very complicated terrain, vaulting verticals of money and shipping empires, the quiet horizontals of the sea and the little handkerchief of a park which was the Dutch acorn that sprouted into the great oak of New York City.

Try to combine with a tip-of-the-island walk (page 52) as a lunch and rest break; it's a long way to go simply for a band concert. *Free.*

FOLK-SONG FESTS

Washington Square

On fine Sundays, as soon as the weather turns comfortable, the intellectual youth of the city—the teen-agers from progressive schools, from the arts high schools, the escapees from too "conformist" homes—pour into Washington Square Park. They don't mingle with the babies or dogs or bicyles or chess-players, or with the couples on the grass; nor do they take up bench space (traditionally the domain of old Italians who, in their Sunday hats, lean forward on their canes and spin out long quiet conversations).

For their theater, the youngsters have picked the very center of the park—a large fountain (usually quite dry, but sometimes achieving a modest trickle). Around this fountain, and in it on dry Sundays, they strum their guitars and sing. Sometimes there are two or three in a group and sometimes a group grows fairly large, surrounding a singer with unusual talent or repertoire. If you can pick your way through the guitar cases strewn around like sarcophagi in a ravished graveyard, you'll be able to hear as many as twenty songs going simultaneously, which seems like uproar, but isn't: the nearby buses won't be outshouted and the members of the trios and quartets sing quietly to each other, with total disregard for the uninitiated gawkers.

You may notice, here and there, a few men quite far from the teens in age, carrying banjos, or bull fiddles, or washbasins for percussion. These may be folklorists hoping to pick up a new version of a song, or simply exhibitionists or, very likely, people who hope to be heard and chosen for jobs in some of the smaller night clubs. Once in a while, they form combinations which leap from the steady rhythms of folk music to surprisingly complex jazz. Recently a young Negro singer has been making fairly steady appearances, dressed in black trousers tucked into heavy black boots and girdled by a broad, studded gaucho belt. He sings sweet popular songs (a bold act in the scornful and devout folklore atmosphere, something like charging into rock-and-roll while the rest of the congregation sings hymns) in the luxuriant manner of an Italian tenor, sustaining a long Bellini line which ends in a Verdi throb. The operatic effect gains immeasurably from the presence of a faithful claque of one, an older man who applauds violently and shouts "Bravo" with unflagging enthusiasm after each number. Try to find the boy and his devoted follower when you go; they put on a good if peculiar show.

The lack of interest in spectators may not be as complete as one thinks, since the costumes show a good dollop of exhibitionism. The boys wear blue jeans or khakis with one or two styles of shirt, brilliant reds or plaids open to the waist, or dark high-necked sweaters for that satanic look. The girls play more variations on the dress theme, with three basic types predominant: the adornment scorner, who wears blue jeans and a dark sweater or her brother's shirt, her hair cut crisp and short, her face free of the nonsense of lipstick; the pre-Raphaelite who lets her lank hair hang poetically loose around her thin shoulders, who wears a wide floating skirt and the facial expression of a Blessed Damozel; then there is the absinthe drinker whose desperate aim is to make her seventeen years look like the abyss of depravity; dead white make-up sets off the black penciling around her burnt-out (she hopes) eyes, and her long paste earrings swing slowly with her exhausted walk. No matter how they see themselves—the pioneers, the late romantics, the dissolutes—they remain to the viewer beguiling bunches of fresh flowers.

OUTDOOR DANCING (POPULAR)

The pony-tails swing free and the blue-jeaned legs scissor through elaborations of rock-and-roll; fun to watch even if you feel your own dancing will be too badly outclassed. Thursdays, in season, Wollman Memorial, Central Park, at 8:30. Enter park at 59th Street and Fifth Avenue.

Also on weekly schedules in parks in the Bronx, Brooklyn, Queens, and Staten Island. Call Department of Parks

(RE 4-1000) for dates and traveling directions, or Visitors Bureau (MU 7-1300).

FOLK DANCING

For outdoor sessions in the city's parks call the Department of Parks (RE 4-1000).

Winter schedules are maintained by the Y's Call PL 5-2700 or the *Metropolitan Duane Church* (CH 3-4636) or the *Henry Street Settlement* (OR 4-1100), which may be far out of your way, but worth the trip for meeting New Yorkers you won't meet at uptown Y's. *Folk Dance House* at 108 West 16th Street (WA 9-0644) carries a full schedule and frequently sports a glittering clientele; good for communing via dance with professors, psychiatrists, and actors.

INDOOR CONCERTS

For superlative concerts at little cost, performed by the Valhalla of artists, watch newspaper announcements of concerts at *Washington Irving High School*, 40 Irving Place, at 16th Street (Lexington IRT subway to Union Sq., walk east one block), and particularly, for the programs offered by the *YMHA* at 92nd Street and Lexington Avenue. The latter's ebullient cultural program includes choice chamber concerts plus recitals of rarely heard ancient music and of very modern. It has also become the showcase of many dancers and the bardic hall of many poets.

New York Historical Society, Central Park West at 77th Street (see page 114). Concerts during the winter months on Sundays at 3 P.M. One-hour concerts designed as showcases for young, but not amateur, talent; in variety of programs—choral groups, chamber, folk music, opera extracts. *Free*. Eighth Avenue IND subway to 79th Street (local); Eighth Avenue bus to 77th Street.

Names like William Warfield, Leontyne Price, Geoffrey Holder, Marian Anderson, Ethel Waters, Harry Belafonte, and the names of others almost equally well known, appear in concerts at the *YMCA* in Harlem (180 W. 135th St.). They are offered twice monthly, at 4:30 on Sundays, and feature a young professional musician, supported in a joint program by one of the established artists. *Free.* (Seventh Avenue IRT subway to 135th Street; Fifth Avenue bus 3 to 135th Street.)

Several chamber music (live) performances in the evening, and recorder concerts of operas, concerti, and symphonies from 12 noon to 2 P.M. on Tuesdays, at *Donnell Library Center* (20 W. 53rd St., near Fifth Ave.; JU 2-6800). A chance for a few quiet, deep breaths before you plunge into the plethora of the Museum of Modern Art across the street. *Free.*

Brooklyn Museum, Sundays at 2 P.M., all year round; chamber music, sonata recitals, soloists of high caliber in a cool, classic setting. *Free.* Seventh Avenue IRT subway to Brooklyn Museum Station.

Frick Collection (1 E. 70th St.), Sundays at 3 P.M. November through March. Same type of programs as Brooklyn Museum (above), with more seasoned performers, sometimes. Admission complicated: separate requests for tickets (one request per one ticket) to be submitted to Collection on Monday (not before, not after) before the concert. It has been known to happen, however, that people just showed up a little time before the concert and were admitted. Worth the chance (and even the effort of ticket requests beforehand) to listen to music as a Medici might have, surrounded by splendid furnishings and great paintings. *Free.* Fifth Avenue bus (not numbers 5 or 15) to 70th Street.

SACRED MUSIC

Some churches offer concerts of sacred music sporadically throughout the year, except summers, with enriched programs for the Easter and Christmas seasons of course. You can find excellent performances of Handel oratorios, Bach Passions, and the more modern sacred music of Stravinsky and Honneger by following the listings in the religious page of the Saturday newspapers. The following churches have especially active programs:

The Church of the Ascension (10th St. and Fifth Ave.)

The Brick Church (Park Ave. at 91st St.)

St. Thomas' Episcopal Church (Fifth Ave. and 53rd St.)

Temple Emmanuel (65th at Fifth), for Hebrew liturgical music

To hear the magnificent bassos of Russian choirs, try to get to the Russian Orthodox churches for Christmas and Easter services (about two weeks after our dates); check especially *St. George's* (22 E. 7th St.) or *St. Vladimir's* (334 E. 14th St.). Some free; some charge, never much.

> NOTE: The Saturday *World-Telegram and Sun* has a complete listing of sacred music in its column "The Choir Loft." The Saturday religious pages of all the metropolitan newspapers are also helpful.

FILMS

Films on art at the *Metropolitan Museum of Art* (see page 107) on frequent Sundays at 3 P.M. Check the bulletin board of events at the museum should you go on a Sunday. *Free.*

Films concerning New York past and present, historical films depicting colonization and early American life, at *New York Historical Society* (see page 114) Saturdays at 2 P.M. *Free.*

The *Museum of Modern Art Film Library* (see page 106) has daily showings at 3 and 5:30. If you are a member it is free—whether member or not if you want to get in it is wise to get your reservation in advance (after 11 A.M. on weekdays and after 1 P.M. on Sundays).

LECTURES

This may not be your idea of how to spend your time in New York, but if it is, you can get considerable enlightenment on art at the *Metropolitan Museum of Art* (see page 107) at 2:30 most weekdays and 3:00 on Sundays; *Brooklyn Museum* (see page 126) on Sundays at 3:45; *Frick Collection* (see page 106) at 3:00 on frequent afternoons.

On historical subjects and American crafts, at *New York Historical Society* (see page 114) on frequent Fridays at 3:00.

On almost any subject, including existentialist psychiatry, at *Cooper Union* (see page 109) several evenings a week.

READINGS

Poetry and drama read by professionals, symposia on these matters, and art lectures, evenings at *Donnell Library Center* (see page 298). Get schedule of events there or at the Central Library or any branch library. For the readings-cum-music variety, see pages 303, 306.

Entertainment: At Variable Cost

THE BIG TIME

Performances at Broadway theaters and the Metropolitan Opera House have been for years their own best advertisers and need no gilding here. People who write ahead for tickets have been known to be pleasantly surprised from time to time with seats for hit shows. And even at short range, there's no harm in trying: first of all, last-minute cancellations do turn up now and again; then there are occasions scattered through the year when heat waves or blizzards or religious holidays (the Jewish New Year and Day of Atonement open up seats for Christians and Easter and Christmas then reciprocate) release a bit of space. An extra Actor's Fund benefit matinee gets scheduled once in a while, too.

Failing all of the above possibilities (but granted strong feet), you might try standing. At the "Met," 280 determined opera-lovers are permitted to stand through each performance (after standing in line outside—for hours on the choicest dates). And most Broadway hit shows also have some standing room tickets available shortly before curtain time.

It goes without saying that if you are desperately in need of tickets and the box office cannot help you, try one of the ticket agencies (see page 347 of "Etcetera" for information).

Should the *New York City Center* (131 W. 55th St., between Sixth and Seventh Aves.; CI 6-8989) be functioning in any one of its multiple capacities—ballet center, opera center, drama and light opera center—while you're around, go. The ballet is world-renowned, the opera is a good balance of the adventuresome and the classic; the drama and light opera repeat shows that one regrets missing; and not one of them will cost over $3.80 for the best seat.

Like minor planets, the off-Broadway theaters have shot off the sun of Broadway into far-flung places. A theater is a bazaar room in a settlement house, a meeting room in a church, an old loft with crumbling board benches, the basement of Carnegie Hall; a converted church contains two theaters—an upper and lower, like berths; one theater lived briefly on the second floor of an old tenement. Some are in the round, some in the oblong, some of classic arrangement, and the seats vary from not-too-comfortable to sway-backed planks. Don't neglect an opportunity to go to at least one performance; the plays and performers are often as good or better than you'll find on Broadway (no guarantee on any specific one, however) and the neighborhood may be one you might not ordinarily visit.

The newspapers, especially the drama section of the fat Sunday *Times* and *Herald Tribune,* and the weekly *New Yorker* and *Cue* magazines (as well as that eccentric of New York weeklies, *The Village Voice*) include reviews and listings of the current off-Broadway offerings. A baker's dozen of these theaters have a central ticket information and reservation service, in addition to their own box offices—call OR 7-1010 (10 A.M-9 P.M., seven days a week).

NIGHT LIFE WITH A DIFFERENCE

As you undoubtedly know, the soil which produces the juiciest bits of columnists' gossip which, in turn, becomes "Broadway" folklore, flourishes in a few famous plots. *The Copacabana* (10 E. 60th St., PL 8-1060) and the *Latin Quarter* (48th St. at Broadway; CI 6-1735) roar extroversion; they are not shy—not their comics, nor their patrons, nor especially their girls. The *Maisonette* of the Hotel St. Regis (55th St. at Fifth Ave., PL 3-4500), the *Persian Room* of the Plaza (58th St. at Fifth Ave., PL

9-3000), the *Empire Room* of the Waldorf-Astoria (Park Ave. at 49th St., EL 5-3000) are, on the other hand, immutably well-bred. No matter how earthy, sexy, folksy or zany any one featured artist may be, they remain sophisticated and decorous. *El Morocco* (154 E. 54th St., EL 5-8769) can often be as noisy and crowded as a cafeteria at lunchtime, but indispensable for anyone who must see and be seen by "names."

NOTE: Always call for reservations. At some of the supper clubs you may not need one if it's a weekday but it does the ego good to be greeted by the headwaiter as though you were a long-lost rich brother.

"Burlesque is dead! Long live burlesque!" is the clarion call that sounds along with the jazz of 52nd Street (W. of Fifth Ave.). Among the pure, undefiled strains of Old Time Dixieland (almost an old-time religion for some devotees) which pour out of *Jimmy Ryan's* (53 W. 52nd St., JU 6-9800) and the Handy-Bartok combinations that often emerge from the *Hickory House* (144 W. 52nd St., CI 7-9524) and the evolutionary stages of jazz in between which soar out of *Birdland* (Broadway at 52nd St., JU 6-7333) come the sinuous sounds which weave around variations of tease. A few fragmented bits of the art of the great Minsky, lightly disguised, can be found at: *Moulin Rouge* (47 W. 52nd St., CI 5-9489), *Pendulum* (51 W. 52nd St., CI 7-8995), *French Casino* (119 W. 52nd St., JU 2-9611), *The Continental* (127 W. 52nd St., JU 6-7549), *Monaco* (133 W. 52nd St., CI 7-6310).

Of a similar kind, a bit more frayed and sometimes sexually uncertain are the *boîtes* on West 3rd Street in the Village, huddled together on the two blocks east of Sixth Avenue. The girls are somewhat ripe for names like "Spring Flowers" but you might be persuaded.

At the other extreme, away from the outspoken fleshly, is the innocence of songs of parting and rue on the banks of the Danube as purveyed by Middle-European cafés. A sweet, moist air of nostalgic tears and the balm of gypsy violins laves: *House of Vienna* (320 East 79th St.; TR 9-6220), *Viennese Lantern* (242 East 79th St.; RE 4-0044), *Chardas* (309 East 79th St.; RH 4-9382), all in the goulash belt (see pages 172-74).

NOTE: A good number of night places are closed on Mondays or Sundays and, in others, some of the entertainers take those nights off; better check. As for prices: entertainment at a table, with drinks and music always requires a well-nourished wallet.

Jazz is everywhere and enjoys the great freedom of being available at odd times: it goes on in the sacred halls of the *Metropole,* the *Village Vanguard,* and *Birdland* at matinees on weekends; it is worshiped at *Eddie Condon's* (330 E. 56th St., PL 5-9550); it blasts through Carnegie Hall at midnight and from the stages of movie theaters after the last show; from avant-garde art galleries, from the auditorium of Cooper Union and from countless little clubs that open and shut with the rapidity of a dusty eye. (The New York *Post* carries a good number of jazz ads, particularly on Fridays and Saturdays.)

A new or stew-form of entertainment has recently begun to emerge, prompted by developments in the *boîtes* of San Francisco: a number of art forms are thrown together into one pot, with resulting confections in varying degrees of palatability. Short stories are read to appropriate music, poetry is declaimed to jazz (page 306), love letters are danced (with or without additional sound), advanced jazz assaults canvases of abstract expressionism, and drama is semi-acted to a web of sounds including the clatter of *espresso* cups. These sorts of performances, while evocative, are, of their special natures, also sporadic and itinerant and not given to loud advertising, so that only the very small notices in newspaper theater sections will herald them, or posters in their neighborhood coffee houses.

As to nightclubs, you probably already know which you would like to visit, but to your private list you might add a number which, as these things go, are lasting and literate:

The Village Vanguard, 178 Seventh Avenue South (CH 2-9355)

Bon Soir, 40 West 8th Street (OR 4-0531)

Upstairs at the Downstairs, 37 West 56th Street (and vice versa at the same address; CI 5-9465)

The Blue Angel, 152 East 55th Street (PL 3-9558)

Showplace, 146 West 4th Street (GR 7-9848)

Central Plaza

Second Avenue (6th St.); AL 4-9800; Fridays and Saturdays only; admission $1.75.

As the young intellectuals move from Dixieland up into the thinner spheres of progressive jazz, the "Marty" set of boys and girls moves up from the sugary ballad to Dixieland. In a huge room, once the scene of neighborhood balls and weddings, now crammed with many minute tables and only a center aisle for possible dancing, the shipping-room boys, the Wall Street runners, the mechanics' assistants with no dates, work their way through pitchers of beer and fifths of gin, exchanging ties on the way, startling each other with trick explosive cigarettes, and working up unsteady gaits and ominous, moist pallors. On the narrow dance floor there is a group of girls whose elaborate coiffures and seeping mascara become Medusa heads as they dance in pairs, trying frantically to keep up with wild pace and sudden shifts of the music. A wan girl from Sarah Lawrence and her escort from Yale struggle to enter the mood of abandon with self-conscious energy.

Up front sit the scholars and devotees, risking deafness as each musician tries to push all of himself through his horn.

When the going gets hot, when the trombone begins to play the trombonist and strains to explode itself and him, when the trumpet coils higher and higher to a last unreachable note, the room becomes frenzied with rhythmic clapping and stamping, the sweat pours and the walls tremble. Through all this a large group of special policemen acts as cordial hosts and benign guardians; they collect tickets, indicate the way to the cloakroom, push the elevator buttons for the guests, and keep a wary, solicitous eye on the over-exuberant boys, maintaining a constant Olympic calm above the shaking floor and the hammer blows of noise.

Whether you like Dixieland jazz or not, you should go. The Central Plaza may be as close an equivalent as you will find to the legendary French dance halls or the Salon Mexico, and the colorful, aging musicians deserve your money and applause; in their small sphere they are great men.

Half Note

289 Hudson Street (near Spring St.); AL 5-9752; closed Mondays.

Set in a dark desert of closed office buildings, the Half Note is one of the temples of enlightened jazz, complex and arid and absorbed by large numbers of serious people with impassive faces. They don't beat out rhythms or stamp their feet or shake their heads or even talk; they just listen studiously as if to a postgraduate lecture on thermodynamics. The music must have great appeal to judge from the numbers of people who pay to listen to it, but, why does it leave them looking so joyless?

Two Guitars

244 East 14th Street (near Second Ave.); AL 4-3838; closed Mondays.
Shows at 8:45 and 11:45, approximately.

Like an adolescent girl, the Two Guitars tries on many rapid changes of guise, seeming to look for one that feels appropriate and capable of lasting. As the girl has a set of physical constants—her height, color of eyes, and so forth —so does the Two Guitars. Its constant is a Russian menu listing *zakuska, kholodyetz,* borsch with *pirozhok* and meats à la Tiflis, à la Stroganoff, and in the styles of Pojarsky and Karsky. The entertainment, though, swings through many places and odd juxtapositions with abandon. A fairly typical conglomeration opens with a trio of minor Moiseyev dancers stamping, twirling, and streaming bright ribbons in ingenuous Ukrainian dances. This could be followed by an act not commonly seen here since the demise of vaudeville, an Apache dance. It is done in the pure, classic manner; the man (very recently a Ukrainian whooper and whistler) wears an evil cap, a striped *maillot,* tight pants, and a red, throttling scarf; the woman wears an assortment of sexy rags. She slinks toward him, threatening, bearing a mean look and a large rubber knife. He slithers toward her, hips first, the proud hidalgo and the most valiant matador, grabs her and throws her over his back and across his shoulders and continues to twist, fold, unfold, and swirl her about himself very much in the manner of Beatrice Lillie with a feather boa.

Sometime later, she (or an identical twin) turns Spanish with the rapid-fire heelwork and bow-arched torso of an Andalusian dance. Somewhere in between, you will have had a sword dancer in the manly full coat of a Cossack warrior. He doesn't dance much, but he is an engaging man who, between shows, wanders from table to table with an accordion which helps him swoop and sob through the sad, heroic ballad of Stenka Razin and the blissfully painful Russian songs of unrequited love and nostalgia, almost all of them decorated with lonely little birch trees. Two lady singers will also have appeared: one a chic Parisienne type with a Hungarian accent who elicits audience participation with "Seeng, you seenairs!" and the other a more seasoned singer who, after singing in German and Russian, dons a kimono and kneeling in a softened light, sings *"Un bel di"* quite well and in good Italian while the rest of Puccini is dealt with by a piano, bass fiddle, and small drums.

There is no lack of variety or surprise, as you can see. On Saturday nights, the piquancy of confusion is added; the place becomes too crowded for its manpower; the waiters, harried by an excess of orders and too little space to move in, retire for long leisurely walks around the block. Try another night instead, or, if possible, the Russian New Year or Easter holidays, when the menu and festivities become more lavish.

Five-Spot Cafe

5 Cooper Square (between 4th and 5th Sts. where Third Ave. becomes the Bowery).

A chameleon; one of the first of the clubs to bring east the San Francisco combination of jazz and poetry but, on Sundays, it changes from its turtle-neck sweater to a formal black suit and purveys chamber concerts and serious modern music.

A not-too-thoroughly converted saloon whose central area has been raised to make a platform for performers, it still attracts old Bowery bums who make an atavistic return to an old haunt, find the dark nest taken over by cuckoos and stumble out in terror, looking for a safer port. To avoid the minimum charge of $1.50, the young devout stand at the bar, the boys protected by unripe beards and heavily masculine coats or big shaggy sweaters out of which their studious faces stare defenseless and beatific. The girls look less rapt, maybe because their exaggerated make-up creates its own salacious expression; their clothing is in the Toulouse-Lautrec-Paris-Apache mode universally adhered to by bohemian girls —high-necked dark sweaters topped by strangling neckerchiefs.

At one table sit four boys in fancy shirts, silent, immobile and blank. Suddenly one throws back his head, closes his eyes, and begins to tremble, gently, ecstatically, to the music. Just as suddenly, he stops, places his head in a more ordinary position, opens his eyes, and then opens a book and begins to read. At another table, three secretaries with bare throats thrust forward in the curves of attraction talk about the surrounding "characters" and try the caresses of their mascaraed eyes on the safe waiter. A lady poet with thin hair and a thick voice holds court for avant-garde publishers and handsome men with pretty boys, while her young escort sleeps sweetly at her side.

After a group of jangling slummers is seated, the entertainment begins. The poet is announced and appears looking proper and healthy, like a young interne assured of a prosperous practice. To the accompaniment of the band (which has been playing right along) he recites satirical poems—not quite poems, not quite prose, but clever. He leaves to enthusiastic applause, which almost shakes the art-exhibition posters off the walls and somehow changes the serious mood into the noisy animation of a night club. When the poet gets to the bar, the bartender (a man who obviously participates) hands him a drink as if it were a sacred chalice and says, "Sir, you were magnificent."

À LA GRECQUE

In another of those mysterious drives to novelty and chic, some of the younger intellectual crowd has begun to abandon the rarefied jazz places for the more earthy pleasures of what are called "Greek" nightclubs, a general term for Near-Eastern entertainment. Most of them, it is true, are Greek restaurants which have extended their hours and pushed back a few unused tables to make room for the entertainers who come in at about nine o'clock; some have been cabarets from their inception, with supper served, if you like, right through the belly-and-hip weaving, the tinkle of finger cymbals, and the low quarter-tone wails of abandoned Nile maidens. Unless the drive has subsided recently, they are likely to be too crowded for an after-theater visit on week-end nights; go during the week or fairly early on the week end, 9:30 to 10:00. It is possible that the fashion may have moved to German beer halls by the time you're ready to use this information and some places may have closed with the collapse. A telephone call or two might save you a fruitless trip.

Egyptian Gardens

301 W. 29th St. (just west of Eighth Ave.; one flight up); LO 5-9839.

As you start climbing the stairs toward the moaning music, a remarkable painting meets your eye. It is ostensibly of a harem dancer, but the torso is thick and square, the thighs masculine, and where the breasts ought to be there is an unmistakable flatness covered by two round plaques. He-she-it may be regarded (take your choice) as the result of inept painting or as suitably suggestive of the Near-Eastern androgyne, past and present.

It is difficult for an occidental to judge, but the music in the Egyptian Gardens sounds more authentic and ancient than it does in some similar places: less Westernized, the melodic line longer and deeper, richer in quarter tones and sad bleating tremolos, and the dancing is more like the subtly shifting sands of the desert than the frantic shaking of the tent show. The most engaging part of the entertainment, however, is a carry-over from the old days when no outlanders visited these cafes, and when any member of the audience rose to dance and sing as the spirit moved him. It still happens in the Egyptian Gardens occasionally; you may see an old man, tieless, unpressed, and still wearing his hat, gravely give the musicians some money and move into a measured solemn dance, graceful and elegant, his eyes downcast and far away in the solitude of remembering. Or an old woman, dressed in black, wearing a nondescript little black hat, will echo ancient beauty with the controlled classic movements of her neck and shoulders and the delicate, understated movements of her still supple body and fine head.

Port Said

257 West 29th Street; CH 4-9322.

Although the musicians use the lovely vase-shaped Arab drums and the dancers punctuate their movements with finger cymbals, the dancing is basically (very basically) of the Little Egypt, carnival and side-show variety, touchingly old-fashioned, recalling the great days of Minsky and Coney Island peep shows. The 29th Street Ouled-Nail-type dancer wears a black bra and a thing below pulled tight under her large flowing belly; her dance consists of pulling a diaphanous veil away from and toward herself as she makes her white masses of flesh shake and shiver, together and separately. If you get a table near the clearing in which she dances and she approaches and shakes her breasts in your face (men's faces, only) you may think and feel whatever your flesh and psyche dictate, but you'll have to pay; it is *de rigeur,* in the circumstances, to push a bill or two into the front of her bra—apparently a rare pleasure considering the avidity with which it is usually done.

In the same neighborhood, there are one or two other possibilities, among them the *Kifisai Restaurant* (250 W. 27th St., AL 5-9854). A bit farther uptown is the *New Byzantion* (see page 175).

NOTE: For additional night-life suggestions, see "Negro Harlem" (pages 84-87).

12
NIGHT FOR
INSOMNIACS

Assuming that all the interest and money allotted for theaters and nightclubs is gone, that there is no one to visit and a long night to fill, there is still much that can be done.

For the Sedentary or Cold-Afflicted

Reading all the columnists in the New York papers, recording repetitions of rumors, denials of rumors, and counter-rumors makes a good game which will absorb many hours. Then there is the radio. From midnight to 6 A.M. "The Happiness Exchange" exudes unremitting comfort and joy (WABC); less sweet and more hot emerges from WOV—rhythm and blues, spirituals, and Negro-slanted news from 8 P.M. to 6 A.M.; WEVD conducts an olio called "Midnight Jamboree" from midnight to 3 A.M.; Spanish soap operas, dramas, weather reports, and news in Spanish are spiced with mambos and merengues on WWRL, from midnight to 10:30 A.M. The rarer items appear on FM stations. As you twist the dial you may catch a group of folk singers talking shop, an artist with esoteric theories and an impenetrable accent trying to explain himself, a frail young poet talking gently of his craft, hasty capsule theater reviews, long discursive rambles by men with some ideas and plenty of time, a full performance of *Fidelio* or a nightful of *Parsifal*, chamber music (with or without careful instruction), and almost always, there is somewhere on the dial Beethoven's *Sixth Symphony*, apparently considered by the longhairs as "music to float to dreams on." One can, of course, turn the radio off and sit quietly in one or more of the movie houses strung along 42nd Street between Sixth and Eighth Avenues. They run late into the morning and by shrewd timing after inquiry, it is possible to see several films (or parts of them) in one inexpensive orgy.

For the Hale and Energetic

Browse among the French books and paperbacks at the **Golden Griffin** (58th St. at Madison Ave.) any time up to midnight, or visit the **Doubleday Book Shop** (Fifth Ave. at 52nd St., DC) or one of the **Marboro Bookshops** (see page 217), which are also Cindarellas. Try to get to **Serendipity** (225 E. 60th St.) for coffee before it closes at 1:00 A.M. If you're permitted to wander, coffee cup in hand, through the arrangements of Tiffany glass and gouty Victorian, look at some of the unbelievable old hats (newly and carefully made to sell—but to whom?), the voodoo kits, the old canisters, and whatever may have drifted in on the whim of the owners. Should you need something lustier in the way of food and atmosphere, there is indefatigable **Reuben's** (6 E. 58th St.). After a raw-meat sandwich at Reuben's, a selection of desserts is available on the all-night fruit-and-vegetable stand just east of Third Avenue on 59th Street.

From here you might dash downtown to sit quietly (hat on head) and watch interminable card games in the Levantine cafes on Allen Street on the lower East Side—the **Istambul,** the **Allen Boulevard,** the **Orient**—at 156, 158, and one upstairs. Should you lack Arabic, however, it might be best to go directly westward to the Broadway area, where you can while away some time (up to midnight) in a chair of the **Dawn Patrol Barber Shop** (816 Seventh Ave.); or, if it is more suitable, have yourself redecorated at **Larry Matthew's Beauty Shop** (47th St. at Seventh Ave.), which never closes. Night-blooming record shops also brighten the Broadway air; the **Colony Record Shop** (1671 Broadway at 52nd St.), for instance, has an extensive range of records available for listening and purchase until 4 A.M. When hunger has mounted beyond possible assuagement by a chocolate bar, and the pizza stalls have dimmed their neon streaks, go to **Gilhuly's** (page 189), which provides Irish fortification up to 2:00 A.M., or look for a Chinese or Latin-American restaurant (pages 149 ff., 179 ff.)—they are unutterably opposed to sleep.

Another possibility is to wait until you get to Greenwich Village, where the hamburgers and talk sizzle all night. There, for a small price, you can sit down to chess at the **Cock-N-Bull** coffee house (147 Bleecker St.) or chess and checkers at the **Cafe au Lait** (90 W. 3rd St.), or imbibe grotesque atmosphere at the *Cafe Bizarre* (106 W. 3rd St.) or take a drink at the *San Remo*—an old, busy saloon, which has helped stimulate and befuddle several generations of artistic brains—or eavesdrop at any of the other coffee houses on Macdougal, 4th, or Bleecker Streets, or try the attempt at ordered calm in the Japanese teahouse at Bleecker and Macdougal. (Some of the specific places mentioned here may have disappeared when you get around to them, but there will very likely be comparable substitutes in possible imitations of Greek *tavernas* or cave restaurants or whatever one's imagination devises, to be swiftly followed by others.) Shopping at the *Paperbook Gallery* (page 274) offers a respite between doses of coffee and existentialism, as does *Rasputin's.* He rarely opens his shop before midnight and doesn't close before 4 A.M., often later. Among some good things of indefinable category, there is much shoddy, or vice versa; the major charm of the place lies in browsing through oddities at 4 A.M.

Four o'clock (yes—A.M.) is about the right time to start for the wholesale produce market, except on Saturday or Sunday mornings. Pick up some rubbers and an extra sweater, then take the IRT Seventh Avenue local to Cortlandt Street. There may not be a seat in the subway train because this is the first small rush hour, when the Polish and Ukrainian women who clean offices start returning home, when hospital workers, short-order cooks, and dockers carrying lunches in brown paper bags start for their jobs. From the station go westward—toward the Hudson River—to Washington Street, which holds much of the city's supply of fruits and vegetables in warehouses covering over a half-mile, north from Cortlandt Street. Earlier in the morning it will have been busier but more confusing; unloading trucks would have made walking hazardous and would have obscured views into the warehouses. Now, at 4:30 or 5:00, the rushing movement, the noise of brakes and shouting, has subsided. Sacks of onions stand in towering rows, one wall of a warehouse is pearled with garlic buds, and a wall of carrots blazes from the other side; odd and lovely fruits, still unmarred by handling, lie in shining, silken rows in their neat boxes. Great bulk gives ordinary vegetables new forms; bunches of Chinese parsley standing upright in tall boxes look like strange swamp flowers.

Outside the warehouses, usually on the corners, stand small pulpits where sales are recorded, almost always preceded by laconic bargaining, more a matter of polite form than trading: "Too much." "I know, but that's what it is." "O.K. Send it." Between these casual sales, the warehouse men are pleased to name and explain their wares; like most of the isolated society of night workers, they are polite, quiet, and unhurried, moving softly in the sleeping city, eager to greet a visitor from the day world.

Turn eastward now, toward the East River, and continue east and south toward Fulton and South Streets. The streets will seem empty and waiting as the early dawn slowly brings dimensions to the black cardboard buildings, but you will never be quite alone; a young policeman walking his somnolent path will greet you, a head will emerge from a manhole and shout "Good morning," a truck driver will tap his horn gently so that you may notice and greet him. When the Fulton Fish Market breaks through the silences with a tremendous roar, it is time to put on your rubbers against the ice spilling and melting all around. (If you've forgotten them, you can buy a pair, or hip boots for that matter, at one of the general stores on Fulton Street; they open at 4 A.M.) From Fulton Street to the Brooklyn Bridge on South Street, under the highway and to the edge of the river, stream stalls on stalls of red snapper, of endless sacks of scallops and scallop-shaped dogfish, of dried slabs of cod in soldierly rows, of silver threads of smelt glittering in gilt cans, of ice nests holding mounds of shrimp and a strayed starfish or two. Weathered men in high boots and heavy sweaters weigh out heaps of fish in suspended 100-pound scoop scales. Two men drag and carry a grouper twice their size, its face still set in the common fish expression of blustering anger. A row of cod, each in its own basket, stands head down with tail fins spread up and out, like precision divers in a water ballet. Out at the very end of the piers rest a few fishing smacks, rusty and worn, their nets hanging limp and dull. At one time, the bulk of deliveries to the market was made by boats, but they have been supplanted by trucks, and it is now the truckmen who are the tough, salty characters while the fishermen become anachronistic shadows.

For breakfast, recross the market (watch out for slashing freight-hooks and heavy swinging scales) to South Street, just below Fulton, where you will find *Sloppy Louie's* (page 55). It will be full of leather-lunged drivers and merchants engulfing extraordinary breakfasts, taking full advantage of the menu's promise: "Sauté dishes with garlic flavor no extra charge."

Walk back to Broadway and take the bus up to 28th Street. One block west (at Sixth Ave.) is the center of the wholesale flower market. At about 7:30 the streets are already filled with autumn leaves (in the fall) and forsythia, apple blossoms, and dogwood branches (in the spring). Delivery boys carry immense boxes of light, loosely-packed flowers with godlike ease, skillfully avoiding the hats of lady florists who walk through the large shops carefully examining roses and orchids and, ladylike, bargaining stubbornly in refined cadences. (Later on in the day, just before the noon closing, the second- and third-string retailers—the subway flower venders, street peddlers, makers of funeral wreaths—will do their shopping from among the more tired flowers.)

From the flower market (at about 8:00), walk up Seventh Avenue toward Penn Station at 33rd Street. On the way, you will pass mobs who look as if gathered for a political demonstration or strike action; they are unbelligerent fur workers for whom the necessary ritual of early sidewalk discussion animates the ensuing working hours. Having listened awhile and passed, avail yourself of the varied facilities of Penn Station, if you like, and end your night by watching the rising flood of commuters pour into the city's new day.

13
A CHRONOLOGY OF PERENNIALS

New York is as great a fiesta town as Oaxaca or Naples; our fiestas are less well-advertised and harder to find, especially through the cold half of the year, when they stay hidden. With persistence, though, one can find any number of public or semipublic events to attend. St. Rosalie's Day doesn't get much attention, but you might enjoy this miniature of the celebrations for Our Lady of Mount Carmel (page 328) in the same neighborhood. Or you might watch or join in the parade from 101st Street to the Cathedral of St. John the Divine on St. George's Day, or listen to a Hans Christian Andersen story on his birthday, or call the Mexican consulate (MU 9-0456) for places where you might help celebrate their Independence Days. You might, also, salute the seasons with us—a group of indigenous New York celebrations, replete with costumed children dancing in Rockefeller Plaza, ballet dancers at the entrance to the Public Library, flower boxes sprouting on the suddenly romantic avenues, proud speeches and civic choral societies; it all has a small-town charm with only the lightest touch of commercialism.

Several big commercial shows have gained, through the years, the status of perennials. Some are frankly industrial and for specialists; some, like the antique and flower shows, spread their appeal more generally. The city's newspapers, *Cue*, and *The New Yorker* carry announcements of these events, which take place sporadically at Madison Square Garden, the Armory at 34th St. and Park Ave., and on a constant schedule at the Coliseum (Columbus Circle), which changes faces dizzyingly—agricultural tools, antiques, yachts, art.

The following list includes events that are generally easily accessible and prepared for public participation.

JANUARY.

A month of convalescence from the crescendo of festivities that starts at Thanksgiving. Nothing much extraordinary happens except good sales in the shops and, toward the end of the month, the beginning of the West Indian carnival season with dances and calypso contests (page 89).

FEBRUARY.

Sometime in February is the Chinese New Year (call Chinese Consolidated Benevolent Assn., CO 7-5780 for exact dates). Undoubtedly the most beautiful free show in town, the Chinese New Year starts on the Eve with firecrackers and the release of silken lions to ward off evil spirits. This is a prelude to the longer sustained greeting and dancing of the lions on New Year's Day when, at about noon, a first high spattering of firecrackers is heard on Mott Street. A group of boys in bright trousers and jackets decorated with Chinese symbols gathers around a large drum; a rhythmic pattern is established on the drum by one of the older men, and then several boys successively take over the wearying job of beating out the heavy insistent rhythm. It is soon joined by the clash of cymbals. When the din is high, a number of dignified gentlemen emerge from a cellar, gently lifting out a lovely silk banner topped with a bouquet of varicolored pompons which bounce and turn in the winter wind. The sound of firecrackers and drums grows heavier and, finally, the first lion emerges. He has a magnificent head of multicolored silk, studded, beflowered, embroidered, and pompom-strewn; his large eyes roll furiously in their sockets and the long fringe on his chin and mouth waves and flutters as the dancer inside the head leaps, turns, and bends to the incessant rhythm of the drums and cymbals. For a body, the lion has only a length of striped silk, held up by another dancer, who echoes the movements of the dancing head.

Lion, cymbals, drums, and banners make their way from store to store, chasing evil spirits; from each establishment, the proprietor emerges with a red-wrapped (for good luck) package of coins for the band and a bundle of firecrackers, which he sets off in front of his shop. From Pell Street another lion emerges, and from Bayard and from the Bowery and from Canal, and everywhere now there are drums and cymbals and lions and the smoke of a million firecrackers. And while you watch, dazzled and deafened, one of the elders may offer you a cigar which he is carrying for the occasion in a small doctor's kit or a child might offer you a bite of his steamed dumpling, stamped with a handsome red symbol which turns out on inquiry to be merely the name of the baking company.

If there is no snow on the ground, the lions will, when they meet, try to outleap and outcavort each other, in the ancient manner of the lion battles of neighboring towns. If there is snow, and the lions are not leaping, you will behold some lovely litter—heaps of red, blue, green, and yellow firecracker shells illuminating the grayed snow.

Household festivities go on for some days and, about a week after New Year's Day, the lions and bands and banners come out for more public celebrations in Columbus Park (one block west of Mott Street). Beribboned, floretted banners form an arena around one lion and a clown in a fat pink smiling mask and a yellow kimono. The clown teases the outraged lion with his broken fan, both starting, backing, and weaving in intricate steps. Near the center of the playground in the meantime, a large area has been cleared for a great fairy-tale dragon whose long sinuous frame is carried by sixteen or eighteen men. The dragon is of black-and-gold scales with a spine of golden spears, a head of gold, and six gold-and-black ears, loosely hinged and undulant. His huge gold teeth and fangs open to a lolling red tongue with a large gold ball dancing over it, black velvet wires spray away from his commanding black eyes, and colored wire flames spurt from his nostrils. Like the lions, he is more beautiful than menacing.

While the dragon rests to be admired and photographed, a music wagon is pushed into sight. It too has a lovely imaginative shape, and from it, the musicians take out viols and lutes and play rueful little Chinese melodies. Off a little way, the stilt-walkers in extravagant costumes and painted faces follow their leader, who twirls and tosses a golden baton as he makes his crane-like progress toward a thoroughly American-style drum-and-bugle corps of local children. Then the whole spectacular entourage—dragon, banners, stilt-walkers, lions, musicians, drummers, and the children make their playful way back through the gray streets of Mott, Pell, and Mulberry, and the mummery is put away for another year.

> NOTE: It can be very cold spending a February afternoon on the streets; wear several pairs of stockings and, if you have them, fleece-lined shoes. To get to Chinatown, take either the IRT or the BMT to Canal Street and walk east a couple of blocks to Mott, which is the main street.

For three days sometime between February 20th and 25th, Village shops join in the Greenwich Village Antique show at Greenwich House (27 Barrow St., CH 2-4140). They show fairly modest objects of vaguely bucolic cast at decent prices.

MARCH.

Dedicated to the Flower Show and the huge Antique Fair; watch the newspapers for publicity and descriptions.

First to second week: the Bock Beer Festival at Luchow's Restaurant (see page 169); German bands and *schwärmerei*.

March 17th: St. Patrick's Day, New York's biggest shindig other than New Year's Eve (and one or two monumental convention invasions). The rivers Shannon and Liffey flow on Fifth Avenue from 44th Street to 96th Street for many hours and with them float many more Irishmen than is statistically possible. Color notes: the white traffic lines on the Avenue's pavement are repainted green for the occasion, and orange ties or scarves are not appropriate garb for the onlooker.

The last Friday of the month (usually—call SU 7-1757 to make sure): The Artists' Equity Ball, though a venerable institution, is still sprightly and imaginative. Not as cheap as you'd like or expect; this is for charity, which is an expensive commodity.

Easter Week: Massive arrangements of Easter lilies and early spring flowers in the Bronx Botanical Gardens; Easter bunnies and eggs for the less aesthetic young.

Easter—Greek Orthodox: Two to three weeks after the Julian dates, depending on the moon. Remarkable choral music, including deep Russian bassos, at the services in the Greek Cathedral (319 E. 74th St.) or St. Vladimir's (334 E. 14th St.) or St. Nicholas Cathedral (15 E. 97th St.). Call the churches for dates and times.

MARCH or APRIL.

Greek Independence Day Parade. (Almost anytime in the spring. The history books say March 25th, but in 1958, the parade took place on April 20th. Phone RE 7-0012 or WA 9-4200 for the current year's date.) Line of march: Fifth Avenue from 60th Street to 74th Street, then east on 74th to First Avenue.

Not anywhere near as big as the St. Patrick's Day Parade, but just as proud and considerably livelier, with much color and a happy minimum of military precision.

A blue-and-white float appears, marked "Maids of Athens and Sons of Pericles." One of the matronly maidens, draped in a diaphanous peplos, her careful hair wreathed in gold leaves, a stretch of green garland in her hand, breaks through the classic calm and, waving an anxious arm, calls to an old couple resting on a 74th Street stoop, "Hey, where'd you leave the kids?" She is followed by a group of girls in graceful long dresses of deep red and yellow, in strong contrast to the cool Hellenic blue and white of still another float, proclaiming "Hellas, the spiritual mother of civilization" and "Greece, the cradle of art, philosophy and poetry"; out of the cradle, latter-day Greeks wave to their friends on the sidelines, shouting arrangements to meet after the parade. History makes a wide leap forward in a wheeled display which discreetly advertises the fur shop of a Greek citizen of New Jersey.

With the floats, around the floats, fore and aft, are the bands—veterans' bands, school bands, scout bands, fraternal organization bands, and drum-majorette corps —most of them with uncanny skill for avoiding a tune. As has become almost customary in city parades, there are a number of adopted participants—Greeks for a day, like a little Negro drummer, for instance.

If you enjoy the game of pulling together disparate times and places and joining them in engaging incongruities—hetaerae in fur coats, a golden Dionysius in a dusty city street—try this one: as the parade goes by you, imagine the haughty Achilles marching out to battle "on the ringing plains of windy Troy," propelled by the martial strains of "That's Why the Lady Is a Tramp," as played by a chromatic-less band of Pans from a church school.

APRIL.

Coney Island opens its social season on the weekend nearest the first of the month.

April 12th: In honor of the birthday of Hans Christian Andersen, his life and a sampler of his stories are presented at the Andersen statue in Central Park.

April 23rd: A parade from the Cathedral of St. John the Divine (101st St. and Amsterdam Ave.) to celebrate St. George's Day.

The last Saturday of April, usually: The Loyalty Day Parade marches on Fifth Avenue from 66th Street to 38th Street in a patriotic demonstration which pleases marchers and spectators and irritates the Fifth Avenue Association; the latter feels that patriotism can be expressed as well on Sundays when shops are closed, or on other less busy streets where overheads are lower.

APRIL into MAY.

Cherry-blossom time in the Brooklyn Botanic Gardens. This is the time of annual house, garden, and private gallery tours organized for various charities; a fine opportunity to get behind doors you might not ordinarily knock on (watch the newspapers).

MAY.

The 4th (or the Sunday nearest): Spanish-American Day Parade. Everyone in New York who can say *"Arriba!"* with the proper trill marches up Fifth Avenue from 26th Street to 70th. Don Quixote appears with Sancho Panza, Queen Isabella and her consort share a float with Columbus, Basque dancers dance, Spanish bagpipers pipe, Carmens strut with flowers in their hair—all in a great show of *Hispanidad.*

The week surrounding the 15th: May Wine Festival at Luchow's Restaurant (see page 169).

May 18th (or the Sunday nearest): I Am an American Day on the Mall in Central Park; music, dancing, speeches by and for new citizens, many of them in attractive native costume.

MAY-JUNE.

From the end of May through the end of June (and again from the end of August through September) is when New York's Bohemia holds its own month-long *festa* of art: The *Festa* of San Leonardo, officially known as the Washington Square Art Show. Once upon a time it was a small show, limited to the confines of the Square itself. It has now achieved the dignity of a catalog and spills over onto the walls of New York University (The School of Commerce was recently hung with lyrical spring scenes) and Italian tenements and proliferates into all the side streets between Sixth Avenue on the west and University Place on the east. If the recent rate of growth continues, the Bowery, several blocks farther east, may find its flop houses and saloons acting as sales cases for canvases of violent seas and disturbed clowns.

Pick a nice clear Sunday, don walking shoes, and go down to the last stop of the Fifth Avenue bus (the one marked "Washington Sq.") and you'll descend into the core of the show. Buy yourself a big pretzel studded with coarse salt or an ice-cream pop from one of the wagons that are almost as numerous as the canvases, and browse. Hardly a type of graphic expression is missing except, maybe, cave paintings: Persian-style miniatures, Japanese landscapes, coats of arms, cartoons, cute sticky kiddy pictures, color encrustations on black velvet, cutouts in felt, paper montages and cutout silhouettes, finger painting, pictures in hammered copper, water colors, and oils—applied to board and canvas with brush, knife, trowel, and fist. Every approach to art is covered, from *trompe l'oeil* to the most secretive abstraction. Styles run from confidently *sui generis* through everyone else's manner of painting, and the levels of quality rise from unspeakable to questionable to promising to the pinnacle of a few solid paintings. Techniques are sometimes competent and often vehement denials of technique; one wonders whether the primitives are such by design or limitation or whether the mystic prose of some of the labels are declarations of purpose or rationalizations.

When the hot sun begins to feel like an enemy, retire for refreshment at one of the local outdoor cafés—the *Cookery* (8th St. and University Pl.; see page 184) or the *Fifth Avenue Hotel* (at 9th St.). Then, restored, you might go back to the show and this time enjoy the people. The artists and their families settle on the sidewalks as if for a long day at the beach. From the yielding depths of beach chairs, shaded by beach umbrellas, and wearing dark glasses, the wives pour milk from the thermos bottles for the children, keep the portable radios going, and chase their dogs from the picnic baskets. Some of the artists with less solicitous helpmeets come armed with portable phonographs, stacks of Telemann and Buxtehude records, and one small ham on rye.

Listen to the artists' wives talk of their hard lots, to the sentences that emerge when the artist turns teacher for the benefit of a potential customer and when the customer turns critic for the benefit of anyone within earshot. Listen to one artist, fringed in beard, say petulantly to another wreathed in pipe smoke, "But I like surrealism!" Another, discussing possible sales, shrugs, "*Que sera, sera;* I'm psychologically prepared." Or, an artist explains to a well-padded woman: "This painting is about how I feel; it's really symbolic of my war with myself and the painting is the gunsmoke of that struggle." She looks awed. The customer-critics are not as wordy, but more pithy: One woman snarls at the Babbitt who is her husband, "For Crissake, don't you know what depth painting is?" A crowd of boys goes by and one shouts, "How can you tell who is the unknown genius here? Show yourself, man." An old Italian gentleman who has strolled over from a local *boccie* game also has a comment, "*Pazzi! Pazzi!*"

On the western fringes of the Art Show, toward the Sixth Avenue boundary, the stepchildren of the arts take

over; the crafts people sit behind tables laden with
conspicuously handmade objects of variable attractiveness—leather wallets and Pony Express pocketbooks;
things in wood, clay, and copper; and jewelry in unexpected materials. As with the painting, the best is not
always here, but you might pick up a "Greenwich Village" gift for an adventurous friend.

NOTE: Sundays have been mentioned as the best days for
visiting the Washington Square Art Show, and the Fifth
Avenue bus as the approach route. But there are other
days and other means of transport. During its two periods
(end of May to end of June, and end of August to end of
September), the Art Show runs right through the week.
Sundays, Memorial Day, and Labor Day are the big days,
with artists and sidewalk critics in mass attendance. Saturdays are next best, but on weekdays there are frequent
gaps in the exhibits; many of the artists are back at their
more mundane activities or busily at work in their Queens
or New Jersey studios building up a fresh stock for the
next week end. (Exceptions are the crafts people and the
sidewalk caricaturists and pastel portraitists—they come
early, stay late, and are hopefully on hand for the thin
crowds even on cloudy Tuesdays.) If the Fifth Avenue bus
isn't convenient, the Sixth and Eighth Avenue IND subways (W. 4th St.—Washington Sq. station, express stop)
or the Lexington Ave. IRT (local stop at Astor Pl., with a
short walk two blocks west to the first canvas propped
against New York University).

JUNE.

First Sunday: The Blessing of the Fleet at Coney Island.
Yachts, sailboats, kayaks, motored rowboats line up to
approach a cabin cruiser from which a rabbi, minister,
and priest join in dispensing blessings, to the puzzlement
of the beach crowd who cannot quite understand Coney
Island's sudden list to holiness. (Some of the craft are
doubly blessed; they had been through a similar ceremony the day before, at Fort Schuyler in the Bronx.)

June 5th through 15th: *Festa* of San Antonio. The
little *festas* surrounding St. Anthony of Padua's Day are
a spattering of block parties (the largest of which runs
southward on Sullivan Street from Houston) which are,
in a way, rehearsal for the greater *festas* of July and

August. Religious observances take place in the local church mainly during the day, but the weekends and evenings are devoted to street dancing, small gambling, entertainment, and eating. Since this is the first sizable *festa* of the season, it is here that the gambling wheels get limbered up, under the supervisory presence of sandal-footed friars from the local convent of San Antonio on Sullivan Street. The children experiment with primitive gambling devices of their own. The favorite is a covered jar full of water, a whiskey glass standing inside the bottom of it. The gambler drops a penny into a slot in the cover and wins 5 cents if his penny lands in the jigger—not as easy as it sounds. Fair novelties are tried out—spumoni on a stick, a mobile pizza wagon ready to bake and dispense pies anywhere, a new kind of balloon, a gaudier type of kewpie doll. By all means go and bring an empty stomach and your dancing shoes. (Via either line of the IND Subway to W. 4th St.; walk south to Houston and a block or two east, following the smell of sausage and the arches of colored lights in flower designs.)

June 10th: St. Patrick's Cathedral steps turn into a flower market this one day in the interests of the valiant Outdoor Cleanliness Association of New York. (In case of rain or other possible dislocating factors, the date is changed; check with St. Patrick's Information Center, PL 5-3082, or Rectory, PL 3-2261.)

June 12th: Rose Day at Bronx Botanical Gardens. Roses in demonstrations, in lectures, in the realm of horticultural problems, in magnificent gardens.

June 14th: (check with Department of Parks—RE 4-1000). Teen-age magicians put on an adroit show on Central Park Mall. There are chinks in the duplicity and an occasional small debacle, but your children will enjoy it very much.

June 21st: Sail Boat Regatta and Design Competition on Conservatory Lake in Central Park. Three classes of competition so spread that anyone with a model boat may enter and play. The rivalry, particularly among the very seniors is tense, and the scene, unless it rains, very appealing.

June 24th—nearest Sunday; Day of San Juan Bautista, patron saint of San Juan, Puerto Rico. From the Bronx, Brooklyn, East Harlem and West, the Puerto Rican populace of the city streams by foot, car, and bus, across the Triborough Bridge to Randall's Island for religious ceremonies in the Stadium there. Afterwards, outside the stadium, a brilliant colored *piñata* is broken by some civic leader and the released toys grabbed by the most swift-legged and swift-handed children. The fiesta ends with a prodigious consumption of hot dogs and Good Humors to the rhythms of mambos and chachas bouncing from an improvised bandstand. When the band stops for breath, the dimmer strains of guitars, small drums, and voices float from groups of pink-shirted girls and shiny-haired boys lolling under the trees. (Take taxi preferably, or special buses, from 125th St. at Lexington Ave.)

The third or fourth Sunday: Irish Feis arranged by the United Irish Counties Association (CO 5-4226); some of the best of carefully chosen Irish dancing and music available locally. Takes place on the campus of Hunter College in the Bronx (via IRT Lexington-Woodlawn subway to Bedford Park Blvd. Station, then two blocks west).

End of the month (check with the sponsors, Brooklyn's Abraham & Straus department store—TR 5-7200): Fishing contest in Prospect Park Lake (Brooklyn) for children (6-15). The lake is freshly stocked with catchable varieties (possibly tranquilized) and the many prizes range from real money, through bicycles, downward.

JULY.

Another good month for watching shop sales.

July 14th: Bastille Day; free champagne for compatriots and linguistically sure free-loaders, served by the French Consulate (934 Fifth Ave.). Inquire while there (or call them at LE 5-0100) about the big dance held in a public hall on the Saturday nearest July 14th.

Week surrounding July 16th: *Festa* of Our Lady of Mount Carmel. From 114th to 116th Streets, Second

Avenue east to Pleasant Avenue. (Third Ave. bus to 116th St., walk east; or Lexington IRT local to 116th St., walk east.)

Since this area is out of the ordinary circles of tourist attractions, the *festa* here is more like a small-town fair, with less gambling and more children's amusements, greater church attendance (crowds stand three-deep, waiting to get into successive services) and much more conspicuous wearing of scapulars. The foodstuffs are less varied, but one or two regional dishes appear which are not seen at other *festas*. And, remarkably, provisions are made for sitting; large oilcloth-covered tables, borrowed from local kitchens, are set out on the wider sidewalks and in the streets, from which traffic has been closed off. For the small price of a cup of *espresso*, you can buy table space for your sausages and *calzone* and the use of a chair. Thus happily off your feet and gorging, you can watch the pleasant, civilized crowd surge by.

The one point of real superiority this *festa* has over its larger counterparts is the variety and quality of the street dancing, enriched by the dance styles of three cultures. First, the very little girls clutch each other in the stiff polite rounds of Anglo-American steps, their cotton-candy-smeared faces set in the immobility their older sisters consider *de rigeur*. Soon the teen-age Italian girls begin to pair off, and a few of the braver boys join them and take over as partners. Though their faces are set in the expressionless flatness that is the current fashion, their feet, seemingly animated by completely different machinery, move in complex little steps, and their shoulders heave and rock as they thrust each other forward and back. More juke boxes are pushed from the backs of candy stores to the sidewalks, more dancing groups form, each circled by spectators who hum and clap with the rhythms or dart witticisms at their dancing friends.

At about nine or ten in the evening, the families from Negro Harlem, Puerto Rican Harlem, and the local housing projects begin to expand the crowds at the *festa*, and the more spectacular dancing shows begin. While the parents and the young children browse through the streets, the teen-agers stay near the juke boxes, ready to show their stuff. And they show it with growing intensity as each nationality group vies with the other two. A three-ring rivalry develops and what can't be expressed in words or with fists or switchblades is danced out with fierce abandon in three modes: the sober reasoned complexity of the local Italian-American style; the intricate, inventive, and deeply humorous style of Lenox Avenue; and the fluid style of controlled heat brought from Puerto Rico.

The contest brings out some of the best amateur dancing in the city, and though it has a bitter *West Side Story* undertone, creates a pleasurable close (and an oddly suitable one) to an evening that began with a solemn parade of a stiff-jointed plaster saint.

July 27th: Anniversary of Puerto Rican Commonwealth; Central Park. Speeches, Latin-American music, and once in a while, a demonstration by dissidents.

End of July: Japanese Feast of Obon on Riverside Drive Mall at 103rd Street. Buddhist homage to the dead in solemn legendary dances; samurai gowns, ancient music, and stiff silken kimonos under the frail light of lanterns.

AUGUST.

During the week of August 7th (check with Department of Parks—RE 4-1000—for exact date): Rowing regatta for 9- to 14-year-olds. Lost oars, progress in circles, damp shirts, serious and appealing endeavors.

Second week: Hardly a New York exclusive but a reminder to watch for the Perseid meteor showers after midnight. See the newspapers for more exact dates or call the Hayden Planetarium (TR 3-1300).

August 17th to 23rd: New York Jazz Festival Week. Jazz concerts (see papers for dates) at Randall's Island.

August 20th: St. Stephen's Day Parade. Hungarian Catholics march from the 60's on Fifth Avenue to St. Patrick's. Recently more political than religious, saints' banners replaced by anathema to Russian officialdom. The girls wear pretty peasant costumes.

AUGUST (end) through **SEPTEMBER.**

Washington Square Art Show (see pages 324-26).

SEPTEMBER.

First week: Field Day of United Irish Counties Association. Fife-and-drum corps competitions open a day of hurling matches, Gaelic football, and concentrated Irish jollity. (Call CO 5-4226 for date and place.)

September 4th: St. Rosalie's Day. A miniature Italian *festa* on and around 116th Street at First Avenue. (See pages 326-30 for similar *festas*.)

Labor Day: West Indies Day Parade. Mrs. Jesse Waddell of Harlem has an unquenchable passion for parties in spite of her years (before there was a parade to organize, she arranged block parties for the children on her street) and a nostalgic yearning for the color and gaiety of West Indian festivals. The parade she whips up emblazons Seventh Avenue from 111th to 142nd Streets with floats, steel bands, baton twirlers, members of the West Indies societies, and almost anyone who cares to march and dance and is—at least in spirit— somewhat West Indian. The men are often in brilliant calypso costumes and the women in the courtly dress of old French island style, with colorful "foulards," high wrapped headkerchiefs, and graceful side-swept bustles. In the parade, too, are likely to be a good number of the city's politicians, particularly in an election year, Labor Day being so propitiously near Election Day. After the parade, which seems to generate energy rather than deplete it in spite of September's heat, the festive day ends and the next begins, with dancing at the Park Palace. (Check with the *Amsterdam News*—AC 2-7800 —before you go. Mrs. Waddell talks of retiring and there may be no parade without her catalytic spirit.)

September 15th and 16th: The Mexican consulate (MU 9-0456) would be delighted to tell you where and when you can celebrate their Independence Day.

Week surrounding September 19th: San Gennaro's Day, street fair in the Mulberry Street area, lower East Side. In essence like the other south Italian *festas* of San Antonio and Our Lady of Mount Carmel, but much larger, more crowded, with exaggerated quantities of everything: several square miles of pizza, a thousand yards of aromatic sausage, huge vats of sizzling, cheese-stuffed *calzone;* ropes of confetti streaming from fire escapes, bright necklaces of lights over the streets, a high florid bandstand, and a Verdi soprano of heroic size and audibility; the saints in the religious processions look more prosperous and bills of larger denominations are pinned to them or thrown in their long, silken trains.

San Gennaro's *festa* has reached the status of being a tourist attraction: Harlem sends a representation, the Village comes east and south for a touch of earthiness, a few Chinatown neighbors come from around the corner, and small-town girls in white shoes and rigid hats move tensely through the robust crowd.

The dense thronging precludes dancing, so the festivities are limited to prodigious eating (of a rather international type to suit a cosmopolitan set of visitors; egg rolls were recently added to the sausages and clams, and hot pastrami is inevitably on its way) and gambling. By the click of a wheel or the fall of a ball, you can win a pale canary in a small cage or a kewpie doll. One never wins very much; St. Gennaro is a poor saint and, being also the saint of agnostics, doesn't embarrass them with miracles.

Finish up at *Ferrara's* (195 Grand St., between Mott and Mulberry). One of the *old* coffee houses, born long before the present wild blossoming, it might easily have been lifted from Palermo and sat down on Grand Street intact—*espresso* machine, *cannolli, cassata,* patrons, clients, noise, explosions of disorganized energy, and all. At its bursting best on *festa* nights, although those are difficult times to get a table. (IRT Lexington or BMT to Canal St.; then walk east to Mulberry St.)

OCTOBER.

During first week: Victory Ball with dance exhibitions at Roseland Dance City (239 W. 52nd St., CI 7-0200).

October 5th (or nearest Sunday): Pulaski Day Parade; Fifth Avenue from 26th Street to 52nd Street. Drums, floats, bands, batons, boy scouts, peasant costumes, this time accented in Polish with political overtones.

October 10th: Ten-Ten Day. Street celebrations of the establishment of the Chinese Republic in 1911. A fragment of the Chinese New Year's Day brouhaha (page 319), including the splurting of firecrackers, the pointillism of confetti, and a shimmery, embroidered dragon looping and dancing to drums and gongs in Chinatown.

October 12th week end: Coney Island Mardi Gras. The usual hoopla whooped up in preparation for the long wintry Lent.

October 12th: Columbus Day. An Italian translation of St. Patrick's Day. It usually starts early in the afternoon and continues on to dusk, filling Fifth Avenue between the 40's and the 80's. Less robust and martial than the Irish parade, it relies more on large contingents from Catholic girls' schools, whose squad leaders whip out military commands in the high querulousness of an older sister scolding a younger.

NOVEMBER.

Early week: Annual Venison Festival at Luchow's Restaurant (see page 169).

November 22nd: St. Cecilia's Day. In honor of the patron saint of music, make a concert pilgrimage to Carnegie Hall, Town Hall, or the YMHA (see page 297).

Thanksgiving Day Parade: Rich uncle Macy throws a gigantic street party of floats, cowboys, television and movie personalities, fairy-tale characters, and huge balloon figures. From West 77th Street at Central Park West, down Broadway to R. H. Macy's, beginning a little before 10 A.M.

DECEMBER.

December is all Christmas. Immediately after Thanksgiving, the tinsel, gaud, shimmer, and dazzle begin to gather into brilliant extravagances of flash and color, while faces become more worried and dour, tearing through the froth and carols unseeing, concentrated on the perfect gift for the very imperfect relative. Beside spending your time, which you will and should, staring at the highly inventive and enchanting fantasies of Christmas decorating in the shopping areas—Fifth Avenue, Madison, 34th Street, 42nd Street, 57th Street, Park Avenue, and Rockefeller Plaza—you might enjoy:

Carols are sung in Rockefeller Center at 5:30 P.M. on several days preceding Christmas. A Carol Festival is held on the Mall in Central Park at 2:30 P.M. on the 22nd, and more informal carol concerts are performed by local groups at Washington Square, during several evenings before Christmas.

A number of churches offer performances of Gregorian chants or Christmas oratorios, often very good; the newspapers list these events.

The Hayden Planetarium (see page 196) has a Christmas show of the stars, usually beginning with a view of the sky at the time of the birth of Jesus.

The Bronx Botanical Garden (Bronx Park) arranges Nativity scenes with live animals and most abundant foliage, a display which lasts from the middle of December to the middle of January.

On December 24th at 4 P.M., a special service is held at the Chapel of the Intercession, 155th Street and Broadway, after which a group of children visit the nearby grave of Clement Moore (who wrote " 'Twas the Night Before Christmas"), where they place wreaths and sing carols.

To wind up the year in an authentic, indigenous fashion, take a short subway ride any time between 3 A.M. and 6 A.M. on New Year's Day. There's no telling what you will find: false eyelashes slipping and black eyes coming into bloom in a field of somnolent sprawling bodies, or a lively, impromptu party where pint flasks are joyfully exchanged and eternal friendship profoundly pledged at first glance.

APPENDIX: ETCETERA

A sampling of the multiplicity of oddities and services available in New York City; some may be useful, others entertaining.

ACTING LESSONS (for teenagers): *Actors Repertory Workshop,* 498 Third Ave. (Saturdays)

ALLIGATOR SOUP: *Allerton Fruit Shop,* 546 Madison Ave.

ALMOND PASTE (canned): *Trinacria,* 415 Third Ave.

AMATORY VERSE: *Fourth Avenue Book Store,* 138 Fourth Ave.

ANIMALS (bizarre but domesticable): *Trefflich Bird & Animal Co.,* 228 Fulton St.

ANIMAL CLINIC: *Humane Society Clinic,* 313 E. 58th St. (Free, 9:30 to noon, Mon.-Sat.)

ANIMAL FORMS (for baking): *H. Roth & Son,* 1577 First Ave.

APRICOT ICES (Syrian style): *Fouad Alwan,* 189 Atlantic Ave., Brooklyn

ARABIAN COPPER EWERS: *Sahadi Importing Co.,* 187 Atlantic Ave., Brooklyn. *Levon Milikian,* 13 E. 7th St.

ARABIAN SLIPPERS: *Bloom's,* 311 Sixth Ave. *Malko Bros.,* 197 Atlantic Ave., Brooklyn

ARMOR: *Robert Abels,* 860 Lexington Ave.

ARTIFICIAL FLOWERS (with fragrance): *Flowers Unlimited,* 125 E. 39th St.

ATTAYEF (Syrian nut-filled pancake): *Fouad Alwan,* 189 Atlantic Ave., Brooklyn

BACON ENDS: *Bozzo Bros.,* 213 W. 103rd St.

BADMINTON: *Theater and Badminton Club,* 498 Third Ave. (Reserve court in advance, OR 9-2479)

BAGEL HOLDERS (for cutting): *Abraham & Straus,* Fulton St. at Hoyt, Brooklyn

BARBERSHOP BOTTLES (old): *Frederick-Thomas,* 210 E. 60th St.

BAROMETERS (repaired): *Yale Clock Co.,* 23 E. 63rd St.

BARRACUDA LOAF: *Oriental Food Shop,* 1302 Amsterdam Ave.

BARREL ORGANS (made to order and repaired): *B. A. B. Organ Co.,* 112 32nd St., Brooklyn

BEAN CAKE: *Chinese Food Fair,* 20 E. Broadway

BEAN CURD (in various styles): *Far East Supermarket,* 5 Division St. *Hsiang Kee,* 220 Broome St.

BEAUTY AT HOME: *William of Park Avenue,* 1026 Park Ave. (24-hour service, TR 9-1130)

BEAUTY PARLORS: *House of Nicky,* 145 W. 47th St. (until midnight). *Larry Matthews Beauty City,* Seventh Ave. at 47th St. (open all night).

BEE'S WAX: *H. Roth & Son,* 1577 First Ave. (82nd St.). *Rohr's Coffee Roasting Est.,* 1492 Second Ave.

BETEL NUTS AND NUT CRACKERS: *Trinacria,* 415 Third Ave.

BIALYS (retail and wholesale): *Kossar's,* 145 Clinton St. (near Broome St.)

BIRD CAGES (tin, in brilliant colors): *Pan-American Shop,* 822 Lexington Ave.

BIRDS' NEST SOUP: *Allerton Fruit Shop,* 546 Madison Ave.

BOCCIE BALLS: 176 Bowery (at Kenmore St.)

BOEUF À LA MODE (to take home): *Le Buffet Français,* 1048 Third Ave.

BOOKS, AMERICANA: *Peter Decker,* 45 W. 57th St. *Eberstadt,* 888 Madison Ave. *Dauber & Pine,* 66 Fifth Ave. *Argosy Book Stores,* 114 E. 59th St.

BOOKS, ARCHITECTURAL: *Architectural Book Publishing Co.,* 883 First Ave.

BOOKS, BRITISH: *British Book Centre,* 122 E. 55th St. *Holliday Bookshop,* 119 E. 54th St.

BOOKS, CHINESE: 65 Bayard St. (in Chinatown)

BOOKS, CZECH: *Czechoslovak Music & Book Shop,* 1363 First Ave. (near 73rd St.)

BOOKS, DANCE: *Kamin Dance Bookshop & Gallery,* 1365 Sixth Ave.

BOOKS, DRAMA: *Drama Book Shop,* 47 W. 52nd St.

BOOKS, FRENCH: *Librairie de France,* 610 Fifth Ave. *Librairie Lipton, Inc.,* 796 Lexington Ave. *Golden Griffin,* 611 Madison Ave.

BOOKS, GAELIC: *Irish Book Shop,* 876 Lexington Ave.

BOOKS, GERMAN: *Arthur M. Adler,* 49 W. 47th St. *Mary Rosenberg,* 100 W. 72nd St. (current, out-of-print, rare). *Stechert-Hafner,* 31 E. 10th St.

BOOKS, HEBREW: Innumerable shops on Norfolk St. (between E. Broadway and Delancey), E. Broadway, and Essex St. (between Grand and Hester)

BOOKS, ITALIAN: *Italian Publications Co. (Vanni's),* 30 W. 12th St.

BOOKS, JAPANESE: *Azuma,* 802 Lexington Ave.

BOOKS, MEDICAL: *George Eliot,* 1302 Second Ave. *Old Hickory Book Shop,* 31 E. 10th St. (for old medicaments).

BOOKS, PORTUGUESE AND SPANISH: *Franz C. Feger,* 17 E. 22nd St. *Casa Gomez,* 53 Seventh Ave. (Spanish paperbacks)

BOOKS, SOVIET: *Four Continents Book Corporation,* 822 Broadway

BOOKS, TIBETAN: Tibetan *Tripitaka* (151 volumes for $5500

plus) from *American Buddhist Academy*, 331 Riverside Drive

BOOKBINDINGS FOR PAPERBACKS: *Yvonne Enterprises*, 106 Bement Ave., Staten Island

BRIOCHE (in sizes suitable for Louis XIV): *Colette*, 1136 Third Ave. (between 66th and 67th Sts.)

BRUSHWORK LESSONS (Chinese): *School of Chinese Brushwork*, 58 W. 57th St.

BURRO, MEXICAN: *Sears, Roebuck & Co.*, Mail Order Dept. (LO 4-2400)

BUTTERFLY WINGS (packaged): *Odyssey Shop*, 101 W. 44th St.

CANDLES (in unusual sizes): *Ajello Bros.*, 100 E. 50th St.

CANES: *Uncle Sam's Umbrella Shop*, 110 W. 45th St.

CARP (preserved Yugoslavian carp): *New International Importing Co.*, 517 Ninth Ave.

CARS, FOREIGN: *Imported Car Rentals*, 524 E. 73rd St. (to rent). *Bucket Seat*, 30 Charles St. (accessories and parts).

CAT BOARDING: *Town & Country Dog Shop*, 201 E. 66th St.

CATS (accessories and toys): *Fabulous Felines*, 141 Lexington Ave.

CHECKBOOK, LEFTHANDED: *Trade Bank & Trust Company*, 8 W. 48th St. and Seventh Ave. at 38th St.

CHEESE DIPS AND LOAFS (hot and cold made to order): *William Poll's Gourmet Shop*, 1051 Lexington Ave.

CHEMICAL GLASSWARE: *Eimer and Amend*, 633 Greenwich St. *Harry Ross*, 61 Reade St. (second-hand).

CHERIMOYAS: *Martin's*, 1040 Madison Ave. (often available)

CHERRY PITTER: *Paprikas Weiss*, 1504 Second Ave.

CHESTNUTS, DRIED: *Trinacria*, 415 Third Ave.

CHICORY, DRIED: *Dick's Coffee Co., Inc.*, 414 W. 42nd St.

CHILDREN'S PARTIES: For entertainment the following magicians are available: *Ward the Wizard* (MU 7-4972); *Clayton Rawson* (OW 8-8090); *Theo Doré* (UN 4-2360)

CHOLENT (to take out): *G & M Kosher Caterers*, 141 Clinton St. (corner Clinton and Broome)

CIGARETTES (Yugoslav, Japanese, Polish, Israeli, Philippine and others): *United Cigar Store*, 42nd St. and Fifth Ave. *Robert Lewis*, 59th St. and Madison Ave. *Russell's*, 56th St. (between Sixth and Seventh Aves.). *Village Smoke Shop*, 24 W. 8th St.

CIGARETTE-MAKING MACHINE: 41 Essex St. (between Hester and Grand)

CLADDAGH RING: *Irish Book Shop*, 876 Lexington Ave.

CLOTHING, OUTSIZE MEN'S: *Tall Men's Shop, Ltd.*, 603 Sixth

Ave. *Barney's Men's Clothes,* 111 Sixth Ave. *Frank Sherwood Co.,* 133 Fifth Ave. (8th floor). *Imperial Wear,* 555 Sixth Ave. *Sig Klein's Fat Men's Shop,* 52 Third Ave.

CLOTHING, WOMEN'S (small sizes): *Kit's,* 58 W. 48th St.

COFFEES (blended to taste): *Schapira's,* 117 W. 10th St. *Schweitzer,* 204 E. 59th St. *Dick's Coffee Co., Inc.,* 414 W. 42nd St.

COFFEE, TURKISH: *Yemen House of Coffee,* 486 Ninth Ave. *New International Importing Company,* 517 Ninth Ave.

CONVERSATIONS WITH SANTA CLAUS: *Macy's,* Herald Square (by appointment only, YU 3-2121)

COQ AU VIN (to take out): *Colette,* 1136 Third Ave. (order early the day before)

CORAL (unworked): *McArthur Shell Shop,* 590 Third Ave.

COUSCOUS: *Trinacria,* 415 Third Ave. *Sahadi Importing Co.,* 187 Atlantic Ave., Brooklyn.

CRYSTAL BALLS (the real thing and expensive): *Long Sang Ti,* 24 E. 55th St.

CRYSTAL, ROCK (as table and lamp bases): *Highlights,* 617 Second Ave.

DATE JAM, GREEK: *Oriental Groceries,* 513 Ninth Ave.

DÉCOUPAGE (an eighteenth-century art form to order): *Carl Federer,* 200 E. 55th St.

DIRECTORIES, TELEPHONE (foreign): New York Public Library, 42nd St. and Fifth Ave.

DIRECTORIES, TELEPHONE (out-of-town): *Concourse of Rockefeller Center,* 30 Rockefeller Plaza (between 49th and 50th St.). *New York Public Library,* 42nd St. and Fifth Ave. (most complete). *Grand Central Terminal,* 42nd St. and Park Ave. *Port Authority Building,* 8th Ave. at 41st St.

DOG-SITTING: *Town & Country Dog Shop,* 201 E. 66th St.

DOG'S SNOW-SUITS AND OTHER INDISPENSABLE APPAREL: *Canine Boutique,* 830 Lexington Ave.

DOLLS, FOREIGN: *United Nations Gift Center* at the United Nations Building, 45th St. and First Ave.

DOMESTICS, CHINESE: *Chinese Domestic Employment Agency,* 1243 Lexington Ave.

DRUMS, ARABIAN: *Fouad Alwan,* 183 Atlantic Ave., Brooklyn. *Malko Bros.,* 197 Atlantic Ave., Brooklyn.

DRUM LESSONS: *Krupa and Cole,* 261 W. 54th St.

EDISON PHONOGRAPHS AND CYLINDERS: *Rita Ford,* 907 Third Ave.

EGGS, EASTER: *Surma Book and Record Shop,* 9 E. 7th St.

EGGS, EASTER (prepared and decorated to order): *Carl Federer,* 200 E. 55th St.

EGGS, GOOSE: *Far East Super Market,* 5 Division St. *Chinese Food Fair,* 20 E. Broadway.

EGGS, TWO OR MORE YEARS OLD: *Hsiang Kee,* 220 Broome St.

ELBOW PATCHES (suede and leather): *Elaine Starkman,* 149 Bleecker St.

ENCHILADA SAUCE: *Casa Moneo,* 218 W. 14th St.

ENTERTAINMENT (for people with special tastes): *Regent's Row,* 136 E. 40th St. *The Barrister,* 47th St. at Lexington Ave. *Ce Soir,* 108 W. 73rd St. *Mais Oui,* 70th St. between Columbus and Amsterdam Aves.

ESSENCES (liquor, baking, or metaphysical): *H. Roth & Son,* 1577 First Ave. *Paprikas Weiss,* 1504 Second Ave.

FABRICS, JAPANESE: *Takashimaya,* 315 Fifth Ave. (at 46th St.)

FABRICS, THEATRICAL AND DISPLAY: *Dazian's, Inc.,* 142 W. 44th St. *Maharam Fabric Corp.,* 130 W. 46th St.

FACE-LIFTING: *Face Youth,* 162 W. 56th St. *William of Park Avenue,* 1026 Park Ave.

FENCING LESSONS: *Masque Fencing School,* 225 W. 46th St.

FETISH BEADS: *Sam Kramer,* 29 W. 8th St.

FHIDARA (ropes for Buddhist robes): *Takashimaya,* 315 Fifth Ave. (at 46th St.)

FIGUREHEADS (for boats, launches, and ocean liners): *Abraham & Straus,* Fulton St. at Hoyt, Brooklyn

FINGERNAILS (patched and repaired): *One Touch of Genius,* 38 E. 63rd St.

FISH CALLERS: *Abraham & Straus,* Fulton St. at Hoyt, Brooklyn

FLOWERS, CRYSTALLIZED: *Allerton Fruit Shop,* 546 Madison Ave.

FOLKLORE INFORMATION (books, music, records, concerts, lessons): *The Folklore Center,* 110 Macdougal St.

FOODS, PREPARED (day-old and cheap): *Horn and Hardart,* 577 Ninth Ave.

FOOT MASSAGE: A vibrator located outside of the Ladies Room in *Macy's Basement* (5 cents for more than a thousand vibrations)

FORTUNETELLING CARDS (with directions in six languages): *H. Roth & Son,* 1577 First Ave. *Paprika Weiss,* 1504 Second Ave.

FOSSILS: *Science Shop,* 1164 Sixth Ave. (at 46th St.) and 126 W. 23rd St.

FRENCH FOOD (prepared to take out): *A La Duchesse Anne,* 806 Madison Ave. *Le Buffet Français,* 1048 Third Ave.

FURNITURE, DO-IT-YOURSELF (chairs, tables, desks, mosaics, etc.): *Door Store*, 161 W. 4th St. and 246 E. 51st St.

FURS TO RENT: *Abet Fur Company*, 150 W. 28th St.

GAME FOWL (partridge, guinea hen, pheasant, mallards): *Midtown Butchers*, First Ave. between 58th and 59th Sts. *Samuel Katz—Venice Market*, 813 Park Ave.

GIFTS FOR THE HOSPITALIZED: *Bedside Manna*, 307 Fifth Ave. (phone orders to MU 4-7740)

GILDING (furniture and objects): *Sal Butta*, 315 E. 74th St. *Michael's*, 235 E. 60th St.

GLASS EYES (for jewelry): *Sam Kramer*, 29 W. 8th St.

GOAT MEAT: *Dos Hermanos Los Pichones*, Stanton St. (E. of Orchard St.)

GOLF HISTORY AND RELICS: *Golf House*, 40 E. 38th St. free; weekdays, 9-5)

GRAPE LEAVES (stuffed or loose): *Sahadi Importing Co.*, 187 Atlantic Ave., Brooklyn

GUIDEBOOKS TO THE ORIENT (old and new): *East and West Book Store*, 132 E. 61st St.

GUITARS (made to order): *Cortesano Instrument Co.*, 106 MacDougal St. *Village String Shop*, 184 Bleecker St.

GUM ARABIC (for chewing): *Malko Bros.*, 197 Atlantic Ave., Brooklyn

HAGGIS: *Drewes Scottish Bakery*, 6815 Fourth Ave., Brooklyn (order in advance, TE 6-1800)

HAIRPIECES (men and women): *Sy Newman*, 131 W. 45th St. *D. Puller*, 28 W. 46th St. *Joseph Fleischer & Company*, 12 W. 27th St.

HANDWRITING ANALYSIS: *Dorothy Sara*, 11 E. 32nd St. (group analysis and via mail, MU 4-1500, ext. 914)

HARDWARE (doorknockers, rods, legs, brackets): *Caster House*, Third Ave. near 49th St.

HARPS: *Victor Salvi Company*, 60 W. 46th St.

HARPSICHORDS (made to order): *Wallace Zuckermann*, 55 Clarkson St. (near Greenwich St.)

HOMEOPATHIC MEDICINES: *Boericke and Tafel*, 140 W. 46th St.

HONEY (acacia, heather, fennel, thyme): *Paprikas Weiss*, 1504 Second Ave.

HORS D'OEUVRES, SAMPLE: *William Poll's Gourmet Shop*, 1051 Lexington Ave. (free tasting every afternoon)

HORSEBACK RIDING: *Claremont Riding Academy*, 175 W. 89th St. *Manhattan Riding Academy*, 32 W. 67th St. (Both adjacent to Central Park; instruction available.)

ICONS: *Juergens,* 1100 Third Ave. *Russian National Book Shop,* 327 E. 14th St.

IGUANA MEAT: *Allerton Fruit Shop,* 546 Madison Ave.

INDIAN, CRAFTS OF THE AMERICAN: *Plume Trading and Sales Co.,* 155 Lexington Ave. (near 30th St.)

INFORMATION (miscellaneous): *New York Public Library,* OX 5-4200. New York *Times,* LA 4-1000.

JEWELRY (tie tacks and cuff links in designs for drinkers): *Merrin,* 530 Madison Ave. (at 54th St.)

JEWELS, SEMI-PRECIOUS (for mounting): *Sam Kramer,* 29 W. 8th St.

JEWS HARPS: *Mattie Haskins' Irish Record Shop,* 1332 Third Ave.

JIGSAW PUZZLES (for adults; to buy and rent): *Par Puzzles,* 18 E. 53rd St.

JUDO FOR JUVENILES: *Judo for Boys Corp.,* 160 W. 73 St.

JUNKS, CHINESE (imported from Hong Kong): *Woodbridge Importing Co.,* Hempstead, Long Island

KANGAROO HIDES: *Connolly Company,* 181 Williams St.

KANGAROO TAIL SOUP: *Old Denmark,* 135 E. 57th St.

KELP (flavored or powdered): *Oriental Food Shop,* 1302 Amsterdam Ave.

KISHKA, KREPLACH, KUGEL (to take out): *G & M Kosher Caterers,* 141 Clinton St.

KOHL: *Sahadi Importing Co.,* 187 Atlantic Ave., Brooklyn

KOSHER CHOW MEIN AND MEATBALLS: *G & M Kosher Caterers,* 141 Clinton St.

KOURABER (Greek pastry): *Poseidon Confectionary Company,* 629 Ninth Ave.

KUZBURRAH (Chinese parsley): *David Saidy Grocery,* 178 Atlantic Ave., Brooklyn

LAMB PIES (small): *Alexander's Syrian Bakery,* 150 Atlantic Ave., Brooklyn

LAMPS (Middle Eastern): *Malko Bros.,* 197 Atlantic Ave., Brooklyn

LEATHER (cleaned and dyed): *Leathercraft,* 62 W. 56th St.

LEG FATTENERS (what this is escapes us, but it sounded engaging): *Modern Methods,* 296 Broadway

LOVE POTIONS: *Kiehl's Pharmacy,* 109 Third Ave.

LOTUS LEAF, DRIED: *Oriental Food Shop,* 1302 Amsterdam Ave.

MAGAZINES (out-of-date): *Back Date Magazine Center,* 1175 Sixth Ave.

MAGIC, LESSONS IN: *Institute of Magic,* 741 Eighth Ave.

MAGIC POTIONS: *Botanicas* in Spanish Harlem

MANUSCRIPT ILLUMINATION: *G. Lange,* 320 Lexington Ave. (LE 2-7269)

MARINE HARDWARE: *Fisher Marine Co.,* 54 W. 45th St. *B. Sack & Sons,* 54-55 South St. *A. L. Don,* 37 South St.

MEDICINE AND TONICS, CHINESE: *Hsiang Kee,* 220 Broome St.

MEDICINES (for dogs): *Pet Remedies,* Lexington Ave. at 91st St.

MEDICINES (herbs): Most Latin-American *Botanicas* in Spanish Harlem

MICROSCOPES (second-hand): *Harry Ross,* 61 Reade St.

MINIATURE FURNITURE AND CHINA: *Eric Pearson,* 18 W. 55th St. *S. Wyler,* 713 Madison Ave.

MOUNTAIN-CLIMBING EQUIPMENT: *White Mountain Ski Shop,* 36 W. 46th St.

MOSAICS, SEED (designed arrangements of colored seeds): *Karl Mann Associates,* 16 E. 55th St.

MOUSSE AU CHOCOLAT (to take out): *Colette,* 1136 Third Ave. *Le Buffet Français,* 1048 Third Ave.

MOVIES, ARABIC: *Lido Theater,* 263 Court St., Brooklyn

MOVIES, CHINESE: *Sun Sing Chinese Theater,* 75 E. Broadway

MOVIES, GREEK: *Cameo,* 693 Eighth Ave.

MOVIES, INTERNATIONAL: *Thalia,* 95th St. and Broadway (watch for summer festival)

MOVIES, ITALIAN: *Cinema Giglio,* 277 Canal St.

MOVIES, POLISH: *St. Mark's Cinema,* Second Ave. bet. 8th and 9th Sts.

MOVIES, RUSSIAN: *Cameo,* 693 Eighth Ave. (once in a while)

MOVIES, SPANISH: *Colon,* Columbus Ave. 85th St. *Azteca,* 1492 Madison Ave. *Metropolitan,* 14th St. near Second Ave.

MUSIC BOXES (repaired): *Rita Ford,* 907 Third Ave.

MUSICAL INSTRUMENTS (repaired, bought, and sold): Numerous places on east side of Eighth Ave. between 48th and 49th Sts.

MUSICAL INSTRUMENTS (harps, lutes, string instruments): *Medina Galleries,* 1037 Third Ave. *Cortesano Instrument Co.,* 106 Macdougal St. *Village String Shop,* 184 Bleecker St.

NARGHILAS: *Sahadi Importing Co.,* 187 Atlantic Ave., Brooklyn. *Connoisseur Tobacco Co.,* 107 W. 47th St.

NAVAHO BOOTS: *Bloom's,* 311 Sixth Ave.

NEW YORK CITY (information on activities): "Around New York," *Radio Station WNYC,* 8-8:30 A.M., Mon.-Sat.

NEWSPAPERS (Irish County newspapers three to four weeks old): *Mattie Haskins Irish Record Shop,* 1332 Third Ave.

NEWSPAPERS AND MAGAZINES (foreign and out-of-town): *Hotaling's,* 54 E. 50th St. and 1475 Broadway (in Times Building)

NIGHTCLUB (kosher): *Arele's New Roumanian,* Horace Harding Expressway at 162nd St. (HI 5-4444)

OBIS, JAPANESE: *Takashimaya,* 315 Fifth Ave. (at 46th St.)

OCTOPUS (canned): *Old Denmark,* 135 E. 57th St.

OFFICES (mailboxes and messages for the peripatetic): *Officette, Inc.,* 215 W. 34th St.

OPIUM BOX (Chinese): *Lar,* 1034A Lexington Ave. (phone to see if available, YU 8-2120)

ORIGAMI LESSONS (Japanese paper folding): *Japan Society,* 18 E. 50th St.

PAINTINGS (for rental): *Museum of Modern Art,* 11 W. 53rd St. (for members only)

PANTS (made to match jackets): *Beckenstein,* 125 Orchard St.

PAPERS, DECORATIVE: *Nelson-Whitehead,* 7 Laight St. (near Canal St.)

PARTRIDGE (stuffed with foie gras): *Allerton Fruit Shop,* 546 Madison Ave.

PARTY FAVORS: *Dennison's,* 411 Fifth Ave.

PATÉ (paté maison): *Baccara Restaurant,* 203 E. 45th St. (to be ordered a day in advance)

PEASANT BLOUSES, UKRAINIAN: *Sirma,* 9 E. 7th St. *Arka,* 48 E. 7th St. (some in black-and-white with drawn work)

PETS (monkeys, wild birds, etc.): *Trefflich,* 228 Fulton St.

PHOTOGRAPHS (dog portraits): *Chi Chi Chien,* 80th St. and Park Ave.

PICKLES, ROUMANIAN-JEWISH: *Roumanian Pickle Works,* 175 Orchard St.

PIDÉ: *Alexander's Syrian Bakery,* 150 Atlantic Ave., Brooklyn

PIÑATAS: *Fred Leighton,* 15 E. 8th St.

PIRANHAS ("man-eating fish"): *Tropical Fish Shop,* 31 Warren St.

PLANTS, INDOOR (planting, care, and feeding of): *The City Gardener,* 437 Third Ave.

PLANTS, SICK (diagnosis and nursing): *The City Gardener,* 437 Third Ave.

PLANTS, TROPICAL: *Plants from the Tropics,* 318 E. 59th St.

POCKETBOOKS (made to order): *Lester Bags,* 669 Madison Ave.

POGO STICK (with automatic jump recorder): *Abraham & Straus,* Fulton St. at Hoyt, Brooklyn

POI (to order): *Oriental Food Shop,* 1302 Amsterdam Ave.

POISE AND ETIQUETTE: *Luella Cuming Studio,* 141 E. 55th St. (EL 5-0276)

POLO EQUIPMENT: *Knoud,* 716 Madison Ave.

POMPANO (cooked, to take out): *King of the Sea Shop,* 53rd St. and Third Ave.

PONCHOS, PERUVIAN: *Pan-American Shop,* 822 Lexington Ave.

PRAYER BEADS, ARABIAN: *Sahadi Importing Co.,* 187 Atlantic Ave., Brooklyn

PRAYERS (individual prayers to individual saints, on newsprint): *Casa Gomez,* 53 Seventh Ave.

PRAYERS (for seamen, longshoremen, truck drivers): *Shrine Church of the Sea,* 21st St. at Tenth Ave.

PRETZELS (very large): *Banks Bakery,* 153-55 Houston St. (between Eldridge and Allen)

PRINTS (old): *Augustin Fries,* 135 E. 56th St. (one flight up). *Walter Schatzki,* 127 E. 56th St. *Old Print Shop,* 150 Lexington Ave.

PRINTS (of Etruscan murals, obscure Renaissance, modern): *Anton's Renaissance Print Shop,* 53 W. 8th St.

PSYCHIATRIC COFFEE SHOP: *The Couch,* W. Third St. (near Thompson St.)

PUPPETS, JAVANESE: *Odyssey Shop,* 101 W. 44th St.

QUEXQUEMATLS: *Pan-American Shop,* 822 Lexington Ave.

QUICHE: *Colette,* 1136 Third Ave. *Le Buffet Français,* 1048 Third Ave.

RABBIT MEAT, SMOKED: *Martin's,* 1040 Madison Ave.

RAVIOLI (homemade and ready to cook): *Tom Ravioli,* 675 Ninth Ave. *Gusto,* 653 Ninth Ave.

RECORDS, ARABIC: *Rashid Sales Co.,* 191 Atlantic Ave., Brooklyn. *Capitol HiFi Center,* 1500 Broadway. *Alamphon,* 182 Atlantic Ave., Brooklyn

RECORDS, CZECH: *Czechoslovak Music & Book Shop,* 1363 First Ave. (near 73rd St.)

RECORDS, HUNGARIAN: *Cosmos Book Store,* 1582 First Ave.

RECORDS, IRISH: *Irish Book Shop,* 876 Lexington Ave. *Mattie Haskins Irish Record Shop,* 1332 Third Ave.

RECORDS, JAZZ: *Original Jazz Record Center,* 107 W. 47th St. (upstairs; also periodicals). *Merit Music Shop,* 13 W. 46th St.

RECORDS, OUT-OF-PRINT: *Merit Music Shop,* 13 W. 46th St. *Bell Music Box,* 847 Sixth Ave.

RECORDS, SOUND EFFECT: *T. J. Valentino,* 150 W. 46th St.

RECORDS, SOVIET: *Four Continents Book Corp.,* 822 Broadway

RECORDS, SPANISH: *La Virgen del Carmen,* Madison Ave. between 107th and 108th Sts.

RECORDS, UKRAINIAN: *Howerla Ukranian Book Store, Surma Book and Record Store, Arka* (all bet. 9-48 E. 7th St.)

RECORDS (to borrow): *New York Public Library,* 58th St. near Lexington Ave. *Donnell Library Center,* 20 W. 53rd St.

REDUCING (legs—thighs to ankles): *Lucille Bouchard,* Hotel Delmonico, Park Ave. at 59th St. *Modern Methods,* 296 Broadway (by mail). *Ann Rudo,* 52 E. 67th St. (spot reducing)

RELIGIOUS ARTICLES, JEWISH: A number of shops are located on Norfolk St. and spill over onto E. Broadway and Delancy St.

RUBBINGS, FISH: *Karl Mann Associates, Inc.,* 16 E. 55th St.

RUSH FURNITURE (recaned and rewoven): *The Associated Blind, Inc.,* 147 W. 23rd St.

SANDALS: *Alan Block,* 171 W. 4th St. (Greek, Roman, and primitive). *Pan-American Shop,* 822 Lexington Ave. (Mexican)

SCOTCH DELICACIES: *Rahmeyer's,* 1022 Third Ave.

SEA FOOD (to take out): *King of the Sea Shop,* 53rd St. at Third Ave.

SEA HORSES (live): *Tropical Fish Shop,* 31 Warren St.

SEA HORSES (dead): *Sam Kramer,* 29 W. 8th St.

SEA URCHINS (Chinese): *Chinese Food Fair,* 20 E. Broadway

SEAWEED, DRIED: *Chinese Food Fair,* 20 E. Broadway

SESAME SEED BREAD: *Alexander's Syrian Bakery,* 150 Atlantic Ave., Brooklyn

SHIPS MODELS (meticulous, expensive): *Nelson's Folly,* 860 Second Ave.

SHIPS MODELS IN BOTTLES (to make): *Seamen's Institute,* South St. at Coenties Slip

SHOES (for dogs): *Canine Boutique,* 830 Lexington Ave.

SHOES (remade and restyled): *B. Nelson and Co.,* 10 E. 39th St.

SHOES (women's; unusual sizes): *Shoecraft,* 603 Fifth Ave. *Chandler's,* 695 Fifth Ave. *I. Miller,* 1552 Broadway. *Coward Shoes,* 20 W. 34th St.

SKINS (bear, cow, and others): *Guccioni's,* 215 E. 19th St.

SKULLS, HUMAN: *Juergens,* 1100 Third Ave.

SOUND EFFECTS RECORDS (to borrow): *Brooklyn Public Library,* Grand Army Plaza, Brooklyn

SPICES: *Tabussi's Grocery,* Vesey St. at Washington St. *Atlas Importing Co.,* 1109 Second Ave.

STAMPS AND COINS: *Du Mont Stamp Company,* 106 W. 47th St. *Broadway Stamp Co.,* 137 W. 47th St.

STOCK MARKET QUOTATIONS: *Radio Station WNYC,* 3:45 P.M., Mon.-Fri.

SWIMMING POOLS: *Henry Hudson Hotel,* 353 W. 57th St. *St. George Hotel,* 51 Clark St., Brooklyn

TAROT CARDS: *Paprikas Weiss,* 1504 Second Ave. *H. Roth & Son,* 1577 First Ave. *Chequer,* 816 Third Ave.

TAXIDERMY: *Guccioni's,* 215 E. 19th St. *Elmer E. Rowland,* 501 Sixth Ave.

TEAS (blended to taste): *Schweitzer's,* 204 E. 59th St. *Schapira's,* 117 W. 10th St. *Dick's Coffee Co., Inc.,* 414 W. 42nd St.

THEATER TICKET AGENCIES: Every sizable hotel maintains a ticket service; Broadway and off-Broadway are lined with reliable agencies which should charge about $1.00 above the ticket price plus a delivery charge if they send tickets to the box office.

THEATER TICKETS, AVAILABILITY OF: Tune in on *Radio Station WBAI* (100 FM), 5 P.M., Mon.-Fri. for off-Broadway offerings, call OR 7-1010, 10 A.M. to 9 P.M. seven days a week.

THUMB SCREWS: *Robert Abels Antiques,* 860 Lexington Ave.

TIES (narrowed and cleaned): *Tie Clinic,* 545 Fifth Ave., 38 E. 57th St., 200 W. 34th St., and 152 W. 42nd St.

TIME (exact): Dial ME 7-1212

TOOTH PICK (golden, leather-cased and even initialed): *Merrin,* 530 Madison Ave.

TURKISH BATHS: *Al Roon's Health Clubs* (call SU 7-0400 for addresses). *Luxor Baths,* 121 W. 46th St. *Reilly's,* 1250 Sixth Ave. *St. Mark's Russian and Turkish Baths,* 8th St. and Third Ave. (men only).

TURKISH CIGARETTES (pure and uncorrupted): 41 Essex St.

UMBRELLAS (repaired): *Uncle Sam's Umbrella Shop,* 110 W. 45th St.

VALENTINES (to order) *Carl Federer,* 200 E. 55th St.

WATCH (with seven interchangeable dials for extra-precision timing): *Abercrombie and Fitch,* Madison Ave. at 45th St.

WEATHER FORECAST: Dial WE 6-1212

WEAVING LESSONS: *Lili Blumenau,* 53 E. 9th St.

WOOD ACCESSORIES (doors, louvers, plaques, trimmings, etc.): *Richardson and Dutt,* Third Ave. bet. 48th and 49th Sts.

WOOLENS, SCOTTISH: MacDougall's, 775 Madison Ave.

WORLD SERIES SCORES: Dial ME 7-1212

YARD GOODS (damask, brocade, and shantungs): *Gunn & Latchford,* 323 Fifth Ave.

ZITHERS: *Rita Ford,* 907 Third Ave.

INDEX